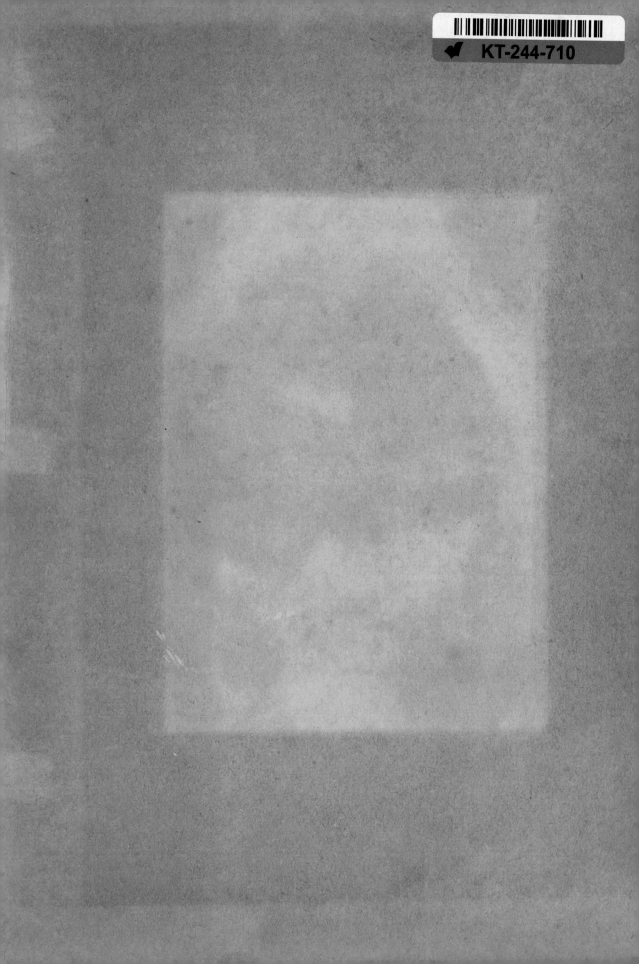

OLYMPIA

Oxford University Press

London   Edinburgh   Glasgow   Copenhagen

New York Toronto Melbourne Cape Town

Bombay Calcutta Madras Shanghai

Humphrey Milford Publisher to the UNIVERSITY

HEAD OF ATHENA

From the metope of the Stymphalian birds, Temple of Zeus, Olympia

OLYMPIA
Its History & Remains

BY

E. NORMAN GARDINER, D.LITT.

OXFORD
AT THE CLARENDON PRESS
1925

Printed in England

To

PERCY GARDNER

PREFACE

MORE than forty years have elapsed since Olympia was excavated by the German Government, and as yet no book on the subject has appeared in English. Admirable summaries are to be found in Guide Books and books of reference, but they are generally without the illustrations that alone can make them intelligible. My first object therefore is to make the results of the excavations available for English readers. That I can illustrate them so fully is due to the generosity of the Oxford University Press.

My second object is to trace the history of Olympia and its festival. With the athletic history of Olympia I have dealt fully in my *Greek Athletic Sports and Festivals*. But the story of Olympia is hardly less important for the study of Greek politics, religion, and art, and it is with these that I am principally concerned in the present work. Our interest in Greek history is apt to be confined to the Eastern side of Greece and the Aegean. But Olympia was in the West, it faced West and North, and the story of Western Greece is very different from that of Eastern Greece. It is for this reason that I have dwelt so much upon the early history of Olympia. Further, both in politics and religion, Olympia stood for unity. Amid the jealousies and factions of the Independent City States of the Greek world Olympia developed and kept alive the feeling of Hellenic nationality, and as the connecting link between East and West it served this purpose long after the liberty of the City States was lost. At Olympia, too, the countless cults of Greek polytheism found themselves harmonized and subordinated under the supremacy of Zeus, and in his worship Greek religion made its nearest approach to Monotheism.

Every book on Olympia must be based on *Olympia : die*

Ergebnisse, the monumental work edited by Ernst Curtius and Friedrich Adler, in which the final results of the Excavations were published. My debt to the eminent archaeologists who contributed to it will be manifest on every page, while my thanks are also due to the firm of Behrend & Co. of Berlin for generous permission to reproduce illustrations from that work.

The various problems raised by the excavations have given rise to an extensive literature, especially in Germany. It is impossible within the limits of this work to discuss the many theories that have been propounded. The reader will find references to the most important articles in the foot-notes. I have always endeavoured to examine the original evidence impartially and to form my own judgement : if I have borrowed without due acknowledgement, I can only crave pardon for the oversight. I must also apologize for adding yet another conjecture to the many that have been proposed as to the origin of the Olympic Games and Festival.

My thanks are due to many friends for the loan of photographs or for advice on portions of the work : to Mr. Bernard Ashmole, Dr. R. Caton, Mr. W. J. Forsdyke, and Professor H. J. Rose ; to Mr. E. S. G. Robertson of the British Museum who helped me in selecting the coins of Elis in Fig. 37, and to Professor H. A. Ormerod who has read through all the proofs. Above all I am indebted to Professor Percy Gardner for the constant help and advice that he has given me from the very inception of this work, and especially for allowing me to inscribe my book to him as a token of personal gratitude and also of appreciation of the great work that he has done at Oxford during his long tenure of the Professorship of Classical Archaeology and Art.

TABLE OF CONTENTS

I. THE DESTRUCTION AND RECOVERY OF OLYMPIA

PAGE

The Destruction of Olympia 3
The Recovery of Olympia 5
    Results of the Excavations 7
    Architectural Terra-cottas 9
    Votive Offerings 10
    Stratification 10

II. THE GEOGRAPHY OF THE NORTH-WEST PELOPONNESE

The North-West Peloponnese 13
    The Mountain Barrier and Coastal Plain . . . 17

Olympia and its Communications 19
    The Upper Alpheios 19
    The Lower Alpheios 22
    Roads to Elis and the North 22
    Roads to the South 24
    Conclusion 25

III. THE PREHISTORIC REMAINS OF THE NORTH-WEST PELOPONNESE

The Prehistoric Village at Olympia . . . 26
    The Pottery of Olympia 28
    Affinities of the Pottery 31
The Remains at Kakóvatos 35
    Conclusion 39

IV. PEOPLES AND CULTS OF THE NORTH-WEST
   PELOPONNESE   PAGE

Mediterranean Elements 40
Northern Elements 42
   Olympia and Dodona 48
Elis and Argolis 51
Pisa and Pelops 53

V. THE ORIGIN OF THE OLYMPIC FESTIVAL

Ancient Legends 58
   Pindar and the Legend of Herakles 59
   Pausanias and Elean tradition 61
   Phlegon and Pisatan tradition 62
Modern Theories of the Games 63
The Evidence of Olympic Custom . . . 68

VI. OLYMPIA AND PISA

Olympia in the Dark Ages 77
   The Votive Offerings before 700 B.C. . . . 77
   The Truce of Iphitos. Elis and Pisa . . . 83
   The Olympic Register 85
The Growth of Olympia, 776–576 B.C. . . . 88
   Archaeological Evidence. Votive Offerings . . . 92
Olympia from 576 to 476 B.C. 96

VII. OLYMPIA AND ELIS

From the Persian War to the Peloponnesian War . 104
   Elean Administration 104
   New Buildings and Monuments 107
From the beginning of the Peloponnesian War to the
   Battle of Chaironeia 112
   Olympia and Panhellenic Unity 112
   Elis and Sparta 115
   Elis and Triphylia. The Pisatan Revolt . . . 121
   The Metroon. New Influences at Olympia . . 123

VIII. OLYMPIA AND MACEDON   PAGE
    Philip and Alexander 129
      The Philippeion 131
      Altis Walls and Stoa 135
    The Hellenistic Age 137
      Olympia and the Diadochoi 140
      The Coming of Rome 145
      The Olympic Festival in the Hellenistic Age . . 148

IX. OLYMPIA AND ROME
    Decline of Olympia under the Republic . . . 152
    Olympia under the Caesars 158
    The Renaissance of Olympia 166

X. THE TOPOGRAPHY OF THE ALTIS
    Temenos and Grove 175
    The Plain and Theatron 178
    The Greek Walls of the Altis 179
    Statues of the Altis 181
    The Roman Walls of the Altis 185
    Processional Entrance, Agora, Proedria, Hippo-
      dameion 188

XI. THE ALTARS AND HERO SHRINES OF OLYMPIA
    Altar of Zeus 193
    Ash Altars of Hera and Ge 195
    The Monthly Offering 197
    The Lists of Officials 200
    Hero-shrines 203

XII. THE HERAION
    The Temple 206
    The Cult of Hera 214

XIII. THE TREASURIES
    What was a Treasury ? 217
    The Identification of the Treasuries . . . 219
    Geloan Treasury 222

PAGE

Metapontine Treasury 225
Megarian Treasury 225
Treasuries of Kyrene, Sybaris, and Byzantion . 229
Selinuntine Treasury 230
Epidamnian Treasury 231
Sikyonian Treasury 231

XIV. THE TEMPLE OF ZEUS

The Temple 234
The Statue and Throne of Zeus 241
The Workshop of Pheidias 243
Sculptures of the Temple 245
The Eastern Pediment 247
The Western Pediment 250
The Greatness of the Sculptures of the Pediments 255
Who were the Artists of the Pediments ? . . 259
The Sculptures of the Metopes 262

XV. THE OFFICIAL BUILDINGS OF OLYMPIA

The Prytaneion 267
The Bouleuterion 269
The Proedria 274
The Hellanodikeon 276
The Theokoleon 278
The Leonidaion 280

XVI. THE ATHLETIC BUILDINGS

The Stadion 284
The Hippodrome 287
The Palaistra 288
The Gymnasion 291

XVII. THE EXEDRA AND THE WATER SUPPLY . 294

XVIII. THE OLYMPIC FESTIVAL 300

INDEX 312

LIST OF ILLUSTRATIONS

PAGE

Head of Athene from Metope of the Stymphalian Birds.
  Photograph by Giraudon *frontispiece*

1. View of Alpheios valley from Drouva. *Photograph by
   Mr. B. Ashmole* . . . . *facing* 1
2. View of Altis from West. *Photograph by Dr. R. Caton* . ,, 1
3. Restoration of Olympia. *After R. Bohn* . . . ,, 2
4. Plan of Olympia 4
5. Geological Sketch-map of North-west Peloponnesus . . 14
6. Olympia and its environs 20
7. Incised pottery from Olympia. *Ath. Mitt.* xxxvi, Pl. V . 29
8. Incised ornament on vases of Timmari. *Mon. Ant.* xvi,
   1906, pp. 88, 130 33
9. Incised bowl from Taranto 33
10. Votive Diskos of Asklepiades. *Olympia*, V. 240 . . . 60
11. The Bouleuterion . . . . *facing* 76
12. The Hill of Kronos . . . . ,, 76
13. Animal figurines in bronze. *Olympia*, IV. 112, 138,
    178, 206, 195, 160, 162, 210 79
14. Copper and bronze bands from the lower stratum.
    Ib. 297, 299, 309, 319 80
15. Bronze plate with birds and fishes. *Ib.* 293 . . . 81
16. Bronze figurines of men. *Ib.* 242, 249, 253, 254, 263 . . 82
17. Bronze bands showing oriental ornamentation.
    Ib. 735, 738, 740 93
18. Lion fibula. *Ib.* 966 94
19–23. Bronzes from Olympia. *Ib.* 696, 717 ; *Funde v.
    Ol.* xxvi, xxvii . . . . *facing* 94
24. Bronze relief. Herakles sacrificing. *Olympia*, IV. 694 . 95
25. Phiale in Ashmolean Museum . . . . . *facing* 96
26–28. Bronze statuettes : Zeus, Aphrodite, Artemis.
    Olympia, IV. 40, 55, 74 . . . . . . ,, 96
29. Bybon's inscription. *Ib.* V. 717 97

PAGE

30. Bronze head of Zeus. *Funde v. Ol.* xxiv . . . *facing* 98
31. Marble head of Aphrodite. *Ib.* xix . . . . „ 98
32. Bronze portrait of Pankratiast. *Ib.* xxiii . . . „ 98
33. Marble head of athlete. *Olympia*, III. liv . . . „ 98
34. Marble head of hoplitodromos. *Funde v. Ol.* xxii . . „ 98
35. Portrait of Elean lady. *Olympia*, III. lxiv . . . „ 98
36. Statuette of Zeus. *Ib.* IV. 45 100
37. Coins of Elis . . . . *facing* 104
38. North-west Corner of Altis . . . . . „ 108
39. Metroon and steps of Treasury Terrace . . . „ 108
40. The Nike of Paionios. *Olympia*, III. xlvii . . „ 118
41. The Philippeion . . . . „ 130
42. North corner of the Stoa Poikile . . . . „ 130
43. Philippeion. Architectural details. *Funde v. Ol.* xxxvii . 132
44. Basis of Statues in Philippeion. *Olympia*, II. lxxxii. 3 . . 134
45. Philippeion reconstructed. *Ib.* lxxx . . . *facing* 134
46. Processional Entrance from West . . . . „ 184
47. Bases of Roman Equestrian Monuments . . . „ 184
48. Shrine at West End of Treasury Terrace . . . „ 196
49. Altar of Ge on Treasury Terrace . . . . „ 196
50. Plan of Heroon. *Olympia*, I. lxxii 204
51. Inscriptions on Altar in Heroon. *Ib.* V. 662 . . 205
52. Heraion from North-east. *Photograph by Dr. R. Caton* *facing* 206
53. Heraion from West . . . . „ 206
54. Archaic Statuette of Zeus (?). *Ath. Mitt.* xxxiii. 186 . . 207
55. Plan of Heraion. *Funde v. Ol.* xxxiv 208
56. Capitals from Heraion. *Ib.* xxxv 210
57. Colossal Head of Hera. *Olympia*, III. 1 . . *facing* 212
58. Pedimental Sculptures of Megarian Treasury. *Ib.* III. ii „ 212
59. The Hermes of Praxiteles. *Ib.* III. xlix . . „ 214
60. Plan of Treasuries. *After J. H. S.* xxv. 294 . . . 219
61. Terra-cotta Akroterion of Heraion. *Olympia*, II. cxv . *facing* 222
62. Terra-cotta cornice from Geloan Treasury. *Ib.* II. cxvii „ 222

PAGE

63. Roof of Geloan Treasury. *Ib.* 224
64. Capital and Entablature of Geloan Porch. *J. H. S.* xxvi. 55 . 225
65. Reconstruction of Megarian Treasury. *Ib.* Fig. 7 . . 226
66–73. Architectural Terra-cottas . . . . . ⎫
66, 67. From Megarian Treasury. *Olympia,* II. cxix. 4, 5 ⎪
68. From Bouleuterion. *Ib.* cxviii. 5 . . . ⎬ *facing* 226
69, 70. From a Treasury. *Ib.* cxx. 1, 3 . . . ⎪
71, 72. From Hellanodikeon. *Ib.* cxxi. 4, 5 . . ⎪
73. From Leonidaion. *Ib.* cxxiii. 1 . . . ⎭
74. Angle of Megarian Treasury. *Ib.* I. xxxviii . . 228
75. Painted Cornice of Sikyonian Treasury. *Ib.* II. cxiii. 3 . 233
76. Fallen Columns of Temple of Zeus. *Photograph by*
    Dr. R. Caton . . . . *facing* 234
77–79. Lions' Heads from Temple. *Olympia,* I. xvii . . ,, 234
80. Plan of Temple. *Funde v. Ol.* xxxii 235
81. Profile of Capitals from Temple. *Olympia,* I. xiv . 236
82. Roof of Temple. *Ib.* I. xvi 237
83. Reconstruction of the Pediments of the Temple. *After Treu*
                                              between 242 *and* 243

84–96. Figures from East Pediment :
84. Pelops ⎫
85. Zeus ⎬ *Olympia,* III. ix . . . . . *facing* 244
86. Oinomaos ⎭
87. Hippodameia ⎫
88. Handmaiden ⎪
89. Charioteer ⎬ *Ib.* III. x, xiv . . . . . ,, 246
90. Sterope ⎭
91. The Seer ⎫
92. Alpheios ⎬ *Ib.* III. xv . . . . . . ,, 248
93. Kladeos ⎭
94. Head of kneeling maiden ⎫
95. Head of Kladeos ⎬ *Ib.* III. xvii . . . . ,, 250
96. Head of kneeling boy ⎭

PAGE

97. West Pediment. Apollo. *Olympia*, III. xxii . . *facing* 252
98. Eurytion and Deidameia. *Ib*. III. xxiv . . . „ 254
99, 100. Lapith women. *Ib*. III. xxxiii . . . . „ 254
101. Kneeling Lapith, centaur, and maiden. *Ib*. III. xxx . „ 256
102, 103. Head of Apollo. *Ib*. III. xxiii . . . „ 258
104. Head of Seer. *Ib*. III. xvi . . . . . „ 260
105. Head of Theseus. *Ib*. III. xxvii . . . . „ 260
106. Head of Lapith boy. *Ib*. III. xxix . . . . „ 260
107. Head of aged Lapith woman. *Ib*. III. xxxiv . . „ 260
108. Head of Lapith maiden. *Ib*. III. xxxi . . . „ 260
109. Head of Athene from Metope of Nemean Lion. *Photograph by Mr. B. Ashmole* . . . . „ 260
110. Metope. Herakles and Stymphalian Birds. *Olympia*, III. xxxvi . . . . . „ 264
111. Metope. Herakles and the Cretan Bull. *Ib*. . „ 264
112. Metope. Herakles and Atlas. *Photograph by Mr. B. Ashmole* . . . . „ 266
113. Metope. Herakles cleansing the Augean Stables. *Olympia*, III. xliii . . . . . . „ 266
114. Plan of Prytaneion. *Ib*. I. xliv 268
115. Plan of Bouleuterion. *Ib*. I. lv 272
116. Painted Cornices from Hellanodikeon. *Ib*, II. cxiii . 277
117. Plan of Theokoleon. *Ib*. II, Figs. 64, 65 . . 279
118. Plan of Leonidaion. *Ib*. I. lxii 281
119. Colonnades of Leonidaion reconstructed. *Ib*. II. lxvi . 283
120. The Stadion. *Ib*. I. xlvii 284
121. Centre of Western Aphesis 285
122. Entrance to Stadion . . . . . *facing* 286
123. Portico of Gymnasion . . . . . „ 286
124. Aphesis of Hippodrome. *Gk. Athletics*, Fig. 164 . 287
125. Plan of Palaistra. *Ib*. Fig. 185 289
126. Capitals from Palaistra. *Olympia*, II. lxxiv . . 290
127. Entrance of Gymnasion reconstructed. *Ib*. II. lxxvi . 292
128. Plan of Exedra. *Olympia*, II. lxxxiii . . . 295
129. Jumping weight found at Olympia. *Ib*. IV. 180 . . 305

SELECTED BIBLIOGRAPHY

(References to special articles will be found in the notes.)

THE EXCAVATIONS.

Die Ausgrabungen zu Olympia. 5 vols. Berlin, 1876–81.

Die Funde von Olympia. Berlin, 1882.

Olympia : die Ergebnisse der von dem Deutschen Reich veranstalteten Ausgrabung. Curtius u. Adler. Berlin, 1887–97.

Vol. I. Topographie und Geschichte.

Vol. II. Die Baudenkmäler.

Vol. III. Bildwerke in Stein und Thon. G. Treu.

Vol. IV. Die Bronzen. A. Furtwängler.

Vol. V. Die Inschriften. W. Dittenberger u. A. Purgold.

GENERAL.

Pausanias. *Descriptio Graeciae.* v, vi.

Bötticher, A. *Olympia : das Fest und seine Stätte*[2]. 1886.

Flasch, A. *Olympia* in *Baumeister's Denkmäler*.

Frazer, Sir James. *Pausanias.* 1898. (Contains excellent summaries of the results of excavations.)

Gardner, P. In *New Chapters in Greek History*. London, 1892.

Krause, J. H. *Olympia.* Vienna, 1838. (A storehouse of literary references.)

Luckenbach, H. *Olympia und Delphi.* Munich, 1904.

ART.

E. Buschor and Richard Hamann. *Die Skulpturen des Zeustempels zu Olympia.* Marburg, 1924.

Hamann, Richard. *Olympische Kunst.* Marburg, 1923.

Schrader, Hans. *Phidias.* Frankfurt, 1924.

Hyde, Walter. *Olympic Victor Monuments.* Washington, 1921.

ATHLETIC HISTORY.

Gardiner, E. Norman. *Greek Athletic Sports and Festivals*. London, 1910.

S. Julii Africani. Ὀλυμπιάδων ἀναγραφή. J. Rutgers. Leyden, 1862.

Förster, H. *Sieger in den Olympischen Spielen*. Zwickau, 1892.

Jüthner, Julius. *Philostratus über Gymnastik*. Leipzig, 1909.

LIST OF COMMON ABBREVIATIONS

Arch. Zeit. = Archäologische Zeitung.

Ath. Mitt. = Mitteilungen des Deutschen Arch. Inst., Athenische Abteilung.

B. C. H. = Bulletin de Correspondance Hellénique.

B. S. A. = Annual of the British School at Athens.

Dar.-Sagl. = Daremberg-Saglio. Dictionnaire des Antiquités.

Ἐφ. Ἀρχ. = Ἐφημερίς Ἀρχαιολογική.

Gk. Athletics = E. Norman Gardiner, ' Greek Athletic Sports and Festivals '.

Jahrb. = Jahrbuch des Deutschen Arch. Inst.

Olympia = Olympia, Ergebnisse.

P. = Pausanias. Descriptio Graeciae.

1. VIEW OF ALPHEIOS VALLEY FROM DROUVA

In foreground Museum and valley of Kladeos.   In centre the Hill of Kronos and the Altis
Behind the Hill of Kronos the Hill of Pisa

2. VIEW OF ALTIS FROM WEST

In foreground the Heroon and Theokoleon.   To right the Byzantine Church
In centre Temple of Zeus.   Beyond it in the distance, faintly visible, Phrixa

I

The Destruction and Recovery of Olympia

ἅπανθ᾽ ὁ μακρὸς κἀναρίθμητος χρόνος
φύει τ᾽ ἄδηλα καὶ φανέντα κρύπτεται.

Soph. *Aias*, 646.

THE Olympic Games have been revived and Olympia is a name familiar on men's lips to-day as it was two thousand years ago. No place makes such an appeal to the modern imagination and no place is more important for the understanding of Greek religion, Greek life, and Greek history. For more than a thousand years it was the national centre of Greek religion and the scene of the greatest athletic festival that the world has ever known. For a thousand years its site remained desolate and its very name was lost. Now the spade has brought to light its ruins, and we can in imagination reconstruct its temples and its monuments and retrace in some sort its history.

There is perhaps no other place in Greece that has such a peculiar charm as Olympia. It lies some ten miles from the sea, in the angle formed by the Alpheios with its northern tributary the Kladeos. About a mile above Olympia the narrow valley expands into a broad alluvial plain, broken only just beyond Olympia by the ridge of Droúva, which, projecting southward to the river bank, cuts off the sacred precinct from the sea. South of the river runs a continuous line of hills covered with corn-fields and vineyards, with villages and farmsteads on the upper slopes. On the north the hills are lower, more broken, and more thickly wooded. Here two conical peaks stand out conspicuously from the rest, forming with the hill of Droúva a semicircle which completely encloses the plain of Olympia. The eastern peak, which comes close down to the river, is the hill of Pisa, on which was the ancient citadel of the kings who ruled the plain. The central peak, standing back a mile from the river,

B

is the sacred hill of Kronos, clothed from head to foot with pine-trees, oaks, and olives, which, stretching southward into the plain, formed the Sacred Grove, the Altis of Olympia. Between the hill of Droúva and the Altis the river Kladeos rushes down from the heights of Pholoe between high banks formerly shaded by plane-trees.

To obtain the best view of the site the visitor should climb the height of Droúva (Fig. 1). Westward the eye travels across the flat plain to the sea, eastward along the valley to the high conical hill of Phrixa and far beyond to the gaunt mountains of Arkadia. To the south, in the gaps of the hills one catches glimpses of the rugged ridge of Kaiapha, while to the north the river extends along the valley of the Kladeos to the mighty mass of Eryman-thos. Immediately below lies the plain of Olympia, a stretch of parkland completely surrounded by the rivers and wooded hills, its quiet charm enhanced by contrast with the grim barrenness of the distant mountains. The vegetation is singularly rich and varied. To-day the dark umbrella-pine has for the most part ousted its rivals on the upper slopes, but lower down the plane-tree and oak still survive, and a multitude of flowering shrubs among which is the wild olive-tree with its small grey leaves and prickly branches, the tree from which the crowns of the Olympic victor were cut. A traveller who visited Olympia in the last century described it as a beautiful wilderness. To the visitor who saw it shortly after the excavations it was no longer a wilderness, but a desolation of trenches and of ruins. From the lower slopes of the hill of Kronos he could trace the outlines of the walls, the ground-plans of temples, treasuries: it was interesting, but unutterably sad, and reft of its beauty. To-day nature has resumed her sway. The Altis is once more a shaded grove, the ruins are embedded in a tangle of flowers and shrubs, the wild olive once more flourishes behind the temple of Zeus. The visitor may find it more difficult to trace out the plans of walls and buildings, the archaeologist may find research less easy, but the loss is more than counterbalanced by the gain of its recovered beauty. Olympia is once more, as it was of old, the garden of Zeus, a worthy setting for the sanctuary and the festival and for the great ideals that they stood for, the ideals of manliness and beauty, concord, and peace.

Such must have been the site when the immigrants from the

Hill of Kronos   Exedra   Treasuries

Philippeion   Heraion   Pelopion   Metroon   Temple of Zeus   Procesional entrance

3. RESTORATION OF OLYMPIA (R. Bohn)

north first brought thither the worship of Zeus. When the festival began we cannot say. Greek tradition placed the first Olympiad in 776 B.C.: the games were celebrated for the last time in A.D. 393. In the next year they were abolished by a decree of the Emperor Theodosius I, and shortly afterwards the great statue of Zeus, the masterpiece of Pheidias, was carried off to Constantinople, where it perished in the great fire. In A.D. 426 Theodosius II issued a decree for the destruction of all pagan temples, and among those that suffered was the temple of Zeus.

THE DESTRUCTION OF OLYMPIA

From this time the work of destruction [1] went on apace. The massive walls and columns of the temple, it is true, resisted the might of the spoiler, but the temple itself was plundered and the building known as the workshop of Pheidias was converted into a Christian church. An apsis was added at the east end, and the interior was divided into three aisles by a double row of pillars. The floor was raised, and in its construction part of the pavement from the temple was employed, besides numerous inscribed slabs and bases of monuments split in two. Other buildings were plundered at the same time for the new church, especially the neighbouring Philippeion with its marble steps and columns, the Exedra of Herodes, the Gymnasion and Palaistra, and the Treasuries of Sikyon and Syracuse. Some forty years later the Altis was again plundered, this time for the construction of a Byzantine fortress. It was about the time when Genseric and his Vandals were ravaging the west coast of Greece, and the fortress was probably intended as an observation post and place of refuge against the raiders. Its north-west corner was formed by the Temple of Zeus, its southern side by the south colonnade, the latter being connected with the temple by massive walls on the west and the east. These walls were three metres thick and, at the time of the excavations, four metres high, and were constructed of blocks of every conceivable shape and size torn from the buildings and monuments of the Altis. West of the fortress the remains of houses and wine-presses point to the existence at this time of a village of peasants.

Flood and earthquake completed the destruction. In the

[1] Adler, *Olympia*, i, pp. 93 ff.

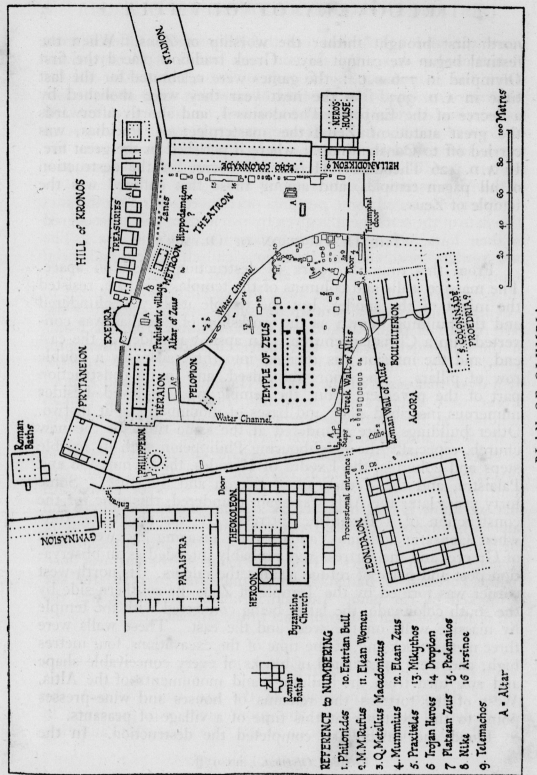

4. PLAN OF OLYMPIA

REFERENCE to NUMBERING

1. Philonides
2. M. M. Rufus
3. Q. Metellus Macedonicus
4. Mummius
5. Praxiteles
6. Trojan Heroes
7. Plataean Zeus
8. Nike
9. Telemachos
10. Eretrian Bull
11. Elean Women
12. Elean Zeus
13. Mikythos
14. Dropion
15. Ptolemaios
16. Arsinoe

A = Altar

years 522 and 551 of our era the Peloponnese suffered from violent earthquakes. We do not know which of the two overthrew the columns of the Temple of Zeus, but in the end the Altis was converted into the field of ruin that we now see. The last earthquake was followed by serious landslips from the hill of Droúva and the hill of Kronos which blocked the course of the Kladeos, and the river bursting its banks swept away the western part of the Gymnasion and covered the western part of the Altis itself with débris.

After an interval some peasants once more settled on the site. The date of the settlement is given by two finds of coins discovered in their huts, belonging to the years A.D. 565 and 575. The new settlers restored the Byzantine church, which had been damaged in the earthquakes, and added a new porch. This village in its turn was swept away by the Kladeos and buried to a depth of four metres beneath the sand. At the same time the eastern part of the Altis suffered in like manner from the floods of the Alpheios. Against this danger it had so far been protected by the embankment of the Hippodrome, and probably by a dyke that guarded the road to Harpina. Road and Hippodrome were swept away completely, but the mass of Roman buildings at the south-east corner of the Altis broke the force of the flood and saved the Altis itself.

Such are the few facts with regard to the destruction of Olympia that we have learnt from the excavations. From this time its history is a blank for a thousand years or more. All that we know is that it served as a stone quarry for Turks and later inhabitants. Blocks from the Altis have been found in the Turkish forts at Miráka, Lála, and Pýrgos, and in the houses of neighbouring villages. Even the name of the site was lost. In the Portulan of Battista Palnese, published in 1516,[1] the site is marked by the name Andilalo, probably because it was the end of the road that led from Lála to the Alpheios.

THE RECOVERY OF OLYMPIA

But though the knowledge of the site itself was lost, the knowledge of its buildings and monuments was preserved in the full and accurate description of the Greek traveller Pausanias,

[1] Weil, *Olympia*, i, pp. 101 ff.

who visited Olympia in A.D. 174. This record early aroused the interest of art-collectors and archaeologists. The first suggestion of an expedition to Olympia was made in 1723 by Montfaucon, who tried to induce Cardinal Quirini, then Archbishop of Corfou, to undertake the exploration of the site. But Quirini left Corfou without acting on the suggestion. A few years later the idea was revived by Winckelmann, who proposed to obtain a firman from the Porte and to employ a hundred workmen to excavate the Stadion. But he died before his plan could be carried out.

Meanwhile in 1766, two years before Winckelmann's death, the site of Olympia had been rediscovered by Richard Chandler. There he found ' the walls of the cella of a very large temple, standing many feet high and well built, the stones all injured and manifesting the labour of persons who have endeavoured by boring to get at the metal with which they were cemented '. ' At a distance before it ', he writes, ' was a deep hollow with stagnant water and brickwork, where, it is imagined, was the Stadium.'

From this time the site was visited by numerous travellers. Fauvel, who visited Olympia in 1787 with Choiseul-Gouffier, was the first to attempt a plan of the site. In this plan the Stadion and Hippodrome were wrongly placed to the west of the temple in the valley of the Kladeos. A more accurate plan was constructed under the direction of Lord Spencer Stanhope, who visited the site in 1813. Meanwhile the work of destruction was going on. Dodwell, who was at Olympia with Gell in 1805, describes the wall of the cella as only two feet above the ground.

The first actual excavation was carried out in 1829, immediately after the War of Independence, by the French Expédition Scientifique de Morée. The expedition did not reach Olympia till the 9th of May, and barely six weeks were available for work, sufficient only for a partial examination of the site of the Temple of Zeus and of the Byzantine church. On the west side of the temple were found some of the metopes of the Opisthodome, on the east portions of those of the Pronaos. A trench dug along the length of the temple laid bare two of the columns of the interior, portions of the pavement of black Eleusinian marble in the cella, and the fine Triton mosaic in the Pronaos. Sufficient was found of the columns, entablature, and roofs for a reconstruction of the general plan of the temple. The sculptural finds were removed to the Louvre.

The honour of completing the work was reserved for Ernst Curtius. He first visited Olympia in 1838, when twenty-four years of age. In 1852 he brought forward a proposal for the excavation of the site, and was fortunate in obtaining the enthusiastic support of King Frederic William IV and his nephew Prince Frederic William. From this time, in spite of many postponements and disappointments, Curtius never relaxed in his efforts, but it was not till 1876 that he at last saw the realization of his dream. The work, which proved far more arduous than was anticipated, lasted six years. The expense was borne by the German Government, and the work was under the direction of a central board consisting of Ernst Curtius, F. Adler, and Dr. Busch, the latter being succeeded in 1879 by Dr. Lindau. The most eminent archaeologists in Germany took part at different times in the work of excavation.

The Results of the Excavations

The excavations fully realized the expectations. For the first time, as Curtius had foreseen, the plan of a Greek national sanctuary was laid bare, and, further, the remains of the buildings enabled us to trace its growth. A glance at the plan will show that nearly all the buildings mentioned by Pausanias were identified and the accuracy of his description was established. The Altis was found to be enclosed by two walls, one of Greek, the other of Roman construction. Within these walls were found the three temples, the Heraion, the Temple of Zeus, and the Metroon, also the Philippeion and the precinct of Pelops. Along its eastern boundary were the Echo Colonnade and the vaulted entrance to the Stadion; along its north side was a stepped wall, above which were the foundations of the Treasuries. The only buildings of which no traces were found were the Hippodameion, the house of Oinomaos, and the great Altar of Zeus. For their sites we must depend on the evidence of Pausanias. The mound of Hippodameia, as we shall see, must have been in the north-east corner of the Altis, the Altar of Zeus to the east of and equidistant from the Heraion and the Pelopion, the house of Oinomaos a little south of the altar.

The only important buildings found that Pausanias does not mention were the so-called Exedra of Herodes Atticus at the north-west corner of the Altis, the triumphal gate of Nero to the east of the Bouleuterion, and the south-east building which seems to have been converted into a palace for Nero. All three buildings are connected with Imperial Rome, a fact which may perhaps explain his silence. As regards Nero, who prostituted the glories of Olympia to his personal vanity, this silence is natural and justifiable ; it is harder to understand his neglect of Herodes, the munificent benefactor of Hellas.

Outside the wall of the Altis on the west are the Prytaneion containing the Altar of Hestia, the Gymnasion and Palaistra, the Theokoleon and Leonidaion. Between the two latter was the Byzantine church in which we may probably recognize the former workshop of Pheidias. Behind the Theokoleon are the remains of an interesting Heroon, not mentioned by Pausanias.

South of the Altis stretched the Agora : outside its south wall are numerous Greek buildings of which nothing is known. In the centre the foundations of the Bouleuterion are clearly visible. South of the Bouleuterion was found a great stoa which I venture to identify with the Proedria of Pausanias.

At the south-east corner of the Altis is a maze of Roman foundations, beyond which must have stretched the Hippodrome. Of the latter not a trace remains, but the starting lines of the Stadion immediately to the north are still visible.

Nothing has been found of the Temple of Demeter Chamyne, which, according to Pausanias, stood near the east end of the Stadion. Nor have excavations on the hill of Kronos produced any results. The Temples of Aphrodite Ourania and of Eileithyia, which were on its slopes, and the Altar of Kronos on its summit, have completely disappeared. Little of the actual buildings remains standing above the stylobate, but we can usually reconstruct their plan with certainty from the numerous architectural blocks found scattered round them or built into the walls of the Byzantine fortress and the floor of the Byzantine church. These remains afford valuable illustrations of all periods and styles of Greek architecture, and throw light especially on the construction of roofs and entablature, the use of terra-cotta for cornices and akroteria, and the use of colour in architectural details.

Architectural Terra-cottas

The terra-cotta remains are particularly interesting, as they enable us to trace the changes of style for more than three centuries.[1] Typical examples, unfortunately not coloured, are collected in Figs. 61–73. The earliest style is represented by the great gable akroterion of the Heraion (Fig. 61). The surface is a dull black-brown on which ornaments are incised with a graver or compass and painted with white, yellow, or violet. Flat bands of geometric ornament are separated by moulded astragals. In the sixth century a new style appears, showing strong oriental influences. The best example of this style is the elaborate terra-cotta casing of the pediment of the Geloan Treasury (Fig. 62). The ground is a rich yellow and the designs are painted in red and black. A very similar cornice (Fig. 68) was found near the Bouleuterion and may possibly belong to that building. The cornice and antefix (Figs. 66, 67) come from the Megarian Treasury. The waterspouts in this cornice were in the form of lions' heads. In a fine cornice showing a later development of the same style (Figs. 69, 70) Gorgons' heads with red lolling tongues serve this purpose. In the fourth century a change took place similar to that from the black-figured to the red-figured vases. The dull yellow ground is replaced by a dark highly polished surface on which the designs are painted in cream or pale yellow. The designs, too, become more naturalistic. Cornices of this type were found in the south-east building or Hellanodikeon (Figs. 71, 72). Towards the close of the century the flat decoration gradually gave place to plastic. The typical cornice of the fourth century is that of the Leonidaion (Fig. 73) with its akanthos scrolls and lions' heads.

With regard to sculpture the sanguine expectations of Winckelmann were doomed to disappointment. Nearly all the statues and works of art which Pausanias describes had been carried off to Rome or destroyed. Still, in the magnificent sculptures of the pediments and metopes of the Temple of Zeus we have an invaluable addition to our knowledge of architectural sculpture and Peloponnesian art, while in the Hermes of Praxiteles and the Nike of Paionios we possess for the first time authentic originals of these two famous artists. A number of marble statues of Roman emperors and others, mostly from the Metroon and the

[1] Borrman, *Olympia*, ii, pp. 187 ff.

Exedra of Herodes, were also found, but of the multitude of Greek masterpieces only a few fragments survive. A few heads belonging to them are reproduced in Figs. 29–34.

But if the statues have perished, hundreds of the inscribed bases on which they stood still exist. Very few, however, are *in situ*. The epigraphical results are rich and varied, ranging from the sixth century B.C. to the third century A.D. From those inscriptions we gain considerable information as to the administration of Olympia and the history of the festival.

Votive Offerings

Lastly, we must notice the lesser finds, objects in metal or terra-cotta. These were mostly votive offerings or vessels used for sacrifices or banquets. An enormous number of votive offerings were found, most of them made of bronze, a few of terra-cotta, and the majority of them belong to the early days of the sanctuary, many of them being older than any known building. The votive offerings consisted of figurines of men and animals in bronze and terra-cotta, bronze groups of dancers, miniature chariots and wheels, miniature tripods, miniature cymbals and double axes ; personal ornaments, diadems, neck-laces, rings, fibulae, pendants, pins ; weapons, spear-heads, arrow-heads, helmets, shields, greaves, swords ; engraved bronze plates and tripods ornamented with griffins' heads. Besides these were numerous bronze vessels, cauldrons, kettles, cups, pans, and large iron tripods.[1]

Comparatively little pottery was found, a remarkable circum-stance considering the quantities that have been found on other sites. It is possible that potsherds were regarded as unimportant and neglected by the excavators. It is only of recent years that we have learnt to understand their value as the chief criterion for determining prehistoric chronology.

Stratification

The distribution of the votive offerings is important. The principal finds were in and around the Pelopion, in the space between the Heraion and the Pelopion, round the Temple of Zeus, round the elliptical foundation formerly identified with the Altar of Zeus, which has since proved to be two prehistoric houses, and to the west of the Metron. Similar but less numerous

[1] *Olympia*, iv.

finds have occurred outside the Altis, especially on the west side and to the west of the Bouleuterion. In the Prytaneion were found, besides a few archaic statuettes and figurines, a variety of domestic and sacrificial vessels, kettles, tripods, cups, weights, lamps, and nails, and similar objects were found in the Bouleuterion and south-east buildings.

The votive offerings were mostly found in a layer of black earth, and we may reasonably infer that the places where they were most numerous were the sites of altars. Unfortunately the stratification of the Altis is, owing to the nature of the soil and its frequent disturbance, very unreliable. Parts of the same dedication were sometimes found in very different parts of the Altis. For example, of three inscribed spears dedicated by the people of Thurii from the spoil of Tarentum, two were found in the Prytaneion and one in the south-east building, while griffin heads belonging to the same tripod were found in front of the building viii on the Treasury terrace and north of the Byzantine church.

In spite, however, of this uncertainty, two strata can be clearly distinguished at two points. First, in the space between the Heraion and the Pelopion, we find an upper stratum of black earth separated by a layer of sand 30 to 45 cm. thick from a lower layer of black earth 20 cm. thick. Both layers of black earth contain votive offerings, and both are older than the wall of the Pelopion which is built above them : the lower stratum is also earlier than the Heraion, since it extends under the foundations of that building, where it seems to be again divided into two thin layers. The discovery of proto-Corinthian sherds by Dörpfeld under the foundation of the Heraion proves that it cannot be much earlier than 700 B.C. We may, therefore, safely date the votive offerings in the lower stratum before 700 B.C.

A second site where the stratification is clear is to the west of the Metroon, where we find a deposit extending slightly to the north of the altar and under the western foundations of the Metroon. Here some 70 to 85 cm. below the altar is a layer of black earth separated by a layer of sand from a second deposit, above which is another layer of sand, on which the altar stands.

The stratification was carried a stage further back by Dr. Dörpfeld.[1] Convinced of the prehistoric character of

[1] *infra*, p. 26.

Olympia he began in 1905 a fresh series of excavations. Trial pits were sunk under the cella and opisthodome of the Heraion. Beneath the level of the Altis at the time of the building of the temple were found numerous terra-cottas, bronzes, and sherds similar to those found in the previous excavations, and a few incised monochrome sherds resembling those that the excavator was finding at Nidri in Leukas. Under the opisthodome were the remains of earlier walls, built of large round pebbles, the walls perhaps of an altar or an earlier temple. Extending his excavations east of the temple he was rewarded by the discovery of six prehistoric houses between the temple and the Metroon. One of these houses was below the north-east corner of the Pelopion, and the settlement seems to have extended under the Treasury terrace, which proves therefore to have been constructed artificially. The structure of these houses and the character of the contents will be discussed in Chapter III. Here we are merely concerned with the stratification. This can be most clearly seen under the Pelopion, where we have first the Greek wall of the Pelopion; then, separated from it by a layer of rubble and stone, the stratum of primitive votive offerings; finally, beneath a layer of sand, the prehistoric stratum, or rather strata, for it consists of two layers of humus and two walls crossing one another. Lower still was a pithos containing the bones of a child, proving that the settlement was of considerable duration. How it came to an end we do not know. It was buried beneath a layer of sand, but whether the sand was brought there by floods or landslip, or whether the village was purposely covered to provide a foundation for altars or buildings, cannot be determined.

II

The Geography of the North-West Peloponnese

Οἳ δὲ Πύλον τ᾽ ἐνέμοντο καὶ Ἀρήνην ἐρατεινήν
καὶ Θρύον Ἀλφειοῖο πόρον καὶ εὔκτιτον Αἰπύ.

Il. ii. 591.

οἳ δ᾽ ἄρα Βουπράσιόν τε καὶ Ἤλιδα δῖαν ἔναιον
ὅσσον ἐφ᾽ Ὑρμίνη καὶ Μύρσινος ἐσχατόωσα
πέτρη τ᾽ Ὠλενίη καὶ Ἀλείσιον ἐντὸς ἐέργει,

Ib. 615.

οἳ δ᾽ ἐκ Δουλιχίοιο Ἐχινάων θ᾽ ἱεράων
νήσων αἳ ναίουσι πέρην ἁλὸς Ἤλιδος ἄντα.

Ib. 625.

THE NORTH-WEST PELOPONNESE

THE north-west Peloponnese is a long triangular strip of hill country and coastal plain extending from Cape Drepanon to Kyparisseia and cut off from the rest of the Peloponnese by the massive limestone mountains that form the western rib of the mountain system of Arkadia. To the north is the mighty mass of Erymanthos, the modern Olonos, which with its northern extension the Panachaikon reaches the shores of the Corinthian gulf, where only a narrow strait divides it from the mountains of Aitolia. To the south again the spurs of the sacred Mount Lykaion reach the sea between the Neda and the Aulon, from which point the limestone ridge continues to the southern promontory of Messenia. Between Erymanthos and Lykaion the mountain system recedes and gives way to a tableland of soft tertiary rocks through which the waters of the Alpheios and its tributaries make their way to the sea along a deep and ever-widening valley.

The contrast between the north-west and the rest of the Peloponnese is striking. Instead of the barren, rugged mountains of the interior we see an undulating hill country of marl, sandstone, and conglomerate cut into innumerable ravines and valleys by the streams that flow down from the mountains, and descending in wooded terraces to a flat coastal plain. In the upper parts this tableland is covered with forests of oak and pine, and owing to the scarcity of water can only support a scanty population of shepherds and hunters. But westwards the hills grow lower, the valleys broader, and their sides less steep. The woods are interspersed with meadows and plough-land, vineyards and olive groves, farms and prosperous villages.

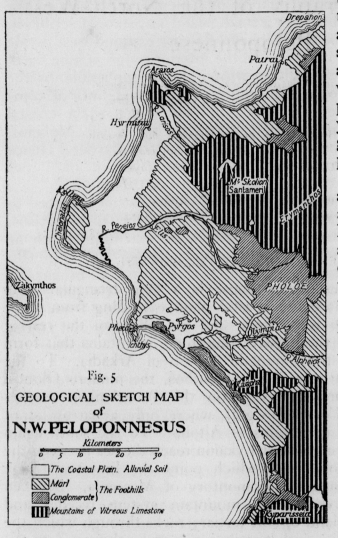

Fig. 5
GEOLOGICAL SKETCH MAP
of
N.W. PELOPONNESUS

Kilometers
0   5   10   20   30

☐ The Coastal Plain. Alluvial Soil
▨ Marl
▧ Conglomerate } The Foothills
▥ Mountains of Vitreous Limestone

Between the hills and the sea stretches a plain of rich, alluvial soil, less than a mile broad at either end, but widening out between the Alpheios and Peneios to a breadth of ten miles, while in the valleys of these rivers the alluvial soil extends many miles inland. The plain is extraordinarily fertile, but in the present day is marshy and unhealthy. Large tracts are covered with forest, and on either side of the Alpheios stretch large salt-water lagoons which cannot have existed in ancient times.

The coastline itself has altered little, for ancient burials have been found between the lagoon of Mouría and the mouth of the Alpheios. A long stretch of sandy shore shelves gradually into a shallow sea. Only at three points is it broken, where three rocky promontories, the remains of former islands, jut out into the sea, Araxos, Chelonatas, and Ichthys. Close to these are the only three harbours on the coast, Hyrmina a little south of Araxos, Kyllene probably to the north of Chelonatas, commanded by the Frankish fortress of Chlemóutsi,[1] Pheia to the west of Ichthys, protected by a small island, as Strabo describes it.

The rivers Peneios and Alpheios flowing east and west divide the land into a series of zones. In the interior progress from north to south is rendered difficult, in winter almost impossible, by the deep valleys and precipitous ravines. The chief lines of communication are along the valleys of these rivers or the coastal plain, and even here the swift broad stream of the Alpheios, fordable only at a few points, offers a formidable barrier. Hence real political union was impossible, and from the time of Homer we find the country occupied by a variety of tribes.

In historic times the northern part of the district belonged to Achaia, which was separated from Elis by the river Larisos. Strabo[2] describes the territory of Elis as extending south as far as the Neda, including besides Elis proper the originally independent districts of Pisatis and Triphylia. Elis proper, or Hollow Elis, consisted in the hill country and plains on either side of the Peneios. The city of Elis, which before the Synoecism in 471 B.C. was little more than a fortress, was situated at the point where the valley opens out into the plain. Farther up the same valley, at the junction of the Peneios and Ladon, was the possibly older fortress of Pyrgos. The boundary between Elis and Pisatis was formed by the brook Elisa or Elison, which has been identified with the Mesolongáki half-way between Chelonatas and Ichthys. Pisatis took its name from the fortress of Pisa, the remains of which have been found on an isolated height a mile to the east of Olympia.[3] It consisted of a loose league of eight towns, all apparently on the northern bank of the Alpheios. South of the river was Triphylia, the land of the three tribes. According to Strabo[4] these were the Epeians, Minyans, and Eleans, but some people, he tells us, substituted the Arkadians for the Minyans. In the extreme south the Lepreatai maintained their independence during most of their history.

[1] This is the view of Partsch, *Olympia*, i, p. 13, and Philippson, *Peloponnes*, p. 299, who maintain that Strabo, p. 338, is mistaken in placing the mouth of the Peneios between Chelonatas and Kyllene. Strabo's account of this district is very inaccurate.
[2] p. 338; P. iv. 36.   [3] Dörpfeld, *Ath. Mitt.* xxxiii, p. 318; xxxviii, p. 137.
[4] P. 337.

The fertility of the country is remarkable. Nowhere in the Peloponnese is so large a proportion capable of cultivation and fit for habitation. To-day, after centuries of misrule and desolation, it is once more recovering its prosperity. Patras is now the chief commercial port of Greece, and from it are exported large quantities of wine, currants, olives, and hides ; a similar commerce is springing up at Katakolo, perhaps the ancient harbour of Olympia.

In ancient times the fertility of Elis was famous. Oxylos, according to the legend, led the Dorians through Arkadia and avoided Elis for fear that the goodness of the land might tempt them to seize it for themselves. Pausanias[1] describes Elis as fertile in all sorts of fruits ; and notes particularly that hemp, flax, and ' byssos ', perhaps a finer sort of flax, were grown everywhere. The land was especially favourable for the breeding of horses and cattle. In Homer[2] the princes of Ithaca have stud farms in Elis, and Augeias holds chariot races there. The name Bouprasion on the coast suggests a cattle market. Nestor tells us how in his youth the Pylians raided Elis and carried off ' fifty herds of kine, as many flocks of sheep, as many droves of swine, and as many flocks of goats, and chestnut horses, a hundred and fifty, all mares with their foals at their feet '.[3] Finally its woods abounded with game, its sea and lakes with fish.

In Homeric times and later the land was kept in a constant state of unrest, chiefly from the pressure of northern invaders, but from the eighth century onwards it enjoyed an exceptional security and freedom from invasion. Living in these easy circumstances the Eleans developed a distinctive character of their own. They were farmers and countrymen living in scattered villages and farms. Their land provided them with all that they required. They multiplied and prospered, but had little incentive to enterprise or adventure. Engrossed in their material comforts, they took no part in the restless activities of their more progressive countrymen. They cared little for politics and never took to city life. They seldom travelled, they founded no colonies, they had no inclination for the sea or for commerce, they won little distinction in literature or art, they took no part in the national struggles of Hellas. So they earned the reputation of

---

[1] vi. 26 ; v. 5. 2 ; vii. 21. 7. For a discussion of the meaning of *Byssos* v. Frazer, *Pausanias*, iii, p. 470.

[2] *Od.* iv. 634, xxi. 347 ; *Il.* xi. 700. [3] *Il.* xi. 677.

being luxurious, addicted to the pleasures of the table, drunken and licentious, unwarlike and cowardly. But they often belied their reputation, and in the administration of Olympia at all events they showed no little ability and vigour.

The Mountain Barrier and Coastal Plain.

The Greeks attributed the security of Elis to the sanctity of Olympia, but history shows that this sanctity was of little avail when more material interests were at stake. The real causes of the security of the land were the protection afforded by the mountain barrier and its remoteness from the Aegean. The whole mountain system of the Peloponnese separated it from the Aegean coast. It is true that this mountain barrier was pierced by the rivers Peneios, Alpheios, and Neda. But while these valleys facilitated peaceful communication with the interior, they were narrow, intersected by deep ravines, and easily guarded. No trade-routes either by land or sea connected Elis with the Aegean. She had no commerce with the interior, nor did she utilize her few harbours. The great trade-route along the Gulf of Corinth passed northwards through the islands before it crossed over to Italy and Sicily, and left the west coast of the Peloponnese untouched. The other route round the south coast was difficult and dangerous, and though known and used even in Minoan times can never have been of sufficient importance to have much influence on the western Peloponnese.

The real key to the western Peloponnese is the coastal plain. This plain faces west and north, and access to the plain was not by land but by sea. Though the harbours were few, the long stretches of sandy coast were eminently suitable for local traffic ; the distances from the islands and Aitolia were but short. Here, as in the Aegean, the sea serves not to separate but to connect. No one who has travelled from Patras to Olympia through the plain can fail to realize how closely connected it is with Aitolia and the islands, and through the islands lies the best route to Italy and Sicily. As far back as we can trace its history we find swarms of northern immigrants crossing the narrow waters, settling among the inhabitants of the plain or driving them farther south or on to the mountains. In the intervals when the land was free from northern invasion, it owed its prosperity to its accessibility to the west. Alpheios pursues the nymph Arethousa beneath the sea, but they rise together in Sicilian Syracuse.

D

How intimately Olympia was connected with the north and the west we shall see in the following chapters. We shall see that the historical Eleans who controlled the festival were Aitolians, and that the growth of Olympia from a local to a national festival was due largely to the participation of the rich colonies of Italy and Sicily. Further, we shall see that when the liberties of Greece were lost and the fortunes of Olympia itself were at their lowest ebb, it was the patronage of the Roman emperors that revived its importance and maintained it till the empire itself was tottering to its fall.

The subsequent history of the land tells the same tale. In the sixth century A.D. a fresh period of immigration from the north began. Hordes of Avars and Slavs crossed the straits and poured into the land. In Elis the native population was so much reduced by war and pestilence that the Greek language fell into disuse, and most of the Greek place-names disappeared entirely. But once more the marvellous vitality of the race reasserted itself. Helped by the Byzantine Government, the Greek inhabitants gradually recovered and drove the Slavs into the mountains of the interior, where, like the Arkadians of old, they maintained their independence for centuries.

The growth of Adriatic trade brought a fresh period of prosperity to the land. Patras, which had been saved from the Slavs by the miraculous intervention of St. Andrew, was now a wealthy and flourishing seaport. Its prosperity excited the cupidity of the crusaders. Guillaume de Champêtre seized the town and, rapidly making himself master of the whole north-western Peloponnese, assumed the title of Prince of Achaia or Morea. His successors extended their power over the whole peninsula, but the centre of government remained in the west. Its capital was Andravída, close to Chelonatas ; the Archbishop of Patras was primate of Achaia. The fortresses of Patras, Clarenza, and Pontikokastro still bear witness to the power of the Frankish princes.

In the fourteenth century we find another northern race appearing in the Peloponnese. The Albanians first arrived there as mercenaries in the pay of the Despots of Mistrà. Some of these settled in the Peloponnese as colonists, and from this time a continuous stream of Albanians poured into the land. They were particularly numerous in the east, but many of them also settled in the plains of Elis, whence they were gradually forced into the highlands of Pholoe. Here they long maintained their nationality and the religion of Mahomet which they had adopted from the Turks.

Lastly, the revived prosperity in the present day of Patras and Pýrgos is due to the advantageous position of these places for commerce with the west.

OLYMPIA AND ITS COMMUNICATIONS

In the whole north-west Peloponnese there is no place so richly dowered by nature, so accessible and yet so secure, as Olympia. The white waters of the Alpheios sweeping through the broad and fertile plain, its tributary the Kladeos rushing down to join it through its wooded valley, the long green ridge of the Triphylian hills, the broken foothills of Pholoe with the pine-clad hill of Kronos overlooking the Altis, all combine to produce a scene of rich and peaceful security. No fairer or more fitting site could have been chosen for a national festival. The Greeks with their natural love of beauty felt its spell, and Pindar never tires of dwelling lovingly on each feature in the familiar scene.[1] But it is not to its natural beauty that Olympia owed its importance. It is the one real centre of the north-west Peloponnese, the place where all roads meet, and more than that, thanks to the Alpheios, it is accessible to every part of the Peloponnese and the greater Hellas of Italy and Sicily.

The Upper Alpheios.

The Alpheios is the main artery of the western Peloponnese. Rising in the plain of Franko-vrýsi, the ancient Asea, it descends into the plain of Megalopolis, where it unites with the many streams that flow from the surrounding hills. The combined waters enter a deep, narrow gorge at the northern end of the plain dominated by the precipitous height on which stands the medieval fortress of Karýtaina. For ten miles the river forces its way north-westward through the massive limestone barrier, and then emerges into a wide, open valley in the centre of which, near the point where the river turns due westward, is the city of Heraia.

---

[1] The Alpheios and its ford, *O.*, i. 92, ii. 14, iii. 22, v. 18 ; *Nem.* vi. 18, &c. ; the hill of Kronos, *O.*, viii. 17, xi. 50 ; παρ᾽ εὐδένδρῳ ὄχθῳ Κρόνου, *Nem.* xi. 25 ; παρ᾽ εὐδείελον Κρόνιον, *O.*, i. 111 ; ὑψηλοῖο πέτραν Κρονίου, *ib.* vi. 64 ; the grove, πανδόκῳ, *ib.* iii. 17 ; εὔδενδρον, *ib.* viii. 9 ; the plains of Pisa, *ib.* xiii. 28 ; the vales, βάσσαις Πέλοπος, *ib.* iii. 24 ; above all the description of the founding of the festival by Herakles, *ib.* xi.

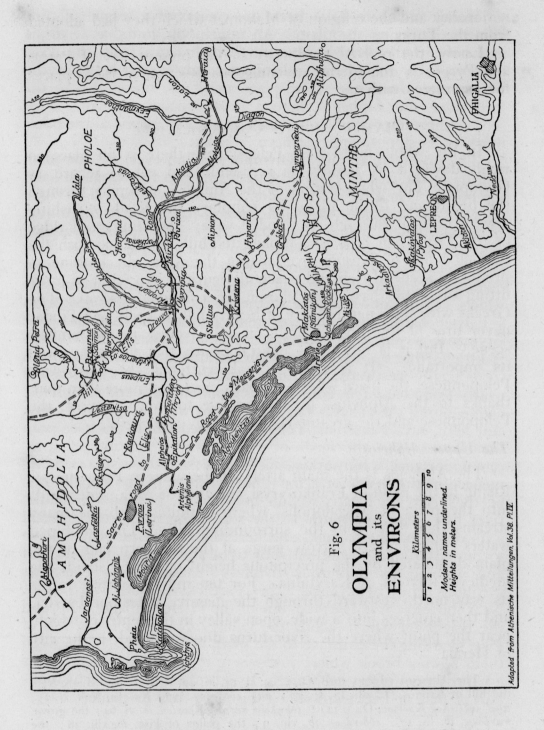

Fig. 6

OLYMPIA
and its
ENVIRONS

Kilometers
0 1 2 3 4 5 6 7 8 9 10

Modern names underlined.
Heights in meters.

Adapted from Athenische Mitteilungen, Vol. 38. Pl. II.

Heraia seems to have been the capital of a league of nine villages occupying the plain. An inscription, found at Olympia and now in the British Museum, which dates from the sixth century B.C., records an alliance for 100 years between the Eleans and Heraians.[1] The place owed its importance to the ford over the Alpheios, here a broad shallow stream. This ford connects two roads, one leading south to Aliphera, the other north to Thelpousa and northern Arkadia.

The road from Heraia to Olympia was, however, well guarded. A little to the east of Heraia two streams join the Alpheios from the north. The first is the Ladon, a stream which in its volume of water far surpasses the Alpheios and has given to the united river its modern name Rouphiá. It is only fordable in late summer, and so swift is the current that the passage by ferry sometimes takes a whole hour. West of the Ladon is the Erymanthos, a smaller stream, but flowing between precipitous cliffs which, coming down almost to the banks of the Alpheios, form a barrier hardly less effective than that of the Ladon. The Erymanthos was the boundary between Pisatis and Arkadia. A little farther on, where the Alpheios after a sweep to the north turns finally westward, there rises on the left bank a conical hill nearly 1,000 feet high, conspicuous from all sides and completely commanding the valley. On the summit was the city of Phrixa, and here, says Pausanias, Pelops sacrificed before his race with Oinomaos.[2] For the lords of Pisa it was a position of first-rate importance, a bulwark against attack from the east, a standing menace in the hands of a foe ; but whether it was actually one of the cities of Pisatis we do not know. Beyond Phrixa the river flows due westwards to the sea. The road from Arkadia follows the northern bank, and here the hills slope gently down to the water's edge, clothed with trees and shrubs of every sort and watered by numerous rivulets. Among these Pausanias mentions the Leukyanias, the Parthenios, and Harpinates. Near the latter was Harpina, one of the Pisatan villages. Beyond the height on which stands the village of Miráka is the hill of Pisa, guarding the entrance to the plain of Olympia, and between them flows a brook which, just where it crosses the road, forms a natural pool of crystal water. It is probably the ancient fountain of Bisa or Pisa from which the place took its name.[3]

---

[1] *Olympia*, v, no. 9.   [2] Hdt. iv. 148 ; P. vi. 21. 5.   [3] Strabo, p. 356.

The Lower Alpheios.

Still more important for Olympia is the lower valley of the Alpheios, its chief means of communication with the west, south, and north. Beyond the hill of Droúva the valley expands into a wide plain extending many miles to the north and watered by numerous streams from the neighbouring hills. This plain is separated from the coastal plain by a low ridge ending to the south of the village of Koúkoura in a bluff of sandstone commanding the river. Here Dörpfeld has found remains of a classical temple and of a prehistoric settlement, and here he would place not only Dyspontion but also the Homeric Thryon.[1] Dyspontion, as its name suggests, was probably the port of Olympia at the point where the river ceased to be navigable. It lay on the road to Letrinoi, which Pausanias states was 120 stades from Olympia, and which was probably therefore in the neighbourhood of the modern Pýrgos.[2] Thryon, or Thryoessa, the place of reeds, is described by Homer as close to a ford over the Alpheios,[3] and here at the present day is a ford and ferry. But on which side of the ford Thryon lay cannot be determined. The important point is the existence of the ford, connecting the coastal plain south and north of the river.

Here, then, near the mouth of the Alpheios, some eight miles from Olympia, is the junction of the three main roads which connect the western Peloponnese with the outer world, the road along the valley of the Alpheios to Arkadia, the coastal road south to Messenia and Sparta, the coastal road north to Patrai and Aigion, whence communication was easy northwards to Aitolia, eastwards to the Isthmus and the Argolis. It is also one of the few points accessible by sea. Not only was the river itself navigable as far as Dyspontion, but a little farther north lay the sheltered harbour of Pheia.

Roads to Elis and the North.

Besides these main roads a network of lesser roads connected Olympia with every part of the north-west Peloponnese. Two roads connected it with the city of Elis, the sacred road and the mountain road. The former followed in the main the modern coast road. Skirting the foot of the hill of Droúva it followed the river to Dyspontion and Letrinoi, and passing through the gap between the hill of Hagíos Johannes and Lasteïka crossed the

---

[1] *Ath. Mitt.* xxxviii, p. 115 ; cf. Partsch, *Olympia*, i, p. 6.
[2] *P.* vi. 22   [3] *Il.* ii. 592.

valley of the Vóvos. A little farther on it crossed another small stream, which is probably the Elisa. In this valley is a copious spring which Partsch identifies with the spring of Piera,[1] and here, too, are traces of an ancient roadway leading north-east which may well have been the actual sacred way. Beyond this point its course is uncertain.

The mountain road to Elis at first followed the line of the modern railway along the valley of the Kladeos, crossed the saddle of Plátanos, and then skirted the hills to the east of Droúva, passing through the villages of Kriekoúki and Broúma. Between these two must be placed the ancient Herakleia,[2] near which was the river Kytherios and the sanctuary of the Ionian nymphs with a fountain credited with medicinal powers. Such a spring exists to-day close to the small village of Pournári. Here, then, Dörpfeld places Herakleia. If this is correct we may probably identify Broúma with Salmone, the city of Salmoneus. The next point mentioned on the road is Aleision, which in Homer is associated with the Olenian rock as marking the southern boundary of Elis.[3] Aleision was one of the Pisatan towns, and Strabo tells us that a monthly market was held there for the district of Amphidolia. We may probably place it therefore in the neighbourhood of Karatoúla at the head of the valley, the most central place in the district. Close to it is a village that still preserves the name Olena, and to the east of this village is a rocky plateau with precipitous sides some 150 feet in height, which must have always been a remarkable feature in the landscape. From Aleision the road crosses the watershed between the Alpheios and Peneios and descends into the valley of the Ladon. Here are a few remains that probably belong to the ancient Oinoe, which was 120 stades from Elis. From Oinoe a road runs eastwards along the valley of the Ladon to Lasion, Psophis, and northern Arkadia. This Ladon was also called the Selleeis, and not far from Oinoe was the Homeric Ephyra.[4] Forty stades from Oinoe was the Elean Pylos, and 80 stades farther on the city of Elis.

[1] *Olympia*, i, p. 7 ; P. v. 16. 8 ; Strabo, p. 338.
[2] P. vi. 22. 7 ; Strabo, p. 356.
[3] In the identification of Aleision and the Olenian rock I follow Partsch, *Olympia*, i. 5, where a full discussion will be found.
[4] The names Ephyra and Selleeis occur in many parts of Greece. Dörpfeld, following Strabo, p. 338, argues that the only Ephyra known to Homer was the Elean Ephyra, but the difficulty of assigning to a single place all the references in Homer seems to me insuperable.

A third important road leads north-east from Olympia along the valley of the Kladeos to the village of Lála, where it meets the northern road from Divri. From Lála it continues eastward, crosses the Erymanthos, and reaches Thelpousa in the upper valley of the Ladon. Through Thelpousa runs the road from Heraia to Psophis and northern Arkadia.

Roads to the South.

Southwards, communication is rendered more difficult during a great part of the year by the swift broad stream of the Alpheios. There was, as we have seen, a ford at Dyspontion, and there must certainly have been communication by ford or ferry nearer Olympia. Various roads crossed the hills at this point. The road to Skillous must have started opposite to Pisa. It ascended the valley leading to the Typaian rock from which women were hurled who trespassed on the Olympia sanctuary during the festival; it then crossed the hills and descended into the valley of the Selinous, where close to the village of Krestena we must place Skillous, where Xenophon retired to hunt and fish and write. Other roads crossing the hills led to Lepreon and Sparta.

The main road south followed the line of the modern railway through the coastal plain. At the western end of the Triphylian hills it passed the Homeric Epitalion. Farther south on the north-west spur of Kaiápha are the magnificent walls of the fortress of Samikon, which occupied the side of the Minyan Makistos. Immediately opposite to it and separated from it only by a narrow marshy pass is a low hill. Here Dörpfeld found traces of a prehistoric settlement which he identifies with Arene.[1] In the marshy land between he places the sanctuary of Samian Poseidon, the federal centre of the Triphylians.[2] South of Samikon stretched the Pylian plain, and here we must look for the Triphylian or Lepreatic Pylos. Here, close to the village of Kakóvatos, Dörpfeld discovered remains of an important Mycenean settlement. Whether it is, as he supposes, the Triphylian Pylos, and whether Triphylian Pylos is the city of Nestor, are perhaps still debatable questions. The important fact is that here, close to the main southern road, the Mycenean civilization was established about 1500 B.C.

[1] *Att. Mitt.* xxxviii, pp. 111 ff.   [2] Strabo, p. 343.

Conclusion.

It is obvious that the accessibility of Olympia to all parts of the Peloponnese must have been largely responsible for the growth of a local festival into a national panegyris. We shall see how the Olympic games were at the first a gathering of the tribes of the western Peloponnese, how their influence extended northwards along the shores of the Corinthian gulf to Corinth, Athens, and even across the Aegean, southwards to Sparta, and shortly afterwards across the sea to Sicily and Italy. But how did Olympia first become a sacred place? To this question geography suggests a clue. We have seen that the movement of peoples in the north-west Peloponnese has always been from north to south, from the plain to the hills. Now if we compare the communications of Olympia northwards with those eastwards and southwards, we shall note an essential difference. Southwards the Alpheios forms a barrier and a protection. Eastwards the narrowness of the valley and the tributaries from the north serve the same purpose. Olympia commands the fords over the Alpheios, it commands the entrance of the upper Alpheios valley. But northwards it is open and unprotected. All the roads from the north—the coastal road, the roads from the valley of the Peneios, the road along the valley of the Kladeos—all converge on Olympia. All peoples moving down through the plain from the north must have come to Olympia, and here they halted till driven by fresh pressure from the north to cross the river or seek refuge in the hills. Here they found a site that appealed to the pastoral habits and the religious instincts that they brought with them from their northern home, and here perhaps on the hill of fair prospect they established the worship of the northern sky-god. Thus Olympia became the religious centre of all folk north of the Alpheios, and for those who were forced to move farther on it still retained its sanctity. So in the first records of the games the victors come not only from the plains of Elis but from Messenia. The evidence for this view will be stated more fully in the next chapter.

III

The Prehistoric Remains of the North-West Peloponnese

'The pillar which the Eleans call the pillar of Oinomaos is on the way from the Great Altar to the Temple of Zeus. . . . This pillar stood, they say, in the house of Oinomaos. . . . A certain Roman senator had won an Olympic victory, and, wishing to leave behind an inscribed bronze statue to commemorate his victory, dug a trench for its foundation close to the pillar of Oinomaos. There the workmen found fragments of armour and bridles and trappings. These I myself saw dug up.'

Pausanias, v. xx. 6–8.

THE only two sites that have so far yielded important results for the prehistoric period are Olympia and Pylos. The minor excavations at Pisa, Koúkoura, and Samikon [1] are chiefly valuable as confirming the results obtained from these two sites.

THE PREHISTORIC VILLAGE AT OLYMPIA

The prehistoric settlement of Olympia discovered by Dörpfeld in 1907 lies between the Heraion and the Metroon. A trench opened here disclosed the walls of six houses, one of them below the north-east wall of the Pelopion. The walls are in places two feet high, and are built of large round stones, probably from the river bed, and flat slabs of limestone. The houses consist of a rectangular chamber ending in an apse. In two cases the apse is cut off from the rest of the building by a cross-wall. It is probable that the elliptical building formerly identified with the Altar of Zeus is nothing more than two similar houses, and perhaps the so-called Altar of Hera between the Heraion and the Pelopion is another such house. Similar walls were found under the opisthodome of the temple and also under the Prytaneion. Within the houses were found numerous stone implements, axes, hammers, knives, flakes of flint and obsidian,

[1] *Ath. Mitt.* xxxiii, p. 319 ; xxxviii, p. 115.

six terra-cotta spindle-whorls, a quantity of hand-made mono-chrome incised pottery, a very few fragments of painted pottery, including one solitary late Mycenean sherd, and fragments of large, coarse pithoi, in one of which were the bones of a child. The only objects of metal found were a bronze horse, and three much corroded fragments of iron spear-heads. The horse had undoubtedly got out of its proper stratum, for there was evidence that the ground where it was found had been disturbed : whether the presence of the iron spear-heads was due to the same cause is uncertain. The settlement appears to have lasted some time, for one of the houses, that under the Pelopion wall, showed two distinct strata with walls crossing one another. It was separated from the stratum of votive offerings by a layer of river gravel. There is no evidence to prove whether this gravel was deposited by a flood which destroyed the village, or whether the deserted village was purposely covered with sand, as Weege supposes, to provide a level surface for some altar or temple. There is no indication of any temple on the site, but somewhere in this neighbourhood must have stood the great Altar of Zeus, if we accept the clear statement of Pausanias.[1]

The masonry of the houses is similar to that found at Kakó-vatos, at Miráka, at Nidri in Leukas, and at Thermon, and seems typical of western Greece, contrasting strongly with the magni-ficent masonry of Mycenae and the Aegean world. A special interest attaches to the ground-plan because it is identical with that adopted centuries later for the two wings of the Bouleu-terion, and we can hardly avoid the conclusion that the very unusual form of the latter was due to the survival of an early architectural tradition. Semi-elliptical buildings have been found in many parts of Greece, at Tiryns in the lowest stratum, near Corinth in a Middle-Helladic stratum, at Orchomenos in the second stratum, in Aegina, at Thermon, and at Nidri. Somewhat similar are some of the houses at Rakhmani in Thessaly, and the elliptical house at Rini.[2]

The parallel between Olympia and Thermon [3] is particularly close. The houses are similar both in plan and masonry. One

---

[1] Dörpfeld, *Ath. Mitt.* xxxi, p. 205, xxxii, p. iv, xxxiii, p. 185 ; Weege, *ib.* xxxvi, p. 163 ; *J. H. S.* xxvii, p. 295, xxviii, pp. 153, 331, xxix, p. 363.

[2] *Year's Work*, 1909, p. 12 ; *J. H. S.* xxix, p. 355, xxxiv, p. 153 ; *Prehistoric Thessaly*, pp. 38, 132, 228 ; *Korakou*, p. 77.

[3] Ἀρχ. Ἐφ., 1900, p. 160 ; 1903, p. 71 ; 1913, p. 236 ; Ἀρχ. Δελτ., 1915, p. 266 ; 1916, p. 184.

of the houses at Thermon has a cross-wall cutting off the apse. Many of them contained pithoi of coarse red clay, sometimes planted in the ground, but there is no evidence that these were used for burials. There is also, at a lower level than the archaic temple, a very large elliptical building with two cross-walls which is the exact prototype of the Bouleuterion at Olympia. Two metres below the surface Romaios discovered two L.M. I vases and other sherds resembling ware found in the shaft-graves at Mycenae. The settlement must be dated therefore in the middle of the second millennium B.C.

Pithoi were used at Olympia both for domestic purposes and for burial. One of the latter was found below the level of house v. It lay on its side, and the mouth was covered with a piece of a large pot and stones, over which was placed a slab of limestone. It contained the skull and bones of a child, much decayed, and also a quantity of charred wood. Hence it is possible that the body had been partially burnt. Close by were a wry-necked jug and a high-handled cup. A large pithos containing a similar jug was found in the earlier excavations south of the Heraion. It also had probably been used for a burial.[1] The custom of burying the dead in pithoi is widespread in the Aegean and on the main-land. Children in particular are often buried thus within or close to the walls of houses. Pithoi burials have been found at Orchomenos, at Zerelia, Sesklo, and Rakhmani in Thessaly, at Nidri in Leukas, in Melos, Aegina, and Crete, and more recently still in Corinthia.[2] Some of these burials go back to Neolithic times; in Phylakopi they are found resting on the rock among foundations of houses of the first city.

The Pottery of Olympia.

The typical pottery of Olympia[3] is a monochrome hand-made polished ware, usually decorated with incised lines filled with white. A few sherds of this ware were found in the earlier excavations. In the prehistoric village Dr. Dörpfeld discovered some forty more or less complete vases. There are two distinct varieties.

A. Most of the vases are made of coarse dirty dark clay, red, grey, or black, roughly modelled, but with thin walls and baked

[1] Weege, *l. c.*, nos. 4, 21, p. 178 ; *Olympia*, iv. 1283.
[2] Bulle, *Orchomenos*, Pl. XXV ; *B.S.A.* xiv, p. 214, xvii, p. 7 ; *Prehistoric Thessaly*, pp. 41, 66, 228 ; 'Εφ. 'Αρχ., 1895, p. 227 ; *B.S.A.* xi, p. 97 ; *Korakou*, p. 110.
[3] Weege, *l. c.*

very hard with a highly polished brown surface. The following shapes occur:

1. One-handled jugs, usually wry-necked and unornamented, precisely like the wry-necked jugs of Troy.

2. Two-handled jugs or amphorae. Two of these have short curved necks with a projecting rim and small handles (Fig. 7 d). One has a long curved neck and long broad flat handles prolonging the curve of the body (Fig. 7 a, b). Another with similar handles has a straight neck and projecting rim. The latter type also occurs with a single handle (Fig. 7 e).

3. Round-bellied cups with projecting rim and a small broad handle (Fig. 7 c).

4. Similar bowls without handles.

5. Cups with one or two high handles resembling the blue cups described below, but of coarser clay and ruder work.

The wry-necked jugs are plain, the rest are decorated with incised lines

7. Incised pottery from Olympia

and punctured points. The commonest ornament is that of single, double, or triple lines arranged in zigzags, step pattern, or meander, combined with dots or small circles. The junction between the body and the neck is marked by rows of lines or dots. The neck is sometimes decorated by a framed panel; the handle has herring-bone decoration or longitudinal lines ending in volutes. One vase has on the bottom a swastika enclosed in a circle.

The chief characteristics of these vases are the sharp break between the body and the neck or rim, sometimes accentuated by the decoration, the sharp-cut projecting lips, the broad flat handles running off into rude spirals or volutes. All these features indicate that the vases were derived from metal prototypes. No less characteristic is the combination of rectangular designs with circles, spirals, and volutes.

B. The second variety of monochrome ware is still more

interesting. It is made of a fine soft clay of a peculiar and very pretty light-blue colour : its surface is slightly polished and has a curious soapy feel that recalls, though with a distinct difference, that of the much harder and more lustrous Minyan ware. There is only one shape, a round-bodied cup with a projecting lip and two high-swung flat handles (Fig. 7*f*). The shape again recalls, but with a difference, the Minyan cups. Nine of these cups were found. Five of them have double volutes incised under the handles. Spirals, circles, herring-bone, lines, and punctured points occur on these cups, which are, however, less decorated than the other vases. This ware is found, I believe, at Leukas, though unfortunately the pottery of Leukas is not yet published, and I have not been able personally to test the truth of the statement. The peculiar blue clay, however, is certainly found in the pottery of Thermon. I saw in the museum there large pithoi made of it, and picked up sherds of the same in the excavations. I also saw there a reddish hand-made cup with a single high handle, somewhat resembling the Olympia cups, but no cup in the blue ware.

Coarser wares were also found. There were a few sherds of rough grey unpolished ware, the whole surface covered with a herring-bone arrangement of incised lines. Similar sherds were found in much greater quantities at Pisa, Kakóvatos, and in Leukas. The pithoi are mostly made of a very coarse gritty clay with a reddish surface, and are decorated with indented bands, or strips of clay notched with the nail to form a rope pattern. There is not the same variety of decoration as on the pithoi found at the other sites.

Painted ware was rare. One large amphora was found of a yellowish clay with a cream slip painted with geometrical patterns in matt black, and a few sherds of the same ware. The earlier excavations produced some wheel-made pottery somewhat similar in character. It is the same fabric as that of the terra-cotta figurines, and continued to be made at Olympia for a considerable period. Two ribbed feet were also found under the Heraion, and numerous jugs of various dates.

One single Mycenean sherd was found, and that of the latest type. Nor have any other Mycenean sherds been found in Pisatis or Elis. Their absence is in agreement with the silence of Homer about Olympia and Pisa, and with the unimportant place that Elis occupies in the poems.

This sherd is important because it enables us to fix approximately the date of the prehistoric settlement. It was found immediately under the wall of house iv, and this house therefore cannot be earlier than the twelfth century B.C. In one of the houses there is, as we have seen, evidence of two strata. But making allowance for this we cannot date the beginning of the actual settlement much before the thirteenth century. This date is confirmed by the discovery of bored celts of Class E according to the classification of Messrs. Thompson and Wace.[1] Such celts rarely occur before the Bronze Age.

The only evidence for an earlier date comes from Corinthia. Here Mr. Blegen found at the top of an Early-Helladic stratum a vase which in fabric and shape so closely resembles the Olympia vase shown in Fig. 7 a that he suggests that it was imported from Olympia. The two vases, however, cannot be contemporary. The flat handles of the Olympia vase—those of the Corinth vase are round—show that it is comparatively late. If the latter really came from Olympia we can only assume that though the actual village was late, the civilization which it represented had existed for centuries in Olympia, and this is quite possible.[2]

Similar pottery to that of Olympia has been found, according to Dörpfeld, at Pylos, Arene, Koúkoura, Pisa, and Leukas. At Pylos and Leukas, he states, all types found at Olympia are represented. Unfortunately little of this pottery has been published. The sherds from Arene and Pisa in the museum at Olympia are mostly of the coarser type. There seems, however, no doubt that the incised ware is characteristic of the north-west Peloponnese. It is also found at Leukas, and probably in Aitolia and Akarnania. One point which these districts have in common with the north-west Peloponnese is the general absence of painted ware other than Mycenean.

Affinities of the Pottery of Olympia.

The incised pottery of Olympia has a distinct character of its own; it is clearly of local manufacture. In decoration it finds its closest parallel in the incised ware of the Bronze Age in southern Italy,[3] which is found along the west coast of the Adriatic from the Terramare of Taranto as far north as Bologna.

[1] Mr. Wace tells me that one of these celts is in the Fitzwilliam Museum at Cambridge.   [2] *Korakou*, p. 14, Fig. 17.
[3] Weege, *l.c.*; Peet, *Stone and Bronze Ages in Italy*, pp. 412 ff.

The ornament consists of incised lines and points filled in with white, sometimes covering the whole vase, sometimes arranged in horizontal bands. Among the favourite designs are the spiral, the meander, and the zigzag. The arrangement of double or triple lines in zigzag with points or small circles in the angles which we notice in the Olympia vases occurs repeatedly on the vases of the Necropolis of Timmari near Matera (Fig. 8). Again, the swastika enclosed in a circle on the bottom of one of the Olympia cups finds a close parallel on the bowl from Taranto (Fig. 9), with its inscribed cross.[1] The swastika itself occurs in Italy at the end of the Neolithic period. Lastly, we may note that an example of the ansa lunata, or two-horned lug so common in the Terramare, was found at Olympia.

How are we to explain the similarity between the incised pottery of western Greece and that of south Italy? Direct importation is out of the question. In both cases we are dealing with wares of local manufacture, and, similar though they are in their system of decoration, they differ both in shape and fabric. Clearly we must look for some common origin to explain their similarity. Here Mr. Peet comes to our assistance. After an exhaustive examination of the possible sources of the Italian pottery, he concludes that it can only be derived from the Balkans.[2] In the pottery of Bosnia and Servia he finds the same spirit of decoration, the same combination of spirals and rectilinear forms that characterizes the Italian pottery, and he shows that from Neolithic times trade was carried on across the Adriatic between the Balkans and the coast of Italy, and that this intercourse continued during the Bronze Age. He supposes, therefore, that this system of ornament was originally imported from the Balkans, and was adopted by the inhabitants of Italy and gradually spread along the whole coast. This being the case, we may reasonably infer that the similar system of decoration that prevails along the west coast of Greece from Pylos to Leukas was also derived from the Balkans. The existence on either side of the Adriatic of a similar civilization derived from the Balkans is confirmed by the evidence of place-names and legends. Fick, working on etymological evidence, arrived at the same conclusion.[3] The earliest migration from the north into Greece

[1] *Mon. Ant.*, 1906, Figs. 78–86, 130–5.

[2] *Stone and Bronze Ages in Italy*, pp. 412–18 ; cp. pp. 85, 108, 217, 287.

[3] *Vorgriechische Ortsnamen*, p. 142. Grote long ago reached the same conclusion, *History of Greece*, ch. xxii.

he argues was due to pressure of the Illyrians. These, in their turn pressing southwards, divided into two sections. One section continued southwards as far as the Peloponnese, the other crossed the Adriatic and settled in southern Italy. It is worthy of notice that in recent times a precisely similar migration introduced an Albanian element both into the Peloponnese and Calabria.

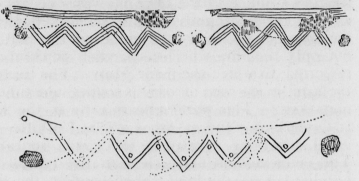

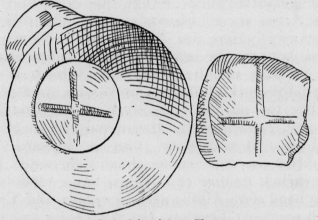

8. Incised ornament on vases of Timmari

We cannot here discuss the affinities of the Balkan pottery. But in view of the similarity between some of the jugs at Olympia and those of Troy it is interesting to note that evidence is gathering to prove the existence of a line of culture extending from Serbia to Troy, 'characterized by the use of incised pottery,

9. Incised bowl from Taranto

weapons of central European types, and probably also by an early knowledge of metal '.[1] Further excavations in Macedonia should throw much light on this problem, and we may expect to find there many parallels to the art of Olympia. The spirals on some of the incised ware of Macedonia bear a distinct resemblance to those on Olympia ware. Further, in both localities we find spectacle fibulae and other bronze ornaments of the Hallstatt type.[2]

[1] *Prehistoric Thessaly*, p. 238, cp. ch. xix ; Vassits, *B. S. A.* xiv, p. 340 ; I. C. Thallon, *J. H. S.* xxxix, p. 193 ; a map on p. 188 shows clearly the distribution of this incised ware. [2] *B. S. A.* xxiii, pp. 33, 49.

If the decoration of the Olympia pottery is derived from the Balkans, its forms are neither those of the Italian nor of the Balkan ware. They are certainly not native to the Peloponnese. Where do they come from ? Once more we must turn to the same district of central Greece which has already provided us with so many parallels, to Orchomenos, the Spercheios valley, and the Pagasaean gulf. The chief forms of the Olympia pottery are those of the Minyan vases, under which name we include not only the fine wheel-made vases sometimes supposed to be imported, to which the name Minyan was formerly confined, but the hand-made ware of various shapes sometimes regarded as local imitations.[1] This ware appears early in the second millennium at Orchomenos and at Argos and at Corinth. Thence it spread in all directions, westwards to Leukas, southwards to Laconia. The connexion is most clear in the typical blue cups. The peculiar colour, the high ribbon-handles, the sharply contrasting curves, the projecting rims, all remind one of the Minyan forms. The parallels which Weege quotes from Orchomenos, Sesklo, and Argos are all Minyan vases. The differences between the vases of Olympia and the finer Minyan ware are no greater than those between the latter and the so-called local imitations.

To sum up, the pottery of Olympia is a local hand-made ware, the work of native potters who imitated to the best of their ability the shapes of Minyan vases brought in from central Greece, preserving the traditional system of ornament that they had brought with them from the Balkans.[1] Thus the pottery confirms the conclusions already suggested by the houses, that the earliest culture of Olympia has a twofold connexion, on the one hand with Aitolia and Akarnania and Epeiros, on the other with southern Thessaly, the Spercheios valley, and Orchomenos. Of the two influences the former is undoubtedly the earlier. Legends, cults, and place-names lead to the same conclusions. But before we examine these we must briefly describe the Mycenean finds in Triphylia.

[1] Tsountas, $\Delta\iota\mu.$ $\kappa.$ $\Sigma\epsilon\sigma\kappa.$, pp. 134 ff., Figs. 39, 50, 54; *B.C.H.* xxx, p. 17; Forsdyke, *J. H. S.* xxxiv, pp. 126 ff. ; Childe, *ib.,* p. 196 ; Blegen, *Korakou*, Figs. 18–22.

[2] Similarly the Lianokladhi geometric ware, $\Delta\iota\beta$, seems to be an adaptation of the Balkan system of decoration to painted ware (*Prehistoric Thessaly*, pp. 20, 180, 216, 246, 254).

THE REMAINS AT KAKÓVATOS

The site that Dörpfeld identifies with the Homeric Pylos [1] is a low spur of hill at the junction of the two streams Kalydona and Glatza, not far from the village of Kakóvatos and separated from the sea by three lines of sand dunes, the vestiges of former coast-lines. On the highest point of this hill are the remains of a palace, a small walled court with the bases of two pillars, magazines containing pithoi, and the angle of a tower, all that is left where the hill has crumbled away towards the south. The floors were unpaved, the walls rudely built of slabs of limestone bonded with earth like the walls of the houses at Olympia. Within and near the palace were found some L.M. I sherds and a quantity of monochrome incised sherds similar to those found at Olympia. To the north of the hill and connected with it by a low ridge are three beehive tombs, the largest of them about 13 yards in diameter. Near the wall of this tomb to the right of the door was a shaft-grave covered by a slab, which had, however, been rifled. The walls are similar to those of the palace, but the dromos walls are better built of large blocks of stone. Although they had been plundered, apparently in Graeco-Roman times, the tombs yielded a considerable number of objects in gold, silver, and bronze: pendants, beads, rosettes, and buttons, a quantity of gold foil, and three bronze swords ; beads of paste, amethyst, and lapis lazuli ; buttons, knobs, and combs of bone and ivory, the buttons incised with circular patterns ; flint arrow-heads ; boars' teeth ; a single iron ring ; a large quantity of amber, and a remarkable series of large painted Mycenean jars of the Palace style. Some human bones were found, and much crushed charcoal. It was stated at first that the bones showed signs of burning, but according to the latest report this statement is not justified and there is no evidence of cremation. [2]

Farther north, on the rock of Kléidhi opposite to Samikon, Dörpfeld discovered some Cyclopean walls and a quantity of sherds similar to those at Kakóvatos, partly Mycenean sherds, partly incised monochrome ware.

It is generally agreed that these finds belong to the L.M. II period or the close of L.M. I, about 1500 B.C. They are somewhat later than the shaft-graves of Mycenae and contemporary

[1] *Ath. Mitt.* xxxii, p. vi ; xxxiii, p. 295 ; xxxiv, p. 269 ; xxxviii, p. 97.
[2] K. Müller, *Ath. Mitt.* xxxiv, p. 269.

with the tholoi of Mycenae, Vaphio, and Thorikos. But how did the Aegean civilization reach the Pylian plain? Was it brought by sea from Crete, or by land from the Argolis? The answer to this question depends partly on the answer to another question. Is the pottery of Kakóvatos of Cretan or local manu-facture? Opinion is divided. Müller, while admitting that two or three vases were probably imported from east Crete, believes that the majority were local imitations of Cretan ware. In technique and fabric, he argues, they resemble other vases found on the mainland, but are quite unlike those of Knossos. They are made of a yellowish local clay full of small stones with a surface of similar but finer clay. They show no trace of the use of the wheel. Further, the arrangement of nine or twelve handles in three vertical zones can be paralleled at Thorikos but not in Crete. He concludes, therefore, that though the motives are Cretan the vases were manufactured on the main-land. Other archaeologists, on the other hand, maintain that they are actual importations from Crete. On the question of the pottery I dare venture no opinion, but that though occasional imports from Crete are possible the settlement at Kakóvatos came by land from the Argolis and not directly from Crete seems to me probable on the following grounds:

The finds bear the closest resemblance to those at Mycenae, Vaphio, and Thorikos, and differ in some important points from those in Crete. For example, the sword type is that of the shaft-graves at Mycenae, the iron ring finds its parallel at Mycenae and at Vaphio. Several bone buttons were found decorated with circular patterns drawn with the compass. A large variety of similar buttons covered with gold was found at Mycenae, but they have not yet been found in Crete. Lastly, while large quantities of amber were found at Kakóvatos and at Mycenae, it hardly occurs at all in Crete.[1]

Again, while Kakóvatos seems to be a most improbable place for a Cretan settlement, for it can never have had even a pretence of a harbour, its position at the southern end of the fertile Pylian plain makes it just the spot that would naturally be selected by invaders from the eastern Peloponnese. It commands the coastal road which communicates through the valleys of the Neda and the Kyparisseis with the plain of Megalopolis and thence with Messenia, Sparta, and Argolis. The earliest settlement of the

---

[1] Many more parallels will be found in Müller's description of the finds, l. c.

Aegean power on the mainland is in the Argolis. Of the extension of this power over the southern Peloponnese we have evidence in the distribution of Mycenean remains.[1] In Homer the power of Agamemnon reaches across the Peloponnese to Messenia : for in an often-quoted passage he offers to present to Achilles seven cities ' all nigh to the sea, on the uttermost border of sandy Pylos wherein dwell men abounding in flocks and kine '.[2] Lastly, at a somewhat later period we have a precisely similar invasion from Sparta, the invasion of the so-called Minyai, who, driven out of Sparta, founded the six Minyan cities, not indeed in the Pylian plain, which was perhaps too strongly occupied, but in the hill country behind the plain.[3]

On these grounds, then, I conclude that the inhabitants of Kakóvatos came not by sea from Crete, but by land from the Argolis. They made themselves masters of the whole plain. At its northern end they built a strong fortress on the rock of Kleidhi. Their progress farther north was barred by the Alpheios. Whether these settlers were the Homeric Pylians is another question.

But whether the Aegean people reached the Pylian plain by land or sea matters little for the history of Olympia. In either case they are of the same race. The important point is that they entered the plain from the south about the beginning of the fifteenth century B. C., and that they found the plain occupied by a less civilized race of northern origin who, even if they knew the use of metals, continued to use weapons and implements of stone, who built their houses of rough stones and earth-mortar, and who manufactured a hand-made incised pottery of a style that they had brought with them from the Balkans, and who possibly may have contained elements from central Greece. The Aegean civilization does not seem to have lasted very long. Did the settlers find the harbourless shore unfavourable for their trade ? Did the northern element prove too strong ? Or was it some fresh wave of northern immigrants that overwhelmed them ? At all events there are no Mycenean remains of the L.M. III period in this district.

It was probably these northerners who first brought to

---

[1] v. Thompson in *Liverpool Annals*, 1912, p. 128.   [2] *Il.* ix. 292.

[3] Hdt. iv. 148. Of the fact of a settlement from Sparta there can be little doubt, but when it took place and whether the Minyai had anything to do with it is quite uncertain.

Kakóvatos the knowledge of amber. The importance of the find of amber on this site has not, it seems to me, been fully appreciated. Nowhere else has such a quantity of amber been found. There were no fewer than 500 pieces, and analysis proves that it is Baltic amber. Hence we may reasonably infer that it came from the head of the Adriatic, the meeting-place of the two great trade-routes by which amber from the Baltic travelled across Europe.[1] Here then we have unmistakable evidence of the existence of an Adriatic trade-route in the middle of the second millennium. At a somewhat later date we find similar evidence in the *Odyssey*. Mentes the Taphian describes how he has put in at Ithaca on his way to Temesa with a cargo of gleaming iron which he intends to exchange for copper.[2] This passage has been fully discussed by Dr. Leaf, and his general conclusions seem to me indisputable.[3]

The main trade-route in Mycenean times passed along the Gulf of Corinth, then followed the coast northwards as far as Korkyra, whence it crossed over to southern Italy.[4] Agamemnon's kingdom in Homer extends as far as Aigion. Beyond this point there are no Mycenean remains in the Peloponnese. There is, however, in the museum at Cambridge a bronze axe found at Patras, which Professor Bosanquet regards as imported from southern Italy.[5] The type which is common in Italy is rare in Greece, and this particular axe bears on either side the marks ப + which occur on a similar axe from Campania. It belongs to the transition period from bronze to iron. North of the gulf Mycenean remains are found as far as Korkyra. With the exception of a few vases of Thermon they all belong to the L.M. III period. North of Korkyra they met the Taphian pirates and Teleboan slave-dealers, who brought down iron from the head of the Adriatic.[6] From this source possibly came the iron rings found at Kakóvatos and Mycenae.

The extension of Mycenean power westwards forced the inhabitants of the Aigialos, Ionians according to Herodotus,[7] to

---

[1] Ridgeway, *Early Age of Greece*, pp. 359 ff. [2] *Od.* i. 179, 259.
[3] *Homer and History*, pp. 173 ff.
[4] M. S. Thompson, 'Distribution of Mycenean Remains', in *Liverpool Annals of Archaeology*, 1912, p. 128 ; *Prehistoric Thessaly*, p. 228.
[5] *Essays and Studies presented to Ridgeway*, p. 269.
[6] Some late Mycenean vases are supposed to have been found at Torcello in the lagoon of Venice ; but the evidence is not sufficient to prove that the Myceneans themselves ever reached the head of the Adriatic (*J. H. S.* xxiv, p. 125).
[7] i. 145, vii. 94 ; cp. Allen, *C. Q.* iii, p. 81 ; *J. H. S.* xxx, p. 297.

retire farther west into Achaia. But the farther advance of the eastern power was checked, we may conjecture, by the resistance of the vigorous northern tribes who occupied the north-west Peloponnese, just as the earlier advance through the Pylian plain had been checked at the Alpheios. Of the attempt to conquer Elis we have perhaps a reminiscence in the legend of the wars of Herakles against the Eleans and Pylians.

Conclusion.

Thus the archaeological evidence leads to the same conclusions as the geographical. Early in the fifteenth century the north-west Peloponnese was inhabited by northerners. The main stock came along the coast from the Balkans ; others, perhaps at a later date, came from central Greece, from the valley of the Spercheios and the Gulf of Volo, bringing with them a civilization influenced possibly by Troy and the northern Aegean. There is contact with the Aegean world at two periods and at two points, south of the Alpheios in the L.M. I period in the plain of Pylos, north of the river in the L.M. III period, when Mycenean influence stopped short at Aigion. In Elis and Pisatis there is no proof of Mycenean influence at all. If this influence did reach Olympia, the single sherd of very late L.M. III ware suggests that it came from Achaia. Of Cretan contact there is not the slightest indication.

IV

Peoples and Cults of the North-West Peloponnese

ἔνθα Διὶ ῥέξαντες ὑπερμενεῖ ἱερὰ καλά
ταῦρον δ᾽ Ἀλφείῳ, ταῦρον δὲ Ποσειδάωνι
αὐτὰρ Ἀθηναίῃ γλαυκώπιδι βοῦν ἀγελαίην.

Homer, *Il.* xi. 726.

μεστὴ δ᾽ ἐστὶν ἡ γῆ πᾶσα Ἀρτεμισίων τε καὶ Ἀφροδισίων καὶ Νυμφαίων
ἐν ἄλσεσιν ἀνθέων πλέως τὸ πολὺ διὰ τὴν εὐυδρίαν, συχνὰ δὲ καὶ Ἑρμεῖα ἐν
ταῖς ὁδοῖς, Ποσείδια τε ἐπὶ ταῖς ἀκταῖς. Strabo, p. 343.

TRADITION and history confirm the predominance of
the northern element in the north-west Peloponnese from
the earliest time. Many writers, however, have attempted
to connect the beginnings of Olympia with Crete, and it has been
freely asserted that the Goddess Hera preceded Zeus at Olympia
and even that the games were first held in honour of Hera.
We must, therefore, briefly consider what tradition and history
tell us of the early inhabitants of the district, and especially of
the religious cults surviving there. It is generally admitted that
the Greeks of history are a product of two stocks, a Mediterranean stock, dark-haired, long-headed, short of stature, and of
a highly artistic temperament, and a northern or central European
stock, fair-haired, short-headed, usually tall, and distinguished by
its physical vigour. The former reached its highest development
in Crete, the latter is represented by the Homeric Achaians.
Let us first see what traces there are of this Mediterranean race
in the north-west Peloponnese.

MEDITERRANEAN ELEMENTS

The earliest inhabitants of whom we hear are the Leleges.[1]
Speculation about this race is, however, as unprofitable as it is
about the Pelasgoi. They have become, as Professor Myres says,

[1] P. iv. 1. 36 ; Fick, *Vorgriechische Ortsnamen*, pp. 107, 136 ; Myres, *J. H. S.*
xxvii, p. 183.

an ethnologist's label for prehistoric peoples. If we want to find evidence of the Mediterranean race we must look rather to the survivals of cults which seem typical of them. Vague though our knowledge of Aegean religion is, we may at least feel sure that the chief deity of Crete and Anatolia was a goddess, and that this goddess was in the first place a goddess of the wild, of mountain, forest, and stream, and all wild things therein. Just such a goddess we have in Artemis, whose shrines and groves were found throughout Elis.[1] She is not the chaste huntress of Homer and Greek art ; rather she is akin to local nymphs of mountain, grove, or stream, many of whose cults she seems to have taken over. Thus Artemis and Arethousa are both beloved of the river-god Alpheios. Her title of Parthenios denotes not the maiden goddess but the goddess of free love.[2] With this phase of the goddess we may connect her titles at Olympia of Κοκκώκα and Κορδάκα.[3] The latter is explained by Pausanias as a lascivious dance introduced by the Phrygian attendants of Pelops. She was also connected with primitive initiation ceremonies at Letrinoi. Such rites are implied in the local legend that the goddess, pursued by Alpheios, smeared her own face and that of her attendants with clay so that he might not recognize her.[4] There, too, she was worshipped as Limnatis, our Lady of the Marsh. The boar, goat, stag, lion, and wolf were sacred to her, and at Patrai a holocaust of these animals was sacrificed every year. As goddess of the wild she was worshipped at Olympia as ἀγροτέρα. She had no fewer than eight altars in the Altis, and every year a festival was held there in her honour.[5]

The goat-god Pan and Hermes belong to the same pastoral religion. At Olympia Pan had a special place of honour in the Prytaneion,[6] where his altar stood on the right of the entrance to the hearth on which burnt the fire of Hestia. At Lykosoura he himself had a shrine with a perpetual fire, and there he gave oracles with the nymph Erato as his priestess. Hermes,[7] too, though not prominent at Olympia, had his pillars or cairns of stones on many a road in Elis, and at Kyllene was worshipped with phallic rites.

[1] Strabo, p. 343. [2] Farnell, *Cults*, ii, p. 447.
[3] P. v. 15. 7 ; vi. 22. 1. [4] P. vi. 22 ; Farnell, *op. cit.* ii, p. 437.
[5] Strabo, *l. c.* [6] P. v. 5. 8 ; viii. 37. 11, 38. 5.
[7] P. vi. 26. 5 ; Farnell, *op. cit.* v, pp. 14 ff.

Lastly we have the cult of Kronos.[1] It is difficult to determine whether he was worshipped at Olympia before Zeus. An established centre of any cult tends to attract to itself kindred cults and legends. It is doubtless thus that the Cretan legend of the birth of Zeus came to Olympia and Mount Lykaion. But there is some evidence of a greater antiquity for the cult of Kronos. We may of course disregard such obviously late inventions as the legend that his temple was built by the men of the Golden Age, or that Zeus wrestled with Kronos at Olympia, a typically athletic and therefore late version of the contest between Zeus and Kronos. Far more important is the fact that certain Basilai sacrificed yearly to Kronos at the spring equinox.[2] From this and similar ritual Dr. Farnell infers that Kronos was a native vegetation god of the Aegean world, and as such we may regard him at Olympia. For centuries perhaps he was worshipped there without a name till a later age identified him with Kronos the father of Zeus. For thus perhaps we may interpret the legend recorded by Pindar [3] that Herakles first named the hill of Kronos : ' for it was without name when Oinomaos was king '.

We find then existing in Elis a number of cults which are certainly not of northern origin,[4] and from these we may infer that the earliest inhabitants were Mediterranean folk. This, however, by no means implies that they were settlers from Crete, only that they were of the same stock and had the same outlook on life. The fact that they never developed like the Cretans rather proves that they had no connexion with that great civilization.

NORTHERN ELEMENTS

For the northern immigrants into the north-west Peloponnese the evidence is much clearer. The Eleans of history were Aitolians who came over with Oxylos. An earlier period is represented in the Homeric poems. North of the Alpheios the Epeians hold sway, south of the river the Pylians. The *Odyssey* also mentions a tribe called Kaukones who inhabited the hill country behind the Pylian plain.[5] From Herodotus [6] we learn

---

[1] Farnell, *op. cit.* i, pp. 22 ff.   [2] P. vi. 20. 1.   [3] O. xi. 50.

[4] As will be seen, I regard Poseidon as a god of northern origin. Dr. Farnell's arguments for this view seem to me to be quite unshaken by the contrary theories of Miss Harrison and other recent writers.

[5] *Od.* iii. 366. When Athene goes off to collect a debt from the Kaukones she disappears in the form of a φήνη. This bird is the bearded vulture of the mountains (*J. H. S.* xxxi, p. 232).   [6] Hdt. iv. 148.

that those Kaukones were dispossessed by the Minyans. The latter, he says, had settled in Laconia, but quarrelling with the Spartans the majority of them migrated to Triphylia, where they drove out the Kaukones and Paroreatai and founded the cities of Lepreon, Makistos, Phrixai, Pyrgos, Epion, and Nodion, most of which were sacked by the Eleans in the fifth century. Herodotos dates this migration a generation or two after the Trojan war.[1]

The name Paroreatai has obviously no ethnic significance. The dwellers on the mountain side are not a race but a shifting population, the inhabitants of the plains being continually driven by the pressure of fresh immigrations into the hills. The plainsmen of one generation are the hillsmen of the next, each fresh migration driving them farther inland. Thus it came to pass that the earliest peoples in the Peloponnese survived in Arkadia and were reckoned as Arkadians.

The Kaukones, however, are a real tribe. They are mentioned in the *Iliad* among the allies of Priam,[2] and a tribe of that name existed in Strabo's time in Paphlagonia. We find traces of them along the western Peloponnese as far as Messenia, but the only place that bore their name was the river Kaukon, a tributary of the Peiros which flowed into the Gulf of Kalydon. The neighbouring city of Dyme was said to have been founded by them. It seems probable then that they came from the north-east, gradually made their way southwards, and crossed over into the Peloponnese near the Gulf of Kalydon.

There is no doubt who the Pylians [3] were. Homer's account of them is clear, and his evidence, confirmed as it is by numerous place-names, is unimpeachable. They came from Iolkos, the home of the Minyai, to whom they were akin. Nestor in his youth fought with Peirithoos against the Pheres, 'the wild men of the mountain caves' in Thessaly. His father Neleus, driven thence by his brother Pelias, made his way to the Peloponnese, where he became King of Pylos. There he helped the Epeians against the attacks of Herakles from Argolis ; but the Pylians afterwards quarrelled with the Epeians, who oppressed them and curtailed their borders, driving them beyond the Alpheios.

---

[1] Cp. Myres, *J. H. S.* xxvii, pp. 184, 202 ; Dickinson, *ib.* xxxii, p. 11. Dickinson assigns the Minyan invasion to the eighth century, but this is a mere conjecture.

[2] *Il.* x. 429, xx. 329 ; Strabo, pp. 321, 342, 345 ; P. iv. 27. 6, v. 5. 5 ; Apollodorus, iii. 8. 1. Dyer, *Harvard Studies*, xix, p. 29, following H. D. Müller, ascribes to the Kaukones the cult of Hades, but there is no evidence for this.

[3] P. iv. 2. 5, v. 3 ; Homer, *Od.* xi. 281 ; *Il.* i. 267, xi. 690 ; Fick, *op. cit.*, p. 160.

Here they had to maintain themselves against their neighbours the Arkadians, and perhaps at a later stage moved southwards to Messenian Pylos. Their movements may possibly be traced in the three places that bear the name of Pylos, though the attempt to connect this name with the gateway of the nether world seems to be fanciful and unsound.[1] From Homer's narrative it is clear that Nestor can never have founded the city of Kakóvatos or of Messenian Pylos, both of which are proved by their remains to belong to the fifteenth century, whereas the migration of the Pylians was a generation or two before the Trojan war. They seem to stand in the same relation to these sites as the Atridai and the Achaians do to Mycenae.

The Pylians, as we have seen, were a branch of the Minyai,[2] whom we meet with at Iolkos and Orchomenos. There is no proof that the Minyai were the makers of the so-called Minyan pottery, nor is any proof possible of the suggested connexion of Mĭnyai and Mīnos. But what we do know about them seems to point to the north-east. They were a restless, adventurous race, fond of the sea and fond of horses. We hear of them in the islands, in Lemnos and Thera, and they can be traced in every part of the Peloponnese. Their principal cults were those of Poseidon Hippios, Hades, and Dionysos. All these cults are found in the north-west Peloponnese, and that they came from northern Greece is clear from their distribution. North of the Alpheios we have abundant evidence of them, in Messenia hardly any.

Of these deities the most important is Poseidon,[3] the special god of the Pylians. When Telemachos landed at Pylos he found the Pylians holding a feast to Poseidon, seated in nine companies, each company with nine tables. In Elis he had shrines on all the headlands, while at Olympia he shared a double altar with Zeus with the title Laoitas, which marks him out as in a special way the guardian of the people. South of the Alpheios near Samikon he had a shrine in a sacred grove of wild olives under the charge of the people of Makistos, and his festival was a time of truce for all the Triphylians. The comparison with Olympia is obvious, and suggests interesting speculations. Was there a struggle between the Poseidon worshippers and the Zeus worshippers? and did the latter when driven south of the Alpheios establish there a rival sanctuary and festival?

[1] Dyer, *l. c.*   [2] Farnell, *Cults*, iv, pp. 23 ff.
[3] Homer, *Od.* iii. 7 ; Strabo, p. 343 ; P. v. 24. 1, 15. 4 ; Farnell, iv, pp. 1–55.

The cult of Hades seems to have been almost unknown outside Elis.[1] There he had a temple opened only once a year, which none but the priests might enter. At Olympia he was worshipped as Zeus Chthonios, and it is significant that the figure of Hades holding the key was represented on the ivory prize table made by Kolotes in the fifth century. The worship of Dionysos, too, was exceedingly popular in Elis. He shared at Olympia an altar with the Charites, but he never attained there the importance that he did at Delphi, and it is probable that he was a late comer in Elis. There are no signs of his cult south of the Alpheios.[2]

Many other legends connect the north-west Peloponnese with central Greece. From Thessaly came Salmoneus, the grandfather of Neleus, and founded the city of Salmone near Olympia. It is not improbable, as we shall see, that Pelops himself came from the same parts. Innumerable place-names[3] are common to the two districts, for example the names of the rivers Peneios, Enipeus, Pamisos. The name of the Minyai was preserved in the river Minyoeis ' that falls into the sea near Arene ', and not far from it was the Lapithos mountain. Taken separately such evidence is weak, but its cumulative effect is overwhelming.

Thus legends and place-names combine with the archaeological evidence to prove the migration of peoples from central Greece into the western Peloponnese. The migrations covered a long period of time, nor were they confined to any one tribe. Just as in the later age of colonization, a chieftain would gather round him a band composed not only of his own kinsfolk but of men of other tribes who found it expedient for any reason to leave their native homes.

Another stream of immigrants came from Aitolia and the north-west, driven south by pressure from the Balkans. To these belong the Eleans of history and their Homeric predecessors the Epeians. The territory of the latter stretched from Hyrmina and Myrtilos on the coast to Aleision and the Olenian rock.[4] The Alpheios valley in Homer appears to belong neither to Epeians nor to Pylians. Later some of the Epeians at least were driven south of the Alpheios, for they were numbered among the three tribes of Triphylia. ' We know ', says Pausanias, ' that the people of Elis originally came from Kalydon and other parts

---

[1] P. vi. 25. 2 ; v. 14. 7, 20. 2.   [2] Farnell, *Cults*, v, pp. 111, 428.
[3] Fick, *op. cit.*, pp. 16, 158.   [4] Homer, *Il.* ii. 615.

of Aitolia ', and Strabo tells us that the Aitolians who came over with Oxylos settled down side by side with the Epeians ' by reason of their ancient kinship '.[1]

The tradition survives in the genealogy of the kings of Elis, an obvious and for the most part worthless fabrication.[2] Endymion, the son of Aethlios the first King of Elis, had three sons, Paion, Epeios, and Aitolos, whom he set to race for the kingdom at Olympia. Epeios won and on his death was succeeded by his brother Aitolos. But the latter had the misfortune to kill Apis by driving over him in the chariot race at the funeral games at Azan, and had in consequence to flee the country. He went to Aitolia, which took its name from him, and was succeeded by his nephew Eleios, the father of Augeias. Six generations later Oxylos, having also killed a man, returned with the Herakleidai and became King of Elis. The settlement of Eleans in Aitolia is of course possible : it was vouched for by two inscriptions quoted by Strabo,[3] one on the statue of Aitolos at Thermon, the other on that of Oxylos at Olympia. There is abundant evidence in Homer of intercourse to and fro between Elis and Aitolia and the islands.[4] But the story bears a suspicious resemblance to that of the return of the Herakleidai. It was flattering to the pride of the Epeians to represent the conquering Aitolians as their own kinsfolk who had migrated from Elis generations earlier. But there can be little doubt that the movement of peoples in western Greece was then, as it has been ever since, from north to south.

The connexion of Elis with Aitolia, Akarnania, and Epeiros is proved by the recurrence of the same place-names and by the similarity of dialect on either side of the Corinthian gulf. The archaeological evidence has shown that there existed all along the western coast from Leukas to Kakóvatos a more or less homogeneous civilization derived from the Balkans, and that Baltic amber and probably iron travelled from the head of the Adriatic to Triphylia as early as the fifteenth century.

Who these northerners were who made their way along the coast to Aitolia and thence into Elis we cannot say definitely. They have been described as Leleges, Illyrians, Achaians. The probability is that they were a very mixed race, the Balkans themselves being inhabited then as now by a variety of tribes. All that we can safely say is that they were northerners with

[1] P. v. 1 ; Strabo, p. 354.   [2] P. v. 1. 2.   [3] p. 463.
[4] *Il.* ii. 627, xiii. 692, xv. 518, xxiii. 630 ff. ; *Od.* iv. 635.

a civilization akin to that of central Europe, speaking probably Aryan dialects and worshipping Aryan gods.

Our knowledge of the cults of western Greece is very fragmentary. It is therefore all the more remarkable that the one god whose worship can be traced all along the coast is Apollo, whose northern origin is more clearly attested than that of any other god except Zeus.[1] The road by which the Hyperborean offerings reached Delos in the time of Herodotus [2] ran westward to the head of the Adriatic, where it joined the two main amber routes from the Baltic, passed southward to Dodona, and thence across Pindos into Thessaly. It is the route by which most of the tribes of Apollo-worshippers entered Greece. Others probably continued their way southwards, and their way can be clearly traced. In almost every case the cult of Apollo is found along the western coast in its oldest and most primitive forms. The cone-shaped pillar of Apollo Ἀγυιεύς, ' the Leader ', appears on the coins of Korkyra, Ambrakia, Orikos, and Apollonia. In Epeiros wild animals were sacrificed to him and omens were taken from pet serpents kept in his precinct.[3] In Kalydon he appears as the god of wild animals with the title Λάφριος. At his festival in Leukas [4] a human victim was thrown from the rock into the sea. At this same festival, too, an ox was sacrificed to the flies, which, glutted with the blood, disappeared. Similarly at Olympia sacrifice was offered to Zeus Ἀπόμυιος, the averter of flies.[5] Aktion and Thermon, too, were early centres of his worship, and there was at Olympia an altar to Apollo Thermios,[6] though whether this was a really ancient altar we cannot say.

Thus we can trace the worship of Apollo from Dodona to Olympia, and the presumption is that Zeus too reached Olympia by the same route.

It is a remarkable fact that, though as far back as we have any record Zeus is recognized as the supreme god of the Greek world, yet his predominance is rarely recognized in local cults. The principal localities where his worship takes the first place are Dodona, Crete, and the western Peloponnese. In the latter three places are peculiarly sacred to him, Mount Lykaion,

---

[1] So Farnell, *Cults*, iv ; Gilbert Murray, *Rise of Gk. Epic*, p. 47. Poulsen follows Wilamowitz in deriving his worship from Lykia, but how the Dorians learnt it from Lykia before they reached Delphi is not clear (*Delphi*, pp. 1, 11).

[2] iv. 33.   [3] Aelian, *N. A.* xi. 2 ; Strabo, p. 459.

[4] *Ib.*, p. 452.   [5] P. v. 14. 1 ; cp. the cult of Μυίαγρος in Arkadia, viii. 26. 7.

[6] Farnell, *op. cit.*, p. 166, points out that the derivation from θεσμός, proposed by Pausanias, is impossible.

Olympia, and Ithome, and in all these places his worship has preserved certain extremely primitive features.

It has been sometimes argued that his worship was brought to Olympia from Crete, and proof of this is found in the legend of the Idaean Herakles and Klymenos, in the cults of Kronos and the Kouretes, in the supposed existence of an Idaean cave at Olympia, and in the legend of the birth of Zeus on Mount Lykaion. The Cretan elements in his story cannot possibly belong to the primitive form of his cult. The claim of Crete to be regarded as the birthplace of Zeus is in direct contradiction to the evidence of Homer, for whom he is essentially a northerner, god of Dodona.[1] It was from the north that his worship came to Crete, where it was associated with certain local cults. Here many of the legends may have taken shape, and hence they may have been transferred to Greece at a later period when it was the fashion ' to derive everything venerable and ancient in the old religion from Crete '.[2] But it is surely inconceivable that his cult should have reached Olympia by this circuitous route instead of the direct route from Dodona. Further, in eastern Greece, where Aegean influence was undoubtedly strong, the chief deity is usually not a god but a goddess, Athene, Artemis, Hera. A comparison of the cults at Dodona and Olympia confirms our view.

Olympia and Dodona.

The few facts that we know about Dodona are as follows. Zeus was worshipped there as an elemental god of the sky, probably therefore as a god of clouds and thunder, certainly as a god of fertilizing rain and dew, under the title of Νάϊος.[3] His partner was not Hera but Dione, probably an ancient title of the earth goddess whose worship was widespread in central Europe. In an early prayer [4] Zeus and Mother Earth are invoked together.

Zeus was, Zeus is, Zeus shall be. Hail, Great Zeus.
O Earth, send forth fruits : therefore call ye on Mother Earth.

To this association with Gaia is due his oracular character at Dodona. Earth is the earliest giver of oracles in Greece, and naturally so. For Earth is the place of the dead, and from the

[1] Homer, *Il.* xvi. 233 ; *Od.* xiv. 327.   [2] Poulsen, *Delphi*, p. 16.
[3] Carapanos, *Dodona*, Pl. XXXIV ; *C. I. G.* 2909.   [4] P. x. 12. 10.

earth rise dreams to those who sleep upon it. And so the spirit of the earth-goddess may be conceived as present in trees that have their root in the earth, and the tree becomes a link between the earth-goddess and the sky-god. So, the ministers of Zeus at Dodona are the Selloi ' with unwashen feet who sleep on the ground ', and Zeus makes his wisdom known in the rustling of the leaves. Thus he was worshipped at Dodona as Φηγωναῖος, god of the oak.[1]

Every feature in the Dodonean worship finds its parallel at Olympia. There, too, Zeus is a sky-god. One of the oldest monuments of the Altis was the ancient pillar which alone remained of the house of Oinomaos blasted by the lightning of Zeus. Not far off was the altar of Zeus Keraunios, the thunder-god, and another altar of Zeus Kataibates, the god who descends in lightning and rain.[2] This altar was enclosed by a fence which marked the place off as having been struck by lightning. On Mount Lykaion prayer was made to Zeus in time of drought, and the priest dipped a branch of oak in the fountain of Hagno, a piece of magic ritual which seems to point to Dodona.[3]

Again, there was at Olympia an oracle of Zeus, and here as at Dodona this oracle may have taken the place of a more ancient earth oracle. Certainly the cult of Gaia was one of the oldest at Olympia. There she had an altar of ashes, and close to it was another altar of Themis, who seems to be an emanation of Gaia personifying her oracular power. At Delphi too, a place of immemorial sanctity, the first oracle belonged to Gaia : there were earth oracles also at Aigai and at Patrai.[4] All three places were accessible from Dodona.

We learn from Pindar [5] that there were two stages in the history of the oracle of Zeus. In historic times Zeus made his will known to the Iamidai in the burnt offerings upon his altar. But at the first the god granted to Iamos a different gift ' to hear the voice that cannot lie ', a phrase which suggests that here as at Dodona Zeus spoke in some mysterious sounds. Whether the sounds were heard in the rustling of the leaves we cannot say.

Certainly Zeus had at Olympia his sacred trees, not indeed the oak, but the wild olive tree and the white poplar, and it is at

---

[1] Steph. Byz., *s.v. Δωδώνη*.   [2] P. v. 14. 7, 10.   [3] P. viii. 38. 3.
[4] P. vii. 25. 13, 21. 11.
[5] *O.* vi. 65 ff. Divination seems to have been also practised at Dodona and Olympia by means of lots. Hesychios, *s.v. Φρυκτὸς δελφίς.*

H

least a curious tradition that both trees were brought to Olympia by Herakles [1] from the land of the Hyperboreans. Lastly, the barbarous Selloi sleeping on the ground may find their Olympic counterpart in the legend of the Kouretes,[2] who when they first came to Olympia made themselves beds of the leaves of the wild olives. But it is not safe to attach much importance to this probably late legend.

Thus at every point the connexion of Olympia and Dodona is proved.[3] One more link uniting the two places deserves notice in view of the theory of the origin of the games which I suggest in the next chapter. Oinomaos, according to the legend, sacrificed before his contest with Pelops on the altar of Zeus Areios.[4] Now the cult of Zeus Areios is excessively rare ; almost everywhere the more peaceful aspects of the god are prominent. Yet there can be little doubt that the chief deity of the warlike tribes who entered Greece from the north was a god of war. It can be no mere coincidence that the only other place where we have any record of Zeus Areios is Epeiros.[5] He is the national god of the Epeirots, and on his altar at the beginning of each new reign king and people took a solemn oath to abide by the customs of the land.

Tradition and archaeology lead us then to the same conclusions. From a very early period a constant stream of peoples from northern Greece flowed into Elis. Some came along the coast from Illyria, others from Thessaly and central Greece ; some came as peaceful settlers, others as hostile invaders. Both movements extended over a long period, and in both there was a considerable mixture of race. With the Illyrian movement, which was the earlier, we have seen reason to connect the introduction of the worship of Gaia and of Zeus. The Thessalian immigrants gave to Olympia its name. From Thessaly came also a tribe of Poseidon worshippers, the Pylians. Homer has left us a vivid picture of the quarrels between the Zeus worshippers and the Poseidon worshippers. It almost seems as if the vale of Olympia, which in Homer belongs to neither party, was the stake for which

[1] Pindar, *O.* iii. 13 ; P. v. 7. 7, 14. 2.
[2] There was a tribe of Kouretes in Aitolia. May it not be that their name gave rise to the legend of the Kouretes at Olympia ?
[3] There is a striking similarity between the cult of Zeus at Olympia and the early cult of Jupiter in Italy. For an account of the latter v. Warde Fowler, *Religious Experiences*, p. 128.
[4] P. v. 14. 6.   [5] Plutarch, *Pyrrhus*, c. 5.

they fought, as it was afterwards in the long struggle between Eleans and Pisatans. But both Pylians and Epeians are found combined to resist the attacks of Herakles, who brings against them the united forces of Argos and Arkadia.

ELIS AND ARGOLIS

Herakles belongs to Argos, and his war against Augeias, his fight with Hades, and his oppression of the Pylians are generally regarded as representing an attempt of the Myceneans to extend their power westwards. Homer places these events a generation or so before the Trojan war ; they may belong to an earlier period. Pindar further represents Herakles as founding the Olympian Games in commemoration of his victory over Augeias. We must notice, however, that Herakles always appears as the enemy of Elis,[1] and we may suspect that the story of his founding the games originated later, when Dorian influence was in the ascendant at Olympia. It was only natural that the great athletic hero of the Dorians should be regarded as the founder of the greatest athletic festival.

The attempt at conquest failed. Agamemnon's kingdom stops at Aigion. But this attack and the constant stream of migration into the eastern Peloponnese possibly caused a movement westwards of the peoples along the shores of the Gulf of Corinth. Herodotus tells [2] us that the Achaians drove out the Ionians from the Aigialos. Of both Ionians and Achaians we have some traces farther west. The plain of Elis seems to have been called Iasian Argos,[3] and at Herakleia there was a fountain of the Ionian nymphs, one of whom was called Iasis. According to Strabo,[4] Olympia was ruled by Achaians before the time of Oxylos, but by Achaians he probably means no more than pre-Dorians. Their name, however, was attached to the Achaian rocks south of Samikon, and Achilles was worshipped as a hero in Elis.

The extension of Argive power westwards must have been responsible for the introduction of Hera at Olympia. Hera is essentially the local goddess of Argolis, and the three cities dearest to her heart are Argos, Sparta, and Mycenae. But when did her worship reach Olympia ? There is absolutely no proof

---

[1] Iphitos is said to have reconciled the Eleans to Herakles, P. v. 4. 6.
[2] Hdt. i. 145 ; vii. 94.   [3] Allen, C. Q., 1909, iii, pp. 86 ff.   [4] p. 357.

of her presence there in Mycenean times, and the absence of Mycenean remains there makes it very improbable. The popular assumption [1] that her worship at Olympia was earlier than that of Zeus rests on most insufficient evidence.

The only real evidence for the priority of Hera is the antiquity of the Heraion. We know now that this antiquity was much exaggerated, and that the temple cannot be much earlier than the seventh century. But even so the Heraion is two centuries older than the Temple of Zeus. This argument, however, is not conclusive. In the first place the Heraion was a joint temple of Zeus and Hera. Secondly, even if Zeus had no temple of his own, there is not a shadow of doubt that during the seventh and sixth centuries Zeus and Zeus alone was supreme at Olympia. His name occurs repeatedly in the earliest inscriptions of the sanctuary, while in the whole range of these inscriptions early and late there is not a single reference to Hera. The earliest literary evidence tells the same tale. We hear often of Zeus of Pisa, not once of Hera. In the face of these facts the argument from the antiquity of the Heraion falls to the ground.

The real reason for the supposed priority of Hera and the Heraia is the preconceived idea that the cult of a goddess in Greece generally preceded the cult of a god. So indeed it often does, and so it may have done at Olympia, where perhaps the cult of Gaia is older than that of Zeus. But the earth-goddess is not Hera, nor were the two cults ever confused at Olympia. Hera was the local goddess of Argos, but there is not the slightest evidence that she was ever the local goddess of the Pisatans or of any other race in western Greece, nor does her cult at Olympia exhibit any of those primitive features which we find in that of Zeus.

On the other hand, while Argive influence might explain the addition of her cult to that of Zeus, it is difficult to conceive what circumstances could have enabled the cult of Zeus to supersede the cult of so powerful a goddess when once in possession. Greece offers many examples of a local goddess triumphing over the most powerful gods ; not a single instance, as far as I am aware, of her cult being superseded. Apollo and Zeus, it is true, may oust an impersonal earth goddess, but Athene, Hera, Artemis can defy all their powers.

[1] This was suggested first by Curtius in *Olympia*, i, p. 17. It has been developed at length by Weniger in *Klio*.

PISA AND PELOPS

We have seen that in the Homeric catalogue the northern bank of the Alpheios belongs neither to Epeians nor to Pylians. Here, according to tradition, was the independent kingdom of Pisa. Homer mentions neither Olympia nor Pisa, but the story of Oinomaos and Pelops is the best accredited of all the legends of Olympia. It was represented on the eastern pediment of the Temple of Zeus, and on the ancient chest of Kypselos ; it was told by Pindar in his first Olympian ode, and must have been told in substantially the same form in the *Kypria*.

Oinomaos, King of Pisa, had a daughter Hippodameia. Warned by an oracle that he would be slain by his son-in-law, he required each of her suitors to compete with him in a chariot race from Olympia to the Isthmus of Corinth. The suitor was to take the maiden in his chariot, and received a start. If Oinomaos overtook him, he slew him. Oinomaos, who had received from his father Ares some invincible horses, had already slain thirteen suitors when Pelops arrived. The latter bribed Myrtilos the charioteer to remove the axle-pins from his master's chariot. Oinomaos was thrown from his chariot and killed, and Pelops married his daughter and reigned in his place.

This is the earliest mention of Pisa. We hear no more of it till we find the Pisatans contesting the presidency of the Olympic Games with the Eleans. A long struggle ended in the destruction of Pisa, and in Strabo's[1] time some people doubted its very existence : Pausanias found its site overgrown with vines. Strabo, speaking perhaps of a late time, describes the district of Pisatis as consisting of eight towns, of which Pisa was not one. He names only five of these towns, Salmone, Herakleia, Harpina, Kikysion, Dyspontion. Aleision may be added as a sixth. The names of the other two we do not know, but it is probable that they, like the rest, lay on the north bank of the Alpheios. It is possible that Pisa was in early times the head of a loose league of village communities united by the sanctity of Olympia.

Who were the Pisatans ? The Eleans who try to oust them from the presidency of Olympia are the latest northern immigrants from Aitolia. The Pisatans, on the other hand, are in sympathy with the Triphylians, and their claims are supported by the Arkadians.[2] It seems probable, therefore, that they

---

[1] Strabo, p. 356.   [2] Xenophon, *Hell.* vii. 4. 28.

represented the earliest inhabitants and settlers in the Alpheios valley. If we are right in supposing that the cult of Kronos preceded that of Zeus, some of the original Mediterranean race may have survived there, and the Basilai may have been the descendants of their ancient priest-kings. The cults of Gaia and of Zeus will have been brought there by the earliest northern immigrants who settled peaceably side by side with the former inhabitants. The legend of Salmoneus points to an early settlement from Thessaly. Each fresh arrival from the north only added to the sanctity of Olympia, and so there grew up in the Alpheios valley a mixed race consisting of all the earliest elements in the population.

Such a mixture of races may explain the curious medley of contradictions that we find in the story of Oinomaos. His grave was shown to the west of the Kladeos, the remains of his palace in the Altis. Some features in his story point to the north, some to Argolis. There are strange elements of barbarism in his story. Like Salmoneus, he seems to have been one of those ancient weather kings who control the thunder and thereby incur the vengeance of Zeus. Sterope, the lightning, is both his wife and his mother. This double relationship to Sterope, and the legend of his incest with his daughter, have been supposed to point to a matriarchal state of society. Lastly, the legend of the chariot race is nothing but a reminiscence of the ancient custom of marriage by capture.

If Oinomaos belongs then to the earliest inhabitants of Olympia, what shall we say of Pelops. Professor Bury [1] believes him to have been a local god of the Peloponnesos. Unfortunately there is not a tittle of evidence for this view beyond the general theory which would people half the Homeric world with these shadowy local heroes or daimons, as if there were not already a sufficient supply of genuine gods. Euhemeros explained the gods as glorified men ; the modern critic reverses the process and explains men as fallen gods. A more reasonable view propounded by Wilamowitz v. Möllendorf regards Pelops as an eponymous hero of a tribe of Pelopes.[2] Unfortunately there is absolutely no evidence that a tribe of this name ever existed. Lastly, to Mr. Cornford [3] the legends connected with Pelops are derived from ritual practices, and Pelops himself, stripped

[1] *Greek History*, p. 55.   [2] *Herakles*, pp. 1, 2, nn. 1, 2.
[3] Miss Harrison, *Themis*, p. 217.

of all reality, becomes ' a figure of saga who has somehow slipped into the place of a year-god, a person of whom nothing is known and who in all probability never existed ', and he scoffs at the idea of deriving the most important of Hellenic festivals from the unrecorded obsequies of this unknown person. He may be right. Yet this unknown person certainly gave his name to the Peloponnese.

I confess that these various dogmas require a degree of faith of which I am incapable, and I prefer to accept the universal tradition of the Greeks that Pelops was a mere mortal, an actual chieftain. Homer knows him only as a ' lasher of horses ', a sceptred king who has received from Hermes a divine sceptre which is handed down from him in succession to Atreus, Thyestes, and Agamemnon. Homer does not tell us of his father : his scholiast adds that Hermes was his father. He is called the son of Tantalos first in the *Kypria*. Nor does Homer connect him with any special place, but we must beware of inferring too much from his silence.

In historic times we find Pelops firmly established at Olympia. There he has a shrine where he is worshipped with the ritual proper to the dead. A black ram is yearly sacrificed over a trench, and no one who has tasted of its flesh is allowed to enter the Temple of Zeus till after purification.[1] It seems too that once a year the youths of the Peloponnese lashed themselves over his altar till the blood ran down,[2] a rite possibly of tribal initiation. It does not appear that the Pelopion was ever regarded as his actual tomb. His bones were said to have been kept in a bronze coffer in a building near the temple of Artemis Kordax in the neighbourhood of Pisa,[3] all except his shoulder-blade,[4] which legend said had been taken to Troy, shipwrecked on the return voyage, and restored to Olympia, whence by the time of Pausanias it had disappeared. Hippodameia also was said to have been buried at Olympia, and she too had a sepulchral shrine where the women offered funeral rites to her every year. Lastly, a mound of stones between Pisa and Olympia was pointed out as the grave of her suitors, to whom yearly rites were paid by Pelops.[5] Another relic of Pelops was his sword, preserved

[1] P. v. 13. 2.
[2] *Schol.* Pindar, *O.* i. 148. Mr. Cornford suggests that this is merely an unfortunate attempt of the scholiast to derive αἱμακουρίαι from αἷμα κουρῶν.
[3] P. vi. 22. 1.   [4] *Ib.* v. 13. 4.   [5] *Ib.* vi. 21. 9.

in the Treasury of the Sikyonians.[1]   We see then that the belief
of the Greeks in the existence of Pelops was attested by an
abundance of relics and monuments which would rival those
of a medieval saint.

Pelops is always represented as a stranger at Pisa, where he
obtains the throne solely by right of his wife.   Neither his father
Tantalos nor his sons have anything to do with the place.   Pelops
alone of his family is connected with Olympia, and he is connected
with no other place in the Peloponnese.   Hence it is extremely
probable that he reached Elis by sea and that the name, island of
Pelops, originated there.   Two legends are told of his origin.
The accepted belief of the fifth century, of Pindar and Thucydides,
brought him from Asia Minor.   He is a Phrygian, Lydian,
or Paphlagonian.   It has been pointed out[2] that the name
Myrtilos is the same as Myrsil, the name of a Hittite king
(c. 1350–1310).   Another tradition makes him an Achaian from
Olenos,[3] and Strabo[4] states that he came to the Peloponnese
as leader of some Achaians or Boeotians.   The name Pelopeia
occurs also in Thessaly and is possibly akin to Pelias.   One
Pelops of Opous is mentioned among the defeated suitors.

The two traditions are not really incompatible.   For the
Phrygians were a branch of the same northern races who pene-
trated into Greece.   The passage of people from south-east
Europe into Asia Minor goes back almost to Neolithic times.[5]
The legends of the Trojan War imply long-standing intercourse
between the coasts of Asia and Greece.   Further, we know that
between 1400 and 1200 B.C. the people on the coast of Asia
Minor were subjected to pressure from the Hittites.   It is
therefore by no means impossible that a Phrygian, Lydian, or
even a Hittite prince may have sailed across to Iolkos or Aulis,
where his abilities or wealth caused him to be accepted as
chieftain of a band of Achaian adventurers, and that, as their
leader, he crossed the Gulf of Corinth to the Peloponnese,
where he married the daughter of the King of Pisa.   Such
a chieftain may have added fresh glory to the worship of Zeus
already established there ; he may have brought from his
Phrygian home the name of Ida and the cult of Rhea, and from
Thessaly the names of Ossa and Olympus.   It may be that he
introduced there the chariot race dear to his Thessalian followers.

---

[1] P. vi. 19. 6.   [2] Hall, *J. H. S.* xxix, p. 19.   [3] *Schol.* Pindar, *O.* i. 35.
[4] pp. 360, 365.   [5] Hogarth, *Ionia*, p. 102.

When Pelops was first worshipped as a hero at Olympia we cannot say. There is no reason for supposing that he was worshipped there before Zeus : there is not the slightest trace of rivalry between them. If a local hero cult in some cases preceded that of an Olympian god, it does not follow that it always or generally did so. The tendency to worship the dead is inherent in human nature, and is perhaps implied in the funeral games of Homeric times. But the actual cult of heroes is unknown to Homer.[1] It probably did not begin until the period of migrations was over, when Greece was once more settled, and the tombs of the dead acquired a new importance. Its growth coincided with the period of colonization in the east and the west, and it was fostered by the oracle of Delphi, which exercised great influence in the founding of colonies. It was the oracle that ordered the shoulder-blade of Pelops to be restored to Olympia, and another oracle bade the Eleans fetch thither the bones of Hippodameia.

We conclude then that Pisa really existed, that there is a historical foundation for the legend of Pelops and Oinomaos, that an oracle of Zeus was established at Olympia by the very earliest Zeus worshippers who entered the Peloponnese, and that it acquired its prestige from the fact that for centuries there was a continuous movement of northern worshippers of the sky-god through the western Peloponnese. The first settlement of any religion in a strange land acquires a sentimental importance in the eyes of later generations which survives all subsequent changes and defies all practical considerations. Thus the site where Augustine founded his church in Britain remains to this day the religious capital of England. So it was with Dodona and with Olympia. The stream of migration flowing southwards had at an early date left Dodona standing as a solitary fortress of Greek religion amid a waste of barbarism. Yet in spite of this its sanctity survived, and though it could never become a centre or panegyris of the Greek race, and though its importance paled before that of Olympia and Delphi, yet its memory was never wholly obliterated, and throughout the history of Greece pilgrims still came to consult its venerable oracle. Olympia might have had a similar history but for that movement of colonization which created a greater Hellas in the west and thus made it the religious centre of the whole Greek race.

[1] Leaf, *Homer and History*, pp. 268 ff.

I

V

The Origin of the Olympic Festival

ἤτοι Πίσα μὲν Διός· Ὀλυμπιάδα δ' ἔστασεν Ἡρακλέης
ἀκρόθινα πολέμου.

Pindar, O. ii. 3.

τό δε σαφανὲς ἰὼν πόρσω κατέφρασεν
ὄπα τὰν πολέμοιο δόσιν
ἀκρόθινα διελὼν ἔθνε καὶ πενταετηρίδ' ὅπως ἄρα
ἔστασεν ἑορτὰν σὺν Ὀλυμπιάδι
πρώτᾳ νικαφορίαισί τε.

O. xi. 55.

ANCIENT LEGENDS

PISA is the abode of Zeus.[1] In these words Pindar gives us the key to the history of Olympia. It was the establishment of the Zeus worship at Pisa that made it at an early date the religious centre of the north-west Peloponnese, and that, when the long centuries of war and migration were over and peace was restored to the land, enabled it rapidly to become the head-quarters of Olympian religion for the whole of the Greek world. The national character of the Olympian religion was elsewhere thwarted by the rivalry of local cults deep-rooted in the soil of narrow city states. But at Olympia, whatever local cults may have existed, no city state arose to give them permanence. In the sanctuary of the Father of the Gods all other members of the Olympic Pantheon could find a home without loss of dignity or feeling of jealousy.

There is no reason to doubt the truth of Strabo's statement that Olympia owed its prestige at first not to its festival but to its oracle.[2] Pindar tells us the same. The oracle existed before the time of Herakles, and the families of the Iamidai and Klytiadai, the hereditary guardians of the oracle, were among the most famous and most ancient in the Peloponnese. Did the festival of Zeus and the games likewise exist in pre-Dorian days ? On this point Greek tradition was unanimous. The founding of the Olympic festival by Iphitos in the ninth or eighth century B. C.

---

[1] Pindar, O. ii. 3.　　　　　　　　　[2] Pindar, O. vi. 353.

was a revival of an ancient festival that had been interrupted and forgotten during the centuries of war and unrest that followed the Dorian invasion. Of one thing we may be certain. If a festival of Zeus existed, and games were celebrated at Olympia before the time of Iphitos, it must have existed before the coming of Oxylos and his Aitolians. For Olympia originally belonged not to Elis but to Pisa, and the latter state maintained a share at least in its control till the sixth, or probably, as we shall see, the fifth century. The claims of Pisa would have been incredible if the worship of Zeus and the Olympic festival had been introduced by the Aitolian Eleans.

In discussing the legends of the founding of the Olympic festival there are two possible sources of error that we must always bear in mind. In the first place there was a constantly increasing tendency to exalt the glory of the festival by exaggerating its antiquity. In Hellenistic and Roman times, from which most of our information about Olympia is derived, mythical origins were eagerly sought for, invented, and combined. The craving for antiquity is well illustrated by the inscriptions on a bronze diskos discovered at Olympia.[1] It was dedicated by a great Corinthian athlete, Publius Asklepiades, and bears on the one side the regular date Ol. 255 (A.D. 241), and on the other the name of the Alytarches Flavius Scribonianus, 'kinsman of senators and consulars', with the extraordinary date Ol. 456, which implies an imaginary chronology according to which the founding of the games took place in 1580 B.C.!

Secondly, our principal authorities are the Elean officials of Olympia. The Eleans had ousted the Pisatans from the control of the Sanctuary, and they tried to justify their usurpation by manipulating the legends, sometimes by omission, sometimes by insertion. Fortunately fragments of the Pisatan tradition have also survived, and by comparing the two sets of tradition we can sometimes arrive at the truth.

Pindar and the Legend of Herakles.

Our earliest authority is Pindar. In his first Olympic ode he tells the story of Pelops, but he never connects him with the founding of the games, nor does he regard the so-called chariot race as the prototype of the Olympic race. The real founder of

---

[1] *Olympia,* v, nos. 240, 241.

the games was Herakles the son of Alkmene.[1] He it was who first celebrated them hard by the tomb of Pelops after his defeat of Augeias, founding them with the spoils of war. He it was who marked out the Altis, who first named the hill of Kronos, who brought to Olympia the sacred olive tree, and who established the laws that ' the Aitolian, the just judge of the games', administered. This tradition was generally accepted. A later age, anxious for a yet greater antiquity, ascribed the games to the Idaean Herakles.

Yet, widespread though the tradition was, we may doubt whether it rested on any historical foundation. It is, as we have

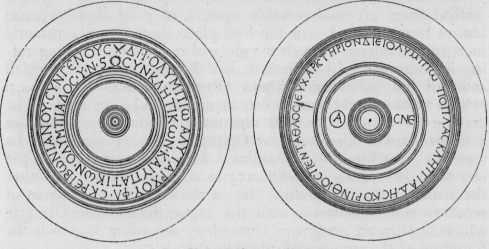

10. Votive Diskos of Asklepiades

seen, inconsistent with the traditional hostility of Herakles to Elis. Moreover, the motive for its invention is obvious. It is part and parcel of the legend of the return of the Herakleidai. Just as the Dorians urged the claims of the Herakleidai to justify their conquest of the Peloponnese, so the Eleans justified their usurpation of Olympia by the plea that Herakles was the original founder of the games which Oxylos and Iphitos revived. Further, there is a suspicious similarity between what is ascribed to Herakles and to Iphitos. Both are represented as promoters of peace and goodwill, both instituted a sacred truce, both introduced the olive crown. If the original legend ascribed the truce and olive crown to Herakles, it is hard to account for the growth of a similar legend ascribing them to a more or less historical

[1] *O.* xi.

Iphitos ; if the original legend ascribed them to Iphitos, their transference to the hero is natural. A further step in the same direction was to transfer them to the Idaean Herakles. We may then agree with Strabo [1] that both versions of the legend are equally untrustworthy.

Still more untrustworthy are the narratives of later historians and antiquarians. The fullest accounts of the mythical history of Olympia are given by Pausanias and Phlegon. In these two narratives we have the rival theories of the Eleans and Pisatans. A brief statement of them will sufficiently reveal their artificiality.

Pausanias and the Elean Tradition.

According to Pausanias [2] the games were instituted by the Idaean Herakles, one of the five Kouretes or Daktyloi who came to Olympia from Crete to take charge of the infant Zeus. Herakles, the eldest of the five, set his brothers to race in play and crowned the victor with a branch of wild olive. In memory of this he instituted games to be held every fifth year because the number of the Kouretes was five. Some people said that gods themselves competed at Olympia, that Zeus wrestled there with Kronos for the sovereignty, and that Apollo defeated Hermes and Ares in running and boxing respectively. Between the founding of the games and their renewal by Oxylos, Pausanias enumerates six celebrations of them under the presidency of the following heroes :

1. Klymenos from Crete, a descendant of Herakles who set up an altar to the Kouretes.
2. Endymion, son of Aethlios, who deposed Klymenos and made his three sons Paion, Epeios, Aitolos, race for the throne, Epeios proving victorious.
3. Pelops, who increased the splendour of the festival.
4. Amythaon.
5. Pelias and Neleus.
6. Augeias and Herakles.

This was the story told to Pausanias by the antiquarians of Elis (Ἠλείων οἱ τὰ ἀρχαιότατα μνημονεύουσι), those priestly officials whose object it was to exalt the antiquity of the festival and to justify the claims of Elis. Their methods are typical of the later mythologists. With the Cretan element in the story we have

---

[1] p. 355 ; cp. Farnell, *Greek Hero Cults*, p. 125. [2] v. 7.

already dealt. The list of those who celebrated the games is concocted of names of eponymous heroes, Homeric chieftains, and local kings. Epeios and Augeias are introduced to substantiate the claims of Elis, Pelops being inserted between them and Oinomaos omitted. The association of Augeias and Herakles is as ridiculous as that of Pylian Neleus and his brother Pelias, who had expelled him from Iolkos. Aethlios is a personification of the games. The stories of Kronos wrestling with Zeus, of the race of the sons of Endymion, have been thought by some writers to imply the existence of some sort of ritual contest for the throne. But the impartial reader with no theory of kingship to establish will see in them little more than athletic metaphors, the natural result of that athletic spirit which made the Greek artist or writer express himself in terms of sport.

Phlegon and Pisatan Tradition.

A very different account is given by Phlegon of Tralles,[1] who compiled his history in the reign of Hadrian. After Peisos and Pelops and Herakles, the first who established the panegyris and the Olympic contest, the festival was neglected until the time of Iphitos. A very ungrammatical parenthesis states that twenty-eight Olympiads were reckoned from Iphitos to Koroibos. Civil strife broke out through the Peloponnese, and Lykourgos, Iphitos, and Kleosthenes, King of Pisa, wishing to restore the people to unity and peace, decided to revive the ancient practice of the games. They consulted the Delphic oracle, which gave its approval and told them to proclaim a truce to the states who wished to take part in the festival. The laws of the games, which the Hellanodikai were to observe, were engraved on a diskos. The Peloponnesians, however, still remained indifferent and obdurate, and were visited by a pestilence. Once more the oracle was consulted and announced that the pestilence was due to the wrath of Zeus at the neglect of his festival. Peisos, said the Pythia, first established the worship of Zeus: after him Pelops appointed a feast and prizes for the death of Oinomaos: thirdly, Herakles son of Amphitryon instituted a feast and games after the decease of his uncle Pelops. The Peloponnesians, still doubting, consulted the oracle again, and were bidden to sacrifice at the altar of Olympia and obey the behest of the Elean seers. Accordingly they entrusted the management of the games to the Eleans. For the first five Olympiads no crowns were awarded,

[1] *F. H. G.*, p. 604.

but in the sixth the Eleans consulted the oracle and sent their king, Iphitos. And the god told him not to give the fruit of the apple as the prize, but to crown the victor with a wreath of the wild olive tree ' which is now clothed with the thin web of the spider '. Returning to Olympia the envoys found an olive tree covered with spiders' webs. They fenced it round, and from this tree were made the victors' crowns.

In spite of many discrepancies it is clear that the first part of this narrative contains the Pisatan tradition. The Cretan legend and the Idaean Herakles disappear, and in their place we have one Peisos, the eponymous hero of Pisa. Epeios, Augeias, and Oxylos are also omitted, while, according to the oracle which Phlegon quotes, games were celebrated by Pelops in honour of Oinomaos, King of Pisa. This oracle is interesting, whatever its date, as the earliest, almost the only, Greek statement of the theory of the funeral origin of the games. Lastly, Kleosthenes, King of Pisa, is associated with Iphitos and Lykourgos in the revival of the games, whereas Pausanias mentions only Iphitos and Lykourgos, and Africanus ascribes the honour solely to Iphitos. In view of the persistent attempts of the Eleans to obscure the claims of Pisa, we are justified in assuming that the Pisatan tradition is here correct.

Further, whereas in the Elean version a strong Cretan element is observable, here we find an equally marked Delphic influence. Not only is the restoration of the games due to the advice of the Delphic oracle, but the statement that the apple was originally the prize at Olympia is borrowed directly from Delphi. The apple was connected with the Pythian games, and is even represented on the prize-table as depicted on the coins of Delphi, but it had nothing to do with Olympia.

MODERN THEORIES OF THE GAMES [1]

Such are the varied and contradictory legends that the Greeks themselves told of the origin of the Olympic festival. In recent years anthropologists have tried to find a religious explanation of the games themselves. Their manifold speculations resolve themselves ultimately into two hypotheses deriving the games

[1] The following section is a summary of a paper read before the Hellenic Society in 1918 and published in *B. S. A.* xxii. 85. My arguments have received most welcome confirmation from the publication two years ago of a most valuable article on the *Greek Agones*, by Professor H. J. Rose in *Aberystwyth Studies*, iii, pp. 1 ff. This article had been actually written in 1914. Professor Rose, working quite independently and without knowledge of my work, had reached the very same conclusions.

either from funeral rites or from a ritual contest for the throne.

The Olympic festival, it is claimed, originated in the funeral games held in honour of the local hero Pelops. These games, which were intended to please the spirit of the dead hero, were afterwards taken over and merged in the festival of Zeus. This theory, which I tentatively adopted in my *Greek Athletic Sports and Festivals*, has been brought into greater prominence by Sir William Ridgeway in connexion with his theory of the worship of the dead.[1]

It is an attractive theory, for it seems to be in accord with widespread Hellenic practice. In historic times athletic festivals were frequently founded in honour of dead statesmen or warriors : in Homer sports were a recognized part of a chieftain's obsequies. It is not improbable that the warlike immigrants from the north brought the practice with them into Greece.

But while these facts make it possible *a priori* that an athletic festival may have originated in funeral games, they are far from proving that athletic festivals as a rule originated thus. Each festival must be judged on its own merits. In the case of Olympia there is no authority for connecting the games with the funeral of Pelops except the probably spurious Delphic oracle quoted by Phlegon. The fifth-century writers know nothing of it. The real objection to the funeral theory is that it offers no explanation of any of the characteristic features or customs of Olympia.

A rival theory strongly advocated by the Cambridge school of anthropologists finds the origin of the Olympic games in a ritual contest for the throne. This theory was propounded in its simplest form many years ago by Mr. A. B. Cook,[2] and it has since been elaborated by Sir James Frazer and Mr. Cornford, the former of whom seeks to harmonize it with the funeral theory. Mr. Cook regards the Olympic victor in the chariot race as the lineal descendant of the divine king or weather magician, whose claim to the kingdom was determined by a contest and who had periodically to defend his title. Oinomaos, he argues, is just such a king, a weather magician who claims to

---

[1] *Gk. Athletics*, p. 27 ; Körte, in *Hermes*, 1914, p. 224 ; Frazer, *Pausanias*, i. 448 ; Ridgeway, *J. H. S.*, 1911, p. xlvii ; *Origin of Tragedy*, pp. 36, 38.

[2] *Folk Lore*, 1904, xv. 398–402 ; *Themis*, pp. 212 ff. ; *Golden Bough*, pt. iii, vol. iii, pp. 89 ff.

control the thunder like Phorbas or Salmoneus. His wife is Sterope, the lightning flash, and his palace is blasted by the thunderbolt of Zeus. He is himself the living embodiment of the tree-Zeus, or, as Mr. Cornford states it, the human prototype of which Zeus is a reflection, and every four or perhaps every eight years he defends his title against the suitors who claim his daughter's hand and his kingdom. Other reminiscences of this same contest are found in the legends of Endymion, and of Zeus wrestling with Kronos. Mr. Cornford finds a further confirmation of the murderous character of the contest in a statement by Plutarch that a single combat with arms to the death once formed [1] part of the Olympic games.

Now though we may admit the possibility that the legend of Pelops and perhaps the other legends do reflect some ancient customs with regard to the succession to the throne, it does not by any means follow that these customs are connected with the origin of the Olympic games or that the latter developed or, as Mr. Cornford would say, degenerated from a contest for the kingdom. The only contest which is connected by tradition with the games is the foot-race of the Kouretes, and there is reason to believe that this legend cannot possibly belong to primitive Olympia. Elsewhere tradition is silent. But if it can be proved that the Olympic victor was treated or regarded as a king, a good prima facie case is established for this theory of the games. This then is the point which these writers endeavour to establish, and as the regal character of the victor is the cornerstone of all their theories it is necessary to examine their arguments carefully : if these arguments prove to be unsound or inadequate their whole theories break down.

The Olympic victor, we are told, received honours regal and divine. The four-horse chariot in which he raced ' assimilated him to the sun-god ' : the crown of sacred olive which decked his brow ' likened him to the great god Zeus himself, whose glorious image at Olympia wore a similar wreath ' ; the spectators pelted the victor with flowers and fruit ' like a tree-spirit or Jack-in-the-Green ' ; hymns were sung and statues erected in his honour. He was feasted in the Prytaneion ; on his return home a breach was made in the city walls through which he drove in a chariot drawn by white horses ; after his death he was in many cases worshipped as a hero, ' not because he was

---

[1] *Quaest. Symp.* v. 2.

a successful athlete but because he had once been an incarnate god '.[1]

I have examined the evidence for these statements in detail elsewhere, and I need therefore only briefly summarize the conclusions.[2] Most of the honours which are supposed to prove the kingship of the Olympic victor are not peculiar to the Olympic victor but are common to victors in all the games, often to others besides. Others have no claim to antiquity, but were the outcome of the hero-worship of athletics which arose in the sixth century and produced its worst excesses in the following centuries in the rich cities of Italy and Sicily.

The four-horse chariot, for example, was not confined to the Olympic games, and if it assimilated the Olympic victor to the sun-god, the same claim might be made for every winner or even competitor in a chariot race. Moreover, the four-horse chariot race was not introduced at Olympia till 680 B.C. The olive crown probably does belong to the very beginnings of the festival, but the practice of crowning the victor was not confined to Olympia, nor was the practice of wearing wreaths confined to athletes, kings, or gods. The same may be said of the custom of pelting the victor with leaves, which seems to have had no ritual significance at all in Greek lands. Again, many others besides victors were publicly entertained in the Prytaneion. Those thus honoured were the guests of the king or of the state, but were never regarded as themselves either regal or divine. The custom of erecting statues in honour of the victor and employing poets to sing his praises arose in the sixth century, but a glance at the odes of Pindar and Bacchylides or the pages of Pausanias is sufficient to prove that neither epinikion nor statue were honours peculiar to the Olympic victor. In fact if the honours enumerated could establish a claim either to royalty or divinity we should have to conclude that kings and gods were scattered broadcast throughout Greece.

The honours paid to the victor tended to become more and more extravagant with the decline of sport and the growth of luxury. The entrance of the victor Exainetos into Agrigentum in a four-horse chariot attended by three hundred chariots drawn by white horses is expressly cited by Diodorus[3] as an illustration of the extravagance and luxury prevalent in Sicily

---

[1] *Themis*, p. 221 ; *Golden Bough*, iii, p. 91.
[2] *B. S. A.* xxii. 88.   [3] xiii. 82.

at the close of the fifth century. As for the purple robe and the breach in the city wall, the first mention of them occurs in the account of the triumphal entry of Nero into Rome after his notorious tour in Greece, and even if some precedent could be found for them in Hellenistic times these excesses cannot be urged as evidence of early Olympic custom.

Of the worship of the victor after death we find only five examples out of some eight hundred victors whose names we know. All five belong to the fifth century, which was characterized by a strong revival of the worship of the dead. Many generals and statesmen were so canonized at this period. The five athletes in question may have been canonized for their athletic prowess, but there is not the slightest justification for asserting that any one of them was worshipped because he had won an Olympic victory and had thereby become an incarnate god.

Thus the only evidence of any real value, the evidence of Olympic custom, completely fails to prove the royalty or divinity of the victor, and the whole theory founded thereon breaks down.

There is no ground for attributing any religious significance to the games themselves. The fact is that Greek athletic sports, though closely associated with religion, are in their origin independent and secular. They are the natural outcome of the universal love of play, love of fighting, love of competition, and their character is determined by the warlike character of the people. We see this in Homer, where sports are the natural recreation of nobles and soldiery alike. Sports in Homer are already fully developed, conducted under definite conditions and regulations. The boxer binds his hands with leathern thongs, the charioteer drives alone in his chariot. Such practices imply a long tradition of sport.

The association of athletics with religion is due to the unsettled conditions of Greek life. The numerous tribes and states among whom the land was divided lived in a constant state of actual or possible feud. Now, an athletic gathering requires a condition of peace, and this condition could only be secured in Greece under the aegis of religion. So in Homer sports were held at funerals, not because they pleased the spirit of the departed, but because a chieftain's funeral drew together all the neighbouring chieftains, and sports were the most obvious means of entertaining the guests. Similarly in historic times sports took place at religious festivals, because these festivals alone provided the necessary security and the assembled crowds required some sort of entertainment. This entertainment usually took the form of some competition, dramatic, musical, literary, or most frequently athletic. But neither in Homer nor in later times were athletics confined to religious festivals. When Odysseus arrived at the court of Alkinoos, impromptu sports were got up in his honour. When the remnant of the Ten Thousand were resting at Trapezous, an athletic meeting was organized, and Alexander celebrated the various stages in his eastern campaigns by sports and competitions for the entertainment of his troops and the inhabitants.

We conclude, therefore, that the origin of the games is not necessarily the same as the origin of the festival. Sports could be added to an old festival, as they were at Delphi. In the case of a new festival sports might be instituted at the same time. Of Olympia all that we know is that Greek tradition attributed to the games a great antiquity : whether they belonged to the very beginnings of the festival or were added later we cannot say. As to the origin and character of the festival itself, the only evidence is to be found in the actual customs of the festival, particularly the time of the year when it was held, the four-year cycle, the olive crown, the sacred truce, the exclusion of women. These I propose to examine in the next section in the hope of finding some clue. At the best our conclusions can only be conjectural.

THE EVIDENCE OF OLYMPIC CUSTOM

Let us first consider the Olympic period. The festival was a penteteris, held as the Greeks expressed it every five, or as we should say every four years. It recurred alternately at intervals of fifty and forty-nine months.[1] The sacred month Μεὺs 'Ολυμπικόs, as it is named in an early inscription,[2] corresponded in the odd Olympiads to the Elean month Apollonios, in the even Olympiads to Parthenios. Apollonios according to the Elean calendar was the eighth, Parthenios the ninth month after the winter solstice. The festival was always held at the full moon. The earliest full moon in Apollonios fell on the 6th of August, the latest on the 5th of September ; the earliest

[1] Weniger, *Klio*, vi. 1–38, where full references are given ; cp. Unger in Iwan Müller's *Handbuch*, i, pp. 714 ff.
[2] *Olympia*, v, no. 16.

full moon in Parthenios was on the 20th of August, the latest on the 19th of September. Consequently the festival always fell between the 6th of August and the 19th of September, and in two years out of three between the 20th of August and the 5th of September, i. e. in early autumn.

Many other festivals such as the Pythia and the Panathenaia were celebrated at intervals of four years. There were also trieteric festivals such as the Isthmia and the Nemea held at intervals of two years. At Delphi and Thebes we find also octennial festivals.

How did these periods originate and what is their relation to one another? According to Geminus the four- and eight-year periods were simply derived by multiplication from the two-year period. But if this were the case we should expect to find that the two-yearly festivals were older than the four-yearly, and the four-yearly than the eight-yearly, and that in the four-yearly festivals there were traces of an older two-yearly festival. But the evidence is all the other way. The Olympic penteteris certainly goes back to the eighth century ; the Pythian festival previous to the sixth century seems to have been held only once in eight years ; there is no evidence that the Isthmia and Nemea were trieteric before their reorganization in the sixth century. Further, no explanation is given why a festival should have been held at intervals of two years.[1] Hence most modern authorities reverse the process and derive the two- and four-year periods by subdivision from the eight-year cycle. The importance of this cycle has been clearly brought out by Mr. A. B. Cook and Sir James Frazer, and in Germany by Weniger, who seem to me to have established the fact that it was closely connected with the origin of the Olympic Games.

The proper regulation of the calendar was a matter of deep religious import to early man, for on it he depended for his knowledge of the right moment for propitiating those unseen powers whose favour was necessary for his welfare.[2] The favour of these powers was especially needful for agricultural operations, and these operations were determined by the seasons of the solar year. The chief points in the solar year, the solstices

[1] J. K. Fotheringham, *J. H. S.* xxxix. 174, maintains this view. Though he proves that no regular system of intercalation was known till a late date, he fails to prove that the eight-year cycle was not known and used at least as early as the eighth century.

[2] Frazer, *Golden Bough*, pt. iii ; *The Dying God*, p. 69.

and the equinoxes, could be easily observed, and with one of them the year usually began. These, with the rising and setting of certain stars, formed the farmers' calendar in the time of Hesiod,[1] and were naturally marked by religious rites. But the early Greeks reckoned time by lunar months and a lunar year, and it was the moon that determined whether a day was propitious or not.[2] Unfortunately the lunar year and the solar year do not agree. The solar year is approximately $365\frac{1}{4}$ days, the lunar month $29\frac{1}{2}$ days, and a year of twelve lunar months is only 354 days or $11\frac{1}{4}$ days short of the solar year. To remedy this deficiency it was necessary from time to time to insert inter-calary days or months. But the arbitrary insertion of such periods by the priests led to endless confusion. The first step towards checking this confusion was the simple discovery that eight solar years were approximately equal to ninety-nine lunar months, i. e. eight lunar years plus three months. It was a discovery easy to make, especially at a time when men regularly observed the heavenly bodies in order to regulate their lives; and it was a discovery of extreme importance, for it provided every eight years a fresh starting-point for the calendar, a means of readjusting it and setting it right.[3]

The cycle of ninety-nine months then formed a Great Year, which brought into agreement the lunar month and the solar year. Now in ancient Italy and Greece the farmer had from time immemorial been accustomed to mark the seasons of the year and the phases of the moon with certain rites. The spring equinox, the beginning of the farmer's year, had everywhere its special rites of lustration. The days of the new moon and of the full moon were also universally observed. It was then only natural that the beginning of the Great Year should be similarly marked, and that in view of its importance as harmonizing the lunar and solar periods it should be associated with the worship of the most important deity of the community. Particularly was this the case when, as at Olympia, that deity was himself a sky-

---

[1] *Works and Days*, ll. 414 ff.   [2] *Ib.*, ll. 764 ff.

[3] The cycle was of course only approximate. In eight years there was an error of nearly three days. We do not know how this was corrected, nor how the inter-calary months were inserted. In late times they were inserted probably in the third, fifth, and eighth years. An improved cycle of nineteen years was introduced at Athens by Meton. His contemporary, the mathematician Oinopodes, dedicated at Olympia a diagram of the Great Year, possibly an improved cycle by which he proposed to correct the defects of the Olympic period.

god. No theory of sun and moon, no sacred marriage between sun-god and moon-goddess, is necessary to explain the rise of such a festival. It was inevitable.

It is by no means improbable that the Olympic festival was originally held every eighth year. It seems certain that the Pythia were so held previous to their reorganization as a penteteris in 582 B. C. Moreover, at Delphi three very ancient festivals, the Stepteria, the Herois, and the Charila, continued to be held octennially in later times. At Thebes there survived another octennial festival connected with Apollo, the Daphnephoria. This festival and the Delphic Stepteria appear from their ritual to have been ceremonies of lustration, and as such might be naturally connected with the beginning of a new cycle.[1] In the *Golden Bough* Sir James Frazer has suggested that in many parts of Greece, particularly at Sparta and in Crete, the kingship was held on an eight-year tenure. But, as I have shown elsewhere, the evidence even for Sparta and Crete is too vague to justify any such conclusion,[2] and there is no proof that the cycle originated in Crete. As it is, its connexion with the festivals of Zeus and Apollo points rather to the north. Its use seems to have survived in the uncivilized district of Dalmatia, where Strabo[3] states there was a redistribution of lands every eight years. According to Unger, the Roman calendar in the time of the kings was based on an eight-year cycle.

But an interval of eight years was inconveniently long. Hence we may suppose the practice arose of celebrating not only the beginning but the middle of the period, just as the beginning and the middle of the month had their special observances. Thus by division of the ninety-nine months of the cycle into fifty and forty-nine months we get the Olympic penteteris. This is perhaps the origin of the legend of Endymion and the fifty daughters whom the moon bore to him. The change took place at Olympia at least as early as 776 B. C., and from Olympia it was copied elsewhere. It was independent of any definite system of intercalation. Such a system did not arise till a later period, when the civil year was arranged in accordance with the cycle, a reform necessitated by the spread of democracies with yearly magistracies.[4]

[1] Farnell, *Cults*, iv. 293 ; Frazer, *The Dying God*, p. 78 ; Harrison, *Prolegomena*, p. 106.   [2] *B. S. A.* xxii. 98 ff.   [3] p. 315.
[4] The failure to realize the gradual growth of the calendar vitiates all the elaborate arguments of Weniger, *Klio*, iv and v. Space forbids me to deal with them here.

If then the Olympic festival marked at first the beginning, afterwards also the middle point of the Great Year, we should expect to find prominent in it rites of lustration. Such a rite was the chief event of the festival, the great procession which starting from the Prytaneion marched right round the Sacred Grove till it reached the great Altar of Zeus where the sacrifice was offered. We may trace the same character, too, in the procession of officials and athletes from Elis to Olympia along the sacred road, which at a later date compassed the borders of the sacred territory. When it reached the frontier of Pisatis it halted, and the Hellanodikai sacrificed a pig and performed rites of lustration.[1]

We pass on to the season of the festival. We should expect the beginning of a Great Year to coincide with one of the solstices or equinoxes. We have seen, however, that the Olympia fell between the 6th of August and the 19th of September. Other important festivals were held at the same season, the Pythia, the Karneia, the Panathenaia. No certain explanation can be given of this fact, but we may notice that all these festivals appealed from the first to a scattered agricultural population. Now the six weeks in question are for the farmer a time of rest. The harvest has been gathered, the corn winnowed and stored before the end of July, and now there is a lull : ' men may rest their knees and unyoke their oxen ' till the rising of Arktouros in mid-September summons them to the work of gathering in the fruits, first the grapes, then the olives. During these six weeks men have leisure to leave their farms and go forth to quarrel with their neighbours or join with them in peaceful gatherings. With the end of July the fiercest heat of summer is past and travelling both by land and sea is easy. It is possible that these festivals coming between the harvest and the vintage were of an agricultural character, a thank-offering for fruits already gathered, a ceremony of propitiation for the fruits to come. The race of the Staphylodromoi at the Karneia seems to point to the vintage, the prize of oil at the Panathenaia and the olive crown at Olympia suggest the olive harvest. But if so we should expect the Olympic festival to have been annual, and of this we have no direct proof.[2] Still, there is at least the possibility that a four-yearly

[1] P. v. 16. 8.
[2] According to Dr. Farnell the Delphic Charila was a vegetation festival of the old and the new year, and the Charila was an octennial festival (*Hero Cults*, p. 32).

festival of Zeus was superimposed on some earlier agricultural festival. The history of Christianity offers numerous examples of Christian feasts replacing earlier pagan festivals.

So far we have offered no explanation of the origin of the games. We have seen that the games had no ritual meaning, but might naturally be attached to any festival. But there is perhaps a special appropriateness in the connexion of athletic sports with the festival of Zeus. Greek sports were in their origin essentially military, and all the tribes who made their way into Elis and Pisatis were warlike tribes. I would suggest that Zeus claimed the allegiance of these tribes not as a tree-god, or a weather-god, or a vegetation-god, but as a god of war, and that his festival was in its very essence an Ekecheiria, a staying of hands from fighting and slaying. We have seen that Zeus was worshipped there as Areios, and that Herakles according to Pindar founded the games as a thank-offering to Zeus for his victory over Augeias. In Homer Zeus is the Lord of Hosts : and his military character is particularly prominent in the account of the raid of the Pylians on Elis. When they reach the Alpheios they pray first to Zeus, then to the river-god, and Poseidon and Athene ; Zeus and Athene aid them in the fight, and when they return victorious they give praise not to their own god Poseidon but to Zeus.[1]

If then Zeus was regarded throughout the western Peloponnese as pre-eminently the God of Hosts, it was but natural that his festival should take the form of a cessation from arms, or that a cessation from arms should be associated with him. Similarly at Rome the close of the fighting season in October, no less than its opening in March, was celebrated by ceremonies of lustration and sacrifices to Mars, and in both months horse races were held in his honour.[2]

The above view offers an explanation not only of the introduction of the games but also of the most characteristic features of the festival, the peculiar stringency of the Sacred Truce, the exclusion of women, and the exclusion of all but free-born Greeks from the actual competitions.

Every festival is a time of peace for those who take part in it, but the Olympic truce was something unique. The peculiarity of the Olympic festival was, if we are right in our argument,

[1] *Il.* xi. 726 ff.
[2] Warde Fowler, *The Religious Experience of the Roman People*, pp. 96, 97.

that it was from the first a festival common to various tribes scattered over a considerable district who normally regarded one another with suspicion or hostility but were united by reverence for Olympian Zeus. In such unsettled conditions men could not leave their farms without some security for their persons outside their own territory or for their homes during their absence. From the first, therefore, the Olympian truce must have extended over all Elis and Triphylia. The Sacred Truce established by Iphitos was regarded by the Greeks as a restoration of the truce inaugurated by Herakles and ratified by a covenant between Oxylos and the Herakleidai.[1] The terms of the truce of Iphitos which were engraved on the ancient diskos preserved at Olympia were particularly stringent. All visitors to the festival were under the special protection of Zeus, and any wrong done to their persons or property on their way to or from the festival was treated as an act of sacrilege. Even Philip of Macedon was compelled to apologize and make restitution to the Athenian Phrynon, who had been plundered by some of his mercenaries when travelling to Olympia.[2] Further, it was strictly forbidden to bear arms in the sacred territory during the truce. During the Peloponnesian war, the Spartans, having attacked Lepreon during the truce, were condemned to pay a fine of 2,000 minae to Olympian Zeus, two for each hoplite. They pleaded in excuse that the truce had not yet been proclaimed in Sparta, and refused to pay. Whereupon the Eleans excommunicated them and excluded them from the Olympic Games.[3] In later times the Eleans put forward most extravagant claims. Their whole territory and their persons were sacred. Any one who invaded the land, or who did not come to its assistance when invaded, was accursed. Any armed force entering Elean territory was forced to lay down their arms on crossing the border, and received them again on their departure.[4] They themselves enjoyed a sacred life, and for this reason they left their cities unfortified. Thanks to this security their land prospered and their population increased. The Elean claims

---

[1] Lysias, *Olympiakos* ; Ephoros quoted by Strabo, p. 358. For the truce compare Weniger in *Klio*, v, pp. 194 ff.

[2] Demosth., *De falsa leg. ὑποθ.*, p. 335.   [3] Thuc. v. 49.

[4] Strabo, pp. 333 and 358 ; Polyb. iv. 73. 10 ; *Diodor.* vii *exc. virt.*, p. 547. The latter's account is distinctly amusing. 'The Spartans were suspicious of the prosperity of the Eleans and their increase in population, and contrived their κοινὸν βίον in order that they might enjoy peace and have no experience in military matters.'

were of course unfounded and they certainly were not respected by the Greek world. Strabo has preserved for us the rival Pisatan version, 'They say that the Pisatans took no part in the Trojan war because they were accounted sacred to Zeus'. From these traditions we can, however, safely infer that the territory of Olympia was at an early date accounted sacred, and that at least during the truce no one was allowed to bear arms within its boundaries. Such a prohibition suggests that from the first the cessation from arms was an essential part of the festival. Some confirmation of this view is furnished by the fact that after 520 B.C. the programme ended with the hoplite race in heavy armour. Philostratos regards this as typifying the conclusion of the truce.[1]

Let us next consider the exclusion of women. No married woman was allowed to be present at the Olympic festival or even to cross the Alpheios during these days under penalty of death by being thrown from the Typaian rock.[2] The only exception to this rule was the priestess of Demeter Chamyne, whose temple probably adjoined the Stadion.[3] For this reason, and perhaps because of the antiquity of her cult, she was allowed to witness the games from a stone altar opposite to the seats of the Hellanodikai. The prohibition did not extend to unmarried women. Further, Pausanias tells us that maidens were allowed to ascend as far as the *Prothysis* of the Altar of Zeus, and so were married women *whenever they were not excluded from Olympia*, but only men were permitted to ascend to the top of the altar.[4] From this passage it seems probable that married women were excluded from Olympia at other times than the festival, presumably at all times when sacrifice was being offered to Zeus.

One of the commonest forms of taboo is that on women,[5] and as such we may regard their exclusion at Olympia. Sometimes their presence is considered dangerous to herds or crops. At Rome they were forbidden to be present at the rites of Mars Silvanus, the primary object of which was the protection of

[1] *Gym.*, p. 264 (ed. Jüthner).

[2] P. v. 6. 5 ; Aelian, *H. A.* 5. 17. The only recorded case of transgression of this rule was that of Kallipateira or Pherenike, a member of the family of the Diagoridai, who disguised herself as a trainer in order to see her son compete. She was pardoned in consideration of the many victories won by her father and brothers (P. v. 6. 5 ; vi. 7. 1).   [3] *Ib.* vi. 20. 9.   [4] *Ib.* v. 13. 5.

[5] Warde Fowler, *Religious Experience*, p. 29 ; Farnell, *Archiv für Religionswissenschaft*, 1904, p. 74, where full references are given.

cattle ; in Greece they were excluded from the temple and grove of the corn-hero Eunostos at Tanagra, and Plutarch states that no woman was allowed to enter the Temple of Kronos.[1] If we were certain that the festival of Zeus superseded an earlier agricultural one, this explanation might hold good. But there is another common cause of a taboo on women. They are excluded from all military rites, the presence of married women especially being prejudicial to warriors on the warpath. At Geronthrai [2] they were excluded from the festival of Ares, and both in Greece and Italy they were excluded from the rites of Herakles. Their exclusion at Olympia was thus only natural if Zeus was a god of war.

The military character of the festival would also explain the rule that none but free-born Hellenes might compete in the games. For the games at first would have been confined to the free-born warriors of the tribe or tribes taking part ; and as the festival developed till it included the whole Hellenic world, this exclusion of all aliens would naturally survive. Taboos against slaves and aliens are also common in agricultural rites. But this explanation seems less applicable to Olympia, for while slaves and aliens were forbidden to compete, there was no regulation against their presence at the festival.

Let us sum up our conclusions. The Olympic festival was a festival of lustration marking the beginning and afterwards the middle point of a Great Year of eight years. It was a festival of Zeus, the predominant god of the district, whose worship had at a very early date been introduced by northern immigrants. These were warlike tribes and their supreme god naturally reflected the character of his worshippers. His festival was a cessation from arms ; no weapons might be introduced within his territory during the Sacred Truce ; no married woman might be present. Games were held at which only free-born warriors of the tribes might compete. The season of the festival was early autumn, a season of rest from agricultural work, and it is possible that it superseded some earlier annual festival intended to promote the prosperity of the vintage or olive harvest.

---

[1] Plut. 300 D ; *F. H. G.* 34.   [2] P. iii. 22. 7.

11. THE BOULEUTERION

12. THE HILL OF KRONOS

To right ruins of Temple of Zeus.   In centre a wild olive tree

VI

Olympia and Pisa

Ἄ τε Πίσα με γεγωνεῖν· τᾶς ἄπο
θεύμοροι νίσσοντ᾽ ἐπ᾽ ἀνθρώπους ἀοιδαὶ
ᾧ τινι κραίνων ἐφετμὰς Ἡρακλέος προτέρας
ἀτρεκὴς Ἑλλανοδίκας γλεφάρων Αἰτωλὸς ἀνὴρ ὑψόθεν
ἀμφὶ κόμαισι βάλῃ γλαυκόχροα κόσμον ἐλαίας.

Pindar, *O.* iii. 9.

Ἀκίνδυνοι δ᾽ ἀρεταὶ
οὔτε παρ᾽ ἀνδράσιν οὔτε ἐν ναυσὶ κοιλαῖς
τίμιαι· πολλαὶ δὲ μέμνανται καλὸν εἴ τι ποναθῇ.

Ib. vi. 9.

OF the history of the Peloponnese during the dark ages that elapsed between the close of the Mycenean age and the revival of Hellas tradition tells us nothing. It was a period of wars and migrations, as the result of which the whole land was changed. The Dorians themselves seem never to have entered the north-western Peloponnese, probably because that district was invaded about the same time by fresh bands of Aitolians who are associated with the name of Oxylos. The new-comers, the Eleans of history, occupied first the plain of Hollow Elis and the valley of the Peneios, settling side by side with or dispossessing the Epeians, many of whom retired south into Triphylia. According to one tradition,[1] these were also joined by immigrants from Achaia. From Elis proper they gradually extended their power eastwards over the hill country of Akroreia, and southwards over Pisatis and the Alpheios valley, and finally over Triphylia till in the fifth century it reached to the boundaries of Messenia. But this was a long process extending over several centuries.

OLYMPIA IN THE DARK AGES

The Votive Offerings before 700 B.C.

The struggle between Elis and Pisa for the control of Olympia was long and bitter. Olympia, we are told, was deserted, and its festival fell into disuse and was forgotten until the time of Iphitos.

[1] P. v. 4. 3.

Some colour is given to this statement by the fact that the pre-historic stratum at Olympia is separated from the earliest stratum of votive offerings by a layer of sand. How long the interval lasted we cannot say, but from the quantity of objects found in the earliest stratum, which as we have seen[1] is earlier than the seventh century, it is certain that Olympia must have been a place of sacred resort for the neighbouring tribes in the ninth or probably the tenth century.

From these votive offerings we can form some idea of the character of the population at this period. The characteristic objects of this stratum are figurines of men and animals in bronze and in terra-cotta, miniature bronze tripods and cauldrons, plates and strips of bronze decorated with punctured, incised, and hammered patterns. Large numbers of other ornaments, fibulae, pins, &c., were also found, but mostly in the later stratum, and their stratification is too uncertain to enable us definitely to assign particular types of them to the earlier period.[2]

These objects show a continuous and unbroken development in both strata, which is most marked in the figurines of animals. The more primitive[3] of these are cut out of a thin sheet of metal, usually copper, and represent as a rule not the profile but the view of the animal seen from above. Sometimes the sheet is folded in two, producing an almost flat profile; sometimes it is rolled over so as to form a rounded body. Side by side with these figurines of sheet metal, which were found only in the lowest stratum, were rude figurines of terra-cotta,[4] moulded by hand from a reddish yellow clay and covered with a dull brown or reddish yellow slip. Horses and oxen alike are thick set, the back marked by a sharp ridge, the legs short, out-spreading, and pointed. Details are shown by lines indented with the nail.

Most of the figurines are cast.[5] The principal types are shown in Fig. 13. Two-thirds of these are imitations in bronze of the terra-cotta type (Fig. 13, *a, b*); the remainder are derived from the rolled and hammered figurines of sheet metal (Fig. 13, *c, e, f, g*). The forms are lighter, the legs are thinner and hollow where they join the body and set upright, the neck flattened, the head long and pointed. Sex is generally indicated and the males

---

[1] v. *supra*, p. 11.

[2] For the votive offerings see the admirable account by Furtwängler in volume iv of *Olympia*.　　　　[3] *Olympia*, iv, pp. 18 ff., Pl. X, 90-104.

[4] *Ib.*, pp. 43 ff., Pl. XVII, 267-78.　　[5] *Ib.*, Pls. XI, XII, 105-96.

are often ithyphallic. They are decorated with engraved lines and zigzags (Fig. 13, *c* and *g*). This type develops naturally into the geometric type of the upper stratum.

The only animals represented are horses and oxen, save for a single bear and a single ram (Fig. 13, *c*). In spite of the limited range of subject these figurines show a remarkable originality and variety which contrasts strongly with the conventionality of the geometric figurines.

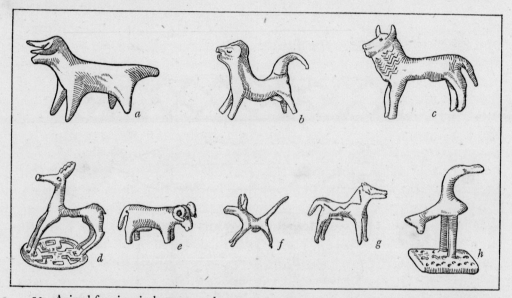

13. Animal figurines in bronze. *a, b,* terra-cotta types; *c, e, f, g,* derived from hammered types; *d, h,* geometric

The latter (Fig. 13, *d* and *h*) are found only in the upper stratum and are comparatively few.[1] Horses are more numerous than oxen, and various other animals occur, stags, goats, hares, sheep, and birds. The type of horse is well known with its cylindrical body and head, flat neck, long legs and tail. Concentric circles take the place of the earlier zigzags. Most of them have rectangular bases in the form of grating. Similar figurines have been found in large numbers at Sparta, Argos, Athens, Delphi, and Thebes, and can be dated to the first part of the seventh century.[2] They are succeeded in their turn by a few figurines of the Archaic type.[3]

Thus the figurines form an unbroken series from the tenth

[1] *Ib.*, p. 34, Pl. XII, nos. 197 ff. xv, p. 144.
[2] v. *B. S. A.* xiii, p. 109; xiv, p. 46;
[3] *Olympia,* iv, p. 149.

to the sixth century, and prior to the seventh century they are distinct from those found on other Greek sites. They are clearly of local manufacture, and we may therefore conclude that during this period there was little change in the character of the population of Olympia, and that before the building of the Heraion it was little affected by influences from the Aegean and eastern Greece. The same tale is told by the remains of bronze tripods and cauldrons.[1] The lower stratum contained miniature

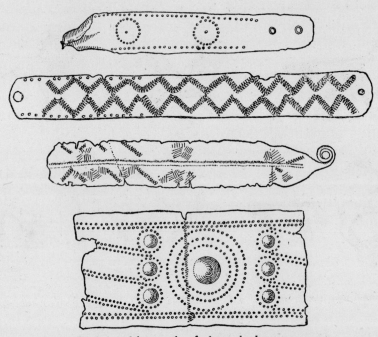

14. Copper and bronze bands from the lower stratum

cauldrons cut from sheet metal, and short, square legs and flat ring-handles of large iron tripods, the upper stratum a variety of geometric types and others showing oriental influence.

The characteristic ornament of the early period is best seen in copper or bronze strips intended for diadems,[2] large numbers of which were found with the primitive figurines. They are decorated with embossed points punched from behind and arranged in straight lines, zigzags, and circles, and with engraved lines and zigzags of what is called 'Tremolierstich'. It is a finely serrated line resembling stitching, and I propose to call it stitch-work. It occurs on some geometric bronzes from Argos and Thebes, but

[1] *Olympia*, iv, pp. 72 ff., nos. 534 ff.   [2] *Ib.*, nos. 297 ff.

nowhere in such profusion as at Olympia, where it is employed on animal figurines, miniature cauldrons, and diadems of the lowest stratum, and on late geometric objects of every sort.[1] It is not found on any object showing oriental influence, and we may therefore assume it to be native to Olympia. It is, I believe, unknown in the Aegean, but a similar ornament occurs on some early Italian pottery.

The same technique is found on some fragments of copper plates.[2] On one of these we see birds and fishes outlined in points (Fig. 15), on another the outline of a bird and an animal embossed and then further defined by lines of stitch-work.

The affinities of this scheme of decoration are not with the Aegean but with Hallstatt and central Europe.[3] Hall-statt is only forty miles from Noricum, the earliest centre of iron mining, and we have seen reason to believe that from the earliest times there was a movement of peoples southwards along the western coast of Greece, and that a trade-route existed from the head of the Adriatic in Mycenean times.

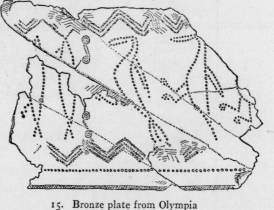

15. Bronze plate from Olympia

From the votive offerings it is clear that the early worshippers of Zeus at Olympia were cattle-breeders and warriors. The figurines of animals always reflect the character of the localities. At Argos the horse predominates, oxen and sheep are rare. At Delphi figurines of men are numerous, but there are few horses or oxen. 'L'Apollon Delphien', says M. Perdrizet, 'ne s'intéressait pas à l'agriculture, ni aux troupeaux.' At the shrine of the Kabeiroi in the plain of Thebes, oxen, goats, and pigs abound. Elis has always been a land of horses and oxen, and these, particularly the ox, are the typical animals of early Olympia. In the seventh century, when the festival is becoming national,

[1] *Ib.*, nos. 116, 136, 162, 171, 252, 292, 297, 362, 380, &c.
[2] *Ib.*, nos. 292–6.
[3] v. Reginald Smith in British Museum *Guide to Early Iron Age*, pp. 14, 15, 35.

M

the number of oxen and horses declines, horses are more numerous than oxen, and other animals make their appearance.

Horses were used both for riding and driving (Fig. 16).[1] Numerous remains of chariots and charioteers, both in bronze and terra-cotta, were found in the very lowest stratum. The chariot (Fig. 16, *d* and *e*) is the two-horse chariot, and we cannot help suspecting that this chariot was used for racing in the plain of Olympia long before the traditional date of the introduction of

16. Bronze figurines. *a*, rider ; *b*, dancing women ; *c*, warrior ; *d*, *e*, chariot horses and charioteer

the four-horse chariot in the 25th Olympiad, and that this was the chief event in the earliest sports held there.

Many of the bronzes represent warriors (Fig. 16, *c*)[2] armed with large helmets, small round shields, and spears. The most primitive figures are naked. Some, especially the charioteers, wear a thick girdle round the waist which suggests the heavy leathern belt of the modern oriental. On their heads they wear the broad flat petasos (Fig. 16, *a*), or a high conical cap (Fig. 16, *e*), which may be ultimately of Phrygian origin. There is no reason to suppose that any of the figurines represent gods.

[1] *Olympia*, iv, p. 39, nos. 248–58, Pls. XV, XVI.
[2] Figures of men, nos. 232 ff., 281 ff.

Figurines of women are remarkably rare. This alone is a strong argument against the view that the earliest cult at Olympia was that of Hera. At Argos and Sparta, where the worship of a goddess undoubtedly predominated, thousands of female figures were found. It is true that a few remarkable groups of dancing women (Fig. 16, *b*)[1] were found at Olympia which certainly suggest the dances of the sixteen women in honour of Hera, but it is doubtful if any of these groups is earlier than the building of the Heraion.

Of the religion of the people the votive offerings tell us little. They were probably hung on the trees of the Sacred Grove. The prominence of the genital organs in both sexes suggests that they were intended to promote productiveness in man and beast. The chariots were perhaps offerings for success in war, or in the chariot-races if these already existed.

The Truce of Iphitos. Elis and Pisa

The history of the struggle between Elis and Pisa for the control of Olympia is very obscure. Most of our evidence is derived from Elean officials who did their utmost to obliterate the claims of Pisa. There can be no reasonable doubt, however, that the sanctuary was originally in the hands of the Pisatans, and we may reject as Elean fabrications the stories that Oxylos,[2] and Iphitos after him, presided over the games single-handed.

Peace between the two peoples was established for a time by the truce of Iphitos, by which the Eleans obtained a share in the control of the festival. The terms of this truce, the sacred Ekecheiria, were engraved on a diskos preserved in the Heraion. This diskos was seen by Aristotle and still existed in the time of Pausanias.[3] From the various statements about it we may conclude that it contained the names of Iphitos of Elis, Kleosthenes of Pisa, and Lykourgos of Sparta. From the mention of the latter it is clear that the diskos cannot have been a contemporary record, for Sparta can have had little or no connexion with Olympia till after the conquest of Messenia, and we may probably assign the diskos to the period of Spartan predominance in the seventh century.

[1] *Olympia*, iv, nos. 263 ff.　　　　　　　[2] P. v. 8. 5.
[3] P. v. 20. 1 ; Plut., *Lycurgus*, i. 1 ; *F. H. G.* iii. 603 ; v. Dyer, ' Olympic Council House ' in *Harvard Studies*, 1908, xix. 41 ff. ; Weniger, *Klio*, v, pp. 184 ff. ; *Gk. Athletics*, p. 44.

From the time of Iphitos, then, the two peoples shared the
control and the two kings presided over the festival. This dual
control was perpetuated in the two Hellanodikai, who were the
chief officials till the fifth century. The two Hellanodikai were
clearly the successors of the ancient kings : they wore royal
robes and one of them seems to have been a descendant of
Oxylos. We do not know when they were first appointed, but
we may be certain that their number was originally two, though
Elean tradition again asserted that there was at first only one
Hellanodikas, and that one the Elean representative.[1]

As to the date of Iphitos ancient authorities differ.[2] Some
made him contemporary with the first Olympiad, 776 B. C., when
Koroibos of Elis won the foot-race. Others placed him 27 Olympiads earlier. Between the two dates we have no means of
deciding, but the vast quantities of votive offerings found at
Olympia prove that it was a sanctuary of much resort long before
the first Olympiad, and it is probable that a festival and games
including a chariot-race had long been held there.

Whatever the date of the truce, it is certain that the Pisatans
were far from content with their divided honours, and made
frequent attempts to regain the sole control. It is impossible,
however, to reconcile the conflicting accounts of the struggle.
According to Strabo[3] the Eleans held the presidency till the
27th Olympiad, when the Pisatans, realizing the importance of
the games, succeeded in recovering their own, and shared the
presidency with Elis till they rebelled and were reduced to
subjection. Africanus asserts that in the 28th Olympiad, Elis
being at war with Dyme, the Pisatans were allowed to preside
over the festival, and that they afterwards held the presidency
from Ol. 30 to Ol. 51. Pausanias,[4] on the other hand, allows
them only two Olympiads, Ol. 8, when they called in Pheidon
the tyrant of Argos, and Ol. 34, when their king Pantaleon presided
over the games at the head of an army. This Pantaleon was said
to have helped the Messenians in their war with Sparta. Later,
in Ol. 48, the Eleans, suspecting the Pisatan king Damophon of
treachery, invaded Pisa. Under his successor Pyrrhos the
Pisatans openly revolted, being assisted by the men of Dyspontion and the Triphylians of Makistos and Skillous. The result

---

[1] v. Dyer, *op. cit.*, and *Gk. Athletics, l. c.*
[2] Weniger, *Klio*, v. 186, where all the evidence is collected.
[3] p. 355.   [4] vi. 22. 2.

was that the Eleans overran Pisatis and Triphylia and razed to the ground Pisa and the other rebel towns. Only once in later times was the power of Elis challenged, when the Arkadians in Ol. 104 occupied Olympia with an armed force under the pretext of restoring the Pisatans to their rights, and a battle took place there while the festival was actually being celebrated. In consequence this Olympiad, together with the 8th and 34th, was declared null and void, or an Anolympiad.

From these contradictory statements all that we can gather is that the struggle was long and its fortunes varying, and that it ended in the destruction of Pisa. But the steady growth of Olympia during this period proves that there can have been no break in the actual management, and this continuity can hardly be explained except by a dual control. The Pisatans had the sympathy of their kinsfolk in Triphylia, Arkadia, and Messenia, the Eleans had the powerful support of Sparta. They seem at some time in the sixth century to have made an alliance with Heraia, the terms of which are recorded on a bronze tablet in the British Museum.[1]

The date of the final destruction of Pisa [2] is uncertain. Most historians, accepting the narrative of Pausanias quoted above, date it about Ol. 50. But in another passage Pausanias states that the Temple of Zeus was built from the spoil of Pisa and the other revolted towns. The temple was built in the middle of the fifth century, and I therefore follow Dörpfeld in connecting the destruction of Pisa with the war recorded by Herodotos [3] as taking place in his own time, when the Eleans laid waste the cities of Triphylia. The fact that he does not expressly mention Pisa need cause little surprise. For Pisa itself had never been more than a village fortress. We may conjecture that its power had already been broken about Ol. 50, but that it had been allowed to maintain a nominal share in the control till the fifth century, when it joined in the revolt of the Triphylian towns. Thereupon Elis seized the opportunity of destroying it, and the dual control came to an end.

The Olympic Register

The real history of Olympia begins with the 1st Olympiad in 776 B.C. How the Greeks arrived at this date we do not know, nor is its significance clear. It is hardly probable that it

---

[1] Dyer, l. c., p. 5, n. 1.   [2] Olympia, ii, p. 20.   [3] iv. 148.

marks the actual beginning of the festival or even the revival
of games that had been long forgotten. Possibly at this date an
eight-year festival was changed into a four-year. Certain it is
that from this time the games were held every four years, and
that from this time its importance grew steadily.

The growth of the festival can be traced in the Olympic
Register[1] even in the imperfect form in which we possess it.
It was first compiled by the Sophist Hippias at the close of the
fifth century. It consisted originally of a historical introduction,
and a list of the victors in the different events, with notes on
athletes of special importance. It was revised by Aristotle and continued and expanded by various eminent scholars, Eratosthenes,
Timaios, Philochoros, and at a later period Phlegon of Tralles and
Sextus Julius Africanus.

The importance of such a record for chronology was obvious.
Even Thucydides twice distinguishes a year as the year in which
a celebrated athlete won the pankration, just as the modern
sportsman dates his year by the winner of the Derby. It is
possible that Ephoros made use of the register for his history.
The first writer who undoubtedly made it a basis for chronology
was Timaios in the third century B.C., who combined with the
Olympic records the lists of the kings and ephors of Sparta,
the Athenian archons, and the priestesses of Argos. Later
writers added brief notices of historical events. The work of
Phlegon ran into sixteen volumes, but he also wrote an epitome
in two volumes. Such an epitome was the work of Africanus
published in the third century A.D. and preserved in the *Chronika*
of Eusebius. A complete list of victors was of no value for
chronology, and Africanus, following the practice of early times,
gives only the name and city of the winner of the stade race,
the first event inscribed on the official lists. From this practice
arose the popular and mistaken idea that the stade race was the
most honoured of all events at Olympia, and that the winner
of it gave his name to the Olympiad.

The list of Africanus exists in full. It is a complete list of
the winners of the stade race down to Ol. 249. Of Phlegon's
more elaborate work we possess two important fragments preserved by Photios.[2] One is the extract from the historical

---

[1] For a full account of the Register, v. Jüthner, *Philostratos über Gymnastik*,
pp. 60–70 ; *Gk. Athletics*, p. 50.

[2] *F. H. G.* iii. 602 ff., Fr. 1 and 12 ; Krause, *Olympia*, p. 412.

introduction quoted in the last chapter. The second is a list of the victors in Ol. 177, the date to which Phlegon brought down his work, and a summary of the events in that Olympiad. Recently a valuable fragment from an Olympic Register by some unknown author has been discovered on an Oxyrhynchos papyrus.[1] It seems to have contained a complete list of the victors from Ol. 75 to 83, and was perhaps copied out by some schoolmaster to aid his pupils in the study of Pindar. The compiler certainly took no little pains with his work; for on three occasions where some doubt as to a name seems to have existed, he quotes the names of his authorities, Krates, Philistos, and Kallisthenes. Notices scattered throughout Greek literature, inscriptions from Olympia and elsewhere, enable us to supplement these lists considerably. In his *Sieger in den Olympischen Spielen*, published in 1891–2, Hugo Förster enumerated no fewer than 634 victors, and to these must now be added the names contained in the Oxyrhynchos papyrus.

Before we proceed let us try to picture the condition of Olympia in the eighth century. The ancient village settlement had long since disappeared, marked only by the solitary pillar of the palace of Oinomaos. There was only the sacred hill of Kronos with his altar on the top, and at its foot the sacred grove of plane-trees and wild olives, and the bare plain sloping down to the Alpheios and stretching eastward to the hill where the kings of Pisa still reigned. There were no temples, unless perhaps some rude shrine already stood on the site of the Heraion. Greek religion centred round the altar and several altars already existed, certainly the Altar of Gaia on the hill slope and the Altar of Demeter Chamyne. Within the grove was the mound of Pelops. But the chief of all the altars, the real centre of Olympia, was the ash altar of Zeus with its perpetual fire. Hither came the country folk to consult the oracle, whose answers were given by the seers of the ancient houses of Iamos and Klytios, and on the trees of the grove hung hundreds of votive offerings. Every four years, when the great festival came round, a procession made its way round the grove to the altar and offered there the sacrifice to Zeus. In the plain to the east games were held, presided over by the kings. The finish of the races was near the altar, and here the victors received the crown of wild olive.

The programme of the games probably included all the

---

[1] Grenfell and Hunt, *Ox. Pap.* ii. 222.

events named by Pindar in his eleventh Olympian ode, the foot-race, the diskos, the javelin, boxing, wrestling, and the chariot-race. We may certainly reject the tradition recorded by Pausanias that the stade race was the first and for thirteen Olympiads the only event. According to this story the games had been forgotten during the centuries of war, and gradually as the memory of them returned event after event was restored. The origin of the story is obvious : it arose from the imperfection of the records. In many cases only the name of a victor was recorded. The first winner whose name was connected with a definite event was Koroibos, the winner of the stade race. So this race must have been the first event introduced. Some Olympiads later a winner of the diaulos was found, and so the date was fixed for the introduction of this event, and so on. At a later period, as we shall see, additions were undoubtedly made to the programme.

THE GROWTH OF OLYMPIA, 776–576 B.C.

The story of the festival as told in the Register[1] is extraordinarily interesting and consistent. For the first fifty years competition was confined to the western Peloponnese. In the first eleven Olympiads two victories only are assigned to Elis. Of the rest one victor comes from Dyme in Achaia, one from Dyspontion in the Alpheios valley, seven from Messenia, which we may take to include all the land south of the Alpheios. The preponder-ance of the pre-Aitolian population over the Eleans is a remark-able confirmation of the claims of Pisa to the original control of the festival.

In the 8th Olympiad the Pisatans tried to recover their power, and called in the aid of Pheidon the Herakleid King of Argos. This ambitious tyrant realized the advantage that the control of Olympia offered for the extension of his kingdom. He invaded Elis and at the head of an army presided over the festival. Of this fact there can be no doubt, nor does there seem any real ground for rejecting the tradition that Pheidon lived in the second half of the eighth century.[2]

If the date of Pheidon is correct, we may with some probability connect with him the building of the Heraion, which was originally a joint temple of Zeus and Hera. The cult of Hera

[1] For a fuller account, v. *Gk. Athletics*, pp. 54 ff.
[2] This is the conclusion of Professor Percy Gardner in his *History of Ancient Coinage*, p. 110.

undoubtedly came from Argos, and this is the only period when Argos exercised any influence over Olympia. It is possible that Pheidon also introduced the worship of his reputed ancestor Herakles, which certainly was not native to Olympia. After his time there seems to have been a distinct estrangement between Argos and Olympia, due perhaps to the influence possessed by her rival Sparta. Certainly no Argive victors figure in the list until the fifth century.

How long Argive influence lasted we do not know. Pausanias [1] states that Pheidon presided only at the 8th Olympiad, which for that reason was expunged from the records. According to Strabo [2] the Eleans recovered their power by the aid of Sparta. Spartan intervention, however, can hardly have been possible before the conquest of Messenia, and with this the athletic records agree. This conquest was completed in 724 B.C., and the first recorded Spartan victory is that of Akanthos, who won the long-distance race in 720 B.C. From this date the Messenians disappear entirely from the list, not to reappear till the restoration of Messenia in the fourth century.

During the next half-century we can trace in the names of the victors the gradual growth of the competition over the whole Peloponnese, southwards to Sparta, eastwards to the Isthmus, thence across the Isthmus to Athens and Thebes and over the sea to distant Smyrna.

The conquest of Messenia gave Sparta the command of the roads to Olympia from the south, and Sparta was not slow to take advantage of this. For a century and a half Spartan athletes were unrivalled. Of the eighty-one victories recorded in this period no fewer than forty-six were won by Spartans. After Ol. 50 their successes cease abruptly. Aristotle [3] explains the early success of Sparta in sports and her sudden decline by the fact that she was the first state to practise athletics seriously, and that when other states followed her example her superiority vanished. But perhaps the explanation lies deeper. The hundred and fifty years of Spartan predominance were the years of her external expansion and internal development. Excavations have shown that Spartan art reached its zenith in the seventh century and in the sixth began to decline. From this time she ceased to expand, ceased to progress, merely seeking to consolidate her power by a narrow and exclusive militarism.

[1] vi. 22. 2.　　　　　[2] p. 358.　　　　　[3] *Politics*, v. 4.

The participation of Sparta raised the standard of athletics and increased the prestige of Olympia. To this period we may assign the legend recorded on the diskos of Iphitos, that Lykourgos had helped to establish the festival. Perhaps, too, we may trace Spartan influence in the Doric hymns sung in the Prytaneion [1] and in the institution of the Hellanodikai, for officials bearing the same name existed also at Sparta. There is, however, no evidence that Sparta ever had any official share in the administration.

The second century of the festival (676–576 B.C.) saw still more rapid expansion owing to the participation of the colonies. It was a time of intense activity. East and west bands of adventurers were sailing forth in search of fresh homes. Early in the seventh century settlers from Megara secured the entrance of the Pontos by founding the colonies of Chalkedon and Byzantion. Other bands from Chalkis, Corinth, and Achaia sailed down the Gulf of Corinth to found a greater Hellas in the west. One of the chief effects of the expansion of Hellas and of contact with barbarians was to make the Greeks conscious of their nationality. Hence arose the feeling of national unity, of Panhellenism. But a nation composed of city states is by its very essence disunited, and, if the idea of nationality was to survive, some common centre was needed where all could meet, some activity in which all could join. Olympia supplied this want.

Olympia was peculiarly suitable to become a national centre by reason of its accessibility to the main waterway that connected East and West, and of its aloofness from the struggles that divided the great city states of the mainland. The athletic sports, which were the chief feature of its festival, were essentially national, and appealed alike to the common feeling of nationality and to the pride of the separate states. For while Greeks of every part and of every class could meet there on equal terms under the sanction of religion, they competed not so much as individuals but as representatives of their states. Above all, Olympian Zeus was the most Panhellenic of all gods. Every state, it is true, had its own peculiar festivals and cults, many of them native to the soil and going back to those primitive forms of religion that preceded the worship of the Olympian gods. Even among the Olympian gods each state had its own especial patron. But Athene and Hera, Apollo and Poseidon, were all members of the Olympian Pantheon as determined for ever by

[1] v. 15. 12.

Homer and Hesiod, and at the head of this Pantheon by universal consent stood Zeus the Father. In his worship alone lay the germ of a monotheism that could counteract the disintegrating effect of Greek polytheism. Of all Greek gods he was the most representative, the most national, and the chief seat of his worship was Olympia.

Thus Olympia became the centre for all the Greeks beyond the seas. The first of them to win a victory was Onomastos of Smyrna, in Ol. 23. In the next century victories are chronicled from Miletos and Samos, from Syracuse, and the rival Achaian colonies Sybaris and Kroton. The hymn with which the victor's friends celebrated his success in the evening revels was the triumphal song of Herakles written by Archilochos of Paros. After Ol. 50 the predominance of the colonies is as marked as that of Sparta in the preceding period. Their interest in Olympia is shown by the Treasuries that they dedicated. Of the eleven Treasuries, eight at least were built by colonies.

Meanwhile the growing importance of the festival could not but attract the attention of the ambitious tyrants and nobles of the seventh century. Like Pheidon, perhaps they hoped to use its influence to further their own schemes of empire, but they employed more peaceful means of penetration. Myron of Sikyon won a victory in the chariot-race and dedicated at Olympia two treasure chests or shrines of bronze weighing 500 talents each. His grandson Kleisthenes won a similar victory in 572 B.C. Myron's contemporary, Kypselos, erected there a golden statue of Zeus, made of gold plates riveted together, and his son Periander, also a victor in the chariot-race, dedicated the famous chest of Kypselos. Kylon, the would-be tyrant of Athens, won the stade race in Ol. 35, and a little later the chariot of Alkmaion the son of Megakles was victorious.

In these two centuries Olympia had become the national festival of Hellas, and was attracting competitors from every part and every class. Meanwhile the programme of the games was growing steadily. In Ol. 14 and 15 the diaulos, or two-stade race, and the long race were added. In Ol. 18 the pentathlon was introduced, possibly taking the place of separate competitions in throwing the diskos and the spear. Wrestling and boxing were added, it is said, in Ol. 23, but we may suspect that they formed part of the original programme. Similarly the four-horse chariot-race introduced in Ol. 25 probably took the place of an earlier race in two-horse chariots. In Ol. 33 the horse-race and pankration were introduced, and shortly afterwards various events for boys, a foot-race and wrestling in Ol. 37 and boxing in Ol. 41. A boys' pentathlon was tried in Ol. 38, but for some reason, perhaps because it was too strenuous, it was abandoned. The introduction of competitions for boys is significant of the growing importance attached to athletic training as a part of education.

Archaeological Evidence. Votive Offerings after 700 B.C.

The archaeological evidence, such as it is, confirms the story of the Register. The only buildings during these two centuries that we can date are the Heraion, which we have connected with Pheidon, and the Treasuries of Gela, Metapontion, and Megara, erected about the beginning of the sixth century. These illustrate the growing influence of Olympia. Some official buildings must have existed in the seventh century : certainly a Prytaneion, possibly also a Bouleuterion. Many fresh altars must also have been added, but of these we know nothing. No inscription found is earlier than the sixth century. Once more we must turn to the votive offerings.

The votive offerings found in the upper stratum date from the seventh to the beginning of the fifth century. The earliest of these fall into two classes, works of late geometric art, and works showing oriental influence. Both classes are found together at Sparta with pottery which enables us to assign them to the seventh century.[1]

The geometric objects include figurines, bronze plates, diadems, fibulae, bracelets, rings, pendants, beads, pins, hair-tongs ; miniature wheels, cymbals, double axes, swords and tripods, and a number of large tripods and bronze vessels including libation bowls. Most of them are similar to the geometric objects found at other sites in Greece, at Hallstatt, and in Italy, and show that Olympia was in close touch with the rest of the Greek world.

But the Greek world at the close of the eighth century was in full contact with the East, partly through the cities of Ionia, partly through Phoenician traders. Oriental influence probably

[1] *B. S. A.* xiii, p. 61.

made itself felt first at Corinth, whence it spread to the rest of
the Peloponnese and to Olympia. Sparta also may have helped
to spread it; for Sparta in the eighth century had connexions
with Egypt, and probably with Cyprus and Crete. Early in the
seventh century Ionian Greeks were competing at Olympia, and
in the votive offerings we find clear traces of the influence of
Assyria and Egypt. We see it in the representation of oriental
motives, lions and griffins, sphinxes and winged daimons, and

17. Bronze bands showing oriental ornamentation

also in the appearance of a new type of ornament, braiding simple
and multiple, volutes and rosettes, palmettes and lotus.[1]

It is impossible within the limits of this work to discuss the
origin of these motives, the claims of Assyrians and Hittites,
Minoans and Egyptians. A few examples must suffice to illustrate
their affinities and distribution.

On the fibula[2] shown in Fig. 18 we see a lion with a tail
ending in a bearded serpent's head. Similar fibulae have been
found at Argos and at Sparta, in the latter place with Laconian II
pottery belonging to the second half of the seventh century.
The intention of the serpent's head is probably apotropaic. In

[1] *Olympia*, iv, pp. 96 ff.

[2] *Ib.*, no. 966; cp. Waldstein, *Argive Heraion*, II, p. 188; *B.S.A.* xiii, p. 114,
xiv, p. 147; Poulsen, *Der Orient u. frühgriechische Kunst*, p. 107.

this figure we have the primitive form of the Chimaira, which according to Poulsen was adopted by the Ionians from the Hittites.

Assyrian influence is clearly seen in the winged figures and griffins that were placed round the rim of large bronze cauldrons.[1] On either side we have a winged figure facing outwards, usually the bust of a man with his forearms resting on a pair of wings (Fig. 23). Between the wings is a bird's tail, and connecting the wings and the tail is a semicircular engraved band. The human figure rising from the wings is an adaptation of the winged circle that was the emblem of the god Asshur. Besides these figures, which served for the attachment of handles, each cauldron had six or eight protomai, usually of griffins facing inwards (Fig. 22). Such cauldrons are found throughout the Greek world from France to Armenia, but wherever they are found they are of Greek manufacture. Furtwängler suggests that they came from Sinope, Poulsen from Rhodes or Cyprus, where Greeks and Phoenicians met.

18. Lion fibula

Sometimes Assyrian and Egyptian influences are blended. A good example of this is a bronze plate with a pair of sphinxes arranged heraldically on either side of a stem crowned with Egyptian lotus leaves.[2]

Mythological scenes sometimes occur, especially scenes connected with Herakles. One early relief (Fig. 24) possibly represents him offering sacrifice at the founding of the Olympic Games.[3] He may perhaps be recognized in the figure of an archer cut out of a sheet of bronze (Fig. 20), a technique common at Olympia but rare elsewhere.[4] On one large relief (Fig. 19)[5] divided into three bands we see in the upper band the winged Artemis holding two lions, in the lowest band two griffins, and in the centre Herakles shooting at a wounded centaur. Another relief representing Herakles and the Old Man of the Sea[6] is interesting because the inscription in early Argive characters written from right to left proves it to come from Argos.

[1] *Olympia*, iv, pp. 114 ff., nos. 787 ff. ; Poulsen, *op. cit.*, pp. 15, 64.
[2] *Olympia*, iv, no. 692 ; Poulsen, *op. cit.*, pp. 110, 132.
[3] *Olympia*, iv, no. 694.   [4] *Ib.*, no. 717.
[5] *Ib.*, no. 696.   [6] *Ib.*, no. 699.

19

20

21

22

23

BRONZES FROM OLYMPIA

Most of the objects described are of Greek workmanship, many of them made locally. But there are also a few imported oriental works. Such are two embossed phialai, one of them in the National Museum at Athens, the other in the Ashmolean at Oxford.[1] The former, on which are depicted various oriental cult scenes, bears an Aramaic inscription of a name, probably that of the donor, ' Nagid, the son of Mepha '. The Oxford phiale (Fig. 25) has two bands of figures. The inner band shows the remains of three lions, originally five. On the outer band a gigantic lion with tongue hanging out follows a chariot drawn by a winged sphinx in which stand a charioteer and an archer who shoots at the lion. To the left of the sphinx a man is

24. Bronze relief : Herakles sacrificing

driving a dagger into the back of a lion, to the right another lion is attacked by two archers.

Both phialai contain a mixture of Assyrian and Egyptian motives, and resemble in style bowls found at Nineveh. Poulsen regards this mixture of styles as typically Phoenician, but as no similar works have been found on Phoenician soil some Egyptologists maintain that they came from Egypt, where, they say, a similar mixture of styles prevailed.

On the same plate are reproduced (Figs. 27, 28) two very interesting statuettes, which if not actually imported show strongly the influence of Ionia and the isles. The first is a statuette of Aphrodite, the pillar-like shape of which recalls the archaic statue of Hera from Samos. The curious round pad on the top of the head probably belonged to some vessel of which the statuette formed part. The other is a very fine representation of Artemis striding forward, probably with her bow in her hands. The Ionian influence is obvious in the careful and elaborate treatment of the drapery.

[1] *Olympia*, iv, p. 141 ; Poulsen, *op. cit.*, p. 23 ; *Ashmolean Museum Guide*, p. 117.

We see then that Olympia in the seventh and sixth centuries was in touch not only with the mainland of Greece but with Asia Minor and Egypt. Of this we have further proof from Herodotos.[1] In the reign of Psammetichos II (594–589 B.C.) Elean envoys were sent to Egypt to inquire if the Egyptians in their wisdom could suggest any improvement in the management of the Olympic Games. The Egyptians inquired if their own citizens were allowed to compete, and on hearing that they did so replied that the rules were far from just, for that it was impossible but that the judges should favour unduly their fellow citizens. The Egyptians clearly did not understand the spirit of Greek sport and of Olympia at this period.

Yet in spite of foreign intercourse Olympia remained purely and exclusively Hellenic ; it never became cosmopolitan. Barbarian potentates might send gifts to Pythian Apollo, but not to Olympic Zeus. No foreign deities found a home in his sanctuary ; if the Eleans poured libations to Libyan Ammon and his consort and Parammon,[2] it was because they recognized in those deities their own Zeus and Hera and Hermes. No alien, however rich or powerful, was allowed to compete in the games of Zeus until that privilege was accorded to victorious Rome. The right to compete belonged to all free-born Greeks and to none other.

OLYMPIA FROM 576 TO 476 B.C.

The next twenty-five Olympiads are the most important period in the history of Greek athletics. The athletic festival was now recognized as a national institution and athletic training as part of the national education. The success of Olympia produced a host of imitations. In the first thirty years of the sixth century the old festivals at Delphi, Nemea, and the Isthmus were reorganized as Panhellenic festivals. Solon showed his appreciation of the value of athletics by offering valuable prizes for the Athenian victors in the games, and under his influence or that of Peisistratos the Panathenaic festival was reorganized. Everywhere local festivals sprang up, and in all of these the athletic programme was modelled on that of Olympia. The result was an amazing development of athletics. Never before or after were they so truly national and democratic, and never was the standard higher. Most of the great athletes whose names

---

[1] ii. 160. [2] P. v. 15. 11.

25. Phiale in the Ashmolean Museum

26. Zeus   27. Aphrodite   28. Artemis

BRONZES FROM OLYMPIA

remained household words for centuries belonged to this period, Milo of Kroton, Glaukos of Karystos, Theagenes of Thasos, and many others. The evils of specialization and professionalism did not yet exist, although the excessive honours heaped on successful athletes provoked an angry protest from Xenophanes towards the close of the sixth century. For the most part, however, the athletes of this age were good all-round men who lived simple, vigorous lives without any artificial system of training, and many of them did good service to their cities in peace and in war.[1]

The typical athlete of the period, as we know him from the records and from the black-figured vases, was the strong man,

29. Bybon's Inscription

wrestler, boxer, or pankratiast. Many stories were told of their feats of strength. One of them, named Bybon, left behind him at Olympia an interesting record. It is a block of red sandstone weighing 316 lb., and on it is inscribed the statement that he threw it over his head with one hand.[2]

At Olympia the chief feature of the period is the number of victories won by athletes from beyond the seas, especially from Italy and Sicily. In the twenty-five Olympiads between Ol. 51 and 75 the stade race was won by them seventeen times, and this event may be regarded as typical of the rest of the programme.

Men of all classes competed in the games, but the chariot-races and horse-races appealed especially to the nobles. In these events Athens was especially prominent. Kallias the wealthy

---

[1] v. *Gk. Athletics*, ch. iv. [2] *Olympia*, v, no. 717.

opponent of Peisistratos, the elder Miltiades, and Kimon the son of Stesagoras were all victors with their horses. The latter is said to have secured the repeal of his banishment by allowing Peisistratos to be proclaimed victor in his stead. It is significant of the close relations between Athens and Olympia that the younger Peisistratos inscribed upon the Altar of the Twelve Gods at Athens the distance from Athens to Olympia.[1]

The athletic programme was completed in Ol. 65 by the addition of the race in armour. In this we may see an attempt to restore the practical connexion between athletics and war. The race was a diaulos of two stades, and the runners wore helmets and greaves and round shields. In Ol. 70 a mule chariot-race (ἀπήνη) was introduced, and a race for mares (κάλπη) in which the rider dismounted in the last lap and ran in with his horse. Both these events were discontinued in Ol. 84. Their introduction was probably in the interest of the local nobles whose wealth was chiefly gained by horse-breeding.

In this period arose the most significant of all honours paid to athletes, the privilege of allowing them to celebrate their success by hymns of victory and by setting up statues in the Altis. Neither of these honours was formally bestowed on the athlete by the authorities. It was the victor himself, his friends, or his city that commissioned the sculptor or the poet and paid him. But the fact that they were permitted by public opinion shows the extraordinary value set upon athletic success. With the hymn of victory we are not here concerned. It began with Simonides in the sixth century and ceased shortly after Pindar and Bacchylides in the fifth century. But the practice of setting up victor statues in the Altis lasted with intervals till the time of Pausanias, and filled Olympia with an array of masterpieces unrivalled except perhaps at Athens. Pausanias enumerates 192 such statues, and Walter Hyde, in his valuable study of Olympic victor monuments, calculates that the total number hardly fell short of 500.[2]

Pausanias tells us that the earliest victor statues at Olympia were those in honour of Praxidamas of Aegina, who won the boxing in Ol. 59 (544 B.C.), and Rhexibios of Opus, the victor in the pankration two Olympiads later. These statues were of wood, and were possibly not the first, but the oldest that had survived, for he mentions statues in honour of yet earlier victors.

[1] Hdt. ii. 7.   [2] *Olympic Victor Monuments*, p. 361.

30. Bronze head of Zeus

31. Marble head of Aphrodite

32. Bronze portrait of Pankratiast

33. Marble head of athlete

34. Marble head of Hoplitodromos

35. Portrait of Elean lady

HEADS OF STATUES

Many of the inscribed bases of these statues still exist, the earliest being that which records the victory of Pantares of Gela in the chariot race towards the close of the sixth century.[1] The statues themselves have all vanished, many of them carried off to Rome, the rest melted down for the value of the bronze. Only a few fragments are left : three heads belonging to them are reproduced. Fig. 34 is an archaic head, possibly of a hoplito-dromos. Hyde[2] identifies the statue as that of one Phrikias of Pelinna, who won two victories, in 508 and 504 B.C. A somewhat similar head he assigns to Phanas of Pellene, victor in 512 B.C. These identifications are of course purely conjectural, but the two heads may be regarded as probably belonging to victor statues of the late sixth century. In Fig. 33 we see a far finer head of a boxer or pankratiast. It belongs to the period of Lysippos. Indeed Hyde, from a comparison of this head with that of the Agias, definitely concludes that it is a work of that master, and assigns it to his statue of Philandridas.[3] It is a typically ideal head, and the majority of athletic statues were of this type. Portrait statues were hardly known before the fourth century. Indeed Pliny[4] asserts that only athletes who had won three victories were allowed to erect portrait statues of themselves. Whether this statement is true of all periods may be doubted. A fourth-century inscription on one Xenombrotos of Cos, a winner of the chariot race, definitely describes his statue as a portrait.[5] Certainly there can be no doubt that our third head (Fig. 32) is a portrait. It is a brutal and life-like representa-tion of some professional bruiser, a work probably not earlier than the third century B.C. Partly on the strength of Pliny's statement Hyde identifies the statue as that of Kapros,[6] the first of the so-called successors of Herakles who won the pankration and wrestling matches on the same day.

Athletic statues were not the only works of art dedicated in the Altis. Olympia was now the national sanctuary of the Hellenes, and votive offerings of every sort were dedicated to Olympian Zeus. These offerings, as was natural, often took the form of statues of the god himself. Pausanias devotes a special section of his work to a description of these statues.[7] One of the earliest appears to have been a statue dedicated by the

---

[1] *Olympia*, v, no. 142. [2] *Op. cit.*, p. 162. [3] *Op. cit.*, p. 298.
[4] *H.N.* xxxiv. 16. [5] *Olympia*, v, no. 170. [6] *Op. cit.*, p. 254.
[7] v. 22 ff.

Spartans for a victory over their enemies.[1] The Aeginetan
sculptor Aristinoos, who seems to have worked at the close of
the sixth century, made a statue of Zeus for the Metapontines.[2]
The god was represented with an eagle in one hand, a thunderbolt in the other. Statuettes of Zeus hurling a thunderbolt are
common (Fig. 36), and it has been suggested that this statue
inspired the representation of Zeus hurling the thunderbolt
on the coins of Elis issued shortly after the founding of Elis
city.[3] We may perhaps recognize a more peaceful type of Zeus
in the archaic statuette of a draped man in Fig. 26. The fine

bronze head of Zeus, somewhat similar
in style, in Fig. 30, probably belonged
to some such statue. Sometimes large
sculptural groups were dedicated. In
the Heraion and in the Treasuries
Pausanias saw groups by several early
artists. In the former building he mentions a group of the Horai by Smilis of
Aegina.[4] Among the bases prior to the
Persian war that have been found are the
bases of a group dedicated by Praxiteles
of Syracuse, that of the Trojan heroes by
Onatas of Aegina, and that of the bronze
bull dedicated by the Eretrians.

36. Statuette of Zeus

To the three Treasuries already existing five more were added during the
second half of the sixth century, the Treasuries of Kyrene, Sybaris,
Byzantion, Selinous, and Epidamnos, a list which sufficiently
indicates the enthusiasm of the colonies for Olympia. These
Treasuries, as we shall see, were partly intended as communal
houses, and we can hardly doubt that the states that dedicated
them hoped thereby to secure for themselves a permanent status
at the national sanctuary and in the national festival.

Further, we learn from inscriptions that it was already the
custom in the sixth century to deposit at Olympia records of
treaties, agreements, and laws, which were thereby placed under
the guardianship of Zeus, any breach thereof rendering the
offender liable to fines or penalties to be paid to the god. These
early inscriptions are for the most part too much mutilated to
admit of full interpretation, but their general drift is clear.

[1] P. v. 24. 3.   [2] *Ib.* 22. 5.   [3] v. *infra*, p. 104.   [4] v. 17.

Some are laws concerning the cult and sanctuary of Zeus.[1] Others are grants of citizenship or other rights. Others are treaties.[2] One of these is a treaty for fifty years between two demes, the Anaitoi and Metapioi, of whom we know nothing. Another is the treaty referred to between the Eleans and Heraians. Such covenants between two states, or between a state and an individual, are described as Fράτραι. These documents are not confined to local peoples. We have an unintelligible inscription relating to Zankle, and another decree of Selinous, or possibly Megara Hyblaia, concerning some Megarian exiles who had taken refuge at Selinous.[3] Both these documents belong to the period before the Persian wars. After this date similar inscriptions are much more numerous.

Of the history of Elis and Pisa during the sixth century, and their relations to Olympia, we have little definite information. It seems certain that about the year 576 the Eleans gained a decisive success over the Pisatans, but did not at that time destroy Pisa. Nor did they deprive them of their hereditary share in the control of Olympia, though this became more and more nominal. Traditions of uncertain meaning point to a certain amount of reorganization. One tradition assigned to this period the first appointment of two Hellanodikai. Another connects with this war the Sixteen Matrons of Elis who wove the Peplos for Hera. They had acted, it is said, as mediators between Pisa and Elis. Far more important is the fact that from this time the monarchy disappears both in Elis and Pisa. Here perhaps we have the true explanation of the appointment of the two Hellanodikai who carried on at Olympia the sacred functions that had formerly belonged to the kings. The Pisatans from this time seem to have lost all political cohesion and to have degenerated into a scattered population of uncultured but turbulent country folk. The Elean monarchy, on the other hand, was replaced by a close and narrow oligarchy of rich and selfish landowners, chiefly concerned with enriching themselves by cattle-breeding and exploiting to their own advantage their connexion with Olympia.

The predominance of Elis at Olympia is evident from the coins of Elis,[4] the earliest of which, numismatists are agreed, were

---

[1] *Olympia*, v, nos. 3, 4, 5, 7, 14.
[2] *Ib.*, nos. 2, 9, 10, 11. [3] *Ib.*, nos. 22, 24.
[4] P. Gardner, *Num. Chron.* xix. 221–73 ; cf. T. Seltman, *The Temple Coins of Olympia*. A selection of these coins is given in Fig. 37.

issued by the Elean oligarchy in the latter part of the sixth century. The coins of Elis form an unbroken series extending over more than three centuries which in variety and beauty is unsurpassed by those of any other Greek state. These coins are one more proof of the existence of a native school of art, of which we find evidence in the early bronze work and in the sculptures of the Temple of Zeus. The connexion of the whole series with Olympia is evident in the types represented. In the earliest coins prior to 471 B.C. the universal type on the obverse is the eagle of Zeus flying with wings outstretched or folded on its back. Usually it holds in its talons a serpent or rends a hare, a fitting symbol of Olympian Zeus, who was from the first regarded as god of war and giver of victory. On the reverse is the equally appropriate symbol of the thunderbolt, while on a few coins we see the figure of Nike striding forward with outstretched wings and holding in her hand a wreath which must surely be the crown of the victor in the games.

Mr. Seltman, in his exhaustive work on the coins of Elis, has argued that these coins were minted at Olympia, where, as we have seen, there must have existed for centuries a school of skilled workmen in metal. The existence of a mint at Olympia is possible, though not proved, but when he describes the coinage as a temple coinage he seems to go too far. Certainly there is no evidence that these coins were like the Temple shekel of the Jews, intended to be used for the offerings or tribute paid to Zeus. Nor is there any proof that they were intended for the use of visitors to the four-yearly festival or pilgrims to the shrine. That such visitors had to change their own money into native currency is very doubtful. Nor is it clear that the Eleans before the founding of Elis city had no need of coins. They were an exceedingly rich and prosperous community, in close touch with the rich cities of Sicily and Italy, and had just as much need for a coinage of their own as any city state.

Nothing is known of the administration of Olympia before the sixth century. Presumably it was left in the hands of the local Pisatans. But the rapid growth of the sanctuary demanded more definite organization. Sixth-century inscriptions mention a council, and also a mass meeting whose consent was required for any change in the laws.[1] One of the principal duties of the council must have been to control the erection of new buildings

[1] *Olympia*, v, no. 3.

and monuments.   Another duty must have been to arrange the programme of the games.   Such a council required permanent head-quarters, and the north wing of the Bouleuterion was built somewhere in the middle of the century for their use.   The two Hellanodikai must have acted as its executive officers.   The fact that a single Hellanodikas is mentioned in one inscription [1] cannot be taken to prove that at this time he had no colleague. Other officials mentioned are the ἱαρόμαοι,[2] who probably had charge of the sacred property, and the Theokolos, who had control of the sacrifices.   One inscription securing protection for the person and property of the Theokolos provides that such protection shall not extend to illegitimate gains (εἰ ἀλλότρια ποιοῖτο).   We may suspect that like Hophni and Phineas this priestly official was tempted to make profit from his office.

The narrow unprogressive aristocracy of Elis seems to have done little for the development of Olympia beyond building the Council House.   The real development came, as we have seen, from without.   But the Elean oligarchy was not to continue long. In the Persian wars they showed a complete indifference to the national cause.   The Elean contingent arrived too late to take part in the battle of Plataiai.   Returning home shamed and angry they proceeded to overthrow the oligarchy and establish a democracy.

In the political changes that followed Olympia was naturally involved.   In Ol. 75 the two Hellenodikai were replaced by a board of nine.   Pausanias tells us that they were divided into three groups in charge respectively of the horse-races, the pentathlon, and the other sports.   We may suspect that the number nine was the number of the Elean tribes.   Another democratic feature—election by lot—may have been introduced at the same time.   The Pisatans thus lost most of their share in the administration, and their discontent was increased by the transference of the political centre to the newly founded city state of Elis in 471 B.C.   The result was the revolt recorded by Herodotus. The Eleans overran Pisatis and Triphylia, sacked the cities, among which we must include Pisa, and added a tenth Hellanodikas to represent the conquered districts.

[1] *Ib.*, no. 2.   [2] *Ib.*, nos. 1, 4, 10.

VII

Olympia and Elis

Ἡρακλέης ἀγῶνα μὲν σωμάτων ἐποίησε φιλοτιμίαν τε πλούτου γνώμης δ' ἐπίδειξιν ἐν τῷ καλλίστῳ τῆς Ἑλλάδος, ἵνα τούτων ἁπάντων ἔνεκα εἰς τὸ αὐτὸ συνέλθωμεν τὰ μὲν ὀψόμενοι τὰ δὲ ἀκουσόμενοι· ἡγήσατο γὰρ τὸν ἐνθάδε σύλλογον ἀρχὴν γενήσεσθαι τοῖς Ἕλλησι τῆς πρὸς ἀλλήλους φιλίας, Lysias, *Olympiakos.*

FROM THE PERSIAN WAR TO THE PELOPONNESIAN WAR

Elean Administration.

THE new relation of Elis to Olympia is asserted in the clearest manner on a coin which numismatists justly connect with the founding of Elis city and the final destruction of Pisa (Fig. 37, 2). On the reverse it bears the figure of Zeus holding in his left hand an eagle and with his right hand hurling the thunderbolt, and the inscription ΛΟΛΥΜΠΙΚΟΝ. On the obverse is the eagle of Zeus fighting with a serpent, and on the oldest specimens of the type Mr. Seltman finds traces of the inscription ϜΑΛΕΙΟΝ, which occurs now for the first time written in full. The claim of Elis could not be affirmed more distinctly. From this time the number and variety of the Elean coins increases greatly, and all the types have reference to Olympia. Some of these are collected in Fig. 37. In no. 1 we see another type of Zeus. He is seated on a rock with a sceptre in his left hand, while from his right hand rises an eagle about to fly away. The type suggests a statue, but is certainly earlier than the statue of Pheidias. Nike too appears, sometimes running, as on the earlier coins, sometimes standing (no. 3). The most beautiful perhaps of all types is the seated figure (no. 4), which Seltman dates 432–421 B.C. Nike is seated on the topmost of two steps. In her right hand she holds the victor's palm-branch. In the exergue is a twig of the Olympic olive.[1]

---

[1] Seltman, *op. cit.*, pp. 19, 21 ; Gardner, *op. cit.*, pp. 226 ff. The coin reproduced in 2 is the Berlin specimen which Seltman dates after 452 B.C. The earliest specimens are placed after 471 B.C. It would be natural to connect this issue with

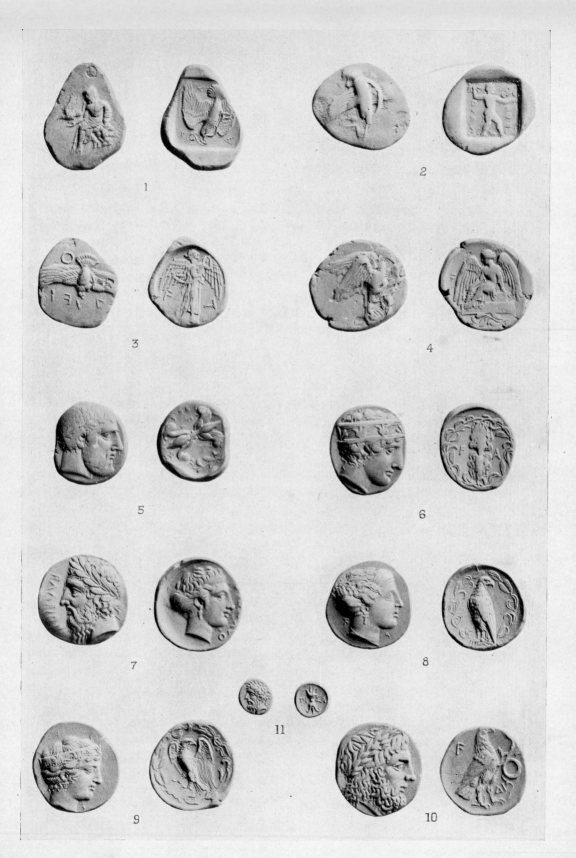

37. COINS OF ELIS

The Eleans fully realized the advantages that accrued to them as guardians of Olympia, and they left nothing undone to identify the new state with the great national sanctuary. They claimed for themselves and their territory the sanctity that belonged to the sacred precinct. Their city gradually became the permanent head-quarters of the Olympian administration. Everything was arranged there solely with a view to the festival.[1] Close to the Agora was the Hellanodikeon, where the Hellanodikai who were now elected by lot received the necessary training at the hands of the Nomophylakes. Thus the tradition of the games was maintained and a supply of duly qualified officials assured. Competitors, too, spent the last month of their training at Elis under the eyes of the Hellanodikai. Three gymnasia were provided for them, equipped with running tracks and wrestling rings. The Agora itself was called the Hippodrome, and was used for exercising horses. It was merely an open space surrounded with colonnades containing no ornaments except a few altars to Zeus and other gods, and even these altars were so constructed that they could be removed when required. A room adjoining the Agora was also set apart for the use of the Sixteen Matrons who wove the peplos presented to Hera at her festival at Olympia. Lastly a sacred road connected Elis and Olympia, and along this when the training was finished the whole body of athletes, trainers, horses and chariots, headed by the Hellano-dikai, went in solemn procession to the festival. When these various arrangements were introduced we cannot say; but we may be certain that the policy that they represented dates from this time, and the history of the festival bears witness to the success of the Elean administration.

The moment when the Eleans secured sole control was for them singularly opportune. The Persian wars had given a power-ful impulse to the Panhellenic festivals and to athletics generally. One of the chief morals that the Greeks drew from these wars was the superiority of the soldier trained in the gymnasia over the

the next Olympic games, 468 B.C., but this does not necessarily mean that they were temple coins. The references of the coins illustrated are :
1. B.M. 13. G(ardner) Series II. 3 ; S(eltman) 101.
2. Berlin = G. II. 1 ; S. 72 (cp. 37).
3. Oxford = G. II. 4 ; S. 71.
4. B.M. 52 = S. 133.
[1] P. vi. 23.

effeminate oriental. Every state had now its own competitions, gymnasia, and palaestrae, and the great national festivals attracted the picked athletes from the whole Greek world. Honours of every sort were heaped upon the victors, poets wrote for them songs of victory, sculptors immortalized their forms. The noblest tribute to the athletic ideal of the fifth century is the art that it inspired.[1]

Some idea of the character and extent of the competition at Olympia can be formed from the list of victors in the 76th Olympiad, the first celebration of the games after the Persian War, when Themistokles himself visited Olympia and received an ovation greater than that of the athletes themselves. The list, somewhat mutilated, is preserved on a papyrus.[2] The stade race was won by a runner from Mitylene, the diaulos by an Argive for whom Simonides wrote an epitaph, the long race and the boys' race by Spartans. The winner of the pentathlon was Ikkos of Tarentum, who is quoted by Plato as an example of abstinence and strictness in training.[3] Pausanias saw his statue in the Altis. The wrestling and boxing were won by two famous athletes, Euthymos of Italian Lokroi and Theagenes of Thasos. The statue of Euthymos was by Pythagoras of Samos, that of Theagenes by Glaukias of Aegina. The winner of the wrestling for boys was an Aeginetan, probably that Theognetos whose victory is mentioned by Pindar in his eighth Pythian ode and who also had a statue at Olympia. Pindar wrote five odes at least for victors in this Olympiad, two for Agesidamos of Italian Lokroi, the winner of the boys' boxing, two celebrating the victory of Theron of Akragas in the chariot-race, and one that of Hieron in the horse-race. Is it a mere accident that in these odes he seems to be even more concerned with the glory of Olympia than with the praises of the victors? In his first Olympian he tells the story of Pelops, in the third and eleventh the founding of the games by Herakles. Hieron's victory was also celebrated by Bacchylides, and a chariot group in his honour was set up later by his son.[4]

Yet even in this great Olympiad we find a warning of the dangers with which excess is fraught in athletics. The hoplite race was won by Astylos of Kroton, who had in previous years won victories at Olympia. On this occasion he had entered

[1] *Gk. Athletics*, ch. v.   [2] *Ox. Pap.* ii. 222.
[3] *Prot.* 316 d ; *Leg.* 840 a ; P. vi. 10. 5.   [4] P. vi. 12. 1 ; Bacchylides, v.

himself as a Syracusan to win the favour of Hieron. It is the first recorded instance of buying athletes. His countrymen in disgust destroyed the statue that they had erected in his honour at Kroton, and turned his house into a common prison.

The vigour of the new administration soon made itself felt. Hitherto individual states had been allowed to arrogate to themselves a privileged position by erecting Treasuries. Between 480 B.C. and 470 three new Treasuries were added, one by the Syracusans to commemorate the victory of Himera, another by the people of Sikyon ; the builders of the third are unknown. But this laxity was now to end. From this time the Eleans took into their own hands the buildings of the Altis, and they were justified by the result.

New Buildings and Monuments at Olympia.

The building of the western Treasuries led to the construction of a stepped retaining wall (Fig. 39). It consisted of nine rows of steps, the object of which was not merely to furnish an approach to the Treasuries but also to provide a commodious grand stand from which the crowds of spectators could view the processions, sacrifices, and sports. A similar line of steps has been discovered in front of the Temple of Didyma, and I suspect that the curious flight of steps to the west of the Parthenon served likewise for spectators of the Panathenaic procession. These steps, together with the Stoa erected a few years later, formed the Theatron mentioned by Xenophon.[1]

About the same time the south wing of the Bouleuterion was built, probably for the accommodation of the new board of Hellanodikai. The architectural remains seem to prove that this addition was made shortly before the building of the Temple of Zeus.

This temple was the greatest of all the works undertaken by the new administration. Hitherto Zeus had shared a temple with Hera ; now he was to have a habitation of his own. It was begun probably in 468 B.C. and finished about 457 B.C. It was of local poros stone, the work of an Elean architect, Libon ; and the sculptures, as we shall see, were probably the work of Elean artists. The cost was defrayed from the spoils of the recently conquered Pisatis, and there is no reason for believing

---

[1] v. Dyer, ' Olympic Theatron ', *J. H. S.* xxviii. 256 ; *infra*, p. 178.

that it was a national work to which the whole of Hellas contributed.   But national it was in that it was dictated by that
spirit of Panhellenism that inspired all the art of the period.
Standing on a solid mass of masonry it rose to a height of more
than sixty feet, dominating the whole Altis, and was a worthy
home for the masterpiece of Pheidias placed in it some years
later.

The next improvement involved a complete reconstruction
of the eastern side of the Altis.   Hitherto the games had been held
in the plain to the east of the great altar.   Now a permanent
level dromos and hippodrome were laid out farther east.   At
the same time the open space between the altar and the dromos
was levelled and a long colonnade built at right angles to the
Treasury terrace.   The date of these improvements must have
been shortly before or after the building of the temple.   For
architectural blocks rejected in this building were used in the
walls of the Stoa and in the water-channel that ran along the
terrace wall, and thence along the eastern wall of the Stoa.[1]

The Stoa,[2] as we shall see, was rebuilt in Macedonian times.
Of the original buildings nothing remains except the back wall,
the side walls, and the foundations of some of the columns.
There seem to have been thirty of these, and the whole length
of the colonnade was 96 metres.   It was probably a double
colonnade, the existing foundations belonging to the inner row of
columns.   The back wall, which was solidly built of poros blocks,
was afterwards buried under the embankment of the Stadion.

Pausanias [3] tells us that the Stoa had two names.   Officially
it was called the Stoa Poikile, or Painted Colonnade, on account
of the pictures which had once adorned it but which no longer
existed in his time.   Some people, however, called it the Echo
Colonnade, on account of its sevenfold echo.   We have no means
of determining which of the two names is the original, nor do we
know if one name belonged to the earlier, the other to the later
colonnade.

Lastly, the so-called south-east building must have been built
a little later than the Stoa, for its alignment is determined by it.
It has been plausibly conjectured that this was the Hellanodikeon,[4] or official residence of the Hellanodikai, and as such
I shall describe it.

[1] *Olympia*, ii, p. 72.   [2] *Ib.*, p. 70.   [3] v 21. 17.
[4] v. *infra*, p. 276.

38. NORTH-WEST CORNER OF ALTIS

Roman west wall to left   Greek wall to right

39. METROON AND STEPS OF TREASURY TERRACE

All these buildings were probably constructed before the chryselephantine statue of Zeus was placed in the temple. According to tradition Pheidias worked at Olympia between the years 438 B.C. and 432 B.C. His workshop was still in existence in the time of Pausanias, and is generally identified with the building converted into a Byzantine church.

In a previous chapter it was pointed out that the rise of Olympia to a Panhellenic festival was largely due to the national character of Olympian Zeus. It was this conception of Zeus as the national god of Hellas that inspired the masterpiece of Pheidias, a statue that embodied the highest ideals of Greek religious thought and may truly be said to have ' added something to religion itself '. His statue of the virgin goddess of Athens in the Parthenon appealed to the Athenians, his Zeus appealed to the whole of Hellas, nay, to the whole world. Every one is familiar with the story how the artist, when asked by Panainos in what type he would embody his conception of Zeus, replied by quoting the lines of Homer :

' The son of Kronos spake and nodded his dark brow, and the ambrosial locks waved from the King's immortal head, and he made great Olympos quail.' (*Il.* I. 527.)

But the Zeus of Pheidias far transcended the Zeus of Homer: he was the Zeus of Homer divested of mythology and human frailty. In him were combined all the attributes under which Zeus was worshipped, all the ideals that poets had imagined of the godhead. This conception is finely expressed in the words that Dio Chrysostom [1] puts into the mouth of Pheidias : ' Our Zeus is peaceful and gentle in every way, as becomes the overseer of an undivided and harmonious Hellas, whom by the help of my art and the wise and good city of the Eleans I set up mild and august, the giver of life and breath and all good things, the common father and saviour and guardian of all men.'

All this artistic activity naturally brought Olympia into touch with Athens, the chief centre of art in Greece. It would seem that some of the family of Pheidias must have settled in Elis, for the office of Burnisher of the Statue of Zeus was an honour hereditary among his descendants.[2] Among the inscriptions of imperial times found at Olympia is one in honour of ' Titus Flavius Heraclitus, descendant of Pheidias, Burnisher of Olympian

[1] *Or.* 74, p. 412.　　　　[2] P. v. 14. 5 ; *Olympia*, v, no. 466.

Zeus '. Many of the master's pupils came with him to Olympia.
Among those who helped him in his work were his kinsmen
Panainos, who painted the panels of the throne, and Kolotes,
who made an ivory and gold table to take the place of the ancient
tripod on which the wreaths of the victors in the games were
placed.[1] It is significant of the influence of Athens that the one
historical scene represented on the throne of Zeus was the sea-
fight at Salamis. Panainos also painted the shield of a chryselephantine statue of Athene at Elis, the work either of Pheidias
himself or of Kolotes.[2]

The list of statues erected during this period baffles the
imagination. The statues themselves are no more, but we can
still read the inscriptions on their broken bases. The most
famous artists of the Greek world were represented there,
Myron and Kalamis of Athens, Glaukias and Onatas of Aegina,
Polykleitos of Argos, Pythagoras of Samos, and many others.
Of the athletic statues alone Pausanias mentions more than fifty
erected between the Persian wars and the end of the century.[3]
They were placed along the road that led from the Bouleuterion
to the Altar of Zeus, the earlier ones mostly to the south. Some
of the statues were grouped together according to the nationality
of the victor or the character of the competition. Not far
from the southern boundaries were groups of chariots including
those of Gelon and Hieron. We can form some idea of their
splendour from the bronze charioteer found at Delphi. A little
farther north, opposite the north-east corner of the temple, was
a group of boxers clustered round the statue of Euthymos.
Another group consisting of Spartan victors stood still farther
north near the Heraion.

Of the statues of Zeus we may mention particularly that
erected by the Greeks who fought at Plataiai in memory of their
victory.[4] On its basis were inscribed, as at Delphi, the names
of the states that shared in the triumph. Part of the basis was
found not far from the south wall of the Altis, with a recess cut
in the front for the bronze plate that bore the inscription.

Statues of other deities were rare. Pausanias mentions two
statues of Hermes.[5] One of these representing the god with
a ram under his arm was the gift of the Arkadians of Pheneos

[1] P. v. 20. 2.   [2] P. vi. 26. 3.
[3] v. Hyde, *De Olympionicarum Statuis*, pp. 73 ff.
[4] *Olympia*, i, p. 86.   [5] P. v. 27. 8.

and the work of Onatas, who also made a colossal statue of
Herakles for the Thasians.[1] The statue of Hermes as a herald
was the work of the Elean sculptor Kallon. Herakles and Hermes
were the special patrons of athletes. There was also a statue of
the youthful Herakles and the Nemean lion, dedicated by a
citizen of Tarentum.[2] The artist Nikodamos of Mainalos, who
lived at the close of the fifth century, also made a statue of
Athene.[3] It was, as far as we know, the only statue of a goddess
erected, and it is significant that it was the offering of the Eleans
themselves.

Numerous important groups were dedicated during this
period. The Messenians of Sicily set up a group representing
a choir of boys and their choragos who had been lost at sea on
their way to take part in some festival.[4] But most of the subjects
were mythological. The people of Apollonia, having conquered
some territory from the neighbouring Abantes, employed Lykios
the son of Myron to make an elaborate group representing the
contest between Achilles and Memnon.[5] It stood on a great
semicircular pedestal. In the centre was Zeus with Thetis and
Eos supplicating for their sons who occupied the two ends,
while in the intervening spaces were pairs of Greek and Trojan
heroes. Another great group dedicated by the Achaians, and
the work of Onatas, had for its subject the Greek heroes drawing
lots to decide who was to accept the challenge of Hector.[6] The
heroes were arranged on a semicircular pedestal which stood
on the left of the road leading from the Bouleuterion to the
temple. On the opposite side of the road was placed the figure
of Nestor drawing lots. The most famous of all the offerings
of the time were those dedicated by Mikythos,[7] the steward of
Anaxilas of Rhegion, as a thank-offering, for the recovery of his
son. These bare records give some idea of the wealth of sculpture
with which Olympia was adorned at this time.

[1] P. v. 25. 12.   [2] P. v. 25. 7.   [3] P. v. 26. 6.
[4] P. v. 25. 2.   [5] P. v. 22. 2.   [6] P. v. 25. 8.
[7] P. v. 26. 2 ; Hdt. vii. 170 ; *Olympia*, v, nos. 267, 268, 269.

FROM THE BEGINNING OF THE PELOPONNESIAN WAR TO
THE BATTLE OF CHAIRONEIA

Olympia and Panhellenic Unity.

The years between the Persian and the Peloponnesian wars
were the most brilliant in the history of Olympia. But the
dream of Hellenic unity was but short-lived. Before the middle
of the century the old feuds had broken out again, and for more
than a century Greece was torn by the strife of rival states, till
unity was imposed upon her by the might of Macedon. In these
struggles Olympia did not escape. The sacred precinct was
twice invaded, building activity ceased, while in the sports we
find traces of the corruption which was becoming prevalent
elsewhere. Yet never was the value of the festival more conspicuous. In spite of the general corruption Olympia maintained
its high tradition of sport, and there almost alone in Greece was
kept alive the ideal of Hellenic brotherhood.

Herakles, says Lysias in his *Olympiakos*, ' founded the festival
because he thought that the gathering of the Greeks there would
be for them the beginning of mutual friendship '. Undoubtedly
Olympia did promote friendship and goodwill. Every four years
the Sacred Truce gave at least a brief respite from war, and
during these months citizens and deputations from hostile states
could travel unmolested to and from the festival. There, in the
words of Isokrates,[1] ' having poured common libations and laid
aside their enmities they joined together in public prayers and
sacrifices, and thus reminded of their common relationship learnt
to be more kindly disposed one to another, renewed ancient
friendships and formed new ones '.

The political value of Olympia was recognized in the making
of treaties. No place was so convenient for the proclamation,
recording, and ratification of treaties and truces. The terms of
the thirty years truce between Athens and Sparta in 445 B.C.
were recorded on a stele in the Altis. So was the peace of Nikias
in 421 B.C., and in the next year the hundred years treaty between
Athens, Argos, Mantinea, and Elis. In the latter case it was
provided that the treaty should be renewed periodically at the
Olympic and Panathenaean festivals.[2]

The Greeks were very sensitive to public opinion, and it was

[1] *Panegyrikos*, c. 43.   [2] P. v. 12. 8, 23. 4 ; Thuc. v. 18. 47.

only at these national festivals that the collective opinion of the Greek world could make itself felt. Hence the supreme importance that states and rulers attached to winning the popular favour at Olympia ; hence the expenditure lavished on Theoriai and teams for chariot-races. Alkibiades [1] argued that by the magnificence of his chariots he had rendered a public service and enhanced the glory of Athens. Contrast this with the account given by Diodorus [2] of the despair of Dionysios at the slights and insults which he received at Olympia. Or take the words that Isokrates [3] puts into the mouth of Archidamos protesting against the re-establishment of Messenia. ' The Spartans have hitherto been objects of admiration and envy at Olympia and the other Panegyreis. But who of us would dare to show himself there if instead of being honoured he is to be treated with contempt, instead of being a centre of attraction to all for his valour he is to be slighted as a coward, if, further, he is to see the slaves of the country that our fathers left to us, offering greater sacrifices than we do ? '

Now the importance of Olympic opinion consists in this, that there were reconciled the opposing ideals of Panhellenism and Autonomy. The failure of the imperial dreams of Perikles was due to the fact that they were inconsistent with autonomy. But at Olympia there was no conflict between the two ideals : it stood for a nation of city states. So at the beginning of the Peloponnesian wars the Mytilenean envoys came to Olympia to protest against the tyranny of Athens in the name of Autonomy, and later when Athens and Sparta were treacherously intriguing with Persia it was at Olympia that on three occasions an appeal was made for national unity.

The first protest came from Gorgias of Leontini at the festival of 408 B.C. [4] Seeing Greece torn by faction he became a counsellor of concord, seeking to turn the Greeks against the barbarians and urging them to take as the prize of their prowess the land of the barbarians, not each others' cities. ' Trophies won against barbarians ', he reminded the Athenians, ' demand hymns, those won against Greeks dirges.'

The *Olympiakos* of Lysias was delivered in 384 B.C. Two years before Greece had been forced to submit to Persian arbitra-

---

[1] Thuc. vi. 16 ; Isokrates, *De Bigis*, 32.
[2] xiv. 109 ; xv. 6. 7. Cf. Grote, *History of Greece*, ch. lxxxiii.
[3] *Archidamos*, 95.　　　　　　　　　[4] Philostratos, *Vit. Soph.* i. 209.

tion and to accept an ignominious peace by which the free Greek cities of Asia were left in the power of the great king. The terms of the peace were inscribed on a stele in the Altis. Sparta, who alone had profited by the peace, had recently sacked Mantineia, and was now in league with another enemy of Greek liberties, Dionysios of Syracuse. The latter, anxious to display his wealth at Olympia, had sent to the festival a magnificent embassy headed by his brother Thearides. His tents of purple and gold were pitched within the sacred precincts, splendid chariots were entered in his name. Skilful rhapsodists had been hired to sing his praises before the multitudes in poems composed by the tyrant himself. But all this ostentation aroused nothing but anger and contempt. These feelings were increased when Dikon, the winner of the stade race, the first race on the programme, was proclaimed as a Syracusan. For Dikon was not really a citizen of Syracuse, but of Kaulon, a free city which the tyrant had destroyed. Such were the circumstances under which Lysias delivered his oration. Warning the Greeks that the real enemies of Greece were Artaxerxes and Dionysios, he urged them not to admit to their sacred games the envoys of an impious tyranny, but to drive the tyrant from his throne and free Sicily, and as a beginning to plunder the gorgeous tents of his embassy. Such an outrage on the hospitality of the festival could not of course be permitted by the authorities ; but the spectators vented their feelings by ridiculing the royal rhapsodists, and they had the satisfaction of seeing the complete failure of his chariots.

Four years later Isokrates distributed at the festival copies of his *Panegyric*, in which he appealed to Athens and Sparta to lay aside their differences and unite in a Panhellenic crusade against Persia.

In these speeches the somewhat vague Panhellenism of earlier days seems to be taking a more definite and practical form. The city state with its factions and feuds was breaking down, and there was springing up a new desire for unity that found its expression in leagues and federations. All Greeks were felt to be brethren, and war between brethren was unnatural. To this feeling we may ascribe the idea that no memorial might be set up in the Altis to commemorate the triumph of one Greek state over another. We trace the growth of this feeling at Olympia. Towards the close of the sixth century the Spartans had set up at Olympia a bronze statue of Zeus twelve feet high as a thank-

offering for some victory. Pausanias connected the victory with
the second Messenian war, but the form of the letters shows
that this must be a mistake.[1] Anyhow, it was a victory over
fellow Greeks. Similarly the Corinthians commemorated their
victory at Tanagra by a shield that they placed over the east
gable of the Temple of Zeus, ' from the spoils ', as the inscription
states, ' of Argives, Athenians, and Ionians '.[2] Yet we hear of
no word of protest. Nor was any protest made when about
420 B.C. the Messenians set up the Nike of Paionios in honour of
a victory over their enemies. Yet a few years later, when Agis
came to Olympia to consult the oracle, the Eleans forbade him
to pray for victory in war, alleging their ancient tradition that
no oracle should be given to Greeks for a war against Greeks.[3]
Finally, after the unsuccessful revolt of Pisatis in 364 B.C., the
Eleans erected a colossal statue of Zeus, with an inscription truly
appropriate to the ideal of the festival, ' The Eleans for Concord '.[4]

Elis and Sparta.

Elis had known little concord since the outbreak of the
Peloponnesian war. She had constantly to contend with two
difficulties, the jealousy of Sparta and the disaffection of the
Pisatans and their Arkadian kinsfolk.

The alienation of Sparta must have begun with the synoecism
of Elis and the overthrow of the oligarchy. Sparta could hardly
view with indifference the independence which the growing
importance of Olympia secured to the new democracy. Moreover, the Panhellenism of Olympia made no appeal to the narrow-
minded Spartans, who had no thoughts beyond the Peloponnese.

On the other hand Athens, with her overseas interests, was in
close sympathy with the ideal of Olympia. The artistic activity
at Olympia could not but draw Elis more closely to Athens and
Argos, the two chief centres of art in Greece and the two most
dangerous rivals of Sparta. Hence, though nominally a member
of the Peloponnesian league, Elis gave but a half-hearted support
to Sparta.

A dispute about Lepreon [5] led to an open quarrel. Lepreon
had refused to pay a yearly tribute of a talent due to Olympian
Zeus in return for help received from Elis against the Arkadians.
When Elis tried to extort it, the Lepreatai appealed to Sparta,

[1] P. v. 24. 3 ; *Gk. Athletics*, p. 138 ; *Olympia*, v, no. 252.   [2] P. v. 10. 4.
[3] Xen., *Hell.* iii. 2. 22.   [4] *Olympia*, v, no. 260.   [5] Thuc. v. 31. 49.

who dispatched 1,000 hoplites to their help. The Eleans complained that the Spartans had violated the Olympic truce, and, disregarding the protest of Sparta that the truce had not yet been proclaimed at Sparta, they imposed a fine of 2,000 minai and, when Sparta refused to pay, excommunicated her and forbade her to sacrifice or compete at the forthcoming festival. In acting thus boldly they relied probably on the recently completed treaty for a hundred years with Athens and Argos. Yet even so the alarm at the festival was great. Would the Spartans accept their exclusion peaceably or not? The alarm was increased by an incident that took place in the games. Lichas, the son of Agesilaos, being debarred from competing, had entered his chariot in the name of the Boeotian commonwealth. His chariot won, and wishing to claim the victory as his own he advanced and himself bound the fillet of victory on the head of the charioteer. The effrontery was too much for the Elean authorities, who ordered the Rhabdouchoi to beat him from the precinct. Yet in spite of this fresh insult Sparta did nothing, and the festival passed off without disturbance. The hundred years' treaty, however, lasted only one year, and after the battle of Mantineia Elis returned to the Spartan alliance, though she henceforth took no part in the war.

Professor Percy Gardner [1] long ago pointed out the connexion between the alliance of Elis and Argos and the first appearance of the beautiful head of Hera on the coins of Elis. But he does not, in my opinion, go far enough. I would suggest that this alliance led to a distinct revival of the cult of Hera, which long survived that short-lived alliance. This will explain the fact that the Hera type continued for nearly a century. Mr. Seltman, indeed, has argued that these coins were issued from a separate mint, possibly, like the Zeus mint, at Olympia.[2] There are numerous buildings at Olympia that might have served the purpose, the workshop of Pheidias, for example, or the buildings south of it. The Hera mint did not supersede the Zeus mint; the two worked side by side without any rivalry, and indeed must have been under the same control. The Hera heads have usually on the reverse the thunderbolt or eagle of Zeus (Fig. 37, 6, 8, 9).

[1] *Op. cit.*, p. 238.
[2] *Op. cit.*, p. 2. Mr. Seltman speaks of separate mints in the precincts of Zeus and Hera. But Hera had no precinct, only a share in a temple. Zeus had the whole Altis, but there was no place for a mint in his temple.

The beautiful heads of Hera and Zeus (5, 6) [1] are clearly contemporary. By their largeness of feature, their noble dignity and simplicity, they belong to the age of Pheidias, and in the Zeus head we may well see a reminiscence of the great statue by Pheidias. It is instructive to compare them with the later types (10).

A further proof of the decline of Spartan influence at Olympia is afforded by the Messenian Nike which was erected about 420 B.C. The inscription states that the Messenians and Naupaktians erected it as a tithe from their enemies. Who were these enemies ? Pausanias [2] thought that they were the Akarnanians of Oiniadai, referring perhaps to the capture of Oiniadai about the middle of the fifth century. But the style of the statue is incompatible with such a date, and we know of no victory won later in Akarnania that would justify such a monument. But Pausanias also informs us that the Messenians themselves claimed that it commemorated their share in the capture of Sphakteria, and that they omitted to insert the name of the enemy from fear of the Spartans. Considering the importance of this victory and the effect that it produced, considering too the intense joy it must have caused to the Messenians, we may well accept their account. But in any case it was a victory won against Sparta or her allies, and we can well understand the feelings of irritation that such a monument must have caused them from the violent protests that they made some fifty years later against the restoration of Messenia.

The figure of Nike and several blocks of the pedestal with the inscription were found *in situ* some thirty yards east of the south-east corner of the Temple of Zeus. The pedestal was composed of twelve triangular marble blocks and was originally about thirty feet high. The goddess was represented flying through the air with outstretched wings, beneath her feet was an eagle, and the rough block that supported her was probably painted blue to represent the air. Her rapid motion is beautifully

---

[1] 5=B.M. 54 ; G. iii. 1 ; S. 147.   6=B.M. 55 ; G. iii. 2 ; S. 264.
    9=B.M. 90 ; G. v. vi. 2a ; S. 301.
[2] P. v. 26. 1.   *Olympia*, v, no. 259 :

Μεσσάνιοι καὶ Ναυπάκτιοι ἀνέθεν Διὶ
᾽Ολυμπίῳ δεκάταν ἀπὸ τῶμ πολεμίων.

Παιώνιος ἐποίησε Μενδαῖος
Καὶ τἀκρωτήρια ποιῶν ἐπὶ τὸν ναὸν ἐνίκα.

expressed by her graceful poise and the thin draperies clinging closely to her body in front and floating out behind in billowy masses. The artist, as the inscription and Pausanias tell us, was Paionios of Mende, ' who also was victorious in a competition for the akroteria of the Temple of Zeus '. Whether he, as Pausanias states, also made the eastern pediment of the temple, will be discussed in connexion with the pediments.

Sparta can have found little satisfaction in the following festival, 416 B.C. For all the public theoriai were completely eclipsed by the extraordinary display of Alkibiades. Never had such a sight been seen at Olympia. For the chariot-race he entered seven chariots, winning first, second, and fourth places, and after his victory he entertained the whole assembly at a banquet in a splendid tent that he had provided. How far he was prompted by personal vanity, how far by a desire to enhance the glory of Athens, or to restore her alliance in the Peloponnese, we cannot say. We are told that he was helped by some of the rich allies of Athens, Ephesos, Chios, and Lesbos. On the other hand, he was accused of borrowing for his own festal procession the plate and vessels belonging to the Athenian Theoria, so that when they appeared afterwards in the public procession the spectators thought that the state had borrowed them from him. Whatever truth there is in such stories, there is no doubt of the deep and abiding impression that he produced.[1]

When the Peloponnesian war was over, Sparta determined to chasten ($\sigma\omega\phi\rho\text{o}\nu\acute{\iota}\sigma\alpha\iota$) Elis.[2] An embassy was sent to the Eleans demanding payment of their share in the expenses of the war, and requiring them to acknowledge the independence of their subject cities. The Eleans retorted that Sparta was trying to enslave Greece. Thereupon Agis, still smarting from his recent rejection at Olympia, led an army from Achaia into Elis and began ravaging the land. But a providential earthquake caused the superstitious Spartan to retreat. Next year, however, reinforced by his allies, he again advanced, this time from the south. He marched through Triphylia received with open arms by the inhabitants, crossed the Alpheios and offered his sacrifice at Olympia, and no one tried any longer to prevent him. He then marched through the rich plains of Elis, the plunder of which attracted to his standard many Arkadian and Achaian

[1] Thuc. vi. 16; Isokrates, *Or.* xvi. 353; Pseudo-Andokides, iv. 29, p. 126. Cp. Grote, *History*, ch. lv.   [2] Xen., *Hell.* iii. 2. 23.

40. THE NIKE OF PAIONIOS

volunteers. But in spite of the assistance of Xenias and the Olympians he failed to take the city of Elis, and retired across the Alpheios leaving garrisons in the land. In the following year, 399 B.C., the Eleans submitted, agreeing to raze the walls of Kyllene and Pheia and to acknowledge the independence of the Triphylian and Arkadian towns. Only the presidency of Olympia was left to them ; for, though the Pisatans claimed it, the Spartans refused to acknowledge their claim, considering them to be mere country yokels and incapable of presiding. Such is Xenophon's account of the war, and in matters affecting Olympia he speaks with first-hand knowledge. Still, his partiality for Sparta some-times leads him into faults of omission. From Pausanias we learn that in the course of the war a battle took place at Olympia in which the Eleans were successful and for which they erected a trophy. He refers to it three times, and his statement is too definite to be rejected. Was this the real reason why Agis retreated first, or why he did not deprive the Eleans of the presidency of the games ?[1]

The effect of the chastening of Elis was soon seen in the games. In 396 B.C. the competition fell off to such an extent that six events were won by local Eleans. It was perhaps to counter-balance the loss of athletic interest that competitions for heralds and trumpeters were introduced in this year. Corruption, too, made its appearance for the first time.[2] In this same Olympiad there was a dispute about the foot-race. Two of the judges awarded it to the Elean competitor Eupolemos, the third to Leon of Ambrakia.[3] Leon appealed to the council, who upheld his appeal and punished the guilty Hellanodikai. There was a similar scandal in 372 B.C. about the horse-race, the winner being himself a Hellanodikas.[4] In consequence a law was passed forbidding a Hellanodikas to compete in the chariot- and horse-races.

There were also cases of an athlete being bribed to transfer his victory from his own state to another.[5] The emissaries of the tyrant Dionysios attempted unsuccessfully to bribe the father of the young Antipatros of Miletos to have his son proclaimed as a Syracusan. Eight years later Sotades of Crete proved more tractable, and accepted a bribe from the Ephesians to transfer

[1] P. v. 4. 8, 27. 11 ; vi. 2. 8.
[2] For the change in the character of athletics produced by the growth of profes-sionalism and specialization v. *Gk. Athletics*, pp. 123 ff.
[3] P. vi. 3. 7.   [4] P. vi. 1. 4.   [5] P. vi. 2. 6, 18. 4.

to them his victory, for which offence he was rightly banished by his countrymen. Such transfers of athletes have their modern analogy in the transfer of professional football players from one club to another. Objectionable as the practice was, there was nothing dishonest about it. It was merely an offence against the competitor's own city, and did not concern the authorities of Olympia. It was different when an athlete took a bribe to allow himself to be defeated. This was an offence against Olympian Zeus, and was punished as such. The first offence of this type occurred in 388 B.C., when Eupolos of Thessaly bribed his fellow competitors to allow him to win the boxing.[1] The fraud was discovered and the guilty parties fined, and from the money six bronze statues of Zeus were constructed and placed at the entrance of the Stadion. These statues were called Zanes, and the row of bases on which they stood may still be seen between the Stadion and the Metroon. The inscriptions on their pedestals warned men that not with money but with speed of foot and strength of limb must prizes be won at Olympia. These vigorous measures were successful. No similar offence took place till 332 B.C., and in the whole history of Olympia few such cases are recorded. The high standard of athletic honour maintained there even in Hellenistic and Roman times is one of the most remarkable features of the festival.

The eclipse of Olympia was only temporary. The power of Sparta was shattered at Leuktra in 371 B.C., and Elis promptly regained her sway over the cities of Triphylia. In the same year under Theban influence the Panarkadian league was formed with its capital at Megalopolis, and the coins of the new commonwealth bear a head of Olympian Zeus closely resembling that on contemporary coins of Elis. The relation of Olympia to the anti-Spartan league is illustrated by an inscription of this period in which some citizens of Thebes, Argos, and Sikyon, who had made rich gifts to Olympia, are appointed *proxenoi* of the Arkadians.[2]

A still more serious blow was dealt to Sparta in 368 B.C., when after centuries of serfdom Messenia was restored to liberty and the harried exiles whom Agis had thirty years before driven from their refuge in Naupaktos flocked back to join in the founding of a new Messene on the slopes of Mount Ithome. The Messenians had played a distinguished part in the early days of Olympia, but for three centuries no Messenian had won

[1] P. v. 21. 5.   [2] *Olympia*, v, no. 31.

a victory at the games. We can imagine their delight when at the first festival after their restoration the Messenian boy Damiskos was victorious in the foot-race.

Elis and Triphylia. The Pisatan Revolt.

But with the decline of Sparta a new trouble arose. The Triphylians were discontented because Elis had seized the opportunity to reassert her authority over them. The Pisatans still cherished hopes of regaining the presidency of the Olympic Games. Both turned for help to the Arkadians ; and when in 365 B.C. the Eleans seized the frontier town of Lasion the Arkadians hastened to its assistance, and advancing as far as Olympia seized and garrisoned the hill of Kronos.[1] The next year being the year of the festival the Arkadians resolved to celebrate the games in conjunction with the Pisatans. They had summoned to their help a force of Argive hoplites and Athenian cavalry, and thought themselves safe from attack from the unwarlike Eleans, though an Elean force was already in the neighbourhood. The first day of the festival passed off uneventfully. On the second day the chariot-races were finished and the pentathlon was going on. Such of the five events as took place on the racecourse were over, and the spectators had returned to the Altis and, crowded on the steps of the terrace and in the Stoai, were watching the competitors wrestling in the open space before the altar, when suddenly the Eleans appeared on the farther bank of the Kladeos. Crossing the stream they attacked with a courage so unexpected that it seemed to be inspired, defeated first the Arkadians, then the Argives, and driving them along the processional way pursued them into the open space where the wrestling was going on. But here they found themselves at a disadvantage. Their opponents had manned the roofs of the surrounding buildings and were plying them with missiles. Their general was killed and they were forced to retreat to their camp. The Arkadians, fearing a renewal of the attack, spent the night constructing stockades and pulling down the booths and tents erected between the Kladeos and the Altis. The next day the Eleans did advance, but seeing the strength of the defences retired home, and the festival passed off without further interruption.

[1] Xen., *Hell.* vii. 4 ; Dyer, *J. H. S.* xxviii. 250.

It has been conjectured that the Pisatans at this time removed the board of Hellanodikai and restored the dual magistracy of earlier times, because, in an inscription[1] already quoted, the names of two Hellanodikai only are mentioned. Diodorus, indeed, states that they did try to restore the ancient customs of the festival, particularly certain musical displays. The latter statement is wholly unsupported, and his whole narrative is inconsistent with the much more reliable account of Xenophon. Moreover, the restoration and date of the inscription are uncertain, and there is more reason for assigning to this period another inscription[2] naming certain Sikyonians *proxenoi* of the Pisatans, and there we find three Hellanodikai mentioned. The number actually mentioned in an inscription is no evidence of the number of the whole board.

The triumph of Pisa did not last long. The religious sentiment of Greece had been violated by the armed occupation of Olympia and the breach of the Sacred Truce. Still greater indignation was aroused when the Arkadians proceeded to seize the Sacred Treasuries in order to pay their mercenaries. Mantinea and other states protested and seceded from the League. In 362 B.C. peace was concluded. The Eleans recovered control of Olympia, and the 104th Olympiad was declared an Anolympiad, though the names of the victors were allowed to remain on the Register.

The Pisatans had celebrated their recovery of Olympia by an issue of small gold coins, the only known coins of Pisa. They bear on one side the head of Zeus, on the other a thunderbolt or three half-thunderbolts with the inscription ΠΙΣΑ (Fig. 37, 11). The head of Zeus is very different from the earlier type. The hair is thick and curly, and he wears a wreath of broad-leaved laurel. When the Eleans regained control they reasserted their presidency by issuing a stater bearing a similar head of Zeus, and on the reverse a head of the local nymph Olympia with the inscription ϜΑΛΕΙΟΝ ΟΛΥΜΠΙΑ (Fig. 37, 7). A corresponding coin, issued from the mint of Hera, bears the same head of Olympia, and on the reverse an eagle within an olive wreath (Fig. 37, 8). The head of the nymph is clearly distinguished from that of Hera : her wavy hair is bound by a simple sphendone, while the goddess always wears her high stephanos.[3]

[1] *Olympia*, v, no. 31. *Supra*, p. 120.   [2] *Ib.* 36.
[3] Gardner, *op. cit.*, p. 246 ; Seltman, *op. cit.*, pp. 56, 61.
  11 = B.M. 1, 2 ; S. 174.   7 = B.M. 72 ; G. v. 1 ; S. 175.
  8 = B.M. 75 ; G. v. 4 ; S. 306.

The Metroon. New Influences at Olympia.

The only building erected during this troubled period was the Metroon,[1] the smallest and worst preserved of the three temples in the Altis (Fig. 39). Little is left of it except in the north-east corner, where the three steps, the stylobate, and portions of two columns are still *in situ*. Fragments of the temple were found in the Byzantine walls. Pausanias describes it as a large temple of the Doric order. Large it certainly was not, as compared with the other temples of the Altis, measuring only 20·67 metres by 10·62. Unless, therefore, a negative has fallen out of the text, we must suppose that Pausanias is thinking of the Treasuries, which were in reality temples.

Small though it was, it had both an opisthodomos and a pronaos, and the cella was divided by two rows of columns. It was surrounded by a colonnade of light Doric columns, six at either end, eleven at the sides. They had an almost straight echinos, and instead of the usual annuli a single recessed band, in which was probably fixed a metal ring. The roof was of terra-cotta with a terra-cotta sima. From the architectural remains it is clear that the temple was built later than the Temple of Zeus, earlier than the Philippeion. A possible clue to the date is given by the pedestals of the Zanes. The six Zanes nearest to the temple were erected shortly after 388 B.C. If they occupy their original position the temple must certainly have been built before this date. Elis was then only just recovering from the effects of the invasion of Agis, and we can hardly suppose that during the preceding years they could have erected a new temple. We may therefore probably assign it to the close of the fifth century.

Weniger[2] argues that the cult of the Great Mother had long existed on the site. He points out that west of the temple and under it is a deep layer, or rather two layers, of ashes containing primitive votive offerings, among which were some miniature cymbals. He infers that the altar of Kybele stood at the west end, and that the entrance of the temple was at this end. But his arguments are very inconclusive. The layer of votive offerings extends right across the north of the Altis. Cymbals have been found in other parts, and are certainly not the monopoly of the great goddess. The position of her altar is quite uncertain : all that we know is that it stood between the Altar of Zeus and

---

[1] P. v. 20. 9 ; *Olympia*, ii, p. 37.   [2] *Klio*, vii. 145 ff.

the Stadion. Further, though the cults of Rhea and Kybele had probably a common origin and were subsequently identified, at this period they were quite distinct. The cult of Rhea probably came from Crete at the time when Cretan influence is found at Sparta. It was but natural that the Mother of Zeus should find a home in the sanctuaries of her son. The cult of Phrygian Kybele seems to have been introduced at a much later date. It was one of the numerous oriental cults that appeared in Greece in the latter half of the fifth century. We know from Aristophanes how popular they were at Athens. Amid the decay of ancient faiths men turned for comfort to the mysticism and orgiastic ritual of the East. Pheidias built a temple of the Mother at Athens, and we have seen how close were the relations between Athens and Olympia. May it not be that from Athens the wave of mysticism spread to Olympia, and that the buildings of the Metroon was one of its results?

It seems that the cult of the Great Mother never really took root at Olympia; for the temple fell into decay, and early in the Roman Empire was rebuilt and dedicated to Augustus. It was but natural. At Olympia the worship of Zeus had been supreme for centuries, and though other deities might be admitted to his sanctuary it was his worship alone that gave to it its peculiar character. Here more than anywhere else in Greece were realized the dignity, the self-restraint, the severity that inspired the religious art of the fifth century, and here more than anywhere the emotionalism that characterized the worship of Kybele must have been felt to be out of place.

We may then regard the building of the Metroon as an indication that Olympia was at this time affected by the influence of the states of eastern Greece. Of this we may recognize another instance in the cult of Hera, if I am right in my suggestion that the appearance of the head of Hera on the coins of Elis and the establishment of a separate mint of Hera which issued these coins continuously from 420 B.C. to possibly 323 B.C. mark not merely an alliance with Argos but the definite revival under Argive influence of the worship of the goddess. The opportunity was certainly favourable. Zeus had now a temple of his own, and the temple which he had hitherto shared with Hera may now have become the exclusive domain of the goddess. The two contemporary heads of Zeus and Hera described above may be symbolic of the change. We know from Pausanias that the sixteen matrons who wove the peplos for Hera had special quarters in the city of Elis, and that before entering on office they went through certain ceremonies of lustration at the fountain of Piera on the sacred road between Elis and Olympia. These facts point to some sort of reorganization of her worship subsequent to the synoecism of Elis, and I would suggest that this reorganization took place towards the close of the fifth century.

The spread of superstition in the fourth century is illustrated by the strange story told by Pausanias of the introduction of the worship of Sosipolis.[1] It was during the Arkadian war, possibly the war of 364 B.C. The Arkadians had invaded Elis and the two armies were facing each other at Olympia, when a woman presented herself before the generals of Elis bearing at her breast a naked babe whom she offered to help them in the battle. The babe was placed in the forefront of the army. When the Arkadians advanced, it changed into a dragon. Terrified at the sight they fled, and the victorious Eleans hailed the dragon babe as the hero Sosipolis, and at the place in the hill-side where it disappeared they dedicated a temple to Sosipolis and his mother, whom they recognized as Eileithyia. This temple, which stood above the Treasuries on the hill of Kronos, has disappeared. We shall see that it cannot be identified with the small shrine to the west of the Terrace.[2] Nor is there any evidence to support Weniger's theory that Sosipolis is the infant Zeus, and that the introduction of his cult and his mother's was a revival of an ancient cult of the Mother and the Child.[3] The cult of Eileithyia is ancient enough; she is perhaps merely a form of Gaia, who was worshipped on the Hill of Kronos at a very early date. But the very title Sosipolis speaks of lateness, certainly in the western Peloponnese, where the Polis hardly existed before the fifth century. Both legend and cult are typical of the superstitious credulity of the fourth century, when men were prone to ascribe good or evil fortune to the influence of some strange god or hero.

But if in spite of outside influences the religion of Olympia remained true to its original character, in other respects the festival reflected all the varied activities of the Greek world. The opportunity for advertisement afforded by so vast a concourse brought to Olympia all who wished to extend their fame or influence beyond the limits of their city state, all who had anything to exhibit or to sell. We have seen the importance

---

[1] vi. 20. [2] *Infra*, p. 220. [3] *Klio*, vii. 145 ff.

attached by politicians and statesmen to the public opinion of
Olympia. The festival appealed no less to artists, writers,
orators, and inventors. For there they could find an audience
that represented the whole Hellenic world.

During most of the fifth century artists from every part must
have been busy at Olympia. Sometimes the execution of some
particular work was put up for competition. Paionios of Mende
claims in his inscription to have been victor in a competition
for making the Akroteria of the temple. At the times of the
festival sculptors could bring their works there for exhibition or
for sale. The athletic statues were not usually portrait statues,
and the sculptor of a diskobolos or boxer might count upon
disposing of his work to some victor or his friends. Painters,
too, resorted to the festival. Zeuxis advertised himself by strutting
about in a robe on which his name was embroidered in letters
of gold. Aetion exhibited at Olympia his painting of the marriage
of Alexander and Roxane, and thereby won for himself the hand
of the daughter of the Hellanodikas Proxenidas.

Public recitation was the surest way by which a writer could
make his works known. Herodotus, says Lucian, was the first
to realize the unique advantages of Olympia. He read his
Histories in the Opisthodome of the Temple of Zeus. His success
produced a host of imitators. Hippias the sophist of Elis,
Prodikos of Keos, Anaximenes of Lampsakos, Polos of Akragas,
and many others constantly addressed the Panegyris and thus
in a short time acquired a reputation. The mathematician
Oinopides went so far as to erect there a tablet on which was
engraved a diagram illustrating his theory of the Great Year.

We should like to know what part Olympia played in the
development of Greek commerce, forming as it did a link between
the East and the West. Latin writers speak of the ' Mercatus
Olympiae ',[1] and we can well understand the opportunities for
profit afforded to those who catered for the crowds at the games.
But did the merchant princes of Greece avail themselves of the
gatherings at the festival ? Of this we have no evidence. But
of one thing we may be sure. The multiplication of horse-races
was not without advantage to the horse-breeding aristocracy of
Elis.

If the growth of professionalism and the decay of the city
states tended to diminish the purely athletic interest of the

---

[1] Vell. Paterculus, i. 8 ; Cicero, *Tusc. Disp.* v. 3.

games in the fourth century, they lost nothing of their attractive-
ness as a spectacle, and the general expansion of interests fully
made up for any loss that there was. It is significant of the change
which had come over Olympia that honorary statues were no
longer confined to athletes. Thus the Samians erected a statue
to the Spartan general Lysander in gratitude for the recovery
of their liberty after the battle of Aigospotamoi.[1] Somewhat
later a statue of the orator Gorgias[2] was set up by his grand-
nephew Eumolpos. The lines inscribed on it illustrate well the
widened outlook. ' No man ever yet discovered a fairer art
to train the soul for virtue's contests, wherefore in Apollo's
glades his statue stands a proof not of wealth but of ways of
piety.'

[1] P. vi. 3. 14.　　　　　　　　　　[2] *Olympia*, v, no. 293.

VIII
Olympia and Macedon

αἰδὼς γὰρ ὑπὸ κρύφα κέρδει κλέπτεται.
                                    Pindar, *Nem.* ix. 33.

THE rise of Macedon which destroyed the independence
of the city states brought to Olympia a fresh period of
splendour.   Once more builders were busy in the Altis,
restoring old buildings, erecting new ones.   The building of
the Philippeion shortly after the battle of Chaironeia led to the
exclosing of the Altis with a stone wall.   On the east side a more
elaborate stoa replaced the simpler building of the fifth century,
and the Stadion was remodelled.   On the west side rose the
Theokoleon, the official residence of the priests ;   north of it
a palaistra and gymnasion stretched from the Prytaneion to the
Kladeos.   South of it the Leonidaion, the princely gift of a private
citizen of Naxos, was perhaps intended for the entertainment of
distinguished visitors.   Below the Bouleuterion a splendid new
stoa was erected commanding a view of the Alpheios valley and
the southern approach to the Altis.   All these buildings were
constructed within a century of Chaironeia.   Their light and
graceful Ionic and Corinthian columns contrasted with the
massive Doric of the fifth century, while the lavish use of marble
bore witness to the wealth pouring in from the East.   With the
single exception of the Philippeion they were all secular in
character, intended to promote the comfort of officials, spectators,
and competitors.

   To the kings of Macedon Olympia had long appealed.   It
was there that their claim to be regarded as Hellenes had been
officially recognized when in the sixth century Alexander the son
of Amyntas established his right to compete in the games.
A century later Archelaos the son of Perdiccas won a victory
in the chariot-race, and by founding a Macedonian Olympic
festival at Aigai he set an example that was widely followed in
Hellenistic and imperial times.

PHILIP AND ALEXANDER

Philip and Alexander were not content to be recognized as Hellenes. They posed as the leaders of a united Hellas, its champions against barbarism. For their policy the support of the national sanctuaries was of supreme importance. They required a capital in Greece itself, and no place offered them such advantages as Olympia. Philip, indeed, had by the Sacred War made himself president of the Amphictyonic League. But for his purposes Delphi could not compare with Olympia. At Delphi the Pythian festival was quite secondary to the Oracle, and the Oracle had been discredited by the unpatriotic part that it had played in the Persian wars and by a long course of political intrigue and partisanship. Moreover, there was something cosmopolitan about Delphi, which received gifts from and gave its answers to Hellenes and barbarians alike. With Olympia it was otherwise. There the festival was all-important, and neutrality was essential to it. Moreover, it was exclusively, even aggressively, Hellenic. It stood for national unity. In the religion of Olympic Zeus the whole of Hellas was united, its sports were part of its national education, its monuments and buildings bore witness to the piety of every age and every part of Hellas. Above all, thanks to its peculiar position and its tradition, the forces of discord which had prevented the realization of political unity, feuds of rival states and party factions, could find no place there. We can therefore readily understand the importance attached to Olympia by those who sought to impose unity on Hellas, by the Macedonians first, later by the Romans. On Philip and Alexander it had an especial claim, in that for a century and a half it had been identified with that very cause of Hellenism against barbarism of which they proclaimed themselves the champions.

Philip showed his interest in Olympia early in his life. In 356 B.C. he won a victory in the horse-race, and on two subsequent occasions he won the chariot-race. Following the example of the tyrants of Sicily he commemorated his Olympic victories by representing his chariot on his coins. The prestige thus obtained doubtless helped him in his intrigues in the Peloponnese. The details of these intrigues are very obscure, but it appears that by bribery he formed a Macedonizing party in Elis.[1]

---

[1] P. iv. 28. 3 ; Demosth., *de falsa leg.* 424 ; *Phil.* iii. 27.

After the battle of Chaironeia he marched into the Peloponnese, the whole of which, with the exception of Sparta, submitted to him. Thereupon he summoned a meeting of all the Greek states at Corinth, where in the year 337 B. C. he proclaimed a crusade against Persia and was chosen commander of the Greek forces. It must have been in this year that he began the building of the Philippeion, his sole memorial at Olympia.

Philip never lived to carry out his crusade. He was assassinated at Aigai, where he was celebrating the marriage of his daughter Kleopatra to Alexander of Epeiros by a magnificent Olympic festival. On his death there was a general revolt, in which Elis joined.[1] But the vigorous action of Alexander crushed all opposition. The Peloponnese submitted, and the Macedonian partisans who had been exiled were recalled to power.

We do not know if Alexander ever visited Olympia in person. He certainly did not advertise himself like Philip by sending his horses and chariots to compete there, much less did he take part himself in the athletics. Every one knows the story told of him by Plutarch, how when asked by his friends if he would not enter for the foot-race he replied that he would do so if he had kings as competitors. The democratic character of the games could not be to his liking. Further, he had little sympathy with the highly specialized athletics of the day, which he considered, rightly, far inferior as a training for war to the field sports of his native land. In the festivals with which he entertained his Macedonians at home and the Asiatics during his campaigns, musical and dramatic competitions and displays and the hunting of wild beasts played a more prominent part than athletics. Yet he fully realized the political and social importance of the national festivals, and he knew how to utilize them. It is related that having taken prisoner at Issos one Dionysodoros of Thebes he set him at liberty on learning that he was an Olympic victor.[2] To Olympia he was especially conciliatory. He regarded it as his capital in Greece. Reports of his campaigns and victories were published and recorded in the Register. Thither in 324 B. C. he sent Nikanor to proclaim to the assembled crowds the royal rescript bidding all the Greek states recall their exiles and bidding them acknowledge his own divinity. Twenty thousand exiles we are told were present, a number which gives us some idea of the size of the gathering.

[1] Arrian, i. 10. 1   [2] *Ib.* 2. 15.

41. THE PHILIPPEION

42. NORTH CORNER OF THE STOA POIKILE

The honorary statues of this period are especially interesting for their variety. There was a group of statues dedicated by the Eleans representing Philip and Alexander and his generals Antigonos and Seleukos.[1] There were statues of the philosopher Aristotle, the historian Anaximenes, and of one Pythes of Abdera, who seems to have been a captain of mercenaries.[2] The two statues in honour of the latter were the work of Lysippos and were dedicated by his soldiers. The most interesting of all the statues connected with Alexander is that dedicated by Philonides, ' courier of Alexander and road measurer of Asia '.[3] Two copies of the inscription on this statue were found, and the lowest block of the pedestal that supported it was found *in situ* at the south-west corner of the Altis. The duty of the road measurer (βηματιστής) was to measure by stepping the distances covered in the march, and probably to note them on a map. One of the inscribed blocks has a sunk panel, probably for the insertion of a bronze tablet, and Curtius plausibly conjectures that on this tablet was engraved a map of Asia on which visitors to Olympia could trace Alexander's campaigns.

The Philippeion.

The most important building of this period is the Philippeion.[4] Pausanias describes it as a circular building of baked brick surrounded by columns and crowned by a bronze poppy that held together the beams of the conical roof. It contained ivory and gold statues of Philip himself, of Amyntas and Alexander, Eurydike and Olympias. The sculptor was Leocharis.

The foundations and steps of the Philippeion may still be seen close to the west wall of the Altis (Fig. 41), and close to them are some of the blocks of the building, among them portions of the richly moulded basis that supported the statues. Other blocks were found in the Byzantine church. From these remains we can reconstruct its plan, and gain some idea of its graceful proportions and of the skill displayed in the workmanship. Steps and roof were of Parian marble, the rest of the building was of poros coated with fine stucco and freely decorated with painting. We learn that Pausanias was mistaken in describing the walls as built of brick. In reality they were of poros, but were painted

[1] P. vi. 11. 1.   [2] P. vi. 4. 8, 18. 2, 14. 12.
[3] P. vi. 16. 5 ; *Olympia*, v, nos. 276, 277 ; *ib.* i, p. 52.
[4] *Olympia*, ii, pp. 129–33, Pls. LXXIX–LXXXII.

to resemble brickwork. This brickwork pattern is found used
as a decoration on the cornice of a much older building, the
Treasury of the Geloans.[1] In the Philippeion it was part of the
colour scheme, intended to throw up the marble steps and the
graceful shapes of the columns.

The foundations were constructed with the greatest care.
They consisted of two concentric rings of thirty-six blocks so

43. Philippeion.   Architectural details

cut as to radiate from the centre. Upon the foundations rested
three steps of Parian marble. They were not of uniform height,
but rose gradually, being respectively 25, 27, 29 centimetres
high. Not only were they carefully undercut, but the upper and
side edges were similarly cut away. Thus both the face and the
tread presented the appearance of a row of panels. Measured
from the lowest step the diameter of the building was 15·25
metres. On the top step rose eighteen slender Ionic pillars
tapering slightly from 65 centimetres at the base to 55 at the top.
They were made of fine-grained poros, covered with stucco and
tinted yellow. The bases were low, of the usual Ionic type, and

[1] *Olympia*, ii, p. 193, Fig. 8.

the shafts had twenty-four flutings. The capitals and entablature, though well proportioned and carefully moulded, are remarkable for their simplicity in form. The same simplicity characterizes the marble sima with its plain antefixes alternating with lions' heads. The geison, like the foundation, was formed of thirty-six radiating blocks which supported the seventy-two beams of the conical roof. The ceiling of the colonnade was similarly divided into cassetted panels decorated with a lozenge pattern. The wall of the cella, as already stated, was built of poros painted to resemble brickwork, save for a low marble sockle on the outside. Its lower part formed a podium 1·92 metres high and 0·72 metre thick. Above this portion the wall was only 0·48 metre thick, but was strengthened on the inside by nine engaged Corinthian pillars, resting directly on the podium without any bases. The half capitals were decorated with four rows of akanthos leaves, while at the corners ' appear for the first time cornucopia-like channelled cauliculi, from which the volutes spring '.[1] There was originally a second row of pillars above, but no remains of these exist. The door was on the south side, the only side where there was a worthy approach. It was about 1·70 metres wide, and was flanked by two windows which served to light the statues opposite.

The statues stood on a curved basis 1·92 metres high, the same height as the podium. It was placed opposite to the door about 1½ metres from the back wall. It was of Parian marble and the upper edges were richly carved (Fig. 44). Philip's statue seems to have occupied the centre, with Amyntas and Alexander on either side. Eurydike must have been next to Amyntas, and Olympias to Alexander.

For the religious history of Olympia the Philippeion is very significant. It has been variously described as a heroon and as a treasury. It is neither. Among the buildings of Olympia it is unique. It has the form of a temple, it is included within the boundaries of the Altis : yet it contains the statues of mortal men.

It has been argued that the Philippeion was built in imitation of the small circular Heroon, and that for this reason its walls were painted to resemble brickwork. Such superficial resemblance proves nothing. With regard to the painting, it is doubtful if it existed, for the walls of the Heroon, if of brick, were of sun-

[1] Marquand, *Gk. Architecture*, p. 212.

dried brick bonded with timber and probably covered with stucco. Nor does the fact that it was round prove anything. All Heroa were not round, nor were all round buildings Heroa. The Pelopion was a Heroon but it was not round : the Temple of Athene Pronaos at Delphi was round but it was not a Heroon. Further, the proper place for the door of a Heroon was the west side : the door of the Philippeion was on the south. Every Heroon had an altar : in the Philippeion there was no altar.

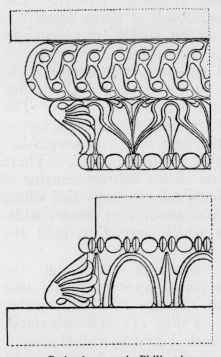

44. Basis of statues in Philippeion

With the Treasuries the Philippeion has more in common. Philip was in part at least inspired by the same motives as the builders of Treasuries, the desire to identify himself with the great national sanctuary and to secure for himself a position of privilege there. Like the Treasuries, too, the plan of the Philippeion proclaimed it to be a temple. But here the resemblance ceases. The Treasuries were, as we have seen, the communal houses of individual states, the Philippeion was the house not of the Macedonians but of Philip, and of Philip not as King of Macedon but in the role that he assumed after Chaironeia as captain-general of the armies of Hellas. Secondly, the Treasuries were dedicated to Zeus, and they contained no cult images as far as we know. The Philippeion contained the statues of Philip and his family. Moreover, these statues were wrought in ivory and gold, a technique hitherto appropriated to the Olympian gods. Add to this the fact that the building itself bore the name of Philip, and that it was enclosed within the boundary of the Altis, and we see that the Philippeion is nothing more or less than a temple of Philip. Thereby Philip asserted his divinity and the Eleans recognized his claim.

This, it seems to me, is the real significance of the Philippeion, and this it is which distinguishes it alike from treasury and heroon. Philip and Alexander received worship not as heroes but as gods,

45. RECONSTRUCTION OF PHILIPPEION

they claimed to be admitted among the Olympians. At the games at Aigai where Philip was assassinated we are told that with the images of the Twelve Gods was carried the image of Philip himself. Alexander claimed to be the actual son of Zeus, and he is said to have obtained acknowledgement of his claim from Zeus Ammon. Finally, in 324 B.C. he demanded at Olympia the recognition of his divinity. For centuries his worship persisted in Macedonia, Asia, and Egypt, and even at Rome in the time of Augustus he was associated with the Twelve Gods by a special decree of the Senate. That the authorities of Olympia should have permitted a mortal to set himself on an equality with Zeus was more creditable to their policy than to their piety. But we may note with satisfaction that there is no sign of any cult of either Philip or Alexander, and that in the following centuries none of the successors of his empire received there the divine honours which were lavished on them in the East and even at Athens. Herein we have another proof that at Olympia Zeus was supreme and unrivalled.

The statement of Pausanias that the Philippeion was built by Philip has been questioned by some modern archaeologists. They urge that the period between the battle of Chaironeia and the death of Philip was too short for the work, and further that Philip would not have dedicated in it a statue of his divorced wife Olympias. But these arguments at the most could only prove that the buildings and statues were not completed in Philip's lifetime, and they certainly do not justify us in rejecting the definite statement of Pausanias. Further, the evidence of the name is conclusive. Had the Philippeion been really the work of Alexander, we can hardly conceive that he would have given it the name of his father and not his own name. It is probable, then, that the building was designed and begun by Philip and completed by Alexander, who erected in it the statue of his mother Olympias.

Altis Walls and Stoa.

The dating of the Philippeion is important for the chronology of Olympia because it enables us to assign to the period of Philip and Alexander a whole series of buildings.

In the first place we may conclude that the extension of the Altis and the building of the first Altis wall, the rebuilding of the eastern Stoa and the enlargement of the Stadion, all took place in the reign of Alexander or shortly afterwards. The architectural evidence proves that the walls are contemporary with the new Stoa, and that the Stoa belongs to the same period as the Philippeion. Further, not only is the line of the western wall obviously determined by the position of the Philippeion, but it seems probable that the sole object of building the wall was to enclose the Philippeion within the sacred precinct. We may conjecture that the wall formed part of Philip's original plan. For the Philippeion stood outside the boundaries of the old Altis. Probably no site farther east was available ; for there was no room on the Treasury terrace, and in the plain below no conspicuous building could be allowed to interfere with the view of the crowds of spectators. Only the hitherto obscure western side remained. But Philip saw that there was no need for it to remain in obscurity. By the simple expedient of a wall he could extend the Altis so as to include his temple within the same boundary as the temples of Hera and Zeus.

The construction of the walls is similar to that of the back wall of the new Stoa. This was built immediately in front of the fifth-century building, which was now dismantled and partially buried under the embankment of the Stadion. The new Stoa was 98 metres long and 12·50 metres broad. In material and style it closely resembles the Philippeion. As in the latter building, the steps and stylobate were of a white, coarse-grained marble, the rest of the building was of poros ; the steps show the same careful undercutting and panellings (Figs. 41, 42). The marble blocks are of a uniform length of 1·075 metres, and the columns were placed in the centre of alternate blocks at a distance from axis to axis of 2·15 metres. Thanks to these measurements it was possible to identify as belonging to the Stoa the remains of a Doric architrave, columns, and capitals which were found in the east wall of the Byzantine fort. There were originally forty-four columns along the front and probably a similar row down the centre of the colonnade. In late Roman times the Stoa was completely rebuilt and two additional columns were inserted, the architrave being shortened accordingly and imperfections concealed by a lavish use of plaster.

What was the pretext for the destruction of the old Stoa and the erection of the new one ? No useful purpose can have been served thereby. It was an act of pure ostentation, and

I would suggest that it was carried out at the behest and perhaps at the cost of Alexander. It may have been in preparation for the festival at which Nikanor proclaimed the recall of the exiles and his master's divinity; it may be that Alexander hoped one day to celebrate himself at Olympia his triumph over Persia and the East.

Meanwhile changes no less important had taken place on the west side of the Altis. The Theokoleon and the Leonidaion both may be assigned to the reigns of Philip and Alexander. Neither building can be earlier than 350 B. C., while the fact that the Leonidaion is not aligned to the western wall suggests that when it was built the wall was not yet in existence. Further, its terra-cotta sima seems to have been the prototype of the sima of the Stoa.[1]

The Hellenistic Age

On the death of Alexander confusion once more reigned. Again Elis revolted, and again she submitted to the Macedonian supremacy. From this time till the final conquest of Greece by Rome she was involved in the intrigues and wars of rival kingdoms and leagues which distracted Greece. Polybios, writing in the middle of the second century, reads the Eleans a lecture on their folly in forfeiting the peace and immunity from war which the sanctity of Olympia had secured for them.[2] He traces the change back to the quarrels with Arkadia about Lasion, which first led the Eleans to have recourse to arms, and he urges them to seize the opportunity offered by the Roman conquest to return to the ways of peace and recover their former privileges. Certainly during the Hellenistic age their territory was no longer sacrosanct, and even Olympia did not escape. In 312 B. C. Telesphoros, the rebellious general of Antigonos, established himself in Elis and even plundered the Treasury of Olympia.[3] But he was shortly afterwards expelled by Ptolemaios the nephew of Antigonos, who restored the treasure to the temple. A century later the Spartan tyrant Machanidas planned to attack Olympia during the festival, but his plans were frustrated by Philip V, who occupied Heraia with his army.[4] Yet for the most part Elis was prosperous, and the sanctity of Olympia was respected by all the rival powers, who courted her support by splendid gifts.

It is impossible to write a connected history of Olympia

---

[1] *Olympia*, ii, p. 198.   [2] iv. 73, 74.   [3] Diodorus, xix. 87.   [4] Livy, xxviii. 7.

during the Hellenistic age. Its prosperity is evident from the magnificence of the new buildings. Unfortunately we do not know the dates of those buildings or the circumstances of their erection. We are forced to fall back on the evidence of the victors' lists and of the honorary statues, the increasing number of which is one of the distinctive features of the age. Scanty though the material is, it enables us to form some idea of the character of the competition and of the relations of Olympia to the rival kings and leagues of the Hellenic world.

Once more the value of the Olympic Register is conspicuously vindicated.[1] It is remarkable how accurately the lists of victors, fragmentary though they are, reflect the changes in the Greek world after the death of Alexander. The great city states of the past, Athens, Sparta, Thebes, disappear almost entirely from the competitions. Their place is taken by Elis, Arkadia, and Achaia. Mercenary soldiers from these parts had brought home with them the wealth of the East, and the result appears in the number of statues dedicated by citizens of these states. Particularly noticeable is the number of victors from Elis. Of thirty-two statues of this period recorded by Pausanias,[2] fifteen are those of Elean victors. Beyond the mainland of Greece the change is still more remarkable. From Italy and Sicily, the Greek colonies of which had played so prominent a part in the earlier history of Olympia, only one victor is known in the third century,[3] and the only offerings recorded are those of the Syracusans in honour of Hiero II, who may perhaps have tried to revive the traditional connexion of his city with Olympia.[4] There is no lack of competitors from afar, but they come from Macedon, Egypt, Asia Minor. The kings and princes rarely compete themselves. Attalos, the father of Attalos I of Pergamon, won a victory in the chariot-race at Olympia,[5] Ptolemy Philadelphos a chariot-race at Delphi, and his mistress Belistiche one at Olympia. But for the most part the kings had more serious contests to occupy them. Not so their subjects. The only event of which we have a complete record is the foot-race, but we may regard this as typical of the whole programme. In the foot-race alone between the years 324 and 268 B.C. we find four Macedonian victories and others won by Philippi and Amphipolis. Then

---

[1] For this section v. Förster and Hyde, *op. cit.*   [2] Hyde, *op. cit.*, p. 75.
[3] Simylos from Neapolis, Ol. 133. But was he from the Italian Neapolis?
[4] P. vi. 12. 2, 15. 6.   [5] Fränkel, *Antiq. Pergam.* viii. 8, 10.

they cease, and in 272 B.C. a similar series of Alexandrian successes begins. Meanwhile there is a constant and ever-swelling stream of competitors from the cities of Asia Minor and the islands. The new cities emulate the old. Early in the second century the names of Alexandria Troas [1] and Seleukeia figure in the lists, while other competitors describe themselves as Carians or Lydians.

The changes which we notice in the character of the competition are the inevitable results of the political changes which were revolutionizing the whole Mediterranean world. The interest and importance of the Olympic games were bound up with the system of independent city states; the competitors contended not so much as individuals but as representatives of their respective states. The rise of Rome and Carthage in the West was fatal to the city states of Italy and Sicily, as that of Macedon was to the city states of Greece; in their place we have leagues like the Aitolian and Achaian, districts like Elis. Only in the East did the city state preserve a semblance of autonomy. The city-state system was a part of that Hellenism which Alexander's conquest had spread through the East; the old Greek cities of the coast recovered their independence, new Greek cities sprang up everywhere. Their independence indeed was merely illusory: but they clung all the more closely to the outward forms of autonomy, among which not the least important were their festivals and games. Every city had its gymnasion, its stadion, its festival; the athletic interest, which had declined elsewhere, gathered fresh life in the East, and, following the examples of the city states of better days, they sent their representatives to compete at Olympia.

An interesting illustration of the close intercourse subsisting between Elis and the East is afforded by a decree in honour of one Demokrates of Tenedos, a noted wrestler who had won victories at Olympia and elsewhere.[2] It records that he and his father had settled in Elis and received the citizenship, that on his return to his native island he had succeeded his father as

[1] P. v. 8. 11 ; cp. *Olympia*, v, no. 184, an epigram of Akestorides, a victor in a chariot-race, who boasts that he was the first Trojan to be crowned with the Pisatan olive.

[2] *Olympia*, v. no. 39. The decree is dated by the Hellanodikai τῶν περὶ Αἰσχύλου, and seems to belong to the first half of the third century. The ἐπιμελητὴς τῶν ἵππων is perhaps one of the Hellanodikai. Demokrates had also a statue at Olympia (P. vi. 17. 1).

Thearodokos and shown great hospitality to the Elean Theoroi visiting the island. In return for this he is to be named Proxenos and Benefactor, to have a place of honour at the Dionysia and a share in the sacrifices. This decree of the Boule is to be set up at Olympia, and the Marshal of the Horses ($\dot{\epsilon}\pi\iota\mu\epsilon\lambda\eta\tau\dot{\eta}s$ $\tau\hat{\omega}\nu$ $\ddot{\iota}\pi\pi\omega\nu$) is to be responsible for this. Further, the Clerk of the Council is to hand a copy of the decree to the Theoroi who were being sent to the festival of the Didymeia at Miletos for transmission to the people of Tenedos.

As to the relations of Olympia with the rival powers of the Greek world we can gather some indications from the list of the non-athletic statues. These are particularly numerous in this age. They are mostly statues of princes and statesmen set up by themselves, or by those who sought to do them honour, some-times by the Elean authorities themselves, or even by individual Eleans. Thus one Tydeus of Elis dedicated statues of Antigonos and Seleukos,[1] and the Iamid seer Thrasyboulos a statue of Pyrrhos.[2] The seer himself was honoured by a statue, represent-ing him with a spotted lizard on his shoulder and a sacrificial dog at his feet.[3] As in the case of the athletic statues the number of statues of individual Eleans is remarkable. They are dedicated by various states, Aitolians, Kephallenians, Pellenians, Psophi-dians, and clearly show the prosperity and importance of Elis in this age.

Olympia and the Diadochoi.

Of the Diadochoi themselves Ptolemaios Soter alone left any monument at Olympia. Pausanias[4] saw a statue erected by him and noted that he styled himself not King of Egypt but a Macedonian. He also saw a group in which he was repre-sented. The other iadochoi were too busy fighting among themselves to have leisure for festivals, and their wars were mostly in the East. There is no record of any offerings made by them at Olympia, but a few statues were erected in their honour by their partisans. We have mentioned the statues of Monophthalmos and Seleukos dedicated by Tydeus; they must have been erected before 316 B.C., when these princes quarrelled. Statues of Monophthalmos and his son Demetrios

[1] P. vi. 16. 2.   [2] P. vi. 14. 9.   [3] P. vi. 2. 4.
[4] P. vi. 3. 1, 15. 9.

Poliorketes were erected by the Byzantines.[1] The inscriptions on these statues and the actual decree of the Byzantines were found. As the decree refers to an embassy to be sent to congratulate Demetrios on some success, we may connect it with his victory over Ptolemaios at Salamis in 306 B.C. The Byzantines had reason to be grateful to Demetrios for help against the Thracians, and possibly they feared that the growth of Egyptian power might prejudice their commerce.

Another monument of Demetrios Poliorketes seems to bring him personally into contact with Olympia, a group representing him in the act of being crowned by Elis.[2] It cannot but have recalled the similar group of Ekecheiria crowning Iphitos, and symbolized thus the restoration of the Olympic peace and the national unity by Demetrios. We can hardly doubt that it was set up about the year 302 B.C., when Demetrios had revived the league of Corinth and had, like Philip and Alexander, been appointed general of the forces of Hellas. Did Demetrios dedicate this monument himself as Philip had on a similar occasion built the Philippeion ? We cannot say. But when we remember the enthusiasm and flattery with which Demetrios was welcomed at Athens, and his extraordinary popularity among the Greeks, it seems likely that it was the gift of his supporters and flatterers among the Eleans themselves. No state but Elis could have taken upon themselves to set up a monument of this type.

After nearly half a century of chaos the kingdom of Macedon was re-established under Antigonos Gonatas.[3] The philosopher king found Athens more attractive than Olympia : he had no ambition to distinguish himself like Philip in the Hippodrome, nor did he aim like Alexander at making Olympia the capital of a world empire. Elis and Olympia lay outside his sphere, but he was forced to interfere there by the intrigues of his enemies.

[1] P. vi. 15. 7 ; *Olympia*, v, nos. 304, 305, 45. Pausanias by mistake gives the name of Antigonos Gonatas instead of Monophthalmos.

[2] P. vi. 16. 3. Curtius, *Olympia*, i, p. 55, conjectures that this group was set up by Antigonos Doson, at the time when he set up a similar group commemorating his victory at Sellasia, and that Doson wished thereby to recall the victory of Demetrios over Ptolemaios at Cyprian Salamis. But there are several objections to this view :

1. There is no evidence at all that the two groups were contemporary.

2. Doson was at peace with Egypt at the time, and this very tactful ruler was not likely to set up a monument which would have offended the feelings of the Ptolemies by recalling their defeat.

[3] For this period v. Tarn, *Antigonos Gonatas*.

He secured his influence by setting up or at least supporting
tyrants in the different states. Elis had welcomed Pyrrhos
when he landed in the Peloponnese ' to restore the liberties of
Hellas, and on the defeat of Pyrrhos Antigonos established there
the tyrant Aristotimos. But the excesses of this tyrant exasperated
the people, who rose against him and murdered him, and thus
ended for the time all connexion between Olympia and Macedon.
The democratic party in Elis was anti-Macedonian, and from
this time the power was in its hands. Elis was in fact continually
in alliance with one or more of the enemies of Antigonos, with
the Aitolians, with Pyrrhos, with Sparta and Egypt. So at
Olympia neither Antigonos nor his son dedicated a single offering,
nor was a single statue erected in their honour, while all the
enemies of Macedon found a place in the Altis. Macedon was
in fact regarded as the destroyer of the liberties of Hellas, and
an interesting illustration of this widespread feeling is afforded
by an inscription in honour of Dropion of Paionia.[1] After the
Gallic invasion Paionia had recovered its independence from
Macedon and established a federation under Dropion, and his
countrymen commemorated their newly won freedom by dedicating at Olympia a statue of Dropion ' their king and founder '.

Aitolia had been closely connected with Elis from the earliest
times, and it was but natural that the Eleans should support the
Aitolian league. They did support it loyally until forced by Rome
to join the Achaian league in 191 B. C. Aitolian treaties were
published at Olympia. When about 275 B. C. Aitolia made a
treaty with Akarnania, a copy of it was set up in the Altis.[2]
Again in 211 B. C., when the Aitolians made an alliance with
Rome, it was enacted that the Eleans might be admitted into
the alliance on the same terms, and that the treaty should be
recorded in the Capitol at Rome and at Olympia.[3] Pausanias
mentions various statues in honour of Aitolians, and statues of
Eleans dedicated by Aitolians in the Altis.[4]

Of all the enemies of Macedonia the most formidable were
the Lagidai of Egypt, and they were the more formidable because
they worked by intrigue and peaceful penetration rather than by
open warfare. They posed as the representatives of Hellenic

---

[1] *Olympia*, v, no. 303 ; Tarn, *op. cit.*, pp. 173, 321.
[2] Tarn, *op. cit.*, p. 210 ; Ἐφ. Ἀρχ., 1905, p. 55.   [3] Livy, xxvi. 25.
[4] Pleistainos, vi. 16. 1 ; Olaidas, vi. 15. 2 ; Kylon, vi. 14. 9 ; Phryskos of
Aitolia, *Olympia*, v, no. 295.

culture, the champions of the liberties of Hellas, and, true to the policy of Philip and Alexander, they sought to win sympathy and support by means of the Panhellenic sanctuaries. Numerous monuments bear witness to their devotion to Olympia. Of Ptolemaios Soter we have already spoken. His successor Philadelphos for some years did not attempt to interfere in Greece. But in 274 B.C. he married his sister Arsinoe, and this ambitious woman soon inaugurated a more vigorous policy.[1] It can hardly be an accident that it is precisely at this time that the series of Macedonian victories at Olympia comes to an end and the triumph of Alexandria begins.[2] In 264 B.C. we find Belistiche, the mistress of Philadelphos, winning a victory in the chariot-race for colts.[3] A conspicuous monument of Philadelphos and Arsinoe was dedicated, as we learn from the inscriptions, by the Nauarch Kallikrates, the son of Boiskos of Samos, either shortly before or after the year 270, when Arsinoe died.[4] The statues of the king and queen were raised on two pillars 30 feet high placed on a great stone platform immediately in front of the Echo Colonnade. Another statue of Philadelphos was dedicated by a Macedonian partisan, Aristolaos.[5] The anti-Macedonian policy of the Ptolemies and their support by Elis are evident from the statues of the period. Philadelphos set up a statue in honour of Areus of Sparta, who fell fighting against Antigonos in the Chremonidean war, ' in consideration ', as the inscription runs, ' of his goodwill to himself and all the Greeks '.[6] Another hero of the same war, Glaukon of Athens, the elder brother of Chremonides, received a like honour from Euergetes. After their defeat the two brothers had taken refuge at the Egyptian court.[7] Euergetes also erected a statue in honour of Kleomenes, who after his defeat at Sellasia also found refuge at his court.[8] Areus was awarded a statue by the Elean authorities, and Aratos himself had a statue erected by the Corinthians,[9] probably not long after his treacherous capture of Corinth when

[1] Tarn, *Antigonos Gonatas*, pp. 261 ff.
[2] v. *supra*, p. 139.   [3] P. v. 8. 11.
[4] *Olympia*, v, nos. 306, 307. For the date of Arsinoe, v. Tarn, *op. cit.*, p. 261, n. 10. For the date of Kallikrates, v. Tarn, *J. H. S.* xxxi. 254 ; he places his death before 265 B.C.
[5] P. vi. 17. 3.   [6] *Olympia*, v, no. 308 ; P. vi. 15. 9.
[7] *Olympia*, v, no. 296. Glaukon had previously won a victory in the chariot-race, which he commemorated by a chariot group at Olympia (*Olympia*, v, no. 178 ; P. vi. 16. 9).   [8] *Olympia*, v, no. 309.   [9] P. vi. 12. 5.

he was still on friendly terms with Sparta and Egypt. To the
same period belong the statues of a son of Pyrrhos and of his
daughter Olympias.[1]

Curtius ascribes to Philadelphos the building of the Gymnasion and the reconstruction of the Stoa Poikile. The latter, as
we have seen, was probably contemporary with the Philippeion.
The Gymnasion and Palaistra and the South Colonnade were all
built in the third century, but there is no evidence for connecting
them with any particular benefactor. The Eleans were rich
enough at this time to dispense with outside help.

The chief bulwark in the Peloponnese against Macedon had
always been Sparta. For over a century she maintained the
struggle against hopeless odds under kings worthy of her best
traditions. From Elis she could always count on support. Elis
had helped her in her struggle against Antipatros in 331 B.C.
She was one of the members of the Peloponnesian league revived
by Areus, and she took part in the Chremonidean war. Statues
of several Spartan kings were set up at Olympia. The Spartans
dedicated there a statue of Archidamos III after his death in
338 B.C., and the Eleans themselves erected a statue to Areus.
Under the heroic Kleomenes it seemed as if Sparta might once
more recover her hegemony. But his patriotic policy was
frustrated by the jealousy of the Achaian league and Aratos,
who called in the assistance of Antigonos Doson, then ruling
Macedon as regent for his nephew Philip. The latter gladly
seized the opportunity of interfering in the Peloponnese. In
222 B.C. he won a decisive victory over Kleomenes at Sellasia.[2]
Kleomenes fled to Egypt, and the Peloponnese once more passed
into the power of Macedon.

It was eighty years since the monument of Demetrios Poliorketes had been set up at Olympia. Antigonos celebrated his
victory at Sellasia by a similar but still more striking monument.
Opposite the group of Elis crowning Demetrios he set up a group
of Hellas crowning himself and his ward Philip,[3] thus asserting
the claims of Macedon as the champion of Hellas in the sanctuary of Panhellenism. It seemed, indeed, as if under this wise
ruler the unity of Hellas might at last be restored, but unfortunately Doson died shortly afterwards, and his ward Philip,

[1] *Olympia*, v, nos. 310, 311.
[2] For the date of Sellasia, v. Holleaux in *Mélanges Nicole*, pp. 273–9.
[3] P. vi. 16. 3.

who now took the reins of government, was a ruler of very different calibre.

The growing power of the Achaian league aroused the jealousy of the Aitolians, and once more Greece was plunged in civil strife. In the wars that followed, the Achaians had usually the support of Philip, while Elis, Messene, and Sparta ranged themselves on the side of the Aitolians. In 218 B.C. Philip made a campaign in Elis, in the course of which he visited Olympia, where he rested his troops and offered sacrifice to Zeus.[1] He conquered Triphylia and laid waste Elis, but in spite of the most friendly offers he failed to induce the Eleans to desert the Aitolian league.[2] Ten years later we find him again in Elis, to protect Olympia from a threatened attack of the Spartan tyrant Machanidas.[3] The latter was in the next year defeated and killed by Philopoimen. Perhaps we may connect with this campaign the dedication by the Achaian *corps d'élite* of a statue to Pythes the son of Antandros, presumably their commander.[4]

The Coming of Rome.

Meanwhile the ambition and intrigues of Philip had brought the Romans on the scene. We have already mentioned the treaty between Rome and the Aitolians in 211 B.C. In accordance with it a Roman fleet was sent to Greece and a force was landed at Kyllene which co-operated for a time with the Aitolians and Eleans, and in 208 B.C. Lucius Manlius was dispatched by the Senate as envoy to the Olympian games to recall to their homes the Sicilian and Tarentine exiles who had been banished by Hannibal.[5] But Rome was too busy with Hannibal to give effective aid to her friends in Greece. In 206 B.C. the Aitolians made terms with Philip, and the next year the Romans too concluded peace. But it was not for long. In 199 B.C. Rome found herself once more compelled to interfere. Titus Quinctius Flamininus was sent to Greece and finally broke the power of Philip at Kynoskephalai. The next year expectant crowds

---

[1] Polybios, iv. 73 ff.   [2] *Ib.* 84.
[3] Livy, xxviii. 7 ; Polybios, x. 41. The date is fixed by the statement of Livy that Machanidas intended to interrupt the games which fell in 208 B.C.
[4] *Olympia*, v, no. 297. The inscription belongs to the third century, during most of which Elis was hostile to the Achaian league. Possibly the dedication may be connected with the battle of Sellasia, but I prefer the date suggested.
[5] Livy, xxvii. 33, 35.

U

gathered at the Isthmian games to learn their fate, and there amid a scene of wildest rapture Flamininus proclaimed that the Greek states were to be free. Two years later he bade farewell to Greece after exhorting the Greeks to use their freedom wisely. But of this the Greeks were no longer capable. Many of the states were discontented with the settlement, in others political faction and class hatred raged. The result was anarchy and chaos.

The few records that we have of Olympia in this period are of considerable interest. Thus Pausanias tells us that Antiochos dedicated at Olympia a purple curtain of Assyrian workmanship which was hung in front of the image of Zeus.[1] There can be no doubt of the occasion. In 193 B.C. the Aitolians invited Antiochos to Greece, and the next year he landed at Chalkis.[2] There he was met by envoys from Epeiros and Elis. The Elean envoy Kallistratos urged him to send aid to them against the Achaian league, and the king at once dispatched a thousand foot soldiers. The league thereupon appealed to Rome, who sent an expedition and easily defeated Antiochos, and as a consequence Messene and Elis were forced to join the league. In 183 B.C. Messene revolted from the league, and in the fighting that ensued the veteran Philopoimen was taken prisoner and was afterwards murdered by the Messenians. The leadership of the league now passed into the hands of Lykortas, the father of Polybios, who defeated the Messenians and with great magnanimity readmitted them to the league. An inscription found at Olympia records the settlement of the boundaries between Megalopolis, Messene, and Thouria which took place at this time.[3] The historian's own name is mentioned in the inscription. He and his father Lykortas were the leaders of the moderate national party in the league who sought to preserve their independence while acknowledging the supremacy of Rome. There was also a Romanizing party under the leadership of Kallikrates. The latter, with two other envoys, was in 180 B.C. sent to Rome to protest against the recall of certain Spartan exiles which had been demanded by the Senate. Arrived there, he betrayed his mission and counselled the Senate not to yield to the demands of the league, but rather to encourage the Romanizing aristocratic party in the various cities and by their aid to make themselves absolute masters of Achaia. The Senate took his advice and restored the exiles, and Kallikrates himself was by

[1] P. v. 12. 4.   [2] Polybios, xx. 1–3.   [3] *Olympia*, v, no. 46.

their influence appointed Strategos of the league. The exiles showed their gratitude by setting up an equestrian statue of Kallikrates, the inscription on which has been found.[1]

When the third Macedonian war broke out, the Achaians, after many heart-searchings, decided to throw in their lot with Rome. In 169 B.C. envoys were dispatched with offers of help to the consul Q. Marcius Philippus in Thessaly.[2] He treated them with consideration, but refused the proffered help, and the Achaians erected in his honour an equestrian statue at Olympia. It is the first of a long series of statues of Roman officials.

No such honour was paid to his far greater successor L. Aemilius Paulus, a sympathetic and broad-minded man, the friend and protector of Polybios. After his defeat of Perseus at Pydna he paid a visit to Olympia, where ' as he gazed on the statue of Zeus he was deeply affected as if in the presence of the god himself ',[3] and offered splendid sacrifices in his honour. This homage paid to Olympic Zeus is typical of the growing influence of Hellenism at Rome, and foreshadows the important role that Olympia was destined to play under the empire.

After Pydna the Romans still hesitated to annex Greece. Acting on the advice of Kallikrates they deported to Rome a thousand of their political opponents, including Polybios. But matters went from bad to worse. Politically, socially, and economically the land was ruined. The return of the remnant of the exiles in 151 B.C. only added to the disaffection, and in 149 B.C. a quarrel between the Achaian league and Sparta in defiance of Rome led to the revolt of the league, which ended in the capture of Corinth by Mummius. The league was dissolved, and Greece, though retaining a certain amount of local independence, became a Roman province under the Roman governor of Macedon.

The memory of Mummius has suffered from the outrages which he permitted his soldiers to perpetrate at Corinth. Otherwise he conducted himself, if we may believe Polybios,[4] with self-restraint and disinterestedness. He restored the holy places on the Isthmus, and enriched the temples at Olympia and Delphi.

[1] *Olympia*, v, no. 300 Λακεδαιμονίων οἱ φυγόντες ὑπὸ τῶν τυράννων Καλλικράτη Θεοξένου Λεοντήσιον καταγαγόντα εἰς τὰν πατρίδα καὶ διαλύσαντα ποτὶ τοὺς πολίτας καὶ εἰς τὰν ἐξ ἀρχᾶς ἐοῦσαν φιλίαν ἀποκαταστάσαντα.
[2] Polybios, xxviii. 13 ; *Olympia*, v, no. 318.
[3] Livy, xxxv. 28   [4] xxxix. 17.

From the spoils of Achaia he dedicated twenty-one golden shields, which were hung on the architrave of the Temple of Zeus. He also erected a statue of Zeus and two equestrian statues of himself, while the state of Elis in return dedicated a third in his honour.[1] A more elaborate monument set up in the time of Augustus represented Mummius himself and the ten commissioners appointed to help him in the settlement of Achaia.[2] These monuments bear witness to the popularity of Mummius and the gratitude of the Eleans. Greece was indeed weary of anarchy, and the better elements in the population welcomed the prospect of peace and order under the rule of Rome.

Finally, we must note the statue of Polybios himself, dedicated by the city of Elis.[3] No one had deserved better of his country than the historian and his father Lykortas. He had eloquently pleaded the cause of his countrymen before the Roman commissioners, preventing them from removing the statues of Philopoimen and securing the restoration of statues of other patriots which had been already removed. On the departure of the commission he was charged to visit the various cities and settle any questions that might arise, and he succeeded after a while in reconciling them to their new constitution.

The Olympic Festival in the Hellenistic Age.

Let us turn now to the history of the games themselves. There was certainly no falling off in their magnificence during this period, nor in the crowds that they attracted ; nor was there much falling off in the number of competitors, though these no longer came from the states that had provided former champions. Rather we may say that in the western parts of Greece, and in the farther East, there was a fresh outburst of athletic enthusiasm due partly to the importance of athletics in the ephebic training of the gymnasia and the growth of new festivals. Further, the tendency which we noticed in the fourth century for other interests to supplant the athletic at Olympia is no longer observable. Literature, science, art, and commerce could now find a permanent home and permanent patronage in

[1] P. v. 10. 5, 24. 4 ; *Olympia*, v, nos. 278, 281, 319.
[2] *Ib.*, nos. 320–4. No. 331 belongs to one Mummius, the son of Gaius, a descendant of Lucius.
[3] *Olympia*, v, no. 302 ; Polybios, xxxix. 14–16.

Alexandria and other cities of the East, and the Olympic gathering for a time lost its value as a means of advertisement and a meeting-place of East and West.

The prestige attached to athletic success is shown by the treatment of the Olympic victor Dionysodoros by Alexander. It is yet more evident in the pages of Polybios, and especially in those casual statements which give such insight into the real sentiments of an author and his age. Thus when he says of Polykrates, who helped to organize the army of Ptolemy IV, that to the advantages of wealth and birth which he possessed was added ' the reputation won by his father Mnasiades as an athlete ',[1] or when he describes the Boeotarch Pytheas as the brother of Akatides [2] the runner, it is as if a modern historian were to describe a prominent soldier or statesman as the son of a famous Blue or the brother of an international football player.

Men of great position still continued to compete in the public games, though their number was small compared to that of the professional athletes. Such were Demokrates of Tenedos, Aratos of Sikyon, who was famed as a pentathlete, and Gorgos of Messene, a victor in the pentathlon, of whom Polybios[3] says that when ' he gave up athletics and devoted himself to politics and the service of his country he gained no less repute therein than in his former dispute ; for he was far removed from the Philistinism that usually characterizes athletes '. In this passage Polybios shows us the real evil in the athletics of the time. They required a severe and specialized training which had a brutalizing effect on the character. In the third century this specialization is evident in the records of professional athletes.[4] Thus Philinos of Cos won five victories at Olympia and nineteen at other Pan-hellenic festivals, Leonidas of Rhodes twelve victories in four successive Olympiads. Still more characteristic is the profes-sional prize-fighter whose over-developed bulk is represented in the Farnese Herakles. The title ' Successor of Herakles ' was actually bestowed on those who won the wrestling and the pankration on the same day. They were further designated as παράδοξος, or παραδοξονίκης, and in inscriptions of the second century the title περιοδονίκης is used of those who won victories in all four Panhellenic festivals.[5] It seems as if the professional

[1] v. 64. [2] xxxix. 7.
[3] vii. 10 ; P. vi. 14. 11.
[4] v. Gk. Athletics, p. 160. [5] Olympia, v, nos. 185, 186.

athlete had sometimes his wealthy patron who kept him in his pay. For Ptolemaios IV had a certain Aristonikos trained and sent to Olympia to contest the boxing championship with Kleito-machos of Thebes.[1] It speaks well for the authorities of Olympia that in spite of professionalism the games were remarkably free from corruption. Indeed, the only instance recorded is that of Kallippos of Athens, who was fined in 332 B.C. for bribing his opponent in the pentathlon.[2] The Athenians actually sent the orator Hypereides to ask the Eleans to remit the fine, and ultimately were compelled to pay by the Delphic oracle. From the fines six more Zanes were erected.

Three more events were added to the programme—the two-horse chariot-race for colts in Ol. 129, eight years later a riding race for colts (both events were introduced in the interest of the Elean horse-breeders), and in Ol. 141 a pankration for boys. It was not a competition suited for boys, and its introduction illustrates the love of sensational and brutal displays that marks the beginning of Roman influence.

In religion the conservatism of Olympia seems to have triumphed over the tendency to innovation which we noticed in the fourth century. One of the chief phenomena of the Hellenistic age was the apotheosis of living men. Philip and Alexander received divine honours in their lifetime. After the death of Alexander the practice spread rapidly.[3] Temples, altars, and games were dedicated and festivals held in honour of the kings of Macedon, Asia, and Egypt. Antigonos, Lysimachos, Ptolemaios Soter, Demetrios were all worshipped in their life-time. At Delos Philadelphos founded a festival in honour of Soter which was to rank with the Olympic (ἰσολυμπία). It may be recorded to the honour of Olympia that after the time of Alex-ander no mortal received divine honours there, no mortal was allowed to claim equality with Zeus. If in this age of scepticism and strange gods the religion of Zeus had little real hold on the Greek world, it was the severe dignity of this religion that appealed to Romans like Aemilius Paulus.

One question remains to be considered before we close this chapter. What influence did Olympia exercise on the Greek world of the Hellenistic age ? Not much, I fear, save in athletics,

---

[1] Polybios, xxvii. 9.   [2] P. v. 21.
[3] Tarn, *Antigonos*, pp. 79, 128, 135, &c. The reader who wishes for full refer-ences and details should consult the excellent index of this work.

where it certainly did keep alive the tradition of athletic honour. It was not merely that Elis had become involved in the political intrigues of the time, but that the ideals which Olympia had represented were dead. In the early days of colonization Olympia had been a real bond of union between the Hellenic states scattered over the Mediterranean world. They saw in it the embodiment of all those ideals, religious, political, social, that distinguished the Hellene from the barbarian. In the fifth century the triumph of Hellenism over barbarism had found its fullest expression in Olympia and its festival ; it was beyond all other places the acknowledged sanctuary of Panhellenism. In the Peloponnesian war and afterwards Olympia still stood for unity and peace. It was as the true centre of Panhellenism that Olympia appealed to Alexander. But in the third century all was changed. When Hellenism had conquered the world, Panhellenism was dead. In the Hellenic kingdoms of the East the distinction between Hellene and barbarian ceased to exist. Rival kings might proclaim themselves the champions of Hellas, the restorers of the Hellenic liberty. But in their wars Hellenism had no place ; they were fought not for Hellenism or any other ideal, but for self-aggrandisement. The liberty which they proclaimed was a mere sham that cannot have deceived even their flatterers ; the autonomy of independent city states was gone for ever. The Hellenistic age was one of intense activity, but it was an age not of ideals but of experiment, in religion, in politics, in art and science. Olympia was no experiment, it stood for an ideal of the past. Hence though magnificent buildings enriched the sacred precinct, though the daily, monthly, yearly sacrifices went on with all their ancient ritual, though as a social and athletic gathering the festival drew crowds as great as ever, we cannot feel that it exercised any real influence on the life and thought of Greece.

IX
Olympia and Rome

Τιβέριος Κλαύδιος Ῥοῦφος ἐπὶ τὸν τῶν Ὀλυμπίων ἀγῶνα περιγενόμενος ἐπεδήμησέν τε μετὰ παντὸς ἐν τῇ πόλει κόσμου . . . . . τάς τε γυμνασίας ἐν ὄψει τῶν Ἑλληνοδικῶν κατὰ τὸ πάτριον τῶν ἀγώνων ἔθος ἀπέδωκεν ἐπιμελῶς . . . . . καὶ διότι παραγενόμενος εἰς τὸ στάδιον ἀξίως καὶ τοῦ Διὸς τοῦ Ὀλυμπίου καὶ τῆς ἀθλήσεως καὶ τῆς ὑπὲρ αὐτοῦ παρὰ πᾶσιν ὑπολήψεως ὑπαρχούσης ἠγωνίσατο μέγα τι καὶ θαυμαστὸν ὥσπερ ἦν ἄξιον ἐπιθέσθαι τὸν Ὀλυμπικὸν στέφανον ἡγούμενος.

Extract from a decree of the Eleans in honour
of T. Claudius Rufus. *Olympia*, v. 54.

DECLINE OF OLYMPIA UNDER THE REPUBLIC

THE century which followed the loss of Greek independence was the darkest period in the history of Olympia. The independence of the city states was vital to Olympia, and its loss resulted in the decline of the competition and interest in the games, in the cessation of building, and finally in the impoverishment of the treasury, which found itself unable worthily to maintain the splendour of its sacrifices and festivals. The decline is due rather to the general conditions of Greece under the Republic than to special reasons ; for on the whole the Romans seem to have treated Elis with exceptional consideration, partly owing to the prudent policy of the Eleans, who appear to have taken to heart the wise counsels of Polybios, and partly owing to a genuine respect with which Olympia inspired its conquerors, a respect due less to its athletics than to the worship of Olympian Zeus, which in its ordered dignity resembled that of their own Jupiter Best and Greatest.

The only Roman who ventured to violate the sanctity of Olympia was Sulla. In the Mithradatic war, finding himself without money or supplies, he plundered the chief sanctuaries of Greece, including the Temple of Zeus at Olympia.[1] He intended, we are told, to compensate the gods by a share of the

---

[1] Plut., *Sulla*, p. 12 ; Appian, *Bell. Mithr.*, p. 54.

conquered territory of Thebes. But worse was yet to come. At the close of the war in 80 B.C. he conceived and carried out the plan of transferring the whole festival, athletes and all, to Rome, the only event left to Olympia being the foot-race for boys. Perhaps he thought that by this act of sacrilege he was conferring an honour on the injured deity. Perhaps he thought permanently to transfer to Rome the greatest of Hellenic festivals. If he did so, his plan perished with him, for before the next Olympiad he was dead.

The good relations existing between Rome and Olympia are shown by the statues of Roman officials dedicated during this period. Those of Mummius have been already mentioned. A statue of Q. Metellus Macedonicus was dedicated shortly afterwards by one Damon of Macedon,[1] but most of these statues are the offerings of states, especially of the Eleans. A statue to Q. Mucius Scaevola, the pontifex, was probably erected by the province of Asia, of which he was governor about 98 B.C.,[2] while the Achaian league conferred the same honour on Q. Ancharius, who was proquaestor of Achaia about 90 B.C.[3] Among the statues dedicated by the Eleans was one in honour of Marius.[4] Why they should have bestowed such an honour on one who boasted of his ignorance of Greek, and who had no connexion at all with Greece, we do not know. It seems like a gratuitous act of flattery. From a very fragmentary inscription it appears that a statue was erected to Julius Caesar [5] by a certain Licinius. The Eleans certainly dedicated statues in honour of Q. Fufius Calenus,[6] who served as Caesar's legatus in central Greece and after the battle of Pharsalus was left in command of the province. He is described by the Eleans as their saviour and benefactor, and on the same basis they erected a statue of his son. A special place of honour was assigned to these statues of Roman officials. They were placed along the south side of the Processional Way, between the Leonidaion and the Bouleuterion.

But the friendliness of Rome could not make up for the loss of independence, and the result is manifest in the decline of competition. We are fortunate in possessing a complete record for the Olympiad of 72 B.C., just after Sulla's outrage.[7] Three foot-races were won by Hekatomnos, who was either a Milesian or an Elean. Two events fell to Sikyon, one to Kos, one to

---

[1] *Olympia*, v, no. 325.   [2] *Ib.*, no. 327.   [3] *Ib.*, no. 328.   [4] *Ib.*, no. 326.
[5] *Ib.*, no. 365.   [6] *Ib.*, no. 330.   [7] Phlegon, p. 12, in *F. H. G.* iii. 606.

Adramyttion, the wrestling to Isidoros of Alexandria, a periodoneikes honoured with the title ἄπτωτος, 'the unthrown' or
'unthrowable'. Of the boys' events two were won by Eleans,
one by a youth from the neighbouring Kyparisseia, one by an
Asiatic. All six equestrian events went to Elis. This list is
typical of the period. The chariot- and horse-races have become
the monopoly of the Elean nobility, the boys' events are mostly
won by local competitors, the others by professionals from the
East, especially from Alexandria. Among them we find three
of the so-called Successors of Herakles.[1] It is a curious coincidence that after Sulla's violation of Olympia, just as after the
crisis at the beginning of the fourth century, corruption reappears.
In 68 B.C. Philostratos of Rhodes was fined for bribery, and from
the fines Zanes were erected.

The falling off in athletics is further shown by the fewness
of athletic statues erected during this period. Of those enumerated by Pausanias it is doubtful if any are later than the middle
of the second century. Among the inscriptions of the period
found at Olympia only three record athletic victories,[2] one the
victory of an Elean in boxing, the others those of two periodoneikai
of Antioch. On the other hand there is a great increase in the
number of inscriptions in honour of victories in the equestrian
events,[3] and without a single exception they are Eleans, and many
of their victories are in events for colts, a striking proof of the
connexion of these events with horse-breeding. Further, there
are numerous inscriptions of honorary statues to private individuals.[4] A few of these are dedications of the Achaian league
or other states in honour of their fellow citizens or benefactors.
One of them is interesting as recording the erection of a statue
to a Messenian by the Dionysian artists from Nemea and the
Isthmus touring in Elis.[5] It is the only reference to these guilds
found at Olympia, though we know that festivals of Dionysos
were extremely popular in Elis. The majority, however, of the
honorary statues are in honour of Eleans, and are erected by
the authorities of Elis or by the relatives of the persons concerned.

These inscriptions throw a flood of light on the lives of the
county families of Elis.[6] They lived on their estates from genera-

---

[1] P. v. 21. 10.   [2] *Olympia*, v, nos. 211–13.   [3] *Ib.*, nos. 191–218.
[4] *Ib.*, nos. 396–423.   [5] *Ib.*, no. 405.
[6] *Ib.*, nos. 62, 85, 415, 456; *C.I.A.* ii. 1155, iii. 2.

tion to generation, intermarrying with one another, busy with horse-breeding, and seldom leaving their farms except to take their colts to compete at Olympia, Nemea, or Delphi, and doubtless selling them profitably, holding various offices at Olympia and Elis, and erecting honorary statues to one another as a sort of mutual admiration society. For example, we can trace the family of Molossos, to whom the Achaians erected a statue, from the fourth century B.C., when the Areopagos of Athens erected a statue to Samippos the son of Molossos, to the second century A.D., when the city of Elis and the Olympic council erected one to Antonia Baebia, daughter of Marcus Aurelius Samippos, who was priestess of the ancient cult of Demeter Chamyne. The name Molossos suggests that this family of horse-breeders came from the north, and they actually claimed descent from Oxylos. In the first century A.D. we find a Samippos serving as Theokolos, and his son Oxylos as Spondophoros.

Still more interesting are the records of the family of Philistos and Theodota.[1] Statues of seven members of the family, three of them women, were placed on one large pedestal. They represent three generations. Most of them had won victories with horses or chariot, one of them, called Theodota like her mother, had married Antiphanes, President of the Board of Hellanodikai.[2] Several other inscriptions refer to members of the same family:[3] some of the statues were dedicated in their honour by the city of Elis or by the Board of Hellanodikai. All the statues seem to be earlier than 36 B.C. Sometimes we find a wife dedicating a statue to her husband. One Menedemos and his son set up statues for one another, the son recording that his father was Theokolos and won the chariot-race at Olympia, the father that his son was Spondophoros and won the chariot-race for colts at Nemea.

While the inscriptions of the period testify to the continued vitality of the old Elean nobility under the Republic, they show no less clearly that the Olympic festival was becoming once more local. This same characteristic may be noticed in another class of inscription. In the days of Greek independence the states had been accustomed to publish at Olympia the text of their

---

[1] *Olympia*, v, nos. 198–204.
[2] *Ib*., no. 406, Ἑλλανοδίκαι περὶ Ἀντιφάνη. Cp. nos. 392–407.
[3] *Ib*., nos. 205–6, 406–10.

treaties with one another. Now in the place of treaties we have merely records of settlements of boundary disputes between neighbouring states, disputes which in the decline of Greek politics acquired an exaggerated importance and lasted from generation to generation. The most interesting of these inscriptions is one concerning the dispute between Sparta and Messene about the *Ager Dentheliates*, a strip of land at the foot of Taygetos.[1] The dispute lasted two centuries or more and was not finally settled till the time of Tiberius.[2] Some hundred and fifty years earlier the question had been referred for arbitration to the Milesians, who had decided in favour of the Messenians, and the latter, in order to give greater publicity to the award, obtained leave to have it inscribed at Olympia. The inscription was placed on the pedestal of the Nike, the most glorious monument of the Messenians in the Altis. It consists of three parts, a decree of the Eleans authorizing the inscription, a letter of the Milesians enclosing an official copy of the award, and the copy of the award itself. Other similar inscriptions relate to disputes of Megalopolis with Sparta and her other neighbours.[3]

As a consequence of the narrowing of the festival the authorities must have been forced to rely on their own resources for its maintenance. The general impoverishment of Greece due to the civil wars cannot but have reacted on Olympia, and possibly the discontinuance for a time of the chariot-races was one of its results. Josephus tells us that in the time of Herod the festival was suffering from want of funds, and that Herod arranged a system of subsidies to keep up its magnificence.[4] Help may possibly have come also from a contemporary of Herod, Archelaos of Cappadocia, to whom the Eleans for some cause or other erected a statue.[5] The impoverishment of the treasury was further aggravated by one of those catastrophes to which Olympia has always been liable. About the year 40 B.C. the district was visited by an earthquake, which caused serious

---

[1] *Olympia*, v, no. 52 ; Hicks, *Gk. Inscriptions*, p. 201.
[2] Tacitus, *Ann.* iv. 43.
[3] *Olympia*, v, nos. 47, 48 ; cp. 50, Tegea and Kaphyai.
[4] *Ant.* xvi. 5. 3. Herod even showed his Philhellenism by founding a quinquennial festival at Jerusalem with athletic, musical, and equestrian competitions. Athletes from every part were induced to come by the offer of rich prizes, and every device was adopted to enhance the splendour of the festival (*ib.* xv. 8).
[5] *Olympia*, v, no. 315. A very much mutilated inscription (p. 363) may perhaps refer to the help given by the two kings.

damage to the Temple of Zeus and other buildings and necessitated extensive and costly repairs.

The evidence of this catastrophe [1] is derived from the repairs of the temple roof. Pausanias tells us that the tiles of the roof were of Pentelican marble. But the excavations have proved that the original tiles were of Parian marble ; so was the sima with its lions' heads, and so were the sculptures of the pediments. At some time or other the Parian tiles were replaced by tiles of Pentelican marble : so were some of the lions' heads, and so were the corner figures of the eastern pediments. These extensive repairs must have been executed at the same time, and they imply damage to the roof that can only have been caused by an earthquake. The builders' marks on the tiles and the style of the lions' heads prove that the repairs took place in Roman times. But a fortunate circumstance enables us to date the earthquake more accurately. The fallen tiles were used for the lists of Olympic officials, which begin in 36 B.C., and the earlier lists are nearly all engraved on these old tiles of Parian marble. Hence there can be no doubt that the earthquake took place about the year 40 B.C., and that the repairs were executed shortly afterwards. It is noticeable that in one of the lists of officials, which dates between 36 and 24 B.C., we find an architect included for the only time. There were further repairs to the roof some eighty years afterwards, for about this time we find Pentelican tiles used more frequently for the lists of officials, and also as facings to the pedestals of statues of Roman officials of that date.

Further light was thrown on the repairs by the discovery near the north-east corner of the temple of fragments of an inscription of Marcus Agrippa.[2] The violet-veined yellow marble of the slab is the same as that used for the Roman pavement of the pronaos, the size of the letters, which are more than six inches high and were probably filled in with gilded bronze, shows that the inscription was set in some prominent place, probably over the entrance of the pronaos or on the architrave of the façade. Hence we may reasonably infer that the restoration of the temple took place with the help of Rome and under the auspices of Agrippa, the friend and counsellor of Augustus.

[1] Fully stated by Dittenberg (*Olympia*, v, p. 696 ff.).
[2] *Olympia*, v, no. 913. Dittenberg dates the inscription before 38 B.C., but his argument is inconclusive.

Olympia under the Caesars

With the advent of the Caesars Olympia once more enters on a long period of prosperity, which reached its highest point in the second century and continued till the invasion of the Goths in the middle of the third century. It coincides with the period covered by the register of officials from 36 B.C. to A.D. 265. After this date we have practically no inscriptions, no names even of victors. The revived prosperity was the result of the provincial organization initiated by Julius and carried out by Augustus and his successors. They understood that if the inheritance of Alexander was to be permanently incorporated in the Roman Empire it must be by encouraging Hellenism and securing its loyalty. This they accomplished partly by granting Roman citizenship to individuals, partly by giving to the cities an autonomy which, while it flattered their vanity, isolated them from one another and bound them all to Rome ; partly, too, by the maintenance of Greek religion, particularly of the worship of the Olympic gods who had long been identified with the gods of Rome. The result was the complete fusion of Greeks and Romans throughout the eastern empire.

This policy was more successful farther east than on the mainland of Greece, which had suffered too much for immediate recovery. Julius had tried to restore the commerical prosperity of Greece by refounding Corinth as a Roman colony, and Augustus founded similar colonies at Patrai and Nikopolis. But Corinth and Patrai, though they rapidly regained their material prosperity, were cosmopolitan rather than Hellenic cities, and their prosperity only aggravated the impoverishment of the land by attracting crowds into the towns. The real centre of Hellenism was in the Hellenic cities of Asia Minor, Syria, and Egypt. To this the records of Olympia bear witness ; during the Empire competitors from the mainland practically disappear, their place being taken by professional athletes from beyond the seas.

In these circumstances the importance of the Olympic festival to Rome is obvious. As in the days of Greek colonization it had served as a link between the colonies of the East and of the West, so now it was a bond of union between Rome and the Hellenic cities of the East.

The revival of Olympia was largely due to the personal interest of the early emperors, particularly of Augustus. The restoration of the religious sanctuaries both of Greece and Italy was an essential part of the latter's policy, but apart from this he seems to have had a genuine taste for athletics[1] quite unusual for a Roman. He was fond of watching competitions, especially boxing, though he seems to have preferred a street fight to the tedious expositions of scientific boxing in the Stadion.[2] He encouraged professional athletes by increasing their privileges and rewards. Not only did he restore the importance of the ancient athletic festivals of Greece, but he founded similar festivals both in Italy and Greece. Thus he commemorated his victory at Aktion[3] by establishing at Nikopolis elaborate quinquennial games, the victors in which received crowns as prizes and bore the title of Aktionikai, while the Aktiads became the basis of a new system of chronology intended perhaps to supplant that of the Olympiads. At Naples in A.D. 2 he reorganized the recently founded Augustalia as a quinquennial festival with the magniloquent title *Italica Romaia Sebasta Isolympia*, and a new era commenced dated by Italids. From a long but unfortunately much mutilated inscription found at Olympia[4] we learn that the athletic and equestrian regulations were closely modelled on those of the Olympic games, while the musical contests followed the lines of the Pythian and Nemean festivals. This close imitation of the ancient festivals is characteristic of the numerous festivals founded during the Empire bearing the names of the Olympic and other Panhellenic games,[5] and in this the example was set by Augustus.

The interest of Augustus in Olympia began long before his principate, if we are right in associating him with Agrippa in the repairing of the Temple of Zeus about the year 40 B.C. It was certainly before 27 B.C. that the Achaian league dedicated a statue in his honour at Olympia.[6] Perhaps we may trace his love of organization in the institution of the register of officials which begins in 36 B.C., from which date, too, the Olympiads are regularly employed as dates in Olympic inscriptions.[7]

That scrupulous observance of ancient ritual and tradition

---

[1] Suetonius, *Octav.* 45.
[2] For a description of boxing at this period see my *Gk. Athletics*, p. 428.
[3] *Ib.*, p. 169.   [4] *Olympia*, v, no. 56.
[5] *Gk. Athletics*, pp. 169–70.   [6] *Olympia*, v, no. 367.
[7] The only earlier instance of the use of Olympiads in inscriptions is *Olympia*, v, no. 530, the date of which is given as Ol. 179 (64 B.C.).

which we note in the inscriptions,[1] and in the writers of the Empire, doubtless owed much to the initiative of Augustus. Much that had been neglected during the chaos of the preceding century was now revived. The chariot-race, which according to Africanus had been abandoned for some time, was restored, apparently for the benefit of the imperial family.

An Olympic inscription records a victory in the chariot-race of Tiberius, the future emperor, which must have occurred some time between the years 20 and 4 B.C.[2] The race, however, seems to have been again abandoned, perhaps from lack of competitors, and it was not permanently restored as part of the programme till A.D. 17, when it was won by Germanicus.[3] The participation of members of the imperial family in the games implies of course the express approval of the emperor.

Again, the custom of erecting statues in honour of athletic victories, which had been interrupted for more than a century, was revived early in the reign of Augustus. An inscription belonging to a statue of this time records a victory of a Milesian in the diaulos.[4]

Besides the Temple of Zeus it is probable that many other buildings underwent repair in the reign of Augustus. It is in most cases impossible to date the many alterations of existing buildings and the new buildings erected in Roman times, but we may probably assign to this reign the building of the vaulted entrance into the Stadion and the pillared gateway of the Gymnasion. From their style they cannot be later, and we can hardly conceive that any such buildings can have been erected during the preceding century. There can be no doubt that the Metroon was now restored.

This little temple was now converted into a temple of the

[1] e.g. *Olympia*, v, no. 54, decree of the Eleans in honour of the pankratiast Claudius Rufus of Smyrna.

[2] *Olympia*, v, no. 220. The statue was dedicated by his client Tiberius Claudius Apollonius.

[3] *Ib.*, no. 221. The dedicator was a member of a prominent Elean family often mentioned in inscriptions, M. Antonius Peisanus. It is in connexion with this victory of Germanicus that Africanus speaks of the chariot-race as πάλαι κωλυθείς. This expression seems to imply a longer interval than that between the victory of Tiberius and Germanicus. Nor does it seem likely that the chariot-race was first abandoned just when the festival was beginning to revive. I conjecture, then, that an attempt was made to restore the event during the early part of the reign of Augustus, but that it was not permanently restored till A.D. 17. For other solutions of the difficulty v. Curtius, *Olympia*, i, p. 60; Dittenberg, *l. c.*   [4] *Ib.*, no. 219.

emperors.   The inscription on the architrave [1] states that the Eleans dedicated it to ' Caesar Augustus, son of a God, Saviour of the Hellenes and the whole inhabited world '.   In it was placed a colossal statue of Augustus, the torso of which was found close to the temple.[2]   The emperor was represented in the guise of Zeus, with sceptre and thunderbolt, and the statue, which was two and a half times life-size, must have filled the whole space at the back of the tiny cella.   Other statues were added subsequently.   A statue of Claudius as Zeus, by the Athenian artists Philathenaios and Hegias,[3] a statue of Titus in richly wrought cuirass, and a statue of an emperor with a kneeling figure at his feet which Treu supposes to represent Domitian and Germania Victa.[4]   These three statues would have filled the whole of one side of the cella, and opposite them, according to Treu, were three draped female statues of the imperial ladies, representing the younger Agrippina, Julia the daughter of Titus, and Domitia.[5]   The whole temple was now full and statues of other emperors were placed elsewhere, in the neighbouring Treasury of Kyrene, in the Temple of Zeus,[6] in the Heraion,[7] and in the exedra of Herodes.

The dedication of the Metroon to Augustus invites comparison with, and was perhaps prompted by, the earlier building of the Philippeion within the Altis.   Both were temples dedicated to living mortals.   But there was an important difference between the two.   The Philippeion was founded by Philip himself, and the recognition of the divinity of Philip and Alexander was imposed by these kings upon the Elean authorities, who had no choice in the matter.   The dedication of the Metroon on the other hand was, if we may trust the evidence of the inscription, a voluntary act of servility on the part of the Eleans, who thereby went far beyond any claim that Augustus would ever have made of them.   The early emperors claimed divinity for their dead predecessors, not for themselves, and in the inscriptions found at Olympia, which doubtless had the official sanction of Rome, Augustus is described not as himself a god but as son of a god, and so are his successors.   Of the organized worship of the

---

[1] *Olympia*, v, no. 366 Ἠλῆιοι Θεοῦ υἱοῦ Καίσαρος Σεβαστοῦ σωτῆρος τῶν Ἑλλήνων καὶ τῆς οἰκουμένης πάσης.   [2] *Ib*. iii, p. 232, Pl. LVIII, 2.

[3] *Ib*., p. 243, Pl. LX, 1 ; *ib*. v, no. 642.   [4] *Ib*., Pl. LX, 2, 3.

[5] *Ib*., Pl. LXIII, 1-3.   [6] Trajan and Hadrian (P. v. 12. 6).

[7] Possibly Nero. The statue of his wife Poppaea Sabina was found there *in situ* (*Olympia*, iii, Pl. LXIII, 6). Fragments of a statue of Vespasian were also found there.

living emperor we have no evidence till the reign of Nerva, when L. Vetulanus Laetus is described as ' chief priest of the Emperor Caesar Nerva '.[1] The explanation must be found in the forbearance of the emperors themselves and their regard for Olympia, for neither the cult of the living nor of the dead emperor could have offended the susceptibilities of the Greeks of this age, who would have regarded him not as a rival of Zeus but as his vicegerent, or human embodiment. It was otherwise with the worship of the goddess Roma, the introduction of which might have seemed a direct challenge to Hellenism, and it is significant that no mention of the cult of Roma is found in Roman inscriptions till the third century, when we find Titus Flavius Polybius, a descendant of the historian, holding the office of priest of the goddess Roma.[2] This absence of the cult of Roma at Olympia is the more remarkable because in the farther East Augustus distinctly refused to allow himself to be worshipped except in conjunction with this goddess.

The gratitude of the Eleans is shown by the numerous statues erected in the honour of the imperial family. The young Tiberius must have been exceptionally popular. The same Apollonius who had commemorated his victory in the chariot-race by a statue dedicated a group in honour of Tiberius and his brother Drusus, to whom he afterwards added his son Drusus, born 15 B.C. Two other statues were dedicated in his honour by the city of Elis, and after the accession of Tiberius the city of Elis and the Olympic Council set up statues to his son Drusus and his adopted son Germanicus.[3]

An interesting inscription belonging to the reign of Tiberius records the erection of a statue by M. Antonius Alexion in honour of G. Julius Lakon, the son of Eurykles.[4] The latter was a rich and powerful Spartan, a friend of the Romans and of Herod, who spent large sums on public buildings and established at Sparta the games called Eurykleia. Shortly before the beginning of our era he fell into disgrace and was banished, but his son Lakon seems to have recovered his position and power. The friendly relations between Elis and Sparta are illustrated by a somewhat

---

[1] *Olympia*, v, no. 437.

[2] *Ib.*, nos. 486–7. If the proposed restoration of no. 317 is correct, the Eleans set up an honorary statue to Rome at least two hundred years earlier.

[3] *Ib.*, nos. 369–72.

[4] *Ib.*, no. 426. Cp. Mahaffy, *Silver Age of Greek World*, p. 307.

later monument set up by the Lacedaemonian people to their kinsfolk the Eleans 'for concord'. The inscription is engraved on one of the blocks of the offerings of Mikythos which were removed by Nero.[1]

Of Olympia under Tiberius and his successors there is nothing to narrate till the time of Nero. The madman Caligula, indeed, gave orders for the statue of Olympian Zeus to be removed to Rome,[2] but the sacrilege was prevented by the emphatic protest of the statue itself, which burst into a mocking laugh which shattered the cranes erected for its removal. A statue of Claudius was erected in the Metroon, and the constant recurrence of the Gentile name Claudius proves the popularity of the Claudii among the Elean aristocracy.

Various inscriptions testify to Nero's interest in Olympia.[3] To the inordinate vanity of the artist emperor no place could offer such scope. Extraordinary preparations were made for his visit to Olympia.[4] The 211th Olympiad, which should have been held in A.D. 67, was postponed till 69 to allow him to compete in person. The building in the south-east corner of the Altis, which had probably served as a residence for the Hellanodikai, was hastily transformed into an imperial villa. The extension of the Altis had probably taken place somewhat earlier ; near the eastern end of the new southern wall a magnificent triumphal gateway was now built. Some of the most famous statues were removed to Rome ;[5] the statues of previous victors were pulled down and thrown into the sewers lest their presence should seem to detract from his own glory. In defiance of all precedent the programme of the games was altered by the inclusion of musical and dramatic contests in which the imperial artist might compete, and in which he was of course victorious. In the chariot-race, again contrary to precedent, he drove himself a ten-horse chariot. He was thrown from his chariot, picked up, resumed the race, never finished the course, but none the less was proclaimed victor. No fewer than seven crowns did he receive from the servile Hellanodikai, who were rewarded by the gift of Roman citizenship and large sums of money. His triumphal entry into Rome was a burlesque of all the extrava-

---

[1] *Ib.*, no. 316.   [2] Suetonius, *Cal.* 22.
[3] *Olympia*, v, nos. 370, 373, 374.   [4] Suetonius, *Nero*, 23 ff.
[5] e. g. the Odysseus from the group of Achaian heroes (P. v. 25. 8), and some of the offerings of Mikythos (P. v. 26. 3).

gances ever perpetrated by the luxury of Sicilian tyrants. After Nero's death every effort was made to obliterate the memory of the disgrace inflicted on the sanctuary of Zeus : the records of the Olympiad were expunged from the Register, the Hellanodikai were forced to disgorge their ill-gotten wealth;[1] the triumphal gateway fell into disuse, if we may judge from the silence of Pausanias. On one of the inscriptions found at Olympia the emperor's name has been carefully erased.[2]

For the next half-century the history of Elis is once more a blank, save for a few statues of Roman emperors[3] and numerous athletic and honorary inscriptions which suggest that in spite of the economic impoverishment of Greece under the Flavii Olympia was still prosperous. Before we come to the age of Hadrian we may pause to consider what changes had taken place at Olympia under the Empire.

Outwardly there was little change. The old forms and ritual were scrupulously maintained or restored. In the honorary inscriptions we find for the first time mention of the old Olympic Council as decreeing or authorizing the erection of statues.[4] They are coupled usually with the city of the Eleans, occasionally with the Hellanodikai. In this we may recognize the influence of Roman organization. In the next century the authorization of the council is represented by the letters ΨB, which remind us of the Roman S.C. Some of these statues are in honour of Roman officials, most of them in honour of prominent Eleans. As in the previous period, members of the same families are mentioned from generation to generation.[5] The statues are erected sometimes by relations, sometimes by the authorities. In the later inscriptions of the first century the offices held by the recipient are enumerated. For example, the city of Elis and the Olympic Council dedicate a statue to L. Vetulanus Laetus,[6] ' archon and priest of the Emperor Caesar Nerva Augustus, and chiliarch of legion . . . and alytarch, and epimeletes and priest of Olympian Zeus, who held the office of agoranomos in Ol. 216 and served as gymnasiarch with distinction '. In another inscription this same Laetus

---

[1] Dio Cassius, 63. 14. [2] *Olympia*, v, no. 287.
[3] *Ib.*, no. 377, Domitian ; no. 378, Trajan. A statue of the latter was erected in the Temple of Zeus by οἱ πάντες Ἕλληνες (P. v. 12. 6).
[4] Dyer, ' Olympic Council ', in *Harvard Studies*, xix.
[5] e. g. family of Peisanos (*Olympia*, v, nos. 426–30) or of Lyson (*ib.*, nos. 431–40). In 432 Lyson bears the title κοσμόπολις.
[6] *Ib.*, no. 437.

is described as the emperor's friend (φιλόκαισαρ).[1] The city of
Elis also dedicated a statue to his daughter.[2] The number of
honorary statues of women is a noticeable feature of the period.
Many of them seem to have been erected in the Heraion. Several
inscribed bases belonging to them were found in the pronaos
of the temple,[3] and among the ruins to the east of the temple
were found four draped statues,[4] one of them a remarkably lifelike representation of an elderly lady of austere type (Fig. 35).
Whether the statues belonged to the bases we cannot say, nor
do we know if any of the ladies thus honoured had any connexion
with the worship of Hera. No priestess of Hera is mentioned
in Elean inscriptions, though the priestess of Demeter is mentioned in several.[5] We may certainly infer, however, that
women played an increasingly important part in Elis.

Yet though its outward forms remained the same, the
character of the competition had completely changed. The
change is expressed in the word οἰκουμένη, which now for the
first time occurs in our inscriptions. The festival was no longer
Hellenic, it was oecumenical. Instead of athletes from the whole
of Hellas we have ' the Xystos of athletes from the inhabited
world gathered at Olympia '.[6] Among these Greece itself was
but poorly represented ; most of the competitors came from
the Hellenized cities of the East, especially from Alexandria ;
even Romans were allowed to compete, though few availed themselves of the privilege. The fiction of Hellenic birth may have
been kept up, but the professional athlete from Alexandria or
Antioch had no more claim to Hellenic descent than the Roman.
If the competitors were cosmopolitan, much more so were the
crowds of sightseers and visitors whom business or pleasure
attracted to the festival from every part of the empire.

As Hellenic feeling and civic patriotism declined, the competitions became more and more the monopoly of professionals.[7]
The professional athlete felt that he was competing for his own
glory and profit rather than for the honour of the state, and this
feeling found its expression in long, bombastic inscriptions in
which the victor enumerates his victories. Athletes were organ-

---

[1] *Ib.*, no. 436 ; cp. no. 373.   [2] *Ib.*, no. 438.
[3] *Ib.*, no. 429, Antonia Kleodike ; no. 435, Claudia Alkinon ; no. 438, Numicia
Teisis.   [4] *Ib.* iii. 253, Pl. LXII, 6 ; LXIII, 4, 5 ; LXIV, 4, 5.
[5] *Ib.* v, nos. 456, 473, 485.   [6] *Ib.*, no. 436.
[7] For a fuller treatment of athletics under the Empire v. *Gk. Athletics*, pp. 172 ff.

ized into clubs, or Xystoi, so called from the covered colonnades where they trained, and these clubs received special privileges from the emperors. We hear of such a club at Olympia, composed of all the competitors. The most popular events were boxing and the pankration, and these under Roman influence became more and more gladiatorial and brutal. Under such circumstances corruption was rampant.

It is a striking testimony to the strength of Olympic tradition and to the rigour of the authorities that in the general degradation of athletics the honour of the games was still maintained. Corruption was severely repressed—only two cases being recorded, the first in 12 B.C., the next in A.D. 125.[1] The guilty parties were punished by fines, from which Zanes were dedicated. The strictness of the administration is shown by the story of one Apollonios of Alexandria, who was fined and forbidden to compete because he arrived too late to enter his name.[2] It seems, too, that the Eleans made some attempt to check the arrogant pretensions and self-advertisement of the professional pugilist, for after A.D. 37 they abolished the title of ' Successor of Herakles ' and decreed that no one should henceforth be allowed to win both in wrestling and in the pankration.[3] Moreover, there were still a few competitors who lived up to the athletic ideals of the past. Such were the young Melankomas and his father, of whom Dion Chrysostom gives us a charming picture ;[4] such, too, was Claudius Rufus of Smyrna, already mentioned, in whose honour the Eleans passed a special decree which is fortunately preserved.[5]

THE RENAISSANCE OF OLYMPIA

Under Hadrian and the Antonines the fusion between Greeks and Romans became complete. Hitherto, in spite of the Philhellenism of the emperors, the Romans as a whole had retained their traditional contempt for the Greeks, and had treated Greece itself with neglect. But from this time there was no longer any difference between Greeks and Romans. Admitted to full citizenship, the Greeks were eligible for the highest offices of the empire. At the court Greek influence was

---

[1] P. v. 21. 15.
[2] P. v. 21. 12.
[3] Förster, *Sieger*, nos. 621, 704, 734 ; P. v. 21. 10 ; Dio Cass., 79. 10.
[4] *Or*. xxix, xxx.
[5] *Supra*, p. 152.

supreme. The emperors themselves, fascinated by the philosophy and art of Hellas, sought to revive its ancient ideals and restore its ancient glory. Under their patronage the cities of the mainland became once more the centre of Hellenism. Everywhere temples and colonnades, aqueducts and baths, gymnasia and stadia, testified to the generosity of the emperors. The old festivals were revived, new festivals were founded, and in old and new the ancient ritual and rules were scrupulously observed.

Nowhere was the renaissance of Hellenism more in evidence than at Olympia, which in the second century of our era attained a popularity and a splendour such as it had not possessed since the days of Pindar. No place bulks so largely in the literature of the age. Dion of Prusa devoted a whole oration to a discussion on the Zeus of Pheidias. Phlegon carried the Olympic Register down to the years A.D. 137, and his work was continued in the next century by Africanus. Lucian in his *Anacharsis* tried to revive the athletic ideal of the past. Pausanias, who visited Olympia in the year A.D. 174, has left us a full description of Olympia and its monuments. Countless allusions in the writers of the second and third centuries bear witness to the widespread interest in Olympia and its games. Indeed, it is to the writers of this age that we owe most of our knowledge of the festival.

These writers leave us in no doubt as to the popularity of Olympia. They tell us of the crowds that flocked there from every part of the inhabited world, of the difficulties of the journey, the scantiness of the accommodation, the heat and want of water, and of the enthusiasm of the spectators who took their places long before daybreak and remained there all day eagerly watching the contests and oblivious to the scorching heat. A fresh wave of athleticism was spreading throughout the empire. Everywhere there was a craving for amusement and excitement, and in the contests of the stadion and the hippodrome men found a spurious substitute for the more serious contests of politics and war. The multiplication of festivals only enhanced the fame of Olympia. For the olive crown was still the athlete's highest ambition, and to Olympia came the picked athletes from all the empire. In Greece itself there seems to have been a distinct revival of athletics.[1] Moreover, under the *pax Romana*

---

[1] The names of Sparta, Sikyon, Aegina reappear in the lists. For the athletic training of the Spartan youths and athletic competitions at Sparta at this period v. *Gk. Athletics*, pp. 183 ff.

travelling by land and sea was easy and safe, and Olympia, as we have already seen, was a natural meeting-place for East and West. Hence, in spite of the depopulation of Hellas the crowds at the festival were as great and as representative as in the time of Hellenic freedom.

It was not merely the love of sport that drew men to Olympia. Many came for private profit, to buy and sell. For the festival was now as always a gigantic fair, attracting traders of every sort from far and near, from the peasant who brought in food and wine to sell among the spectators, to the horse-breeder and the art dealer who hoped to find patrons among the wealthy visitors from Rome. The greater the multitude the greater the possibilities for trade. Hence it is significant that Roman writers translate the Greek *panegyris* by *mercatus*, and speak of the Olympic festival as *maximus mercatus*.[1]

Once more Olympia was the resort of poets, rhetoricians, and philosophers, and once more statues in their honour were set up in the Altis. In an inscription belonging apparently to the middle of the second century one Glaukos of Athens claims that he was honoured with a statue by the decree of the council for ' singing an Olympic hymn ', and another inscription, dated A.D. 233 and written in characteristically archaic style, records that ' the men of Peisa set up a statue of Spercheios on account of his blameless song '.[2] It looks as if in these late days the hymn of victory had been revived. Among several sophists similarly honoured we find the name of Flavius Philostratos of Athens, probably the elder of the two writers of the name.[3] We do not know if these rhetoricians gave public displays at Olympia. It is not improbable that they did. Certainly the rival schools of philosophers, especially the Cynics, took full advantage of the opportunities afforded by the festival for spreading their propaganda. Philostratos tells us how the mystic enthusiast Apollonios of Tyana, escaping from the persecution of Nero, came to Olympia, and from the steps of the temple discoursed on wisdom, manliness, and temperance.[4] There, too, came the Cynic Peregrinus to immolate himself like Herakles on a funeral pile before the assembled multitude, whether from pure vainglory and love of notoriety, or, as Professor

---

[1] Cic., *Tusc. Disp*. v. 3 ; Justin. xii. 5 ; Vell. Paterc. i. 8.
[2] *Olympia*, v, nos. 457, 482.
[3] *Ib*., no. 476 ; cp. nos. 462, 463, 464.   [4] iv. 31.

Dill [1] suggests, from a sincere desire to prove the triumph of philosophy over death. Little did he dream that he would owe his immortality to the pen of the scoffer Lucian. The latter describes how when he came to Olympia on the first day of the festival, he found the opisthodome of the temple full of the Cynics and their opponents, extolling and abusing Peregrinus with such vehemence that they actually came to blows.[2] It was, says Lucian, his own fourth visit to the games, and surely nowhere else could he find such scope for studying the foibles of his fellow men. It says much for the authorities of Olympia that while little else escapes his satire, for the Olympic games and ideal he has nothing but genuine admiration.

It was not only at times of festival that visitors resorted to Olympia. Every day, says Pausanias, the Eleans and others offer sacrifice on the Altar of Zeus. With this altar was connected the oracle under the charge of the Manteis, still chosen from the ancient families of the Iamidai and Klytiadai. Hitherto there had been two seers, but towards the close of the second century we suddenly find this number raised to four.[3] We know that at this time there was a general revival of the oracles throughout the Greek world, and from this increase in the number of the seers we may surely conjecture that the oracle at Olympia shared in the revival. Athletes have always been a superstitious class. Moreover, it was an age of travel. It had long been the fashion for Romans of good family to visit Greece, but hitherto the chief attraction had been Athens, where they went to study philosophy and rhetoric. Now, however, the example of the emperors had aroused an interest in the antiquities and art of Greece, and no tour to Greece could be complete without a visit to Olympia. It was probably to meet the increasing requirements of tourists that towards the close of the century a second exegetes was appointed.[4] The original function of this official was to expound the religious law of the sanctuary, and he acquired therefore an intimate knowledge of the traditions of the place. Thus he naturally developed into a sort of official guide. What sort of information these officials gave we may gather from the pages of Pausanias, especially in the opening chapters. Like all guides, they sought to excite the wonder of their hearers by exalting the antiquity of what they described. They revelled in mythical origins.

[1] *Roman Society*, pp. 353 ff.   [2] *De Morte Peregrini*, 31.
[3] *Olympia*, v, p. 140.   [4] *l. c.*

Of the antiquarian spirit of the age, inscriptions of Olympia furnish two very interesting examples. The first is an inscription in honour of the historian C. Asinius Quadratus, who wrote a history of Rome called ' the Thousand Years ', in which he made the foundation of Rome coincide with the first Olympiad. For this act of flattery the Eleans erected a statue to him ' because he had honoured Olympia both in word and deed '.[1] The second inscription is that on the diskos dedicated by Asklepiades,[2] according to which the origin of the festival goes back to 1580 B.C. ! This inscription is further interesting from the fact that it is dated not by the Hellanodikas but by the Alytarches, and the name of the official is Flavius Scribonianus, kinsman of senators and consulars. The office of Alytarch, originally a sort of superior police officer, had attained much greater importance in the third century. The same love of antiquity is seen in the care with which all the ancient ceremonial of the games and sacrifices was maintained.

In all matters of athletics the Elean authorities enjoyed a prestige similar to that possessed to-day by the M.C.C. in cricket, and they certainly justified their reputation. Though elsewhere corruption was rife, they succeeded, thanks to the religious associations of the games, in maintaining at Olympia the purity of sport. The last recorded case of bribery occurred in A.D. 125, and Pausanias makes thereon the significant comment : ' It is strange that any person should be found to despise the god at Olympia and to receive or give bribes in connexion with the games.' [3] The same exalted view of the games is evident in the parting words which, according to Philostratos, the Hellenodikai addressed to the competitors when they left Elis for Olympia : ' If you have exercised yourselves in a manner worthy of the Olympic festival, if you have been guilty of no slothful or ignoble act, go on with a good courage. You who have not so practised, go whither you will.' [4] What a contrast between this ideal and the actual condition of athletics. Of the hopeless artificiality of the athletic revival, of its vicious and unscientific system of training, of the moral and physical deterioration of the athletes, of the general corruption, we have abundant proof in the writings of Philostratos, Plutarch, and Galen, but for these evils Olympia was not responsible.[5]

[1] *Olympia*, v, no. 356.   [2] *Ib.*, nos. 240, 241 ; v. *supra*, p. 59.
[3] P. v. 21. 16.   [4] *Vit. Apoll.* v. 43.
[5] For the condition of athletics in this period cf. *Gk. Athletics*, pp. 178 ff.

Not the least of the attractions of Olympia was the statue of Zeus by Pheidias, which seems to have fascinated the thought of the age. Philosophy and religion were drawing closer together. Metaphysical speculation had given place to a more practical philosophy, which sought to find some moral guidance for life, and with this object to justify and unify the many cults of paganism. All schools alike were seeking after God, and the tendency of all was towards monotheism. The Stoic conception of the world-spirit helped in this, for all existing deities might be regarded as partial expressions of this spirit.[1] Of none could this be said more easily than of Zeus, whose cult, as we have seen, was bound by no narrow limits of locality. Hence in the writings of the later Stoics, Nature, Fate, God, Zeus, are almost interchangeable terms. Thus in the often-quoted rhapsody of Marcus Aurelius on Nature : ' For thee are all things, in thee all things, to thee all things return. The poet says Dear City of Kekrops ! and wilt thou not say Dear City of Zeus ? ' Moreover, the impersonal world-spirit of the older Stoics had itself been transformed into an infinitely benevolent providence, and this providence becoming more and more personal was invested with attributes borrowed from the Platonic conception of God and the Stoic ideal of the philosopher king. It was this moral ideal that men found expressed in the Zeus of Pheidias. ' Its beauty ', says Quintilian, ' seems to have added something to the received religion ',[2] and Epiktetos bids his disciples journey to Olympia to see it, and account it a misfortune to die without having done so.[3] The ideal is fully developed in an oration of Dion of Prusa inspired by a visit to Olympia, in which he arraigns Pheidias for daring to give plastic form to the deity.[4] The sculptor in his defence sets forth the conceptions which he tried to express in his art in terms which, according to a recent French writer, are little more than a rhetorical exposition of the Stoic conception of the ideal king.[5] It was doubtless the general reverence for the statue that prompted Hadrian to represent it on his coins, some of which bear the head of Zeus, others a copy of the whole statue, the god seated on his throne.

But we must not be led into exaggerating the influence of this ideal, or supposing that there was a real revival of the worship of

[1] For the philosophy and religion of this age cf. Dill's *Roman Society*.
[2] *Inst. Orat*. xii. 10. 9.   [3] Arrian, *Epict*. i. 6. 23.
[4] *Or*. xii. Cp. Dill, *op. cit*., p. 380.   [5] *Rev. Et. Gr*. xxx, p. 105.

Zeus. The crowds of visitors were attracted by love of excite-ment, love of sport, love of gain, not by religion. The worship of Zeus by virtue of its immemorial antiquity, an asset of the greatest importance in religion, inspired now as always universal veneration but little enthusiasm. The ideal of Pheidias appealed to the thinker and philosopher, above all perhaps to the emperors of the second century, but it had no message for the masses, who were eagerly turning throughout the length and breadth of the empire to those mystical oriental cults which by a promise of future blessedness offered them some compensation for the miseries of the present. These cults established themselves every-where : even Delphi had its Temple of Osiris. But at Olympia, though we may trace in the inscriptions some revival of the ancient worship of Demeter,[1] no foreign cult could find a place. There Zeus still ruled without a rival, and it was this unique supremacy of the Father of Gods and Men that made Olympia the last bulwark of philosophic paganism in its struggle with Christianity.

With the exception of the Exedra we have no clue to the dates of the various Roman buildings erected during the empire, but the majority of them probably belong to the second and third centuries. They are all secular in character, intended for the accommodation and comfort of the numerous resident officials and visitors. Their extent indicates a considerable resident population. Among them we may notice two *Thermai*, one to the north of the Prytaneion, another farther south on the banks of the Kladeos. They contained some fine mosaic floors. Many of the Greek buildings were enlarged and reconstructed. The Leonidaion and Theokoleon underwent reconstructions, and colonnades were built in front of the Prytaneion and Bouleuterion.

It is remarkable that Hadrian, who scattered his benefactions broadcast throughout Greece, left no conspicuous monument at Olympia. The Achaian league erected his statue in the Temple of Zeus, and an inscription of the league in his honour was found at Olympia.[2] Another statue was placed in the Exedra, but not a single building bears the emperor's name or the name of any of his successors.

It was otherwise with the great private benefactor of Greece, Herodes Atticus, who built an aqueduct to bring the water of

---

[1] The priestess of Demeter is mentioned in several inscriptions (*Olympia*, v. nos. 456, 473, 485, 610.   [2] P. v. 12. 6 ; *Olympia*, v, no. 57.

the Alpheios to the Altis, terminating in two pools crowned by a vast half cupola overlooking the Heraion. This so-called Exedra contained the statues of the imperial family dedicated by Herodes, and those of his own family erected by the Eleans. In the centre stood a marble bull, the inscription of which states that it was dedicated by his wife Regilla, priestess of Demeter Chamyne. In honour of his wife's priesthood he also replaced the ancient statues of Demeter Chamyne by new statues in Pentelican marble.[1]

Why does Pausanias make no mention of so conspicuous a building? It certainly was in existence when he visited Olympia. It can hardly be that it was too modern to interest him, for he mentions buildings erected by Herodes elsewhere and his statues in the Temple of Demeter at Olympia. Can it be that he was offended by its utter incongruousness and ostentation? or that a party of the Eleans themselves resented a monument which proclaimed so arrogantly the subjection of Hellas, just as they had at an earlier date resented the triumphal gate of Nero? That some such feeling did actually exist appears from the story told by Lucian of Peregrinus, who on his first visit to Olympia violently denounced Herodes for introducing effeminate innovations at Olympia.[2] The people, says Lucian, who appreciated the benefits of the new water-supply, tried to stone the Cynic. But the protest suggests that there may have been a strictly conservative party opposed to any innovation that would interfere with the traditional discomforts of the festival. There was a similar dispute in the fourth century at Antioch. Certain people had proposed to transfer the local Olympia, which was modelled in every detail on our Olympia, from Daphne to Antioch itself.[3] The proposal, which was evidently made for the convenience of the dwellers in the city, was violently opposed by the conservative party, who protested against any change as a violation of the true Olympia.

The revived prosperity of Olympia lasted till the middle of the third century, if not later. This at least is clear from the inscriptions, which, if few, are interesting from their varied character. They show that the chariot-races were still attracting wealthy competitors from a distance. A couplet engraved on the pedestal of a statue of one Theopropos, a winner of the horse-race, tells us that he was ' a Eupatrid of Rhodes, the father of

[1] P. vi. 21. 1.   [2] *De Morte Per.* 19.   [3] *Olympia*, i, p. 53.

Senators '.[1]   An Athenian inscription records the victory in
chariot-races of T. Domitius Prometheus of the deme of Oa, who
held the office of *Antikosmetes* in A.D. 245.[2]   We may note, too,
the increased importance attached under the empire to the flute-
players and heralds.   Their bombastic inscriptions [3] rival those of
the professional athletes.   The latest inscription of a victor that we
possess is that of the herald Valerius Eklektos of Sinope, who won
four successive victories at Olympia, A.D. 245–261, was three times
periodoneikes, besides winning victories at Rome, Athens, and other
festivals, amounting to no fewer than eighty.   He further records
that he was councillor of his native city, of Smyrna, Philadelphia,
Hierapolis, Tripolis, Perga, and had received the citizenship of
Athens and Elis.   The last honorary inscriptions belong to the
same period.   They refer to two statues dedicated by the Achaean
league and by the Messenians to Titus Flavius Polybius,[4] a
descendant doubtless of the historian.   He is described as priest
of the goddess Roma and as a true Heraklid.   Another member
of the historian's family had been similarly honoured at Olympia
a century earlier.

In A.D. 267 Greece was invaded by the Goths.   The danger
awoke the nation from its sloth to fight in defence of its homes.
But though the invaders were repulsed by the valour of Dexippos,
the land must have suffered severely from barbarian raids.   The
security of the *Pax Romana* was no more.   From this time our
records are silent save for an occasional reference which tells
us that the festival still went on.   But a power greater than that
of the Goths threatened Olympia, the all-conquering power of
Christianity.   Olympia was doomed.   By a strange irony of fate
the last recorded victor in the national games was Varazdates,
a Persian Arsacid from Armenia, who won the boxing in A.D. 385.
Eight years later, in the 293rd Olympiad, the festival was held for
the last time.   The next year it was abolished by a decree of the
Emperor Theodosius I.   According to another account it lingered
on till the reign of Theodosius II, who in A.D. 426 decreed
the destruction of all heathen temples throughout the empire.

[1] *Olympia*, v, no. 239.   [2] *C.I.A.* 758 a.
[3] *Olympia*, v, nos. 232, 237, 242.
[4] *Olympia*, v, nos. 486, 487 ; cp. nos. 449, 450.

X

The Topography of the Altis[1]

Διὸς ἄλκιμος
υἱὸς σταθμᾶτο ζάθεον ἄλσος πατρὶ μεγίστῳ· περὶ δὲ
πάξαις Ἄλτιν μὲν ὅγ᾽ ἐν καθαρῷ
διέκρινε τὸ δὲ κύκλῳ πέδον
ἔθηκε δόρπου λύσιν.

Pindar, O. xi. 44.

TEMENOS AND GROVE

THE Altis, as we see it to-day, is clearly defined as a rough quadrilateral at the foot of the Hill of Kronos. Within this space were the most sacred buildings and monuments of historical Olympia, but the walls of the Altis are comparatively late, and certainly do not contain all the sacred territory. From the description given by Xenophon of the battle of Olympia in 364 B.C., it is clear that the *temenos* extended beyond the Kladeos. For the Eleans, he tells us, before they crossed the river ' were already *in the temenos* '.[2]

Moreover, there were many ancient monuments outside the Altis. Just outside the west wall was the small circular Heroon : across the Kladeos was a cairn of stones said to be the tomb of Oinomaos, and close to it were the remains of his stables. To the east again was the Temple of Demeter Chamyne, and beyond it Pisa itself with its fountain and stream. A stade farther on was another cairn, the tomb of the suitors of Hippodameia. Lastly, there was to the north the Hill of Kronos with its ancient cult of Kronos and priestly Basilai. We may, then, fairly infer that the Altis or grove was the holy of holies, and that the *temenos* included all the sites that we have mentioned.[3]

We have no means of determining the exact extent of the temenos or sacred territory. Its southern boundary must have been the Alpheios, which women were not allowed to cross during the festival. On the north it certainly included the Hill of Kronos.

---

[1] v. Plan of Altis, p. 4.
[2] *Hell.* vii. 4. 29 παρῆσαν ἤδη εἰς τὸ τέμενος.   [3] P. vi. 21.

If, as we may conjecture, it included the whole territory of ancient Pisa, it must have extended eastwards as far as that place and westwards probably as far as Dyspontion, which was closely connected by tradition with Pisa [1] and was the ancient port of Olympia.

Before the fifth century most of the buildings that we can date, with the exception of the Bouleuterion, lay along the southern slope of the Hill of Kronos. In the north-west corner was the Prytaneion, along the slopes of the hill was the terrace of the Treasuries, cut out of the hill-side. Below the terrace was the Heraion, and farther east probably the Hippodameion. South of the Heraion was the Pelopion. In front of these two buildings was the Altar of Zeus. Between the Pelopion and the Bouleuterion was a low ridge sloping down to the river, and there was the Sacred Grove which Herakles measured for the Sovereign Father and marked the bounds thereof.[2] In the time of Pausanias the sacred wild olive-tree grew near the south-west corner of the temple. To the north of the temple, about the middle of the precinct, was a grove of plane-trees. There was also a grove within the Pelopion.[3]

What was the boundary of the Grove? It was probably marked only by a hedge. The only clue that we have is the line of certain ancient water-channels, which seem to preserve the lines of still more ancient roads.[4] They are constructed of blocks of poros, many of them rejected fragments of ancient buildings, triglyphs from the Temple of Zeus, drums of pillars split in two, and down the centre is an open semicircular runnel. These runnels served in the first place to carry off the rain-water, afterwards also to distribute water from a reservoir above the Heraion. There were three main lines. One passed eastwards along the foot of the Treasury terrace. The other two ran southward to the south-west corner of the Heraion, where they parted. One branch continued southwards to the south-west corner of the Bouleuterion. The other followed the north and east walls of the Pelopion, and after a long sweep ran due south, crossing the line of the Altis wall a little to the west of the Triumphal Arch of Nero. In this road we may recognize the main approach to Olympia from the south. If we prolong the line of the western runnel in front of the Bouleuterion, the two

---

[1] P. vi. 22. 4.
[3] P. v. 15. 3, 27. 11.
[2] Pindar, *O.* xi. 46.
[4] *Olympia*, i, p. 77; ii, p. 171.

roads completely encircle the site where the ancient grove lay. Is it fanciful to recognize in them the ancient boundary of the grove, the earliest Processional Way?

Confirmation of this conjecture may be found in the fact that the few statues earlier than the building of the temple, the site of which we can fix, all lay close to the eastern half of this circuit. A little south of the east end of the temple, buried under the rubble of the terrace, was found the basis of the statue set up by Praxiteles of Syracuse and Kamarina.[1] Farther east, five yards in front of the Altis wall, was the basis of the Zeus dedicated in memory of Plataiai.[2] Close to it were the foundations of the chariots of Gelon and Kleosthenes.[3] A short distance to the north was the semicircular foundation on which stood the group of the Trojan Heroes.[4] The remains of the Eretrian Bull were found still farther north,[5] and close to it was the inscribed pedestal which bore an ancient statue of Zeus dedicated by the Spartans for some victory over their enemies.[6] From Pausanias we learn further that close to the group of the Trojan Heroes was the statue of Herakles fighting the Amazon, dedicated by Evagoras of Zankle, and also the Thracian Herakles by Onatas.[7]

The most important series of statues described by Pausanias is that of the victors in the games, which occupies eighteen chapters of his sixth book. By a careful study of the text Walter Hyde succeeded in fixing approximately the positions of most of these statues.[8] He enumerates thirty-one statues earlier than the temple. Of these all but four must have stood east or southeast of the Temple of Zeus. If we may judge from existing remains, there were hardly any statues much farther east than the line of the water-channel. Of the remaining four two, the ancient wooden statues of Praxidamos and Rhexibios, stood close to the house of Oinomaos, i.e. farther north but still close to the water-channel, on either side of which there are numerous foundations at this part. The other two statues seem to have been moved from their original position at the time when the temple was built.

[1] *Olympia*, ii, p. 144, v, nos. 266, 630, 631.
[2] *Ib.*, i, p. 86 ; P. v. 23. 1.
[3] *l. c.* ; P. vi. 10. 6, 9. 4.   [4] *Olympia*, ii, p. 146 ; P. v. 25. 8.
[5] *Olympia*, ii, p. 147, v, no. 248 ; P. v. 27. 9.
[6] *Olympia*, i, p. 86, ii, pp. 78, 147 ; P. v. 24. 3.   [7] P. v. 25. 11.
[8] *De Olympionicarum Statuis*, pp. 71-3.

The fact that all the monuments the position of which we can determine stood close to the line of the road running from the Bouleuterion to the north-east corner of the Pelopion justifies our conjecture that this was part of the original Processional Road which, starting from the Prytaneion, encircled the Sacred Grove and ended at the great Altar of Zeus somewhere in front of the Pelopion and the Heraion.

THE PLAIN AND THEATRON

East of this road and bounded on the north by the Hill of Kronos stretched an open plain. There are no signs within it of any buildings,[1] altars, or statues before the building of the Stoa, and even after this date such monuments are only found along its northern and eastern sides. In the earlier plans it is misnamed the Agora. The latter, as we shall see, lay farther south. The plain was a far more important place. For here from the earliest times the spectators crowded to watch the sacrifices, processions, and games. This was why its western side was the favourite site for statues and monuments, and why the Treasuries were built on a terrace cut out of the hill-side. This was why the stepped retaining wall was built and the eastern Stoa, which together formed, as I have already said, the Theatron of Xenophon.[2]

The Eleans, he says, drove the Arkadians into the space between the Bouleuterion, the shrine of Hestia, and the Theatron adjoining these buildings. The shrine of Hestia is in the Prytaneion at the north-west corner of the Altis. East of the line joining the Prytaneion and the Council House stretches the open plain. The Theatron forms the other two sides of the triangle. The stepped wall extends almost to the Prytaneion. The Stoai extend south to a level with the Bouleuterion. The intervening space may have been occupied by temporary stands. At all events it formed part of the ground for spectators, which is all that the word Theatron implies.[3]

One point deserves notice. Xenophon makes no mention

[1] Hyde, ignoring this fact, supposes that the statues stretched right across to the eastern colonnade.

[2] *Hell.* vi. 4. 29. Cf. Dyer, *J. H. S.* xxviii. 250 ff. ; *Gk. Athletics*, pp. 53, 120.

[3] Philostratos, *Vit. Apoll.*, p. 192, expressly states that there was no theatre in the modern sense at Olympia.

of any wall west or south of the Altis. Had it existed at the time, it would have played an important part in the fight. Nor does he show any horror at the sacrilege involved in fighting within the Altis. From this I infer that the building of the Stoa was not felt as extending the bounds of the Altis, and that the plain enclosed was not regarded as more sacred than the rest of the Temenos.

Certainly there was no change in the processional way. Statues continued to be erected along the same line. The triangular basis of the Messenian Nike was found some thirty yards east of the south-east corner of the temple,[1] and the pillar of the Elean statue to Concord a little north of its north-east corner.[2] The favourite site for honorary statues, as Hyde[3] has shown, was still to the south between the Bouleuterion and the temple and opposite its east end. As the sites in the south became overcrowded, the dedications were placed farther and farther north, till in the middle of the fourth century there was a line of statues between the Heraion and the Pelopion.

THE GREEK WALLS OF THE ALTIS

We come now to the walls of the Altis. Two walls are marked on the plan. The outer wall, which is constructed of blocks of concrete bonded with mortar and wooden dowels, belongs to Roman times ; the inner wall, built without mortar, to Greek times. The two can be best compared at a point a little north of the Philippeion, where they begin to diverge. In our illustration (Fig. 38) the Roman wall is seen on the left, the Greek wall on the right.

The south Altis wall,[4] marked in most plans as the south terrace wall, runs from just above the later processional entrance almost parallel to the line of the temple and at right angles to the line of the Stoai. From its western end it extends without a break for 137 metres to the point where the water-channel crosses it. It is built of large blocks of conglomerate and is 0·82 metre thick. Beyond the channel it is continued eastward for 34 metres by a thinner wall of conglomerate only 0·36 metre thick, which ends in a broader block bearing a small conglomerate

---

[1] *Olympia*, i, p. 49, ii, p. 153, v, nos. 52, 259.
[2] *Ib.* i, p. 86, v, no. 260 ; P. v. 24. 4.   [3] *op. cit.*, pp. 75, 76, 78.
[4] *Olympia*, i, pp. 69 ff., ii, p. 61 ; Dörpfeld, *Die Altismauer v. Ol., Ath. Mitth.* xiii. 327.

pillar. The difference in thickness between the two walls is due perhaps to the fact that the western section served also as a retaining wall for the temple terrace.

Of the west wall only small portions still exist, sufficient however to enable us to trace its course with certainty, a small portion 8 metres long at the south-west corner, and a longer stretch of 40 metres north-west of the Philippeion. It ran parallel to the later Roman wall at a distance of $2\frac{1}{2}$ metres to a point north of the Philippeion, where it makes a bend eastwards in a line with the west wall of the Prytaneion.

In structure both south and west walls resemble the eastern wall of the Stoa, which was built at the same time as the Philippeion. In spite of their thickness the walls must have been quite low. For immediately within them numbers of statues were placed, and the Philippeion itself was only five yards from the wall. After the Roman wall was built the Greek south wall served only as a retaining wall for the temple terrace, and can hardly have been more than 18 inches high ; for the foundations of monuments were found immediately above it.

No traces of any gateways have been found in either wall, and we must suppose that such gateways as existed were simple openings without any portico either inside or out. It is clear that there must have been a gateway to the north of the Philippeion giving access to the Prytaneion, and perhaps another farther south opposite to the Palaistra. A third gateway probably existed at the west end of the south wall where two steps lead up to the terrace. There was certainly an entrance north-east of the Bouleuterion leading through an avenue of statues to the entrance of the Great Temple. Lastly, there was a gateway a little farther east, for there is a break in the wall at the point where the ancient water-channel crosses it. This, I conjecture, was the entrance of the Processional Way which, starting from the Prytaneion, passed out of the Altis and followed the line of the west and south walls to this point, whence it continued, as it always had, northwards to the Altar of Zeus. This conjecture is supported by the fact that Nero's great triumphal gateway stood a little south of this opening, and there can be no doubt that this gateway was intended to be the processional entrance, though not used after his time.

STATUES OF THE ALTIS

In a former chapter we saw that the enclosing of the Altis with a wall and the extension of its boundaries were connected with the building of the Philippeion. The date of the walls is confirmed by an examination of the list of statues erected after this period, and of the remains of their bases and inscriptions. The west and south walls offered new and honourable sites for the erection of statues for which there was no room farther east, and they did not remain vacant long.

No section of the chapters in which Pausanias enumerates the athletic statues is so consistently clear as that dealing with the statues to the south of the Temple of Zeus. It begins with the notice of Telemachos of Elis in chapter xiii, and ends with that of Philonides in chapter xvi. The bases of both these statues have been found *in situ*, that of Telemachos inside the Altis wall to the east of the entrance from the Bouleuterion, that of Philonides in the south-west corner of the Altis.[1] A little beyond the latter, just outside the Altis wall, was found the inscription of the statue of Leonidas,[2] which Pausanias mentions next to Philonides. It must have stood just inside the wall. Between Telemachos and Philonides Pausanias enumerates thirty-two statues of athletes and nineteen honorary statues, and he enumerates them from east to west. Next to Telemachos he mentions Aristophon of Athens, whose name was found on a broken block close to that of Telemachos. Of the next fifteen statues ten at least belong to the early part of the fifth century, and probably stood to the south and south-east of the temple opposite to the Bouleuterion.[3] The one extant inscription belonging to them, that of Xenombrotos, was found to the north-east of the Bouleuterion.[4] The remaining sixteen athletic statues and the fifteen other statues all belong to Macedonian times, and may be placed inside the south Altis wall. First comes the statue of Aischines of Elis, whose inscription was found in the north wing of the Bouleuterion. Next comes Archippos of Mytilene, and his basis was found between the temple and the Bouleuterion. Opposite the sixth pillar of the

[1] *Olympia*, v, nos. 177, 276, 277. [2] *Ib.*, no. 294.
[3] Not, however, as Hyde supposes, east of the water-channel.
[4] *Olympia*, v, no. 170. The victory of Xenombrotos belongs to the fifth century; the verses of the inscription cannot be earlier than the fourth century. Cf. Hyde, *op. cit.*, p. 53.

temple from the west were found the inscription of Epitherses and part of the basis of the statue of Antigonos dedicated by the Byzantines, the decree of the latter being found a little farther west.[1]   Thus at every point where we can test it the accuracy of Pausanias is vindicated.   From the list of statues which he gives it is clear that the southern terrace has now become the place of honour.   Mingled with the statues of athletes are those of kings and statesmen.   Besides the statues of Demetrios and Antigonos mentioned above, this terrace contained the statues of Hiero II of Syracuse, Archidamos III of Sparta, Seleukos of Syria, Antigonos Doson and Philippos III of Macedon, and Areus.   The inscription on the statue of Areus, which was set up by Ptolemaios Philadelphos, is the only one that has been recovered.[2]

Leaving the south wall Pausanias proceeds northward along the west wall, and here he enumerates fifteen athletic and four non-athletic statues.[3]   Of these all but two belong to the fourth or third century.   None of the bases of these is *in situ*, but several inscriptions belonging to them were found in the buildings outside the Altis wall.   The most interesting of these is that of Deinosthenes,[4] winner of the stade race in 316 B.C., who recorded on the basis the distance from Sparta to Olympia.   This inscription was found in the Palaistra, that of Glaukon of Athens in the Byzantine church.[5]   Just to the north of the Philippeion, actually abutting on the wall, are two large bases not mentioned by Pausanias, one of which bore the equestrian statue of Kallikrates, the Achaian envoy to Rome in 180 B.C.[6]

Another conspicuous site for statues was in front of the eastern Stoa.   Numerous bases were found here, but unfortunately none of them inscribed.   The long basis wrongly identified with the Proedria seems undoubtedly to have supported the two lofty columns on which stood the statues of Philadelphos and Arsinoe, and probably monuments of the Ptolemaic age occupied some of the other bases in front of the Colonnade.

Finally, the statues of the Hellenistic age enumerated by Pausanias in his last section must, as Hyde has shown, be placed between the Pelopion and the Temple of Zeus.   The one inscribed base of this group, that of Gorgias, was found just where we

[1] *Olympia*, v, nos. 45, 173, 176, 186, 305.   [2] *Ib.*, v, no. 308.
[3] Hyde, *op. cit.*, pp. 21, 28.   [4] *Olympia*, v, no. 171.
[5] *Ib.*, nos. 178, 296.   [6] v. *supra*, p. 146.

should expect to find it from the context, at the east end of this passage, not far from the house of Oinomaos, close to which were the statues of Praxidamas and Rhexibios. Dörpfeld, on the other hand, places all the statues of this section outside the Greek wall of the Altis, and assigns to them a row of large bases along the south side of the Processional Way. We must, therefore, briefly examine this section.

In the first sixteen chapters of Book VI Pausanias has described a circular tour of the Altis. He enumerates in order the statues of victors :

1. In front of the Heraion, i. e. on its southern side (1. 3–3. 7).
2. Between the Heraion and the east end of the Temple of Zeus (3. 8–13).
3. Opposite to the east end of the temple (3. 13–14. 13).
4. South of the temple (14. 13–16. 5).
5. To the west of the temple (16. 5–9).

He then proceeds : ' These are the most remarkable monuments if you go the round of the Altis as described (ποιουμένῳ τὴν ἔφοδον ἐν τῇ Ἄλτει), but if you should wish to reach the Great Altar from the Leonidaion by the right-hand road, there are the following monuments deserving notice.'

What is the right-hand road from the Leonidaion to the Great Altar? According to Dörpfeld Pausanias is distinguishing the statues inside the Altis from those outside, and the road is none other than the processional road along the south side of the Altis. The objections to this view are insuperable. It makes Pausanias practically retrace his steps along the south side of the terrace, pass through the crowd of statues he has already described, following the Processional Way till he reaches the house of Oinomaos. Moreover, at the time of Pausanias this road was not outside but inside the Altis. Finally, Hyde has convincingly proved that the statues in question were between the Pelopion and the Temple of Zeus.

But why should this road be called the right-hand road ? The reason is perfectly simple. There was another road on the left, and Pausanias has already been along it in his first ἔφοδος. To reach the altar from the Leonidaion you entered the Altis by the south-west door, and mounted the two steps that led to the level of the terrace. From this point two ways were open to you, and in distance there was little to choose between them. You might go straight north to the north-west corner of the Pelopion and then pass between the Pelopion and the Heraion, the last and first portions of the ἔφοδος. This was the left-hand road. Or you might go in a north-easterly direction between the Pelopion and the Temple of Zeus, precisely the ground that Pausanias had not covered in the ἔφοδος. This was the right-hand road. Thus the whole difficulty is solved and there is no need with Hyde to seek refuge in emendation.[1]

We must now return to the row of bases lying between the Bouleuterion and the Leonidaion which we have mentioned above. As can be seen from our illustration (Fig. 47) and from the plan, they form a remarkably uniform and clearly defined group, the only parallel to which is the row of bases for the Zanes at the entrance of the Stadion. They are made for the most part of sandstone, and Weil assigns them to the late Greek or early Roman period.[2] They are large and oblong, intended evidently for equestrian statues. Moreover, they are placed close together, and carefully aligned, thirteen of them forming a line on the south side of the Processional Way parallel to the south wall of the Altis. At the west end is a further line of four statues almost at right angles to the first line and parallel to the Leonidaion, immediately in front of which was another row of statues apparently belonging to the same period, the two rows forming an avenue of statues on either side of the road. As Hyde has shown, the statues at Olympia were not erected haphazard, but were arranged in groups determined either by date or by the nationality of the victor or by the character of the competition.[3] Hence we may be certain that a group of bases so remarkably distinct belonged to some special class of dedications. To whom then are we to assign these bases? The answer is hardly doubtful. They were the bases of the statues of those Roman officials and benefactors some of whom we have noticed in a former chapter.[4] Two inscribed bases were actually found *in situ*. The first, which was found in the main line, is that of L. Caecilius Metellus Macedonicus, consul in 143 B.C.[5] The second, found in the southern extension, is that of one Marcus Maecilius Rufus,[6] of whom unfortunately we know nothing. Again, to the east of the Bouleuterion was found

[1] *Op. cit.*, p. 70.
[2] *Olympia*, i, p. 141.
[3] *Op. cit.*, p. 1.
[4] *Supra*, p. 153.
[5] *Olympia*, v, no. 325.
[6] *Ib.*, no. 334.

46. PROCESSIONAL ENTRANCE FROM WEST

47. BASES OF ROMAN EQUESTRIAN MONUMENTS

the large basis erected in the time of Augustus, on which stood the statues of Mummius and the ten *legati* who assisted him in the organization of Achaia.[1] Hence we are justified in inferring that the other bases in the group supported the statues of Roman officials. The bases were intended for equestrian statues, and the statues of Roman officials were usually equestrian.

Further, let us note the unique advantages of the site. It would be hard to find a site calculated in so high a degree to flatter the pride of the Romans without hurting the suscepti- bilities of the Greeks. We can easily understand the unwilling- ness of the jealous authorities of Olympia to place the statues of barbarians, however distinguished, within the boundaries of the most exclusively Hellenic of all sanctuaries. At the same time no site could be found in the crowded Altis at once so conspicuous and so honourable. The statues stood in full view of the temple terrace, by the side of the sacred road along which all the proces- sions passed. No monuments could be placed in front of them or obscure their view ; there were no monuments of earlier times to challenge comparison. By its southern extension this road was directly connected with the Leonidaion, which probably served for the entertainment of distinguished visitors, and which was perhaps already the residence of the Roman officials. Finally, if our view is correct, we can understand why it was that in the early days of the empire, when the distinction between Greek and Roman was being obliterated, the Altis wall was extended so as to include the statues of those officials to whom in the first place was due the incorporation of Greece in the Roman Empire.

THE ROMAN WALLS OF THE ALTIS

The Roman walls involved a considerable extension of the Altis. On the west the extension was but slight, the new west wall running parallel to the old wall at a distance of about 3 yards except in its northern part, where it continues almost straight instead of turning to the right. But on the south a long strip was added to the Altis some 30 yards broad at the west end and little more than 5 yards at the east end. As a result the broad street that ran along the west side of the Altis was narrowed to such an extent, especially in front of the Leonidaion, that Pausanias could not understand how such a lane could be called

---

[1] *Olympia*, v, nos. 320–4.

a street (ἀγυιά) and explained it as a peculiarity of Elean speech.[1] On the other hand, the southern part of the processional way with all the statues to the south of it was included in the Altis.

The walls stand on a foundation of small stones[2] and mortar, and are built of blocks of conglomerate held together by mortar and wooden dowels. In some places the blocks are the thickness of the walls, in other places two thin blocks are set edgewise side by side. On the inside they are supported by buttresses set at regular intervals of about 8 metres. The walls themselves are 0·55 to 0·57 metres in thickness; they are at present about 3 feet high, but must have been originally at least three times as high.

In the west wall there are three entrances, one at the north end close to the Prytaneion, another precisely similar to it opposite the Leonidaion and immediately below the old south wall, and between the two a third small door opposite the road running between the Palaistra and the Theokoleon. The latter was a simple doorway fitted with folding doors, with a small threshold of conglomerate in front but no portico. Of the other two entrances the best preserved is the southern one (Fig. 46), the processional entrance of Pausanias. It consists of three equal openings 1·40 metres broad, divided by square pillars faced by Doric half-columns, the lowest stones of which are still standing. In front of it on the outside is the stylobate of the porch formed of blocks of conglomerate set on a foundation of *opus incertum*, at the edge of which are the marks of four pillars arranged opposite to the pillars of the doorway. Of the pillars and the superstructure nothing remains. Two pillars standing on the inside in front of the central door pillars belong to a late aqueduct built when this door had fallen into disuse, later therefore than the time of Pausanias.

In the southern wall there were two entrances, one forming the approach from the Bouleuterion, and a large triumphal gateway farther east. Of the latter all that remains is the foundation of the platform and part of the pavement. The foundation is of *opus incertum*, and forms a rectangle 4·43 metres deep by 16·65 metres broad. The pavement consists of blocks of limestone and conglomerate, the latter marking the site of four massive piers that supported the arches. From these we learn that there were three doors, a large central one flanked by two smaller

---

[1] v. 15. 2.

[2] *Olympia*, i, p. 70, ii, p. 62; Dörpfeld, *Die Altismauer v. Ol., Ath. Mitth.* xiii. 327.

ones, and that the structure was of the usual type of triumphal arch.

From the similarity of their building and plan it is certain that all these gates and the walls belong to the same period. Many of the blocks of stone employed for the pavement of the doors bear traces of previous use and seem to have been taken from earlier Greek buildings. In particular the pavement of the triumphal door is largely composed of bases of statues of various dates. Dörpfeld, therefore, conjectures that these bases belonged to the statues carried off to Rome by Nero, and that this gateway was constructed on the occasion of his visit to Olympia in 67 B.C. This conjecture is supported by the fact that the south-east building close by was reconstructed as a dwelling-house for the use of Nero. Further, while it is evident that this archway must have been intended for the processional entrance, Pausanias entirely ignores it, and places the processional entrance in the south-west of the Altis. The abandonment of this stately entrance is quite intelligible if it was erected by Nero, for we know that on his fall the Eleans did all in their power to obliterate the traces of one who had brought such dishonour on their sanctuary and the games.

We may therefore consider it almost certain that the triumphal arch was the work of Nero. It does not, however, seem to me to follow that the whole of the new wall and the gates were his work. I should suggest, as more probable, that at the time of his visit they had been recently erected, and that the portion between the Bouleuterion and the south-east building was altered at his behest. We may notice that this section of the wall is not in line with the western section, and that there are no buttresses on the inside as in all other parts of the wall.

If Nero's gateway was intended for a new processional entrance, it must have involved a considerable alteration of the processional way. Instead of following the line of the Greek south wall between the avenue of statues, it must have been carried farther south, probably along the south side of the southern colonnade till it met the main road from the south leading past the Bouleuterion to the new triumphal arch. Such an innovation would certainly have aroused intense resentment among the conservative Eleans, and it was only natural that on Nero's death both the new road and the new gateway should be abandoned. Certainly in the time of Pausanias the processional entrance was the less pretentious gateway opposite the Leonidaion, and the processions once more followed their traditional way. As, however, the position of the processional gateway has given rise to much discussion and many different views, we must carefully examine the evidence. In doing so we shall have to deal with three other topographical difficulties, the position of the Hippodameion, of the Agora, and of the Proedria.

PROCESSIONAL ENTRANCE, AGORA, PROEDRIA, HIPPODAMEION

Pausanias refers three times to the processional entrance ἡ πομπικὴ ἔσοδος.[1] The first two passages occur in the second chapter, in which he enumerates the altars. At the beginning of the chapter [2] he notices the workshop of Pheidias outside the Altis. He re-enters the Altis by the south-west door opposite to the Leonidaion. Here comes a parenthesis about the latter building. ' It is outside the sacred precinct, but near the *Processional Entrance into the Altis, the only road along which the Processions pass.*' The position of the Leonidaion is definitely known. Hence the processional entrance referred to can only be the south-west door. The emphatic statement that this is the only processional road perhaps reflects a surprise that so insignificant an entrance was preferred to the triumphal arch of Nero. After this digression he starts again at the point where he has entered the Altis, i. e. at the south-west door. To his left is the terrace. Here he sees an altar of Aphrodite and the Horai, probably the altar which still exists by the side of the steps leading up to the terrace.[3] Close to this altar he notices the Sacred Olive-tree ' to the right ' [i.e. the south side] ' of the opisthodome of the Temple ', and near it is the Altar of the Nymphs, close probably to the open water-channel that runs south from the Heraion to the south wall. As he is standing with his back to the gateway all these objects are obviously to his left. Next he turns to the right and sees, ' still inside the Altis but to the right with regard to the Leonidaion ', an altar of Artemis Agoraia (ἔστι δ᾽ ἔτι ἐντὸς τῆς ῎Αλτεως, ἐν δεξιᾷ δὲ τοῦ Λεωνιδαίου). The description ' to the right with regard to the Leonidaion ' means, as so often in

---

[1] v. Dörpfeld, *Olympia*, i, pp. 74, 83 ; Weil, *ib.*, p. 153 ; Heberdey, *Eranos Vindob.*, p. 38 ; Flasch in Baumeister, p. 1097 ; Weniger, *Klio*, vi, p. 380 ; Wernicke, *Jahrb.* ix, p. 88.   [2] v. 15. 1.

[3] *Olympia*, ii, p. 164, n. 13. Curtius identifies this altar with that of the nymphs (*Die Altäre v. Ol.*, p. 24).

Pausanias, to the south with regard to it : it is readily intelligible if we remember that he is standing with his back to that building. Not far off is the Altar of Zeus Agoraios. These altars must be somewhere in the south angle of the Roman Altis wall.

Here, then, to the south of the Greek wall we must place the Olympic Agora, the place where the merchants set up their booths and the country folk brought their provisions to sell to visitors at the festival. In Xenophon's time the booths extended as far as the Kladeos,[1] but this space had been much curtailed by the building of the Leonidaion. Southwards the Agora may have stretched to the Alpheios. The Altars of Zeus and Artemis of the market-place had stood outside the earlier Greek walls, but were now included with a section of the Agora within the Roman boundary. There is, then, absolutely no necessity with Roberts to emend the text of Pausanias by altering ἐντός into ἐκτός.[2]

Pausanias next mentions an altar of the Pythian Apollo in front of ' what is called the Proedria ', after which he proceeds to the Aphesis of the Hippodrome. From this passage, as Roberts [3] has shown, it is clear that the Proedria lay between the south-west gate and the Hippodrome, presumably in the group of buildings to which the Bouleuterion belongs. But what is the meaning of προεδρία ? Most writers interpret it as either the residence [4] or the business quarters [5] of the πρόεδροι or presiding officials who at Olympia were the Hellanodikai. This, though not the usual meaning of the word, is a possible one. That the residence of the Hellanodikai should have been called Proedria seems, however, most improbable. Their residence at Elis was called the Hellanodikeon, and we may assume that if they had a residence at Olympia it bore the same name. Wernicke accordingly regards the Proedria as the business quarters of the Hellanodikai, and he identifies it with the southern wing of the Bouleuterion. That one of the two wings did serve as business quarters of the officials is extremely probable, but that it was called the Proedria there is no proof. Wernicke, indeed, tries to show that when Pausanias speaks of the Bouleuterion he means the north wing, not the south wing, but his argument depends on the assumption that the two wings had different names, and it

---

[1] Xen., *Hell.* vii. 4.   [2] *Hermes*, xxiii, pp. 435 ff.
[3] *l. c.*   [4] Flasch in Baumeister, pp. 1071, 1104.
[5] Wernicke, *Jahrb.* ix, pp. 101-14, 127-35 ; Dyer, *Harvard Studies*, xix, p. 55.

is equally or more probable that by Bouleuterion Pausanias means the whole group of buildings, the two wings, and the central block and the colonnade that united them. Indeed, this conclusion is inevitable if we hold that the statue of Zeus Horkios was in the central block, for he definitely states that this was ' in the Bouleuterion '.[1] The third interpretation is that of Sir James Frazer, who translates Proedria ' Grand Stand ', meaning thereby ' the stand of the officials ', though he does not identify it with any building. This was the view of Curtius,[2] who identified it with the long stone platform in front of the Echo Colonnade, a topographical impossibility. Against this view Dyer urged that προεδρία never has this meaning. It is, however, commonly used for the ' front seats occupied by officials ',[3] and from this meaning to that of a stand for officials the transition is easy. Moreover Pausanias, by the expression ' *what is called the Proedria* ', seems to suggest a slightly unusual use of the term. Now the only building south of the Altis that can possibly be so described is the southern colonnade.[4] This colonnade was closely connected with the Bouleuterion, and I conjecture therefore that it was built for the convenience of the members of the council and the officials, partly perhaps as business quarters, partly as a stand from which they could view all that went on in the plain below.

In the next two sections (§§ 5, 6) Pausanias enumerates the various altars in the Hippodrome. He then returns from the portico of Agnaptos which formed the western boundary of the Hippodrome, re-enters the Altis by the processional gate (ἐσελθόντων δὲ αὖθις διὰ τῆς πομπικῆς, § 7), proceeds due north to the back, i. e. the west end, of the Heraion, and ends up where he began at the Prytaneion, close to the ἔξοδος opposite to the Gymnasion ', i. e. the north-west gate.

It has been suggested that the gate by which Pausanias re-enters the Altis is not the south-west gate but the old Greek gate east of the Bouleuterion, or the triumphal arch.[5] Now, even if this were the most direct way, it does not follow that it is the

---

[1] v. 24. 9. [2] *Olympia und Umgegend*, p. 39.
[3] Hdt. iv. 88 ; vi. 57. An official chair found at Lesbos bears the inscription προεδρία, and the name of Potamon, son of Lesbonax, a noted rhetorician. Dar. Sag. s.v. Proedria.
[4] If ' proedria ' means nothing more than a stand for officials, we might identify the proedria with the semi-circular exedra north of the Bouleuterion, but it seems hardly of sufficient importance.
[5] Dörpfeld, *l. c.* ; Heberdey, *l. c.*

way that Pausanias describes, for he is describing the course taken by the Elean priests in their monthly visitation of the altars, and such a round is not determined by considerations of distance. But, even in point of distance, in going to the back of the Temple of Hera from the west end of the Hippodrome, which we must remember was at least 300 yards across and extended far south of the Altis, it makes very little difference if you enter the Altis east of the Bouleuterion and go round the Temple of Zeus and the Pelopion or enter at the south-west gate and go straight to the Heraion. Moreover, Pausanias is absolutely clear and explicit. At the beginning of the chapter he enters by the processional gate : when later on in the same chapter he speaks of ' *entering again by the Processional Gate* ', he can only mean the same gate at the south-west, opposite to the Leonidaion. It is inconceivable that he should have used the same expression twice in the same chapter of two different gates, especially after the careful description of the position of the gate in the first passage.

We pass on to the third passage, which is the cause of the whole difficulty.[1] ' Inside the Altis,' he tells us, ' close to the Processional Gate is an enclosure called the Hippodameion about a plethron square surrounded by a wall. Here once a year the women enter who sacrifice to Hippodameia and perform other rites in her honour.' If, disregarding for the moment the reference to a gate, we look only at the context, we unhesitatingly place the Hippodameion in the north-east of the Altis. In the preceding chapter Pausanias has described the Treasuries from west to east : he has then climbed to the summit of the Hill of Kronos. Descending he notices on the slopes between ' the hill and the treasuries ' a temple of Eileithyia and Sosipolis, and, close by, the ruins of a temple of Aphrodite Ourania. Then comes the account of the Hippodameion, and immediately afterwards he enters the Stadion by the κρυπτὴ ἔσοδος, at the extreme end of the Zanes. The same position is implied in the only other passage [2] in which Pausanias mentions the Hippodameion, namely in his account of the statues of Zeus. Here, too, he mentions it immediately after the Zanes and certain other statues at the entrance to the Stadion. A coincidence so remarkable can hardly be accidental.

The only difficulty then is the statement that the Hippodameion

[1] P. vi. 20. 7.   [2] P. v. 22. 2.

is near the Processional Gate. To suppose that Pausanias means here the south-west gate is, even apart from the context, impossible practically. There is no room for such an enclosure in the south-west corner. To suppose that he means the triumphal archway, or the old south-east gate,[1] is to impute to him almost incredible carelessness, and does not really help matters. For why after coming down from the Hill of Kronos should he cross right over to the south-east of the Altis before visiting the Stadion? The fact is that the only entrance that can possibly be near the Hippo-dameion is the entrance into the Stadion, and we can only suppose either that by the πομπικὴ ἔσοδος Pausanias here means not the processional entrance into the Altis, but the processional entrance into the Stadion—a much less violent supposition than to suppose that he mentions two processional entrances into the Altis—or we must suppose that the text is corrupt and that instead of πομπικὴ we should read κρυπτὴ or δρομικὴ or some other expression describing the entrance to the Stadion.[2]

We may conclude then that there is only one processional entrance at the south-west of the Altis, and that the Hippodameion is in the north-east corner close to the entrance to the Stadion. It was probably little more than a mound supposed perhaps to contain the bones of Hippodameia and surrounded by a low wall, and its complete disappearance need cause us no more astonishment than that of the Great Altar of Zeus.

[1] As does Dörpfeld with considerable hesitation, and Heberdey, *op. cit.*
[2] The former proposed by Bötticher (*Philolog. Wochenschrift*, 1882, p. 1209), the latter by Weniger (*Klio*, vi. 380 ff.). Hirschfeld, quoted in *Olympia*, i, p. 152, reads τὴν ἐς τὸ στάδιον ἔσοδον. I have for the most part followed Weniger.

XI

The Altars and Hero Shrines
of Olympia

Βωμοὺς ἐξ διδύμους ἐγέραιρεν ἑορταῖς Θεῶν μεγισταῖς
ὑπὸ βουθυσίαις ἀέθλων τε πεμπταμέροις ἁμίλλαις,

Pindar, *O.* v. 5.

PAUSANIAS enumerates more than seventy altars, and his list is still incomplete. Some altars, we know, had already fallen into disuse at the time of his visit : for example, a circular Greek altar was found buried under the Roman porch in front of the Bouleuterion. Most of the altars have disappeared entirely, and we can only conjecture their sites from the indications that Pausanias gives and from the layers of black earth that are found in certain parts of the Altis. They were often made of perishable materials, and, as the chief symbols of paganism, it was natural that they should have been absolutely destroyed by the Christians. They were generally constructed of blocks of coarse conglomerate covered with plaster, which owing to the stains of blood and smoke required constant renewing. They were usually rectangular but sometimes round, and their foundations can be recognized by the fact that beside the altar proper there was a platform for the officiating priest. Some sixteen altars have been thus recognized, but of these only three or four can be identified with those mentioned by Pausanias.[1]

ALTAR OF ZEUS

The Great Altar of Zeus [2] was the most sacred and perhaps the oldest object in the Altis. Tradition said that it was founded by the Idaean Herakles or two generations later : certainly it existed long before there was any temple at Olympia. It was the altar of prophecy βωμὸς μαντεῖος,[3] where the sacred seers, the Iamidai and the Klytiadai, practised divination from the burning

---

[1] *Olympia*, ii, p. 161.   [2] P. v. 13. 8.   [3] Pindar, *O.* vi. 5.

of the skins of the victim. As the altar of divination it was the natural resort of strangers (πολυξενώτατος).[1] Pausanias states that daily offerings were made upon it not only by the Eleans but by private individuals, and one of the earliest inscriptions found at Olympia directs strangers visiting the sanctuary to sacrifice sheep upon the altar and make payment to the god.[2] The penalty for violating the sanctuary or breaking an agreement placed under the safeguard of the god was excommunication from the altar. Thus in an agreement made between the Anaitoi and the Metapioi,[3] apparently two local communities, it is laid down that if either party violate the agreement they shall be excluded from the altar by the Proxenoi and the Manteis. In a somewhat later inscription the same penalty is imposed on a certain Timokrates, who had ill-treated some Theoroi.[4] In this case the penalty is enforced by the priest and the Proxenoi. The Proxenoi are concerned as responsible for the conduct of those whom they represent ; the priest of Zeus and the Manteis as the officials in charge of the altar. The taboo which excluded married women from the Olympic festival applied also to the altar.[5] They might ascend the prothysis but not the upper part of the altar.

'The Altar of Zeus is almost equidistant from the Pelopion and the Temple of Hera, but situated in front of and before both buildings.' It is no longer necessary to discuss how far this description is compatible with the identification of the altar with the elliptical foundations farther south. That site is now recognized as belonging to the prehistoric settlement. There is, therefore, no justification for distorting the absolutely explicit statement of Pausanias.[6] The altar stood a little to the east of the angle between the Pelopion and the Heraion.

From his description it seems probable that the altar itself was circular. It stood on a raised platform, or prothysis, 125 feet in circumference, enclosed probably by a stone wall, covered like other altars with several layers of stucco. The altar itself was built up out of the ashes of the sacrifice, cemented together by a paste made of ashes and water. Every year on the nineteenth day of Elaphios, about the time of the spring equinox, the Manteis

[1] Pindar, O. i. 93. [2] Olympia, v, no. 5. [3] Ib., no. 10.
[4] Ib., no. 13. [5] P. v. 13. 10 ; v. supra, p. 75.
[6] Weniger, for example, still places the altar farther south, utterly disregarding Pausanias, although he usually relies implicitly on his accuracy (Neue Jahrb. xxxi, 1913, p. 241 ; Klio, xiv, p. 411.

collected the ashes from the hearth of Hestia in the Prytaneion, kneaded them together with water from the Alpheios, and plastered them on the altar. No other water might be used, for no other water had the same binding power, a miraculous property due probably to the quantity of lime that the flooded river contains at this season. The prothysis was approached on either side by a flight of stone steps or more probably by a ramp, and on either side of the altar steps were cut in the ashes. The initial rites, the slaughter and dismembering of the victims, took place on the prothysis. The thighs only were taken to the top of the altar and there burnt, the rest of the flesh being removed to the Prytaneion, where it was cooked for the feast.

It is difficult to understand the dimensions given by Pausanias. He gives the circumference of the altar proper as 32 feet, the total height including the prothysis as 22 feet. It is generally supposed that the prothysis was only 6 feet high, though I see no reason why it should not have been higher. Now it is obvious that a base of 32 feet in circumference is quite inadequate for an altar built up of debris 16 feet high. This then must be the measure not of the base but of the top of the altar. The various reconstructions [1] that have been attempted are purely conjectural. We do not know the height of the prothysis, we do not know the shape of the altar. Even if, as is possible, the prothysis was rectangular, it seems to me most improbable that the altar of debris was so, unless it was confined by some sort of wall. But in the absolute dearth of evidence further discussion is futile.

ASH ALTARS OF HERA AND GE

Hera, like Zeus, had her ash altar.[2] This has been identified either with the foundation wall of small stones found in a layer of black earth full of votive offerings south of the Heraion, or with the large double foundations of conglomerate due east of the temple. Recent excavations make it doubtful whether the former remains are those of an altar : they are certainly older than the Heraion, and if the cult of Hera already existed, and if

[1] Weniger, *l. c.*, reconstructs it as circular, square, and rectangular. Cp. *Olympia*, ii, p. 212.

[2] *Olympia*, ii, p. 163, nos. 2, 5 ; Weniger, *l. c.*, p. 416. He identifies the eastern altar with the double altar of Apollo and Hermes.

the temple was originally Hera's, these remains may be those of
her altar. If on the other hand the cult of Hera was, as I have
argued, introduced when the Temple of Zeus and Hera was
built by Pheidon, there can be no doubt that her altar stood on
the foundation to the east of the temple. It is in a line with its
axis, and its size is quite suitable for an ash altar. It consists of
two rectangles, the smaller one to the west being probably the
platform for the priest.

The third ash altar was that of Ge.[1] It stood, says Pausanias,
on the Gaion, and near it was a Stomion and an altar of Themis.
He has just mentioned the Altar of Herakles or the Kouretes
close to the Treasury of the Sikyonians, and next, with an apology
for his zigzag course, descends from the terrace probably in the
centre, where an easier flight of steps appears to have existed, to
the Altar of Zeus Kataibates close to the Great Altar. Presumably, then, the precinct of Ge was on or above the Treasury
terrace, and just at the point where he descends stands the small
building VIII, the so-called Treasury of Kyrene (Fig. 49).
This building Dörpfeld identified with the Gaion. It is too small
and its walls are too thin for a treasury. Also they seem to have
been covered with several coats of stucco, and portions of a
stucco moulding were found, both of which are features rather
of an altar than a treasury. Moreover, it stands on the highest
point of the terrace, and Pausanias appropriately uses the expres-
sion ' on the Gaion ' ($\epsilon\pi\grave{\iota}\ \tau\hat{\wp}\ \Gamma\alpha\acute{\iota}\wp$). Here, then, we may place
the Altars of Ge and of Themis and the Stomion, which was
probably an artificial cleft like that in the Gaion at Athens into
which honey-cakes were thrown.[2]

The ash or earth altar is the simplest and most primitive form
of altar, and the cults with which it is associated are as a rule
extremely ancient.[3] Certainly this is true of the cults of Zeus
and Ge, while the ritual of Hera in this as in other details reflects
the ritual of Zeus. Pausanias always notices such altars when
he finds them.[4] He compares the Altar of Zeus with the ash
altar of Hera at Samos, which he describes as hardly more
conspicuous than what the Athenians call temporary hearths
($\alpha\grave{\upsilon}\tau o\sigma\chi\epsilon\delta\acute{\iota}\alpha s\ \grave{\epsilon}\sigma\chi\acute{\alpha}\rho\alpha s$). He mentions ash altars of Apollo Spodios

[1] P. v. 14. 10 ; *Olympia*, i, pp. 75, 84, ii, p. 48.
[2] Weniger, *op. cit.*, p. 426 ; P. i. 18. 7. He, however, places the Gaion above the
Treasury of Sikyon.   [3] Curtius, *Altare v. Olympia*, p. 43.
[4] P. v. 13. 8 ; ix. 11. 2 ; viii. 38. 7.

48. SHRINE AT WEST END OF TREASURY TERRACE

49. ALTAR OF GE ON TREASURY TERRACE (VIII)

at Delphi, and of Zeus Lykaios on Mount Lykaion. There was a conical ash altar on Mount Ainos in Kephallenia, and an ash altar of Hermes on Mount Kyllene.[1] The great altar of Apollo at Thermon was also probably an ash altar, if we may judge from the thick layer of ashes that marks its site.

THE MONTHLY OFFERING

Once a month a solemn sacrifice was offered at all the altars.[2] ' They sacrifice ', says Pausanias, ' after an ancient fashion. They burn upon the altars frankincense and cakes kneaded with honey, and they place upon them branches of olive and pour libations of wine. Only to the nymphs and the Despoinai they do not offer wine, nor upon the common altar of the Gods.' Pausanias gives a list of seventy altars, and though few of them can be identified we can trace the general course of the procession.[3] Early in the morning it gathered in the court of the Prytaneion, headed by the Theokolos, the Seers, the Libation pourer, with other subordinate officials. First they offer sacrifice on the Hearth of Hestia, then make their way to the Temple of Zeus, within which was a small altar. Thence they move northwards to the Great Altar of Zeus and the Altar of Hera, then eastwards to the entrance of the Stadion. Next they mount the Treasury steps ; then returning into the Altis again they make their way to the south-west corner, thence to the Hippodrome, from which they return to the processional entrance and so to the Prytaneion. It has been suggested that the course of the procession was divided into two halves with an interval between. But there is no evidence of any such division, nor, considering the simplicity of the ritual, does it seem necessary. The Greeks were not a sedentary people, and were accustomed to long processions and ceremonies.

If we only knew the history of these altars we should know the religious history of Olympia. We can see that they represent every stage in that history, but we do not know who founded them or why or when. Altars of Zeus of course occur with various

---

[1] *Schol.*, Apollonios Rhodios, ii. 297 ; Geminus, i. 14. The great ash altar of Pergamon is an instance of the love of archaism so common in Hellenistic times.

[2] v. 15–16.

[3] v. Weniger, *Klio*, ix. 291 ; xiv. 398. His general conclusions are sound, though I disagree with him in many details. Want of space forbids me to discuss these articles here.

titles. But next to him in importance comes, as I have already pointed out, not Hera but Artemis. Athene, too, has four altars, while Hera, besides her ash altar, has only one. The gods of the Palaistra, Hermes and Apollo, have several altars. There are altars to the nymphs, to the rivers Alpheios and Kladeos, and to such late abstractions as Tyche and Kairos. Very occasionally we can guess the historical occasion of an altar. The altar of Ergane, for example, suggests the work of Pheidias, that of Concord the Elean statue to Concord.

Three, possibly four, double altars[1] figure in the list. Herakles, according to tradition, founded six double altars. Pindar mentions them in his Fifth Olympian Ode ; it seems to have been the custom for victors in the games to celebrate their victory by sacrificing upon them. They were dedicated to the following pairs of deities :

1. Zeus and Poseidon. P. v. 24. 1 (14. 4 ?)
2. Hera and Athene.
3. Hermes and Apollo. P. v. 14. 8.
4. Dionysos and the Charites. P. v. 14. 10.
5. Artemis and Alpheios. P. v. 14. 6.
6. Kronos and Rhea.

This group of altars is certainly not primitive, the conception of a Pantheon of Twelve Gods, though widely spread, being a comparatively late development of Olympian religion. The earliest definite recognition of it is the founding of the Altar of the Twelve Gods at Athens by the younger Peisistratos. The establishment of such a Pantheon was particularly appropriate at Olympia, which was a resort for the whole of Hellas. It was a definite assertion of its national Panhellenic character, and as such was not likely to have taken place before the beginning of the sixth century, when the national character of Olympia was first fully recognized. Weniger assigns the founding of the six double altars to the 50th Olympiad, when, as we have seen, important changes were taking place at Olympia, and no time seems more probable. I cannot, however, agree with him in

---

[1] The text of P. v. 14. 4 is defective. We may with safety restore the mention of Zeus Laoitas and Poseidon Laoitas. Cf. Wernicke, *Jahrb.* ix. 90. Weniger would insert the other two missing altars (*Klio*, ix. 291). For the six double altars v. Mauer, *De Aris Graecorum plurimis deis in commune positis*, pp. 5 ff. ; Roberts and Preller, *Gk. Myth.*, p. 110.

regarding the double altars as symbolical of the union of Elis and Pisa, a union which, according to him, was effected by the complete destruction of Pisa. Were this the case, we should expect to find an Elean and Pisatan element represented in each pair, and this we certainly do not find : it is doubtful, indeed, if a single pair can be so divided. We must be content to see in the twelve deities a local Pantheon in which the local deities of Olympia are united with the chief deities of Hellas.

The local character of this list is evident when we compare it with the much more symmetrical list given by a scholiast in a note on Apollonios Rhodios, which is generally supposed to be the list of the twelve gods worshipped at Athens to whom the younger Peisistratos dedicated an altar. This list is as follows :

1. Zeus and Hera.
2. Poseidon and Demeter.
3. Hephaistos and Athene.
4. Apollo and Artemis.
5. Ares and Aphrodite.
6. Hermes and Hestia.

This list, however, certainly does not correspond to that of the gods represented on the Parthenon pediment, where the local element is again prominent. These variations show how very fluid was the conception of the Greek Pantheon.

The list of altars on which the monthly offerings were made does not include all the altars. There were various reasons why an altar might be omitted. Thus the Altar of Zeus Horkios in the Bouleuterion was felt perhaps to be reserved for the solemn oath-taking by competitors in the games. Other altars had priests or priestesses of their own, for example the altars of Kronos, of Eileithyia, and of Demeter Chamyne. Such altars were known as hieratic : the monthly offering was non-hieratic in that it was not offered by the priest of any special god but by the religious officials of Olympia.

A sanctuary like Olympia, with its multitude of altars and sacrifices daily, monthly, yearly, required a considerable number of such officials. Pausanias enumerates those responsible for the monthly offering, the Theokolos, the seers, the Spondophoroi, the Exegetes, the flute-player, and the wood-cutter. These and many others are all mentioned in a series of inscriptions which record the names of the officials.

THE LISTS OF OFFICIALS

This remarkable series of inscriptions [1] contains no fewer than eighty-four lists, beginning with Olympiad 186 (36 B.C.) and ending with Olympiad 261 (A.D. 265). They are inscribed on gable-headed stelai of marble, made from tiles of the Temple of Zeus. The gables are decorated with Akroteria and contain in the field a wreath or other emblem and the inscription ΔΙΟΣ ΙΕΡΑ, or after the close of the first century ΔΙΟΡ ΙΕΡΑ.[2]

The date is given by the number of the Olympiad. Each period of four years was divided into three periods, ' the Olympiad ', ' the interval before the Truce ', ' the interval after the Truce ',[3] each period having its own list of officials. We have no means of determining the length of these three periods. The officials serving during the ' Olympiad ' would naturally be responsible for the festival. The preparation of the festival was a lengthy business ; the athletes, we know, had to undergo ten months training. At Delphi invitations to the Pythia were sent out six months before. It is probable, therefore, that their period of office fell mostly before the festival and began at least ten months before it. It appears to have ended in the month of Athenaios [4] following the festival, but we do not know when this month fell. ' The period after the truce ' seems to have lasted till two years after the festival,[5] and it is therefore probable that the three periods were of equal length, i. e. sixteen or seventeen months.

The officials named are those who officiated at the daily, monthly, and yearly sacrifices at all non-hieratic rites. We do not know what part they played in the Olympic festival or what were their relations to the Hellanodikai or to the priest of Olympian Zeus. The principal officials appear in all the lists. Chief of these were the three Theokoloi. The earliest inscription found at Olympia makes mention of the ' Theokolos who was officiating at the time '.[6] They seem to have been elected by lot [7] from

---

[1] *Olympia*, v, nos. 58–141.

[2] The archaistic revival of the Rhotakismos is typical of this period (*ib.*, pp. 86, 176).

[3] The formulae in twelve lists are ἐπὶ τῆς . . . ’Ολυμπιάδος; in ten lists μετεκεχήρου τοῦ πρὸ τῆς . . . ’Ολυμπιάδος; in fourteen lists μετεκεχήρου τοῦ μετὰ τὴν . . . ’Ολυμπιάδα.

[4] Inscription 111 has the unusual formula ’Αθαναίω τῷ μετὰ τὴν σμη´ ’Ολυμπιάδα.   [5] *Olympia*, v, p. 208.

[6] *Ib.*, no. 1 ὁ Θεοκόλορ ὄρτιρ τόκα θεοκολέοι.   [7] *Olympia*, v, no. 107.

the noblest families in Elis and to have been men of ripe age, for their sons and grandsons appear sometimes in the same lists holding subordinate posts. They officiated in turn for a month at a time,[1] and had an official residence, the Theokoleon.

The Theokoloi were assisted in the sacrifices by the Spondophoroi, who were sometimes their sons and were possibly nominated by them. The word spondophoros has two meanings, (1) a libation pourer, (2) a truce bearer. The proclamation of a truce was always accompanied by libation, and Pindar describes the heralds who proclaimed the Sacred Truce as the Spondophoroi of Zeus. It is clear that the spondophoroi of the inscriptions were primarily libation pourers. Whether they were also the heralds who proclaimed the truce we cannot say. The basis of a statue of a spondophoros found at Olympia bears a herald's staff.

The younger members of noble families officiated at the sacrifices as dancers, Epispondorchestai. Of these there were also three. They danced to the strains of the flute. The flute-player, auletes, or spondaules also played at the games during the pentathlon. In the third century the flute-player and the dancers were often temple slaves, and so was the scribe or grammateus.

Next in importance to the Theokoloi were the seers or Manteis.[2] Of these there were at first two, but after A.D. 180 four, usually divided evenly between the two families, the Iamidai and the Klytiadai. The seers held office for life. Their office was hereditary, and when the true succession failed recourse was had to adoption. Having knowledge of the will of Zeus they were the special guardians of his altar, and their presence was necessary at all sacrifices. With the seers is associated the Exegetes, whose duty it was to give decisions on all questions of religious law and ritual, to expound oracles and omens. Hence he was an authority on local tradition and history, and came to be recognized as a sort of guide. In some of the lists he even bears the title of Periegetes, or guide.

Of the officials whose names occur only occasionally or disappear in the later lists, the most important are the Kathemerothytes and the Epimeletes. The former was obviously the

---

[1] P. v. 15. 10.
[2] v. Weniger, *Die Seher v. Olympia*, in *Archiv für Religionswissenschaft*, xviii. 53–117.

official who offered the daily sacrifice on the Altar of Zeus. It may be that he was regarded merely as an assistant of the Theokoloi, and like other subordinate officials his name was omitted after the first century.[1] On some of the lists his name is the last. The Epimeletes, on the other hand, was perhaps the most important official at Olympia next to the priest of Zeus. The two titles are sometimes coupled together as the climax of the Elean *Cursus honorum*.[2] On two of the lists his name appears at the head as the eponymous magistrate of the year,[3] while on a third list, one of the latest, the priest's name is similarly used.[4] Elsewhere he occurs immediately after the Spondophoroi or the Manteis. Though the office is mentioned in no list after the first century A.D., we know from other inscriptions that it continued to exist with undiminished importance. The full title is given as $\epsilon\pi\iota\mu\epsilon\lambda\eta\tau\grave{\eta}s$ $\tau\hat{\omega}\nu$ $\tau o\hat{\nu}$ $\Delta\iota\acute{o}s$ or $\epsilon\pi\iota\mu\epsilon\lambda\eta\tau\grave{\eta}s$ $\Hry'O\lambda\upsilon\mu\pi\acute{\iota}as$,[5] from which we gather that he was the keeper of the Sanctuary and its treasures, and responsible for the upkeep of the buildings and repairs. A series of tiles, one of which is certainly earlier than our era, is dated by the name of the Epimeletes.[6] Such being the duties of the Epimeletes he had no direct concern with the ritual of Olympia, a fact which may explain the omission of his name in the later lists. The same explanation perhaps holds for the Kleidouchoi, or key-keepers, who varied in number from one to five and who were perhaps assistant-treasurers to the Epimeletes. They are not included in any lists later than A.D. 63. For the same reason these lists make no mention of officials connected with athletics such as the Gymnasiarchos or the Alytarches or of the political magistrates of Elis.

The other officials are clearly subordinate. The woodcutter, who provided the white poplar wood used for sacrifices, is mentioned in two of the earliest lists, and only reappears in the third century. Similarly the Mageiros, or cook, whose duty it was to cook the meat of the sacrifice for the feast in the Prytaneion, is not mentioned in any list of the second century, and at the beginning of the third century we find that two cooks were required. The Oinochoos, or cup-bearer, who may have assisted the Spondophoroi, also disappears after the first century. One of the earliest lists (62) mentions also a chief cook ($\alpha\rho\chi\iota$-$\mu\acute{\alpha}\gamma\epsilon\iota\rho os$), an architect ($\alpha\rho\chi\iota\tau\acute{\epsilon}\kappa\tau\omega\nu$), and a physician ($\iota\alpha\tau\rho\acute{o}s$).

---

[1] *Olympia*, v, p. 138.   [2] *Ib.*, no. 437.   [3] *Ib.*, nos. 65, 80.
[4] *Ib.*, no. 124.   [5] *Ib.*, nos. 65, 80, 568.   [6] *Ib.*, nos. 728–52.

None of these titles occurs again. The menial character of the duties performed by these officials fully explains their omission from the lists, in which we trace perhaps the spirit of aristocratic and priestly exclusiveness which is noticeable also at Athens after the time of Hadrian. When, however, temple slaves were included in the lists as flute-players or dancers, there could be no longer any objection to the inclusion of free men holding other subordinate offices.[1]

HERO SHRINES

' The Eleans ', says Pausanias,[2] ' pour libations also to heroes and wives of heroes who are honoured in Elis and among the Aitolians.' The altars of heroes are properly termed ἐσχάραι, not βωμοί, and they had no share in the monthly offerings. Their sacrifices were usually annual. The principal heroes worshipped at Olympia were of course Pelops and Hippodameia. To Pelops a black ram was offered once a year by ' the yearly officials '.[3] Once a year, we are told, the youths of the Peloponnese lashed themselves over his grave till the blood ran down.[4] Mr. Cornford suggests that this latter statement is a mistaken attempt on the part of a scholiast to explain Pindar's αἱμακουρίαι ἀγλααί (O. i. 90) : but in view of the similar rite on the Altar of Orthia at Sparta we are hardly justified in rejecting the statement. We have no evidence that these yearly rites were in any way connected with the Olympic festival, but it seems likely that sacrifice was offered to Pelops at the festival ; if so, presumably on the eve of the festival. A scholiast tells us that sacrifice was offered to Pelops before Zeus, and we know that sacrifice to the Olympians was offered before midday, sacrifice to the heroes after midday.

Of the worship of Hippodameia [5] all that we know is that there was a yearly ceremony conducted by the women. The officiating women were possibly the sixteen matrons who presided over the Heraia, for they were divided into two companies, half of them forming the chorus of Physkoa, half that of Hippodameia. There is no evidence, however, for connecting this yearly ceremony with the Heraia.

---

[1] *Olympia*, v, p. 139.   [2] v. 15. 12.   [3] P. v. 13. 2.
[4] Schol. Pind., *O.* i. 146 ; *Themis*, p. 213.
[5] P. vi. 20. 7. Weniger (*Klio*, vi. 380 ff.) conjectures that the ceremony was an *enagismos* that took place on the eve of the Heraia, and consisted of burnt offerings and libations into a trench, an *anaklesis* by means of a hymn and a dance.

Pausanias describes the Pelopion [1] as a grove surrounded by a stone wall with an entrance on the west side, and containing the altar of Pelops and some statues. Only a small portion of the wall remains, but from the foundations we learn that it had the shape of an irregular pentagon. In the south-west corner was the entrance with a Doric propylaion raised on three steps and approached by a stone ramp. Dörpfeld assigns to this porch some pillars and architectural blocks found in the Byzantine wall. It seems to have been built in the second half of the fifth century and to have taken the place of an earlier building.

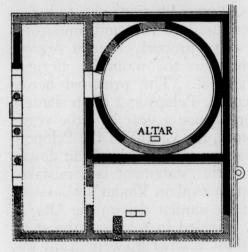

50. Plan of Heroon

Many other heroes were doubtless honoured at Olympia. To some hero or heroes unknown belonged the small heroon and altar [2] discovered to the north of the Byzantine church (Figs. 50 and 2). It is a circular chamber 8·04 metres in diameter, contained within a square enclosure. To the south was another room which may have contained an altar. Along the west stretched a pillared entrance hall, giving access to the circular chamber. The latter is well preserved. The foundation was formed of a ring of stone slabs sunk into the ground, on which was set another ring of stones 1·25 metres long, 68 centimetres high, and 47 centimetres thick. The outside of these blocks was left rough, the inside was rounded off, while the inner half of the upper surface was carefully levelled to a uniform height of 63 centimetres. From this we may infer that the superstructure was built of woodwork and sun-baked brick, protected probably by a conical roof to which belong numerous triangular tiles found in the interior.

The most interesting feature of this heroon is the small earth altar [3] found against the centre of the south wall. It is 54 centimetres long, 35 centimetres high, and 36 centimetres wide. The top is covered with thin bricks which show traces of burning; the side is coated with a thick layer of stucco. This

[1] *Olympia*, ii, p. 165.   [2] *Ib.*, pp. 105, 165   [3] *Ib.*, v, no. 662.

was found on examination to consist of some thirteen or more thin layers on which were remains of painting. The painting in all cases was similar in character. Around the bottom of the two sides and front of the altar ran two branches meeting in the centre, usually in a knot, in one case in a rose. Above the branches was inscribed ΗΡΩΟΡ, ΗΡΩΟΣ, ΗΡΩ ; in one case the plural ΗΡΩΩΝ occurs. Why the plural is used we do not know : nor do we know who was the hero to whom the altar was

dedicated. Curtius supposed that the hero was Iamos, and that the heroes were Iamos and Klytios. But there is no evidence to support this theory, nor is it probable ; for in the Roman period to which the inscriptions belong the Iamidai and Klytiadai are regularly mentioned together in official lists.

51. Inscriptions on altar in Heroon

Though the inscriptions are late, the shrine itself is evidently old, how old we cannot say. Hero worship was prevalent at all periods of Greek history, and especially so in the Peloponnese.[1] Separated as the Heroon is merely by a narrow lane from the west wall of the Theokoleon, we should certainly conjecture that it was older than the latter building. If so, it must have stood by itself apart, and its site was perhaps determined by the fact that the ancient road from the west ran close by. Shrines of heroes were frequently placed along roads, especially in the neighbourhood of towns, and this heroon stood appropriately on the road to the Grove of Zeus.

[1] Cf. *B.S.A.* xi. 89–90 ; xii. 288–94 ; Roscher, ii. 2493–6.

XII
The Heraion

Παῖ Ῥέας ἅ τε Πρυτανεῖα λέλογχας Ἑστία
Ζηνὸς ὑψίστου κασιγνήτα καὶ ὁμοθρόνου Ἥρας.

Pindar, Nem. xi. 1.

THE Heraion is the earliest temple, probably the earliest historic building, of Olympia; and it is likewise the best preserved. The stone socle on which the walls of the cella rested is standing, and the lower drums of the columns of the colonnade are still in position, some of them 9 feet high. Two of the columns at the east end have been completely restored. Standing out against the dark background of pine-trees they are the most imposing monument in the Altis to-day.

The temple, according to Elean tradition, was built by the people of Skillous eight years after Oxylos became king,[1] and Dr. Dörpfeld long maintained therefore that it belonged to the tenth or eleventh century.[2] But, as has been already mentioned, this date is no longer tenable. The discovery of Proto-Corinthian sherds under the foundations has proved that the existing temple cannot be earlier than the close of the eighth century, and this date is confirmed by the differences between the bronzes and other votive offerings found in the upper stratum, which is later than the building of the temple, and those in the lower stratum, which is earlier.

It is, however, quite possible that a more ancient temple already existed on the site, and to this the Elean tradition may refer. Dörpfeld discovered under the floor of the Opisthodome remains of an earlier wall built of large cobbles, which from the thick layer of ashes surrounding it seems to have been an altar.[3] At a still lower level, under the rubble formed by the levelling of the site for the temple, there was a thick layer of ashes containing numerous fragments of bronze and iron, terra-cotta figurines, and pottery, including a remarkable figure of a helmeted warrior which very probably represents Zeus (Fig. 54). The

[1] P. v. 16. 1.   [2] Olympia, ii, pp. 35, 36.
[3] Weege, Ath. Mitt. xxxvi, p. 191. For Dörpfeld's latest excavations v. infra, p. 216.

52. HERAION FROM NORTH-EAST

53. HERAION FROM WEST

deposit seems to cover a considerable period. For, while some of the pottery resembles the archaic pottery of the prehistoric village, the bronzes and terra-cottas are similar to those found in the earlier excavations. The fact that a layer of river-gravel separates the two deposits suggests that the site was for a time deserted.[1]

It is now generally agreed that the Heraion was originally a joint Temple of Zeus and Hera, and contained the cult images of Zeus and Hera, the latter seated on a throne, the former standing beside her bearded and helmeted. Such is the obvious meaning of an unfortunately mutilated passage in Pausanias,[2] and his statement is corroborated by the discovery at the west end of the cella of the large limestone base on which the two cult images stood. It was only after the Temple of Zeus was built in the fifth century that the Heraion became the monopoly of Hera. The failure to recognize this fact, and the belief in the extreme antiquity of the Heraion, have been the cause of most of the wild speculations about the cult of Hera at Olympia.

Why was the first great temple built in the sanctuary of Zeus a joint temple of Zeus and Hera? The centre of the worship of Hera was Argos, and I have therefore ventured to suggest that her worship was introduced by Pheidon of Argos when he usurped control of the festival.[3] With this conjecture the date of the temple agrees. Further, it may explain the traditional connexion of the Skilluntines with the building of the temple.

54. Archaic statu-
ette of Zeus (?)

For Pheidon invaded Elis as the ally of the Pisatans and Arkadians, and the chief fact that we know about Skillous is its constant hostility to the Eleans.[4] It is quite in accordance with the Panhellenic policy of the tyrant that he should have endeavoured by means of his Arkadian allies to secure the

[1] *Ath. Mitt.* xxxi, p. 205 ; xxxii, pp. iv–vi ; *Year's Work*, 1906, p. 6 ; 1907, p. 14 ; *J. H. S.* xxvii. 295 ; xxviii. 331.
[2] P. v. 17. 1 τῆς Ἥρας δέ ἐστιν ἐν τῷ ναῷ Διός ... τὸ δὲ Ἥρας ἄγαλμα καθή-μενόν ἐστιν ἐπὶ θρόνῳ, παρέστηκε δὲ γένειά τε ἔχων καὶ ἐπικείμενος κυνῆν ἐπὶ τῇ κεφαλῇ· ἔργα δέ ἐστιν ἁπλᾶ. From the emphatic position of Διός it looks as if Pausanias was surprised to find the place of honour in Hera's temple occupied, or at least shared, by Zeus. [3] *Supra*, p. 88. [4] P. v. 6. 4 ; vi. 22. 4.

association of his native goddess with the god of Olympia. Further, this conjecture explains how it is that the worship of Hera played so little part in the history of Olympia. The influence of Argos was but short-lived. With the conquest of Messenia Sparta became the predominant power in the western Peloponnese, while the power of Pisa steadily declined till in the fifth century Triphylia became a dependency of Elis and the control of Olympia became the monopoly of that state. Hence, though Hera sat beside Zeus in the Heraion, though she had her earth altar, and her games modelled on those of Zeus, no fresh

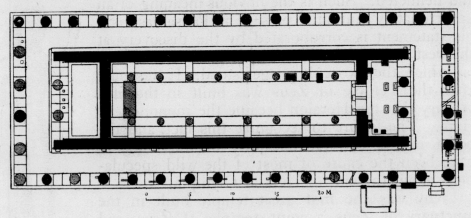

55. Plan of Heraion

altars, no statues, were erected to her in the Altis, not a single mention of her occurs in the whole range of Olympic inscriptions. The only record of her cult is the occurrence of her head on the coins of Elis when Argive influence revived towards the close of the fifth century.[1]

The Heraion [2] was a long, low, narrow temple of the Doric order, and it is interesting architecturally for the many archaic features which it presents, and especially for the evidence it affords of the transition from wood to stone.

The foundations were constructed of a coarse local conglomerate, which may be distinguished from that used for the Temple of Zeus by the presence of numerous oyster shells. To secure a level site a terrace was formed by cutting away the lower slope of the Hill of Kronos. At the western end the foundation was strengthened by an additional layer of large stones

[1] *Supra*, p. 116.   [2] *Olympia*, ii, pp. 27 ff. ; P. v. 16-20.

bonded with clay, but in spite of this precaution the western and southern portions of the temple show considerable settlement.

Like the old Temple of Athene at Athens, the Heraion had only a single step. Even this step was, on the north side, buried beneath the soil washed down from the hill, while on the south side the soil was washed away, laying bare part of the foundation and thus producing the appearance of a second step. In consequence easy flights of steps were arranged at either end of the south side to give access to the temple, that at the east end being still in existence. The stepped retaining wall, built along the foot of the hill in the fifth century, checked the further washing down of the soil.

Measured along the top of the step the temple is 50·01 metres long by 18·75 wide. The colonnade consisted of sixteen pillars on either side, six at either end. The pillars have a height of of 5·22 metres, or 16 Pheidonian feet,[1] half the height of those of the Temple of Zeus, while the diameter varies from 1·02 to 1·29 metres. The intercolumniation measured from axis to axis is 3·26 metres, or 10 Pheidonian feet. The long and narrow proportions of the temple, the number of pillars on the sides, their lowness in comparison with their diameter, and the wide intercolumniation are all features characteristic of archaic temples. The chief peculiarity of the pillars is their remarkable variety. They differ from one another in style, size, structure, and material. Not only are the pillars at the end thicker than those at the sides, but those at the sides are all different in diameter. Most of them have the usual twenty flutings, one has only sixteen, and there is considerable difference in the depth of the flutings. The drums are usually low, but in three columns they are three times the usual height, and three were apparently monoliths. Some have small dowel-holes, some large, others have none at all. Lastly, the eighteen capitals found represent every type of Doric capital from the bulging echinus of the earliest period to the flat, straight outlines of Hellenistic and Roman art.

The explanation usually accepted of these variations is that the temple was originally constructed of timber, and that as the wooden pillars decayed they were replaced by stone. This explanation seemed satisfactory as long as it was supposed that the temple was built in the tenth or eleventh century. Now that

---

[1] This may be a mere coincidence. If not, the use of the scale attributed by tradition to Pheidon is significant.

we know that it cannot be much earlier than the seventh century
it is difficult to understand the early date of some of the stone
pillars, and the theory requires some modification. The Heraion,
it is pointed out,[1] was probably the earliest large temple in
Greece : large temples were not needed till large stone images
began to be made. Hence the Heraion was somewhat of an
experiment. The builders tried to use both stone and timber,
of which there was an abundant supply in the locality. But
the wood proved unsatisfactory, possibly from warping, and so at an early date it had to be replaced by stone.

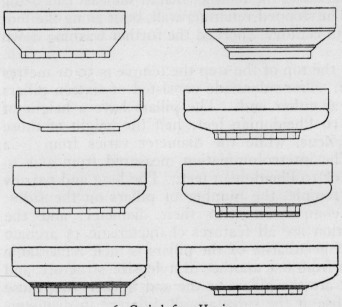

56. Capitals from Heraion

Of the entablature not a trace has been found, and we may conclude therefore that it too was of wood and that being protected by the roof it never required to be replaced by stone. This conclusion is
confirmed by the absence on the top of the capitals of the
holes that would be necessary for fixing a stone architrave, and
also by the unusual distance between the columns. Indeed,
it was only the fact that the architrave was of wood that
rendered the substitution of stone columns a comparatively easy
task. We may further feel certain that it was surmounted by the
usual triglyph frieze : for the intercolumnar distance at the
corners is 0·20 to 0·30 metre less than that along the sides, and
this well-known peculiarity of Doric temples is a necessary
result of a frieze of triglyphs and metopes.

Dörpfeld supposed that the temple had originally a flat clay
roof. This conclusion seems less probable, since we know that

[1] G. Rodenwaldt in *Ath. Mitt.* xliv. 183. His argument is an additional
confirmation of the later date of the temple.

the still earlier temple at Sparta [1] had a gable roof. Certainly the Heraion had at an early period a gable roof of terra-cotta tiles. These tiles were slightly concave, so that when placed together their edges formed a ridge which was covered by narrow semicircular tiles. The ends of the ridges were closed by terra-cotta disks. The roof-ridge was similarly protected, and ended in large circular akroteria of terra-cotta. One of these has been reconstructed. It is 2·24 metres in diameter, and richly ornamented with geometric bands in painting and relief (Fig. 61). p. 222

The temple proper was symmetrically arranged with opisthodomos and pronaos formed by the projecting walls of the cella. The ends of the antae were encased in wood, and between them were two pilasters which were also originally of wood and supported a wooden entablature. The opisthodomos could only be entered from the colonnade, and the spaces between the pillars were closed with doors, the marks of which are still visible on the floor.

The walls of the cella are of unusual thickness, 1·18 metres. They are built of four courses of squared blocks, faced on the outside with upright slabs. The blocks are slightly concave at the sides, so that only the edges meet, and the upper surface is similarly hollowed except in the blocks of the top course, which were left flat, probably because baulks of timber rested on them. No clamps or dowels were used in the building. From the thickness of the walls and their uniform height it is clear that the superstructure was of a different material, probably of sun-dried brick strengthened by horizontal baulks of timber which dovetailed into the wooden casing of the antae. Sun-dried brick was widely used for private dwelling-houses and also for palaces and temples. When the roof of the temple fell in, the action of the weather rapidly dissolved the unprotected wall, and converted it into the thick layer of clay that was found within and around the temple. Possibly this upper wall was covered with stucco, which was freely used in the buildings of Olympia.

The ceiling of the cella must have been flat, for Pausanias [2] tells us that the body of a soldier was found in the space between the ceiling and the roof. There was no means of lighting the temple except the door : but in the clear atmosphere of a Greek summer such light is amply sufficient.

A wide doorway gave entrace to the cella from the pronaos.

[1] *B. S. A* xiv. 20.　　　　[2] v. 20. 4.

The doors were probably of wood covered with bronze, as were the door-posts, which were secured to the walls by horizontal beams, the marks of which are still visible. The cella was divided by two rows of eight pillars set in a line with the outer pillars. The alternate pillars were originally joined to the walls by short cross-walls. These walls served to support the great beams of the roof, which probably reached right across the temple. Similar cross-walls ending in pillars occur in the temple of Bassai. When the wooden pillars were replaced by stone these cross-walls became unnecessary and were cut away. The binding stones of the central course which were let into the main wall were cut in half, as can be clearly seen in the existing wall. Three small Doric capitals found near the temple probably belong to these pillars. When the change took place we cannot say. It has been suggested that the cross-walls were intended to separate the temple into eight chapels which were used by the sixteen women who wove the peplos for Hera. In the time of Pausanias these women did their work at Elis. But we do not know whether the weaving of the peplos was part of the original ritual of Hera. If we are right in supposing that the Heraion was originally a temple of Zeus and Hera, and that Zeus was the chief deity, it is hardly probable that the temple should have been planned with a view to the worship of Hera. Certainly there is no sufficient evidence for connecting the division of the cella into chapels with the weaving of the peplos. Moreover, architectural considerations are quite adequate to account for the building of the cross-walls.

Near the west end, between the last pair of pillars, was found the large limestone base on which were placed the images of Zeus and Hera. As it completely blocks the space between the pillars it cannot have been placed there before the removal of the cross-walls. If it existed previously it must have stood against the west wall, unless, as Treu supposes, it was originally shorter. Zeus, as has been already stated, was represented standing, bearded and helmeted, an unusual type which we may possibly recognize in the archaic bronze figure found under the temple (Fig. 54). Hera was seated on a throne. A lion's claw with a foot resting on it, also found under the temple, possibly formed part of her footstool. It is of the same limestone as the basis, and also as a colossal head of a goddess found to the west of the temple in the Palaistra which is generally supposed

57. COLOSSAL HEAD OF HERA

58. PEDIMENTAL SCULPTURES OF MEGARIAN TREASURY

to belong to the statue of Hera (Fig. 57). A statue of such soft material could hardly have been set up in the open air, and at the period to which the head belongs no temple existed at Olympia large enough to receive it except the Heraion. Moreover, the head itself is eminently appropriate to the statue of Hera.

The goddess wears a high crown of upright leaves. Her hair, which is confined by a fillet, is worked in parallel locks ending in a row of flat curls. The eyes are large, the eyeballs flat and sloping downwards, the pupils marked by circles incised with a compass. The nose is broken off. The mouth is thin and very slightly curved, ending on either side in a dimple. The cheek-bones are prominent, but the cheeks and chin are full and rounded. In spite of its roughness and archaism there is something very lifelike and natural about the face, which is good-humoured and strong. There are indications that as in other archaic statues the head was painted: there were remains of dark red on the fillet and of a brighter red on the hair.

The temple was crowded within and without with votive offerings and works of art. The opisthodome, which served as a treasury, contained the chest of Kypselos, an ivory bed supposed to have been a toy of Hippodameia, the diskos of Iphitos, and the ivory and gold table on which the prizes were placed.[1]

In the cella between the pillars were numerous works of art of different periods, including chryselephantine statues by Smilis, Dorykleidas, Theokles, and other early sculptors. The group of the Hesperidai by Theokles had been transferred to the Heraion from the Treasury of Epidamnos, and the Athene of Medon probably from the Megarian Treasury. Other statues came from the Philippeion. We do not know when or why they were transferred. It has been suggested that at a late date, possibly before Nero's visit, the Heraion was turned into an art museum, where statues of various periods were collected and arranged historically. But there is no evidence for this conjecture.

Of all the statues enumerated by Pausanias the only one surviving is the famous Hermes of Praxiteles, which was found in front of its pedestal between the second and third columns from the east end of the north side. Between the first and

---

[1] P. v. 20. For the reconstruction of the chest of Kypselos, which is described at length by Pausanias, v. Gardner, *Gk. Sculpture*, i. 74; Stuart Jones, in *J. H. S.*, xiv, Pl. I; Furtwängler, *Meisterwerke*, Fig. 135.

second columns was found the statue of a Roman lady. Treu
identifies her with Poppaea Sabina, and supposes that the statue
of Nero was placed opposite to her.

In the pronaos were found six pedestals covered with marble.
The inscriptions on three of these show that they bore the statues
of noble Elean ladies.[1] They belong to the second half of the
first century A.D. At the south-east corner of the temple there
were found four contemporary statues[2] of such ladies, including
one remarkably lifelike and well-preserved head of an elderly
lady of dignified and severe type (Fig. 35). Were they priestesses
of Hera ? We cannot say. Poppaea Sabina was represented as a
priestess. Regilla was a priestess of Demeter, and other priestesses of this goddess are mentioned in inscriptions. But it is
a remarkable fact that there is not a single mention in any inscription of a priestess of Hera.

Under the south colonnade and between the pillars are the
marks of numerous statues, while on the pillars themselves may
still be seen rectangular depressions which must have held reliefs
or votive tablets. Traces of all sorts of bases and stelai are visible
too at the east end, in front of which Hera's altar stood.

THE CULT OF HERA

Of the ritual of Hera and her festival we know only what
Pausanias tells us in a very obscure chapter.[3] We hear of no
priestess of Hera, only of sixteen matrons assisted by sixteen
maidens. These matrons in the time of Pausanias were selected
from the Elean tribes—two from each tribe ; but tradition said
that they had once represented Elis and fifteen other cities, and
had acted as peace-makers in the war between Elis and Pisa.
As these matrons formed two choral bands, one named after
Physkoa, a nymph of hollow Elis, another after Hippodameia
of Pisa, it is generally supposed that they represented eight cities
or villages of Elis and eight of Pisa. Another legend connected
them with Hippodameia, who was represented as the founder of
the Heraia as Pelops was of the Olympic Games. The account
of these sixteen women is further complicated by the assumption
that they are the same as those whom Plutarch[4] calls the Sixteen
Women of Dionysos, perhaps the same as those women of Elis

---

[1] *Olympia*, v, nos. 429, 435, 438.
[2] *Ib.*, iii, Pl. LXII, 6 ; Pl. LXIII, 4, 5 ; Pl. LXIV, 4.
[3] v. 16.   [4] *Mul. Virt.*, p. 251 ; *Is. et Osir.*, p. 35.

59. THE HERMES OF PRAXITELES

whom he represents as invoking the bull god Dionysos to come rushing with his bull feet. There is, however, nothing to indicate that this worship of Dionysos had anything to do with Olympia, and it is not easy to see what the matrons of Hera had to do with the worship of Dionysos.

Before commencing their duties, the sixteen, like the Hellanodikai, purified themselves by the sacrifice of a pig and by lustrations at the fountain of Piera on the sacred road between Elis and Olympia. Their duties were threefold. First they had to weave a new peplos for Hera, to be presented to her every fifth year. Secondly, they presided over the games of Hera. Lastly, they took part in certain religious dances, when and where we do not know.

The practice of presenting a goddess with a new robe is familiar to us from the Panathenaic festival. It was probably known to Minoan ritual, and is found in many parts of the world. We do not know when or why it was introduced at Olympia. It is tempting to connect it with the alliance between Athens, Argos, and Elis in 420 B.C., from which we have dated the revival of Hera's worship, but unfortunately there is no evidence to support the guess.

The games of Hera are an exact counterpart to the Olympic Games. There were foot-races for maidens, divided according to age into three classes. The victors received crowns of olives and had the right of dedicating their statues to Hera. There is in the Vatican a beautiful statue of a girl runner, represented just as Pausanias describes, with hair hanging down her back, short tunic reaching to the knees, and right shoulder bare. The length of the course was less than the Olympic Stadion by a sixth. It is difficult to understand on what ground Curtius and Weniger maintain that the games of Hera were the prototype of the Olympic Games.[1] There is no evidence that athletic sports for women were a feature of a matriarchal age in Greece or in any other land, or that man learnt his athletics from women! The only people in Greece who did encourage sports for women were the Spartan Dorians. If the girls' foot-race at Olympia was introduced by the Dorians it was certainly not the prototype of the race for men. Athletics for women are unknown to Homer, but every Achaian warrior is an ' athletes '.

As the presenting of the peplos was the central rite of the

[1] *Olympia*, i, p. 21 ; *Klio*, xiv. 418.

festival, it follows that it was held every fifth year. We do not
know in what month it was held or whether it was held in the
same year as the Olympic Games or not. From the exclusion
of married women at the latter we should suppose that the two
festivals were perfectly distinct. Weniger[1] argues that the month
of Hera was Parthenios, and that her festival fell on the new
moon of Parthenios alternately a fortnight before or after the
Olympic Games. It is impossible here to examine his argument
in detail; it consists of a series of conjectures, each one of which
is more or less problematical. It implies the existence at the time
of the founding of the Olympic Games of a fully developed
calendar with a definite system of intercalation. It is really
based on the assumption of the antiquity of the cult of Hera at
Olympia, as is his theory of the games of Hera. These theories
thus established are then used as arguments to prove that
antiquity.

ADDENDUM

Since this chapter was written Dörpfeld[2] has again investi-
gated the problem of the Heraion. As the result of further
excavations he concludes that there were three temples on the
site. The first, which he dates at the beginning of the orientalizing
period, i.e. the close of the eighth century B.C., occupied the
site of the cella of the existing temple. It was a temple *in antis*
built of mud-brick walls on a rough stone foundation. To this
he assigns the cult image or images and the lion's claw mentioned
above as forming part of the throne. This temple was burnt
down and was succeeded by a larger temple built on a higher
level with wooden columns and cross-walls to support the roof.
The tradition of these wooden columns was continued in the
existing third temple, which was built at a still higher level,
certainly not later than the seventh century B.C.

[1] *Klio*, iv. 128; x. 28; xiv. 418.
[2] Buschor, in *Kunst. Chronik*, i, p. 307; *Year's Work*, 1923, p. 94. For the
smaller finds and pottery v. Buschor and Schweitzer, *Ath. Mitt.* xlvii, p. 48.

XIII[1]

The Treasuries

WHAT WAS A TREASURY?

NO group of buildings is so instructive for the early history of Olympia as the Treasuries. Standing as they did in a line on a terrace overlooking the Altis, they were a lasting witness to the Panhellenic character of Olympia, and to its connexion with the Greeks beyond the seas. The earliest Treasury was built at the close of the seventh century, the latest shortly after the Persian wars. They were the gifts of the free states of Hellas. Of the eleven states that built them eight were colonies, and they represented the length and breadth of the Greek world. The only two states of the mainland, Megara and Sikyon, owed their prosperity to the trade that passed east and west along the Gulf of Corinth. That Corinth herself built no Treasury at Olympia may perhaps be due to a certain rivalry that we can trace between the Isthmia and the Olympia. The intense devotion that Olympia inspired may be judged from the fact that the terra-cottas, sculptures, even the stones of the Treasuries were often fashioned at home, and transported to Olympia at a cost which we can hardly conceive.

What was a Treasury? The name is somewhat misleading. The Treasuries did not always contain treasures, and it is doubtful if they were primarily intended to do so. Pausanias[2] felt this. Speaking of the Treasury of the Sikyonians at Delphi, he says, ' You must not expect to find any treasures there, nor in any other of the treasuries '. What then were they? In the first place they were temples. They had the form of a temple : the earliest Treasury at Olympia, that of the Geloans, faced east and west like a temple : it is not improbable that altars were attached to some of them. The ancients, too, spoke of them as temples. Polemon, for

---

[1] In this chapter I have in the main followed the two careful studies of the Treasuries by Louis Dyer, *J. H. S.* xxv, p. 294 ; xxvi, p. 46.

[2] P. x. 11. 1.

example, speaks of the temple (ναός) of the Byzantines and the temple of the Metapontines at Olympia. Strabo, after describing the Temple of Hera at Samos, adds that there were close by several little temples (ναίσκοι), obviously of the same type as the Treasuries. Pliny uses the Latin equivalent ' aedes ' of the Treasury of the Cnidians at Delphi.[1]

Here we must note a difference. We associate a temple with the name of some deity or deities, of Zeus, of Hera, or of the Mother—it is the house of the god ; we associate a treasury with the name of some people or state—it is the house of a community. The reason of the difference is clear. The temple is a religious centre for the people dwelling round about it : it is built by them and in honour of the god or gods whom they themselves worship. It bears, therefore, the name of the god : there is no need to ask who built it. The treasury, on the other hand, is an offering dedicated in some sanctuary of exceptional and national sanctity to the presiding god of that sanctuary : and it is dedicated not by the people who dwell around the sanctuary and therefore control it, but by members of distant states or lands who wish to avail themselves of the sanctuary, to keep in touch with it. It bears, therefore, the name of the people who dedicate it : the god to whom it is dedicated is known to all, at Olympia Olympian Zeus, at Delphi Pythian Apollo. Hence the treasury contains no image of the god.

But the Treasuries were not merely temples : they were also οἶκοι. This is the word used for them in the Delian inventories. An οἶκος, in the religious meaning of the word, is a communal house, a building which serves as the religious centre of a community and where its *sacra* are kept. The Treasuries were communal houses for the use of members of the state that dedicated them, and especially for the official Theoroi when they came to the festival. We know how these Theoroi vied with one another in displaying their wealth and splendour, and how they brought with them costly vessels of silver and gold. The state that had a treasury kept in it these sacrificial vessels. The possession of such a house gave to its Theoroi a certain advantage over others, in prestige at all events, even if it conferred no formal privileges. The site of the Treasuries at Olympia was itself calculated to minister to their vanity. Commanding a unique view of the Altis, they were so many royal boxes from the

---

[1] Athenaeus 480 a ; Strabo, p. 637 ; *J. H. S.* xxv, pp. 301 ff.

porches of which the Theoroi or distinguished citizens could watch the processions and sports below. These advantages of course entailed certain responsibilities. The builders were responsible for the upkeep and repairs of the buildings. The existing remains bear evidence of such repairs, and even of more elaborate restorations and additions.

But why were these buildings called θησαυροί? The word may mean either a treasure-house or a treasure, and according to Dyer, these buildings being ἀναθήματα, offerings were them-

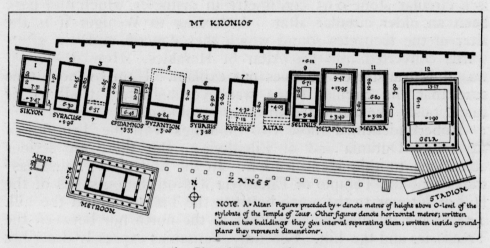

60. Plan of Treasury Terrace

selves described as treasures. A votive offering might take the form of a miniature shrine, and such were the bronze θάλαμοι of Myron preserved in the Sikyonian Treasury. The Treasuries, he argues, were but larger offerings of the same type. Yet though it seems improbable that the Treasuries were originally or exclusively intended to hold treasures, it is certain that before the fifth century rich offerings were placed in them, and this fact alone is sufficient explanation of the name.

THE IDENTIFICATION OF THE TREASURIES

Pausanias enumerates eleven Treasuries[1] from west to east: the excavations have revealed the remains of fourteen buildings on the terrace. Of these the two at the west end are certainly not Treasuries. One of them was destroyed and partly buried

[1] P. v. 19.

in the building of the Exedra. The other is a tiny shrine consisting of a cella about 9 feet square and a portico [1] (Fig. 48). The
walls of the cella were built of blocks of marly limestone carefully
dressed on the inside but left rough on the outside. Towards
the back of the cella is the foundation for an altar or cult image
with a wooden barrier in front. The portico was of wood. In
front of the shrine was a large altar.

This must be the Altar of Herakles or the Kouretes described
by Pausanias as close to the Treasury of the Sikyonians.[2] In it
is a circular stone 0·95 centimetre in diameter, which may have
been an older circular altar. According to Weniger it is the
altar of the Kouretes round which they danced, and was afterwards converted into the Altar of Herakles. How or why it
was thus transferred he does not explain. I am by no means
sure that the circular stone was ever an altar at all: it is
suspiciously like a rejected drum of a column.

Robert identified these two buildings with the Temples of
Aphrodite Ourania and of Eileithyia.[3] But there are serious
objections to this identification. In the first place, Pausanias[4]
states that the Temple of Eileithyia was on the outskirts of the
Hill of Kronos to the north between the Treasuries and the hill.
The shrine in question is neither to the north nor between the
Treasuries and the hill. Secondly, Pausanias expressly describes
the Temple of Eileithyia as consisting of two parts. In the
outer temple was the Altar of Eileithyia, in the inner temple was
worshipped the hero Sosipolis. The outer temple was open to
the public, but none might enter the inner temple except the
aged priestess of Sosipolis, who entered with a white veil over her
head to make lustrations and offer honey-cakes to the hero, while
in the outer temple maidens and women sang a hymn. The
description of the double temple and the ceremony that took
place there is quite inconsistent with our tiny shrine, nor is
there any justification in identifying the altar in front of it with
the Altar of Eileithyia, which Pausanias expressly states was
inside the temple.

Robert's theory is developed by Weniger,[5] who sees in our
small shrine the Idaean cave where he supposes the Cretan cult
of the Mother and the Child to have been long established. No

[1] *Olympia*, i. 75, ii. 48 ; *J. H. S.* xxv. 295.   [2] v. 14. 7.
[3] *Ath. Mitt.* xviii. 37–45 ; Frazer, *Pausanias*, iv. 76.   [4] vi. 20. 2.
[5] *Klio*, vii. 145 ; cp. Miss Harrison, *Themis*, p. 239.

natural cave of course can have ever existed on the hill : it is possible that an artificial grotto existed, and it is just conceivable that our shrine with its rough-hewn walls may have been regarded as such. The whole theory, however, is a series of conjectures quite incapable of proof. There is no proof that the Mother and Child were ever worshipped at Olympia. The very existence of an Idaean cave at Olympia is uncertain. It depends on a statement of Demetrios of Skepsis quoted by a scholiast on Pindar,[1] and the scholiast adds, ' Others say that Demetrios does not refer to Olympia but to Crete.'

To whom then did the shrine belong ? Dörpfeld connects it with the neighbouring altar, and suggests that it was a shrine of Herakles. Yet we have no evidence that Herakles had a shrine at Olympia. Had Pausanias seen one, he must surely have mentioned it. Possibly, like the building to the west of it, it had fallen into disuse and perhaps been buried when the Exedra was built. If so, Pausanias would never have seen it.

Of the twelve foundations that remain, numbered from west to east on the plans of Olympia, we have already seen reason to believe that VIII is not a Treasury but an ancient earth-altar, the Altar of Gaia.[2] I and XI are identified beyond any doubt by actual inscriptions with the Treasuries of the Sikyonians and Megarians : for the rest we must fall back on the list of Pausanias. II will accordingly be the Treasury of the Carthaginians, or more properly of the Syracusans, erected by the latter to commemorate a victory over the Carthaginians, probably that of Himera in 480 B.C. Here comes a difficulty owing to a manifest confusion in the text of Pausanias. He assigns the third and fourth Treasuries to the Epidamnians. Then follows a lacuna, and at the end of the same section he speaks of ' *the* Treasury of the Epidamnians ', implying that there was only one. At the beginning of the next section he states that the Sybarites built a Treasury next to that of the Byzantines, though he has made no mention of a Byzantine Treasury. We are therefore fully justified in assuming that the text is corrupt, that the Epidamnians had only one Treasury, probably IV, and that the name of the people who dedicated III has fallen out of the text. Louis Dyer, whose careful study of the Olympian Treasuries[3] I have in the main followed, conjectured that the anonymous Treasury was that of the Samians,

---

[1] *O.* v. 17. [2] *Supra*, p. 196.
[3] *J. H. S.* xxv. 294 ff. ; xxvi. 46 ff.

and he assigned to it a block of some unknown building found to the north-east of the Heraion, inscribed in Hellenistic characters ΣΑΜΙΩΝ.[1] This is, however, as he fully recognized, merely a conjecture. In the German official publication it was assumed that foundations III and IV had been destroyed and buried under a Roman road leading up the hill at the time when Pausanias visited Olympia, but the evidence for such a road is very doubtful.[2] Assuming then that IV is the Treasury of the Epidamnians, we may now follow Pausanias and assign V to the Byzantines, VI to the Sybarites, VII to the Kyreneans, IX to the Selinuntines, X to the Metapontines, XI to the Megarians, XII to the Geloans. We shall find some of these identifications confirmed by the existing remains.

For the date of the buildings we must depend partly on the evidence of existing remains, partly on the levels and relative positions of the various foundations. From such considerations Dyer arrived at the following order and date, which is in my opinion approximately correct.

1. Geloan, XII, *c.* 610 B.C.
2. Metapontine, X ⎫ *c.* 590 B.C.
3. Megarian,   XI ⎭
4. Kyrenean, VII ⎫
5. Sybarite,   VI ⎬ *c.* 550 B.C.
6. Byzantine,   V ⎭
7. Selinuntine, IX, *c.* 530 B.C.
8. Epidamnian, IV, *c.* 525 B.C.
9. Syracusan, II ⎫
10. Samian ? III ⎬ 480–470 B.C.
11. Sikyonian, I ⎭

GELOAN TREASURY, XII [3]

This, the oldest of all the Treasuries, is also the largest. It occupies the lowest point on the terrace at its extreme east end, commanding a view of all the plain below. Its plan is unique. It consists of a broad shallow cella 13·17 metres by 11·19, with a spacious Doric portico in front. The reason for these unusual proportions is that the portico was a later addition,

---

[1] *Olympia*, v, no. 652. Cp. the similar inscription 653 of the Megarian Treasury.
[2] *l. c.*, p. 295, n. 2.   [3] *Olympia*, ii, pp. 53, 215 ; *J. H. S.* xxvi, p. 47.

61. TERRA-COTTA AKROTERION OF HERAION

62. TERRA-COTTA CORNICE FROM THE GELOAN TREASURY

and the cella formed the whole original building, which, like most temples, faced east and west, the entrance being at the east end. All the neighbouring Treasuries are aligned to its south wall. Only the foundations remain, but the entablature of both cella and portico and the columns of the latter were found built into the walls of the Byzantine fort, and from these we can reconstruct the whole building.

The remains of the cella indicate that it was built shortly before 600 B.C. Gela was then at the height of its prosperity. Founded by Rhodian colonists in 690 B.C., it acquired such powers that in 581 B.C. it founded the still greater colony of Akragas. The southern porch, intended to adapt this old-fashioned building to the type of the later Treasuries, cannot have been built later than 491 B.C., when Gelon, having usurped the throne, transferred the seat of government to the newly captured city of Syracuse. Dyer connects its building with the victory of Pantares in the chariot-race, *c.* 500 B.C.

Of the interior of the cella we know nothing, but the entablature and roof are of exceptional interest. All round the building horizontally and also along the slopes of the gable ran a stone cornice or geison encased in a painted terra-cotta sheathing and surmounted by a terra-cotta sima (Fig. 62). The cornice consisted of two bands, the lower one recessed so as to leave a narrow soffit between them.[1] The lower band and the broad sloping soffit underneath it were covered with stucco painted red. The upper band was sheathed in terra-cotta plaques attached by iron nails. The sima,[2] too, was composed of two upright bands separated by a hollow moulding or cavetto, a type which finds parallels at Gela and Syracuse. Both geison and sima were richly decorated with maeanders, guilloche, palmettes, and other ornaments, painted in red and black on a yellow ground.[3] Along the sima was a row of waterspouts projecting from the centre of disks painted as rosettes. This sima, without the waterspouts, was actually continued along the horizontal geison of the gables in an artistically effective but utterly illogical manner, seeing that its only effect must have been to catch and retain the water.

[1] Marquand, *Gk. Architecture*, p. 115, Fig. 143.
[2] *Ib.*, p. 123, Fig. 156.
[3] *Ib.*, p. 234, Fig. 289 ; *J. H. S.* xxvi, p. 51, Fig. 2. For a similar guilloche in temple C at Selinous v. Koldewey and Puchstein, *Griechische Tempeln*, Fig. 71 ; cp. *Olympia*, ii, p. 200.

The use of terra-cotta veneering to protect the surface of stone is probably a survival from the days of timber construction. The wooden eaves, as being most exposed to the weather, required most protection, and it was to them that the veneering was first applied. This practice, which was probably of oriental origin, was widely spread in Italy and Sicily, and survived there for a long time. In Greece it had been superseded before the fifth century by the use of stucco.

The roof itself was no less striking. It was covered with large flat terra-cotta tiles with raised quadrant-shaped edges on either side. The ridge formed by these edges was capped by semicircular tiles. Along the ridge-pole ran a row of much larger almost cylindrical tiles, producing the effect of a

63. Roof of Geloan Treasury

great pipe from the top of which rose a row of terra-cotta palmettes.

These terra-cottas were made of a local Geloan reddish clay quite distinct from the yellow clay of Olympia, and we may infer that they were manufactured at Gela and brought by sea to Olympia. The extraordinary brilliance of the colours that they still possess is due to the mixing of the clay with a certain amount of black metal.[1] The effect of the roof with its many-coloured gables seen against the dark foliage of the trees must have been gorgeous in the extreme. Its gorgeousness was indeed oriental rather than Greek, and naturally so ; for the art of Sicily was strongly influenced by the East.

A more Hellenic appearance was given to this many-coloured building by the addition about 500 B.C. of a Doric hexastyle porch along the south side. At the same time the builders were careful not to conceal the brilliant terra-cottas of their fathers,

[1] Graef, *Olympia*, ii, p. 189 ; *J. H. S.* xxvi, p. 49, n. 7.

and therefore provided the new porch with a low lean-to roof. The portico was made as spacious as possible, the half-pillars actually overlapping the side-walls of the cella. Seven of the eight pillars have been found. They have a pronounced entasis and are decorated round the neck by four deeply cut grooves.[1] The capitals have a beautifully curved echinus (Fig. 64).

METAPONTINE TREASURY, X [2]

The position of this Treasury half-way between the altar and the Geloan Treasury makes it probable that it was the next one to be built, and we may date it early in the sixth century. But we do not know why or on what occasion it was dedicated. Little smaller than the Geloan Treasury, it differed from it in that it faced south. Its very scanty remains tell us only that it was a temple *in antis* and built in the undeveloped Doric style. We do not even know how many pillars there were between the antae. Among the foundations were found fragments of metopes and triglyphs of a soft marly limestone, above which ran a rudimentary cornice which recalls the veneered cornice of the Geloans. The Treasury contained an ivory statue of Endymion and a collection of gold and silver vessels for the use of the Metapontine Theoroi at the festival.[3]

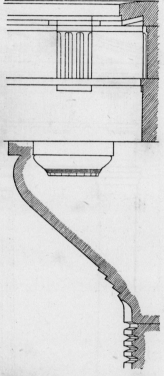

64. Capital and entablature of Geloan porch

MEGARIAN TREASURY, XI [4]

The Megarians selected a site for their Treasury between those of the Geloans and Metapontines, which were undoubtedly already in existence. Pausanias records that over the gable was

---

[1] Marquand, *op. cit.*, p. 191 ; *J. H. S.* xxvi, p. 55, Fig. 4.
[2] *Olympia*, ii, p. 50 ; *J. H. S.* xxv, p. 294, xxvi, p. 56.
[3] Athenaeus, xi. 479 ; P. vi. 19. 11.
[4] *Olympia*, ii, p. 50 ; *J. H. S.* xxv, p. 298, xxvi, p. 58.

a shield with an inscription stating that the Treasury was dedicated to commemorate a victory over the Corinthians. This victory was also commemorated by a sculptured group in cedar-wood overlaid with gold by the Spartan artist Dontas, possibly a mistake

65. Reconstruction of the Megarian Treasury

for Medon. Pausanias, misled perhaps by an exaggerated idea of the antiquity of this artist, dates the Treasury in the archonship of Phorbas, i.e. before the first Olympiad. The date is manifestly absurd. The Treasury cannot have been built earlier than the sixth century. At the same time it is not likely to be later than 570 B.C., when Athens captured Salamis, a blow from which Megara never recovered. In the seventh century Megara was one of the chief colonial and commercial states in Greece.

66   Megarian Treasury   67

68   69   70

Bouleuterion   One of the Treasuries ?

71   Hellanodikeon   72

73   Leonidaion

ARCHITECTURAL TERRA-COTTAS

Megarians had at an early date competed at Olympia. Two of her colonies, Byzantion and Selinous, erected Treasuries there in the sixth century. Her victory over Corinth was probably won in the long commercial war at the end of the seventh century between Chalcis and Eretria, in which Corinth and Megara took opposite sides.

The Megarian Treasury is the best known of all these buildings.[1] Most of its materials were found together in the south-west wall of the Byzantine fort, including the pedimental sculptures and an architrave block bearing in Hellenistic characters the inscription ΜΕ[ΓΑ]ΡΕΩΝ.[2]

Its foundations were especially strengthened at the south end, where they project beyond the buildings. Possibly an altar stood here. Its plan was that of a temple *in antis* with a cella and a porch with two pillars between the antae. It measured 12·29 metres by 6·80. Its narrowness as compared with the two earlier Treasuries was due to the limited space between these two buildings. The space between the two pillars of the porch was closed by folding doors, the marks of which are still visible on the stylobate.

The chief characteristic of this Treasury is the economy of labour shown by the builders. Realizing that the view of the sides was obstructed by the existing Treasuries they confined the ornamentation severely to the front. Thus of the twenty flutings of the pillars only the eleven visible from the front were completed, and the grooves round the neck were only cut half-way. The architrave and triglyph frieze again were confined to the front, the latter being represented at the sides by two abortive metopes. Even the mutules were omitted along the sides (Fig. 74).

A plain flat geison ran round the whole building, but only at the gable ends was it provided with a terra-cotta sima (Figs. 66, 67). The latter was of a simple archaic profile, a flat band surmounted by an outspreading convex band decorated with palmettes, and ending on either side in remarkably fine water-spouts in the form of lions' heads, the prototype of those of the Temple of Zeus. Along the sides ran a plain terra-cotta band, the tile ridges ending in palmette antefixes. These terra-cottas were made of a pinkish clay found at Megara and must have been

[1] *Olympia*, v, no. 653.
[2] The roof can be entirely reconstructed, but the problem of roof construction is too technical to discuss here.

manufactured there. They were painted in the same three colours as those of the Geloan Treasury. A similar palmette frieze was used in the interior of the pronaos to decorate the long wooden beams which divided the ceiling into narrow panels.

So far the Megarian Treasury shows resemblances to the Geloan Treasury and to the early Doric temples of Sicily. The columns of the porch, however, are of a later type, approximating to that of the Temple of Zeus. The shafts, 3·50 metres high, are five times their diameter, with slight diminution and no entasis. Their delicately curved echinus is almost identical with that of

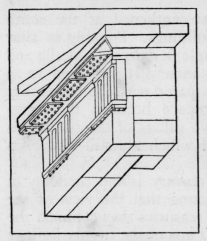

74. Angle of Megarian Treasury

the temple columns. Further, in the architrave ├───┤-shaped clamps were employed such as are rarely found before the fifth century. Finally, the pedimented sculptures can hardly be much earlier than 500 B.C. It seems probable, then, that about this time the Megarians for some reason or other made some alterations and improvements in their Treasury. Possibly they were stimulated by the enlargement of the Geloan Treasury.

The pediment, of which all five blocks have been found, measured only three-quarters of a metre in height and less than six metres in length. Consequently the figures were somewhat less than half life-size. They were carved in high relief on soft local limestone similar to that used for the archaic head of Hera, and colour was freely employed to hide defects of material and workmanship. The background was painted light blue, and there were traces of red on the armour and heads of the giants, while a lighter colour seems to have been used for the foot of Athena.

The subject was the battle between the gods and the giants. There were five groups, each consisting of a god and a giant, and the corners were filled by a dragon and a sea-monster. The central group represented Zeus in the act of striking down a wounded giant (Fig. 58). Of the god nothing remains but his left leg and a shapeless mass that was once his torso. The figure of the giant is the best preserved of the whole pediment. He is sinking on his left knee, defending himself with his uplifted right arm. He is fully armed with helmet, breast-plate, and greaves, and carries on his left arm a shield. The other groups are still more mutilated. To the right apparently is Herakles, armed with bow and club, advancing against a prostrate foe. Beyond him a kneeling god, probably Ares, is plunging a spear into a giant. To the left of the central group is Athene, her left foot planted on the leg of a fallen giant in which a gaping wound is visible, and beyond her is Poseidon. The general composition is vigorous and dramatic, but the execution, like the material, is crude. The body of the giant fighting with Zeus is far too small for his head, and the eyes are impossibly elongated. These sculptures show some resemblance to those of the Megarian colony Selinous, and it is probable that though made at Olympia they were the work of Megarian artists.[1]

TREASURIES OF KYRENE, SYBARIS, AND BYZANTION, VII, VI, V

The Treasury of Kyrene[2] is generally identified with the altar No. VIII. This identification is precluded by the one fact recorded of it by Pausanias, that it contained the statues of Roman emperors, for which august purpose this tiny building is quite inadequate. There is nothing in the scanty remains of these three buildings that enables us to identify or date them apart from the evidence of Pausanias. The Sybarite Treasury must have been built before 510 B.C., when Sybaris was destroyed; the Byzantine before 513 B.C., when Byzantion was captured by Darius. The Treasury of Kyrene, if we may judge from its position, was the earliest of the three. We may date them c. 550 B.C. All three were of the usual type.

Treu and Studniczka[8] have assigned to the Treasury of Kyrene two sculptured fragments of African limestone. One of these is the mutilated torso of the nymph Kyrene struggling with a lion, as she was when ' he of the wide quiver, far-darting Apollo, found her '. Her breast and arms are bare, and long curls fall over her shoulders. There are traces of red on her dress and of blue on the background. If, as is conjectured, she was the central figure of a pediment group, we must suppose

---

[1] *Olympia*, iii, pp. 5 ff., Pls. II, III. I have followed Treu's reconstruction.
[2] *Olympia*, ii, p. 48, iii, pp. 19–23 ; *J. H. S.* xxvi, p. 66 ; Studniczka, *Kyrene*, pp. 28–39 ; and in Roscher's *Lexicon*, s.v. Kyrene, p. 1724.

that Apollo was standing by. The other fragment is the headless and tailless body of a cock such as is often seen on vases of Kyrene. Treu suggests that a cock and hen were placed at either end of the gable. Studniczka assigns the sculptures to the middle of the fifth century. Being made of African limestone they must have been carved at Kyrene. A slab of similar limestone inscribed ϘVPA[NAΦN][1] must have belonged to some monument in the Treasury.

The Treasury of Sybaris was similar in plan. Treu assigns to the pediment some limestone reliefs of birds, a waterfowl, a cock, and a hen.[2] It contained a cedar-wood figure of Triton holding a silver cup, a silver Siren, and numerous vessels of silver and gold.[3]

Of the Byzantine Treasury [4] only the southern part of the foundations is left. Owing to the treacherous nature of the soil they had been strengthened by a deep footing of pebbles embedded in clay-mortar. Its width is greater than that of any Treasury except the Geloan, and it must have had a façade of six pillars or four between antae. Treu assigns to it a limestone relief of a horse painted yellow with a red mane.

SELINUNTINE TREASURY, IX[5]

Most of the Treasuries already described must have been built before the Selinuntines resolved to occupy the narrow space between the altar and the Treasury of Megara. Perhaps the experience of the Byzantines warned them against attempting to build farther west, or perhaps they wished to be near their mother city Megara. The foundations, part of the walls, and the pavement still exist. The lowest course of the walls consists of a double row of slabs placed upright. The stone used is a hard poros of finer texture than that found near Olympia, and it was probably quarried near Selinous. The peculiarity of this stone enables us to recognize as belonging to this building the blocks of a Doric entablature. They are of a simple archaic style : the mutules have no guttae and the tops of the glyphs are almost flat. Two capitals of the same material were found of a spreading archaic type. They differ somewhat in profile, but considering the variations found in Greek temples this is not a serious objection.

[1] *Olympia*, v, no. 246.   [2] *Ib.* ii, p. 47 ; iii, pp. 23, 25.
[3] Athenaeus, xi. 480 a.   [4] *Olympia*, ii, p. 46 ; iii, pp. 16–18.
[5] *Olympia*, ii, p. 49 ; *J. H. S.* xxvi, p. 73.

Epidamnian Treasury, IV [1]

This building is usually identified with the Syracusan Treasury founded after the battle of Himera. The architectural remains, however, undoubtedly belong to the sixth century, and are therefore far more appropriate to Epidamnos, which reached its greatest prosperity during this century.

The treacherous nature of the ground necessitated foundations of exceptional strength. They consisted of two courses of poros blocks resting on a deep bed of pebbles, 6 feet deep at the south end. Numerous fragments of dazzling white limestone were found among the foundations, and we are thus enabled to assign to this building various blocks of the same material. They were probably quarried and worked at Epidamnos. The Doric column shows particularly interesting variations from the usual type. It has thirty-two flutings, and they are divided alternately by the usual sharp arris and by a recessed astragal moulding. The latter motive is repeated above the architrave, a detail which we find elsewhere only at Selinous. The capital shows the prominent curve typical of the sixth century. Treu further assigns to this building a fragment of a limestone relief, representing a naked leg with an arm grasping it, but there is no definite evidence for this attribution except the material. [2]

Pausanias tells us that the Treasury contained certain statues, the work of Theokles and his son, representing Atlas upholding the world, and Herakles in the garden of the Hesperides. The latter had been removed to the Temple of Hera.

Of the anonymous Treasury No. III, which Dyer assigns to the Samians, and of the Syracusan Treasury, No. II, nothing remains except a few blocks of their foundations. They seem to have been destroyed in Roman times, as traces of a Roman pavement and walls were found above them, but the date of this destruction is quite uncertain, and there is no evidence to connect it with the building of the Exedra of Herodes or to show that they did not exist in the time of Pausanias.

Sikyonian Treasury, I [3]

The preservation of this Treasury is in striking contrast to the ruinous condition of the neighbouring houses. The foundations are almost perfect except in the south-east corner. Many of

[1] *Olympia*, ii, p. 46 ; *J. H. S.* xxvi, p. 76.   [2] *Olympia*, iii, p. 15.
[3] *Olympia*, ii, p. 40 ; *J. H. S.* xxvi, p. 76.

the larger blocks of the superstructure were found close by, and smaller blocks near the Prytaneion and the Byzantine church. This identification was rendered certain by their material, a tawny limestone, almost resembling sandstone, probably quarried near Sikyon.

Pausanias states that the Treasury was dedicated by Myron to commemorate his victory in the chariot-race in the 33rd Olympiad. He also dedicated two chambers (θάλαμοι) of bronze, one of Ionic, the other of Doric architecture. These we may suppose to have been model shrines such as have been found at Athens. They were, however, of exceptional size and weight, the smaller of the two weighing 500 talents; and the floor of the Treasury required to be especially strengthened to support their weight. In ascribing a seventh-century date to the building itself, Pausanias was misled by the legend with regard to these *thalamoi*. No fact is more certain than that the existing Treasury is not earlier than the fifth century. Hence the *thalamoi* must have been placed originally in some other building, possibly in an older building on the same site.

The foundations rest on a solid bed of concrete 10 feet deep at the south end. The temple was 12·80 metres long by 7·31 broad. It was surrounded by two steps, and at the south-east corner was a projecting pavement which possibly supported an altar. The northern half of the cella floor is paved with stone slabs resting on two foundation courses. It was especially strengthened to support the weight of Myron's *thalamoi*.

The columns between the antae were 3·84 metres high with very slight entasis and with capitals very similar to those of the Temple of Zeus. One of the centre blocks bears the inscription ΣΙΚΥΟΝΙΟ[Ν]. The letters are those of the Sikyonian alphabet in use between 500 and 450 B.C., and the same is true of the stonemasons' marks. A Doric frieze of triglyphs and metopes ran all round the building. The pedimental metopes were broader and higher than those along the sides, and the abaci above them were therefore of different height. To counteract the effect of this irregularity the architect introduced continuous astragal moulding above the abacus. There were no sculptures in the pediment. The roof was formed of marble tiles, and along the gable ends ran a marble sima similar to that of the Temple of Zeus. The wall of the cella was decorated inside with a cornice consisting of an abacus painted with an elaborate maeander and a Doric cymation (Fig. 75).

The architectural and epigraphical evidence agrees with the date proposed by Dyer, 480–470 B.C. Dörpfeld, however, on the strength of the astragal moulding, argues that the Treasury was built after the Parthenon, where this same moulding is used. But, as Dyer showed, it is very unsafe in the imperfect state of our knowledge to draw an inference from a single architectural detail. Moreover, while the cessation of the building of the Treasuries after the Persian wars admits of an easy explanation, it is by no means

■ Red □ White ▨ Neutral ▥ Blue ■ Grey

75. Painted cornice of Sikyonian Treasury

easy to explain the building of an isolated Treasury forty years afterwards. We may conclude, therefore, that the Treasury was built between 480 and 470 B. C.

Besides the *thalamoi* of Myron, Pausanias describes other votive offerings stored in this Treasury: a bronze shield, helmet, and greaves dedicated by the Myanes, the sword of Pelops with a golden hilt, and the ivory horn of Amalthea, offerings of Miltiades the first tyrant of the Chersonnese, whom Pausanias confuses with his more famous nephew the son of Cimon. There was also a boxwood statue of Apollo dedicated by the Epizephyrian Locrians, and the three diskoi used in the pentathlon. Why these various objects found a home in the Sikyonian Treasury, and when they were placed there, we do not know.

XIV

The Temple of Zeus

Χρυσέας ὑποστάσαντες εὐτειχεῖ προθύρῳ θαλάμου
κίονας ὡς ὅτε θαητὸν μέγαρον
πάξομεν.

Pindar, O. vi. 1.

THE TEMPLE

PINDAR, in his sixth Olympian ode, compares the proem of his song to the pillars and façade of a stately temple. This ode was written in honour of Agesias of Syracuse, who won the mule chariot-race in 468 B.C. In this very year the Eleans were building, or about to build, the Temple of Zeus, and it is no idle fancy to suppose that the building of this temple suggested the poet's comparison.

The temple and the image of Zeus, says Pausanias, was built with the spoils of war when the Eleans sacked Pisa and such of the perioikoi as joined the Pisatans.[1] We have seen that the war referred to took place shortly after the synoecism of Elis about the year 470 B.C. For before the next Olympiad a tenth Hellanodikas was appointed to represent the conquered district. The temple must have been completed before 456 B.C., for in that year the Spartan allies dedicated a gold shield to commemorate the victory of Tanagra. This shield was placed over the eastern gable of the temple, into which an inscribed block[2] was built to support it.

The twelve years between 468–456 B.C. afforded ample time for the work. The architectural and sculptural remains, the letters used upon the roof-tiles as builder's marks, the bases of statues found buried under the rubble of the temple terrace, all agree with this date. There is no reason to suppose that an older temple existed on the site. There are traces of altars, and in the rubble were found quantities of early votive offerings. The

---

[1] P. v. 10. 2 ; v. *supra*, p. 85 ; *Olympia*, ii, p. 5.
[2] This block was found bearing the inscription quoted by Pausanias, *Olympia*, v, no. 253.

76. FALLEN COLUMNS OF TEMPLE OF ZEUS

77

78   79

LIONS' HEADS OF DIFFERENT PERIODS FROM TEMPLE OF ZEUS

site was, as we have seen, part of the Sacred Grove, on the trees of which these offerings were hung.

Nothing of the temple remains standing save a few blocks of the cella walls. Yet even so the massive platform surrounded by the huge drums of fallen pillars and blocks of the architrave is an impressive sight and gives some idea of its grandeur. Owing to the raising of the level of the site the foundation walls were of unusual depth. Though only 1 metre below the original level of the ground, they measure some 4 metres to the top of the stylobate. They were built, like the rest of the temple, of a coarse shell conglomerate quarried locally, and were bonded with |——|-shaped iron clamps. The spaces between the walls were filled with earth and rubble. Above the foundations are the usual three steps, the two lower steps 0·48 metre in height and the same in width, the upper step 0·56 metre high. The stylobate is formed of blocks 2·60 metres wide, or about half the width of the space between the centres of the columns, so arranged that each column stood in the middle of a block. The length measured along the top of the stylobate was 64·12 metres, or exactly 200 Olympic feet,[1] its breadth 27·66

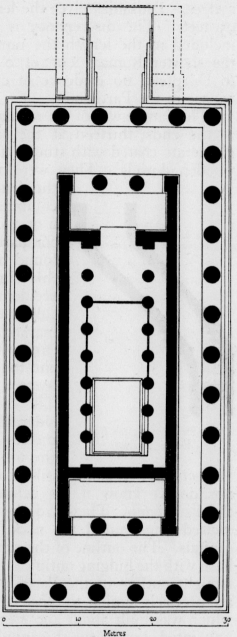

Metres

80. Plan of Temple of Zeus

[1] Two measures appear to have been used at Olympia : (1) the Olympic foot of 0·3216 metre, determined by the length of the Stadion, possibly regarded as a sacred measure ; (2) the Pheidonian or Aeginetan foot of 0·327 metre, which appears to have been used for most of the measurements. *Olympia*, ii, p. 19.

metres. Pausanias gives the length as 230 feet, the breadth as 95 feet. The discrepancy is due to the fact that Pausanias included in the length the ramp at the eastern end, and used the shorter Roman foot of 0·296 metre. There is, according to Dörpfeld, no evidence of curvature in the stylobate such as we see in the Parthenon.

The temple was of the regular hexastyle type, with six columns at the ends, thirteen at the sides. These were built of conglomerate coated with stucco, and the drums were fastened with wooden dowels. They were 10·43 metres in height, or twice the distance between the centres of the columns. The distance varies only by 2 or 3 centimetres, a very small variation compared with the 20 or 30 centimetres found in some older temples. Yet even this slight variation cannot have been accidental, for the distance between the columns was most carefully measured and marked. A small hole was made on the surface of the stone and filled with lead, and the centre of the column was marked by two lines intersecting at right angles. The diminution of the columns is considerable. Those at the ends measure 2·25 metres in diameter at the base, 1·72 at the top, those at the sides 2·21 and 1·68

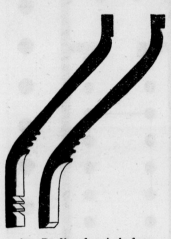

81. Profile of capitals from Temple of Zeus

respectively. It is impossible to determine the amount of entasis, nor do we know if the columns were inclined inwards as in the Parthenon. They had the usual twenty flutings and three incised rings round the neck. Four similar rings encircle the capitals. The outline of the echinus is especially fine, contrasting both with the bulging outline of earlier capitals and with the almost straight outline of the Parthenon. Their curve and proportions are precisely similar to those of the Temple of Aphaia in Aegina,[1] which was built about 490 B.C. The columns and capitals were unpainted, except for the annuli, which were red.

The architrave and triglyph frieze were massive and simple, but their severity was relieved by the use of colour. There were traces of red on the upper band of the architrave and between the mutules, the mutules and triglyphs being blue. The metopes

[1] Furtwängler, *Aegina*, Pl. XLII.

were covered with white stucco and without any other decoration. At a later period the twenty-one shields dedicated by Mummius were fastened to the ten metopes of the east end and the eleven adjoining metopes of the south side, these being the most conspicuous parts of the temple as facing the processional road.

The roof and sima were of marble. The original tiles were of Parian marble, but these were replaced in the time of Augustus by the tiles of Pentelican marble which Pausanias saw and described. They were flat with raised edges, capped by triangular cover-tiles, and fastened together by pegs. A peculiarity of the roof is the absence of the usual anthemia. Instead we find a continuous marble sima almost upright and interrupted only by lions' heads that served as water-spouts. The lower part of

82. Roof of Temple of Zeus

the sima was perpendicular and was decorated with a maeander pattern: the curved upper portion had a band of palmettes and a string of beads and reels. These patterns were painted with a reddish yellow colour that possibly served as a foundation for gold ; the ground was coloured light blue.

The lions' heads bear witness to the frequent repairs required by the cornice and roof. Thirty-nine more or less complete heads have been found, and some three hundred fragments. Of these the earliest are of Parian marble and show two distinct types, one with drooping, pointed ears and the hair divided into three rows, the other with upright, rounded ears and four bands of hair. Both types are contemporary with the building of the temple. The execution is fine and careful. The types are not slavishly copied, but the different heads are executed with freedom and vigour. The other heads are of Pentelican marble, mostly of Roman times and lifeless imitations of the original types, degenerating finally into coarse and barbarous monstrosities. The details of the types can be seen in our illustrations (Figs. 77–9).

The height of the gables was one-eighth of the length, or about 10 feet. At either end golden vases were placed as akroteria, and over the centre golden statues of Victory, the work of Paionios. These statues must have been erected later in the fifth century, for originally the golden shield dedicated by the Spartan allies served as akroterion at the east end.

The main approach to the temple was at the east end by a broad stone ramp with three broad steps in front and narrower steps at the sides. The colonnade and the spaces between the pillars, especially on the south side, were full of votive offerings and bronze statues ; it was paved with blocks of poros covered by a concrete floor of pebbles and mortar. In Roman times a fine floor of coloured marbles cut in hexagons was laid down, of which some traces still remain. The ceiling was made of wood.

The temple proper stood on a low step and was 46·84 metres long and 16·39 metres broad. It was symmetrically planned with two pillars flanked by antae at either end. Above them rose a Doric entablature of six metopes at either end in which the labours of Herakles were represented. These metopes must have been inserted before the completion of the temple, for the grooves in the triglyphs into which they fit do not extend to the top.

The opisthodome was open at the end and provided with a stone bench. It served as a sort of assembly room where orators, poets, and philosophers might recite their works, or explain their theories to the spectators. It was here that Herodotus published to the Greek world his History.

The pronaos was similar in plan but closed by three pairs of folding doors of bronze. The sockets of the hinges and the holes for the bolts are still visible on the thresholds. Here under the Roman marble floor a fine Greek mosaic was discovered by the French expedition. The principal subject is a Triton with a boy seated on his tail. It was constructed for the most part of rounded pebbles from the river beds, shaped stones being only used for details. In the north-east corner was another mosaic representing fishes and sea-birds. The date of these

mosaics is unknown : they are undoubtedly Greek work, perhaps
the earliest work of this sort that we possess. They are certainly
later than the building of the temple : for in laying them account
was taken of a large basis found in the north-west corner.

The pronaos was full of votive offerings. Here was the group
of Ekecheiria crowning Iphitos, and close to it were some offerings of Mikythos and the horses of Kyniska. Here, too, was
the throne of the Tyrrhenian king Arimnestos, the first foreigner
to make offerings to Olympian Zeus. The bronze tripod on which
the crowns of the victors were originally placed was probably
preserved here, and so too were the twenty-five bronze shields
used by competitors in the race in armour. There were pillars
recording treaties, among which was the Hundred Years' treaty
between Athens, Argos, Elis, and Mantineia.

A mighty doorway 5 metres broad led from the pronaos into
the cella and was indeed its only source of light. As one entered,
the full glory of the statue of the god burst upon the sight, filling
the whole breadth of the central aisle and almost touching the
ceiling. On either side was a row of Doric columns, seven in
number, with half-columns at either end, and above them rose
a row of lighter columns. In the corners winding staircases led
up to the roof and to galleries which ran along the side aisles at
the point probably where the upper row of pillars began. Whether
these galleries belonged to the original plan or were added later
to afford a nearer view of the statue we cannot say.

The cella was 28·74 metres long and 13·26 metres broad, the
central aisle 6·50 metres broad. A comparison of this aisle with
that of the Parthenon leaves no doubt that it was altered and
arranged under the direction of Pheidias for the reception and
effective display of the statue of the god.

This aisle, like that of the Parthenon, was divided into four
sections. First there was an antechamber 7·50 metres long in
both temples, and extending at Olympia as far as the second
pillar. Beyond this a barrier of poros prevented nearer approach
to the image of Zeus except through doors. Similar barriers
extended from this point between the pillars to a point beyond
the basis of the statue, leaving a space at the west end which with
the side aisles formed a continuous passage round the two
central sections of the cella. The second and most important
section was again the same length as that of the Parthenon,
9·50 metres, and extended to the basis of the image. Immedi-

ately in front of the basis was a square of 6·50 metres paved with black Eleusinian limestone and surrounded by a raised border of Pentelican marble. Pausanias supposed that this marble border was designed to catch the drippings of the oil with which the statue was anointed, but we can hardly doubt that its real purpose was artistic, as a setting to throw into relief the black limestone of the floor and the basis. In this section there were traces on the floor of numerous monuments and altars, among which we may be sure was the Altar of Olympian Zeus at which the monthly offerings were made.

The third section was completely occupied by the basis of the statue, 6·65 metres broad, 9·93 metres long, and 1·09 metres high. The spaces between the columns were here closed by metal screens, which seem to have been continued at the back of the image. A border of Pentelican marble surrounded the basis, which was lined with black Eleusinian stone with projecting top and foot. The upper surface of the projecting foot was left rough and had dowel holes, probably for fastening the gold reliefs with which the front was adorned. The central scene represented Aphrodite rising from the waves and received by Eros and Peitho. On either side were groups of deities, and at the ends, as on the pediment of the Parthenon, Helios and Selene.

Lastly, behind the statue is a fourth section only 1·74 metres deep, forming, as we have seen, a passage connecting the two side aisles. In the larger cella of the Parthenon this section is considerably deeper.

The similarity of this arrangement with that of the Parthenon, the agreement of the actual measurements, the use of Eleusinian limestone and Pentelican marble, are convincing proof that the interior arrangements of both temples were designed by Pheidias himself. It is certain that at Olympia the laying down of the floor was not contemporary with the building of the temple. Unfortunately the excavations do not enable us to settle the disputed question whether the statue of Zeus was an earlier or later work than that of Athene.[1] But so far as it goes the evidence does corroborate the view that was prevalent in antiquity that Pheidias worked at Athens till 438 B.C., when the Athene was dedicated, and then went to Olympia, where he worked from

[1] The evidence is clearly stated by Professor E. A. Gardner, *Gk. Sculpture*, pp. 251 ff.; cf. Overbeck, *Schriftquellen*, pp. 114–16.

438 to 432 B. C.[1] With this agrees the definite statement of
Pausanias that he took as a model for one of the figures on the
throne the youthful Pantarkes, who was victor in the boys'
wrestling match in 436 B. C. Now we have seen that the measure-
ment of the length of the first two sections of the cella is the same
in both temples. In the Parthenon the second section is a square
of 9·50 metres determined by the width of the aisle : at Olympia
the length is the same, but the aisle is only 6·50 metres wide.
Hence it seems certain that the length was borrowed from the
Parthenon and not vice versa. We may further note that the
portion of the floor paved in Eleusinian stone does form a square
determined as in the Parthenon by the width of the aisle.

THE STATUE AND THRONE OF ZEUS

Of the ideal represented by the Zeus of Pheidias and of its
effect on those who saw it I have already spoken.[2] The statue
itself and the throne are lost. For its details we must rely on the
description of Pausanias, who gives us more information about
the throne than about the figure of the god. The only representa-
tions of the statue existing are on certain bronze coins of Elis
issued under Hadrian. Some of these show the head of Zeus,
others the whole statue. Of the latter three views are given,
and small though they are the evidence of these coins is of great
value for the interpretation of Pausanias.

The pedestal, as we have seen, was 3 feet high and 22 feet
broad, occupying the whole breadth of the central aisle. The
statue, which we are told almost touched the roof, must have been
nearly 40 feet high, or eight times life-size. But measurements,
says Pausanias, can give no idea of the effect that the statue
produced. The god was seated on his throne, his feet resting
on a footstool. In his right hand, which was raised, he held
a gold and ivory figure of victory. His left hand rested on a
sceptre inlaid with many metals and supporting an eagle. His
sandals and his mantle were of gold, the latter decorated with

[1] Both Plutarch, whose authority is probably Ephoros, and Philochoros, as
quoted by the scholiast to Aristophanes, agree in this. Whether the trial of Pheidias
took place before or after his visit to Olympia is immaterial to our purpose. We may
note that the story that he was tried for embezzlement by the Eleans and put to
death seems a mere variation of the Athenian story, and is quite incompatible with
the honour in which his descendants were held at Olympia.

[2] *Supra*, p. 171.

a variety of animals and flowers. The gold and ivory plates were fastened on a strong framework of wood, and arrangements were made by which the latter could be kept constantly oiled to prevent it from shrinking and so disarranging the plates or to protect the ivory from damp. The care of the statue seems to have been a hereditary privilege of the family of Pheidias.

The throne was wrought of gold and precious stones, ivory, and ebony. The legs were adorned with figures of Victory, either in relief or as caryatids; the arms were formed by sphinxes bearing in their clutches their Theban victims. Along the edge of the seat was represented, probably in relief, the slaughter of the Niobids by Apollo and Artemis. On the back of the throne, above the god's head, were placed the Graces and the Horai, three on each side. The throne was strengthened by cross-bars which ran from leg to leg, while further support was provided by four pillars placed probably under the centre of the seat where the weight was greatest. These cross-bars are clearly visible on the coins; the pillars are not so, the reason being that they were hidden by screens which enclosed the space between the legs so that it was impossible to walk under the throne. On the cross-bar in front were placed eight figures representing athletic contests. One of them was a portrait of the youthful wrestler Pantarkes. One figure had disappeared in the time of Pausanias, probably having been stolen. Above the cross-bars on the other three sides was represented the war of Herakles and the Amazons. There were twenty-seven groups of combatants, nine probably on each side. These figures on the cross-bars were probably made of gold and in the round, and stood out clearly against the dark-blue background of the screens. The panel below the cross-bar in front was hidden by the footstool; the lower panels on the sides and at the back were filled with paintings by Panainos, the brother of Pheidias. As Pausanias enumerates nine groups, we may reasonably suppose that there were three groups on each side, each group consisting of two figures.[1] They are as follows:

A. 1. Atlas and Herakles.
   2. Theseus and Peirithoos.
   3. Hellas and Salamis.

[1] Of the many arrangements of these pictures proposed I have adopted that of Mr. H. G. Evelyn White, *J. H. S.* xxviii. 49. Following Professor E. A. Gardner, *J. H. S.* xiv. 233, he rejects the view of A. S. Murray and Dr. Dörpfeld, who placed the pictures not on the sides of the throne but on the screens between the pillars

Eastern

Western

83. RECONSTRUCTION OF THE PEDIMENTS OF THE TEMPLE OF ZEUS

(After Treu, *Jahrb.* 1888–9)

    B. 1. Herakles and the Nemean Lion.
       2. Aias and Kassandra.
       3. Hippodameia and Sterope.
    C. 1. Prometheus and Herakles.
       2. Penthesileia and Achilles.
       3. The Hesperides.

Lastly, the footstool was flanked by golden lions, and on its front bore in relief a representation of the battle of Theseus against the Amazons, the first conflict in which the Athenians displayed their bravery.

THE WORKSHOP OF PHEIDIAS

A work so colossal and so complicated required something more than a temporary workshop. The workshop of Pheidias was still existing in the time of Pausanias.[1] It contained an altar to all the gods. It lay outside the west wall of the Altis, apparently between the Palaistra and the Leonidaion. Hence it is usually identified with the Greek building afterwards converted into a Byzantine church.[2] Thanks to this conversion it is exceptionally well preserved. It is 32·18 metres long, or 100 Olympic feet, and 14·50 metres or 45 Olympic feet broad. Owing to the

of the cella. This view is quite inconsistent with the description of the throne by Pausanias. According to Professor Gardner the pillars which helped to support the throne were placed between each pair of legs, and thus with the cross-bars divided each side into four metope-like panels. In each of the two upper panels he places one group of two figures, in the two lower panels the two figures of the third group. This reconstruction of the throne is, as Mr. Evelyn White shows, inconsistent with the evidence of the coins, which in every case show the cross-bars but not the pillars. A further variation is proposed by Mr. C. H. Tyler, *J. H. S.* xxx. 82. Accepting Mr. Evelyn White's reconstruction of the throne, he follows Professor Gardner in dividing the three groups, but places two groups or four figures below the cross-bar and the third group above it. Any such division of the three groups, and the placing of any paintings above the cross-bar, seem to me open to the following serious objections :

(1) *The pictures above the cross-bar could not be seen.* Assuming the statue to be eight times life-size, the distance between the legs would be not less than 16 feet, and the height of the seat about the same, seeing that the god's feet rested on a stool. Hence the cross-bar would be 8 feet above the top of the basis, and 11 feet above the temple floor. The space between the wall of the cella and the base on either side was not more than 11 feet (3·3 metres), that at the back was about 6 feet (1·74 metres). At a distance of 11 feet it would be practically impossible to see a picture the lower edge of which was 11 feet above the ground, especially in the dim religious light of the temple.

(2) *A panel 16 feet by 8 feet would require at least six figures to fill it properly.*

[1] v. 15. 1.   [2] *Olympia*, ii, pp. 93 ff.

slope of the ground and the danger of floods from the Kladeos the foundations are of unusual strength ; they are more than 5 feet deep and are supported on the outside by twelve massive buttresses. The walls consist of a stone socle, 1·12 metres thick and 1·60 metres high, with a superstructure of brick tiles and stone rubble. The unusual thickness of the walls suggests that they were of considerable height, an inference further supported by the size of the doorway, which was 4·54 metres broad and therefore could hardly be less than 9 metres high. As the length and breadth of the hall are approximately those of the cella of the Temple of Zeus, we may reasonably suppose that it was about the same height, or 14 metres. A studio of such dimensions was eminently desirable if the artist was to judge of the general effect of his work. The arrangement of the interior seems equally appropriate for the purpose. It was divided into two rooms, 10·30 and 18·47 metres long, separated by stone walls projecting 2·20 metres from either side, the space between being closed by a movable partition. As in the cella, there were two rows of stone pillars which seem to have supported galleries. These pillars must have been at least 7 metres high. From the character of the masonry it appears that the building belongs to the fifth century.[1]

Against the identification of this building with the workshop of Pheidias various objections have been raised. In the first place it is urged that the building is too substantial for such a purpose. This objection does not take sufficient account of the time required for the execution of the statue, the number and variety of the craftsmen employed or the costliness of the materials. Moreover, the workshop was certainly still in existence six centuries afterwards. Further, it is argued that, however well adapted such a hall was for enabling the artist to judge of the general effect of the work, it was by no means suitable for the various technical processes of work in gold and ivory, which required a number of separate compartments. Just such a workshop is found in the long, narrow building to the south, 57 metres long, 7 metres broad, which is divided by cross-walls into a series of small rooms. But the necessity of such small studios for the making of the separate parts does not obviate the necessity for

---

[1] From the use of ⌐-shaped clamps it is argued that the building is earlier than the Temple of Zeus, in which case it must have been originally erected for some other purpose. But the evidence of the clamps by itself is not conclusive.

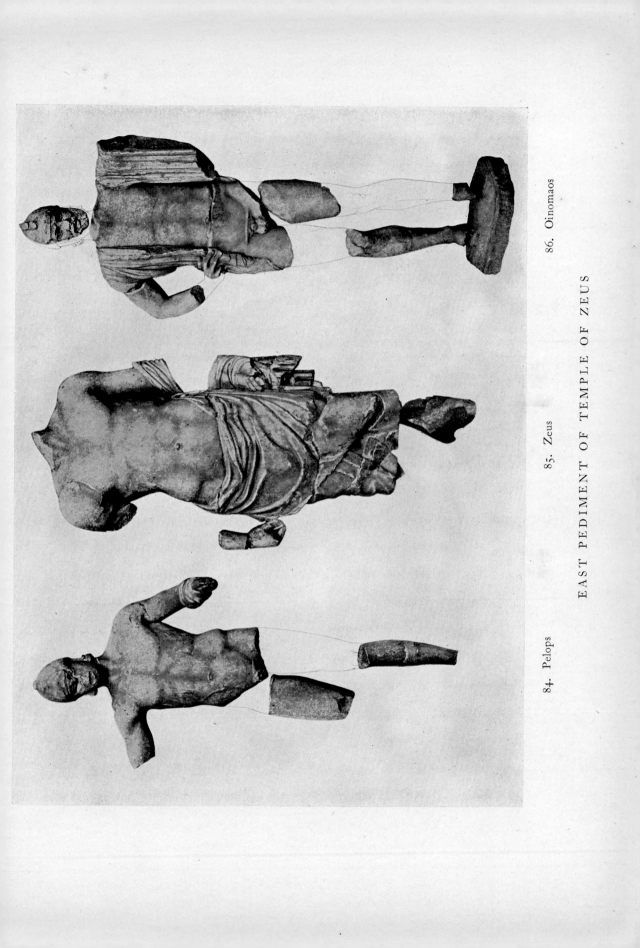

84. Pelops   85. Zeus   86. Oinomaos

EAST PEDIMENT OF TEMPLE OF ZEUS

a hall where the whole statue could be safely erected. Both are equally necessary, and if the main hall was the workshop of Pheidias we may with Adler regard the long, narrow building as an annexe to it.

SCULPTURES OF THE TEMPLE

We must now turn to the sculptured decorations of the temple.[1] The pediments are described at some length by Pausanias, who ascribes the eastern pediment to the sculptor Paionios, the western to Alkamenes. In the eastern pediment were represented the preparations for the contest between Pelops and Oinomaos. Pausanias mentions twenty-one figures, if we count each chariot as four, and of all these figures portions were recovered. The subject of the western pediment was the fight between the Lapiths and the Centaurs. Pausanias does not enumerate all the figures, but the excavations have shown that this pediment likewise contained twenty-one figures, which completely fill the available space.

In attempting to reconstruct the pediments we must be guided partly by the description of Pausanias, partly by the measurements of the tympanon, partly by the evidence of the actual remains. Some archaeologists have based their reconstruction on the position in which the fallen blocks were found. But, as Treu has pointed out, after the fall of the temple the site was occupied by a Byzantine village, and it is certain that many of the blocks of the pediments were moved from the places where they were lying, and even used in the building of the village. Hence no reliance can be placed on such evidence.

For the arrangement of the figures the description of Pausanias is invaluable, but, as we shall see, he makes some undoubted mistakes. Some of these are due to imperfect observation : thus on the east pediment he describes a kneeling maiden as a groom, a mistake perfectly intelligible when we consider that the pediments were some 60 feet above the level of the ground, and therefore could only be seen from a distance. Moreover, he probably paid little attention to the subordinate figures ; indeed, in describing the western pediment he omits most of them. Other mistakes are due to misinterpretation, or perhaps to wrong information on the part of his guides. The most glaring mistake of this type is his description of the Apollo of the western pediment

[1] *Olympia*, iii.

as Peirithoos. It must have been to the official guides that he owed the probably unfounded statement about Paionios and Alkamenes. One more point must be noticed. In using the terms right or left Pausanias always speaks from the spectator's point of view.

The tympanon had a length of 26·40 metres, or 80 Pheidonian feet, and a height of 3·30 metres, or 10 Pheidonian feet. Its depth was at least 0·84 metres, and may have been more. To the height must be added some 11 centimetres due to the hollowing out of the surface of the sloping geison blocks. But this gain was counterbalanced by the fact that the figures were not placed directly on the horizontal geison blocks but on marble slabs at least 0·10 metre in thickness.

The position of the figures is determined partly by their height and shape. Thus there can be no doubt that Zeus and Apollo stood in the centre and the recumbent women occupied the angles. A comparison of those figures that can be definitely placed proves that they were arranged in symmetrical pairs on either side of the centre, and it is probable that the remaining figures were similarly arranged. The assignment of a figure to the left or right of the gable can be often settled by observing the difference in working between its two sides. The sculptors of Olympia practised considerable economy of labour, and those parts which were not meant to be seen were usually less carefully worked and often left quite in the rough. Sometimes an accurate clue to the position of a figure is afforded by the shape of the basis. Most reliable of all is the evidence of corrections made by the workmen when putting a figure into position in order to fit it in with the adjacent figures. Examples of these various kinds of proof will be found in our description of the pediments.

In the following pages I have followed the reconstruction finally adopted by Treu after a long and careful study of the actual remains (Fig. 83). His arguments appear to me conclusive. Other arrangements may offer a greater variety and may therefore appeal more to modern taste. But the strict symmetry of Treu's reconstruction appears to me not only more in accordance with the Greek spirit of the period but also more dignified and more appropriate to the massive simplicity of the temple.[1]

[1] It is impossible to discuss at length the various reconstructions of the pediments. For Treu's arrangement v. *Olympia*, iii. 114 ff. The arrangement adopted in the museum at Olympia is that of Curtius, *ib.*, p. 280. The references to the earlier

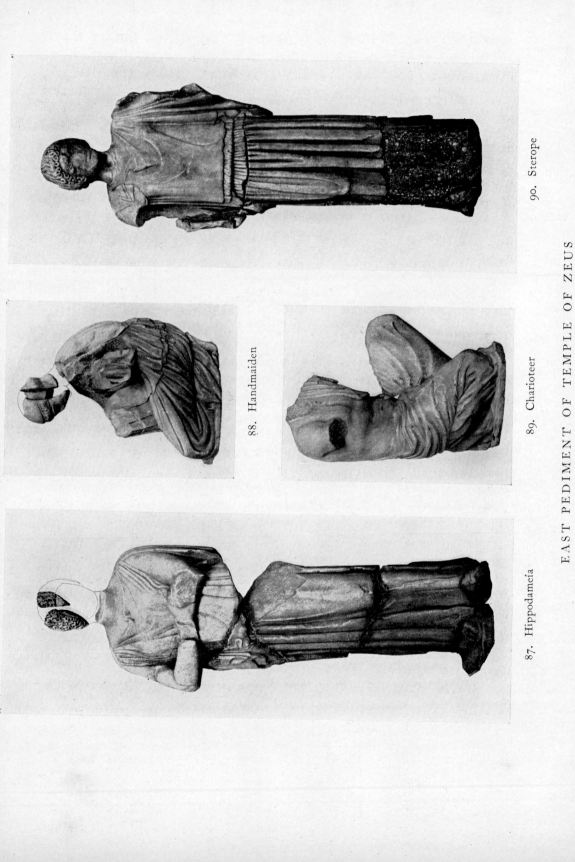

90. Sterope

88. Handmaiden

89. Charioteer

87. Hippodameia

EAST PEDIMENT OF TEMPLE OF ZEUS

THE EASTERN PEDIMENT

Greek religious feeling demanded, we are usually told, that the scene represented on the principal or eastern pediment of a temple should be calm and stately. The artist of the Olympic pediment has chosen for his subject not the actual contest between Pelops and Oinomaos but the moment of preparation. To the spectator's left and right respectively stand the two combatants with their chariots and attendants. Between them stands the majestic figure of Zeus, the arbiter of the contest, uniting the two groups but invisible to the competitors, who are turned away from him towards their chariots. The upper part of the god is naked, his left arm and lower limbs swathed in his mantle (Fig. 85). In his right hand he held a sceptre, probably of gilded bronze. The head is unfortunately lost, but the torso of the god is boldly and powerfully modelled and his attitude dignified. The back is only roughly carved and almost flat, an indication that the figure was placed close against the back wall of the tympanon. The bend of the neck shows that he is looking to his right, towards Pelops, the destined victor, and away from Oinomaos, who stands on his left (Figs. 84, 86).

Both heroes are helmeted and hold spears the shafts of which were probably of bronze. Pelops also bore on his left arm a round marble shield, of which portions have been found. From the careful modelling of his body both back and front it seems probable that the artist originally intended it to be naked, but changed his mind, perhaps after the figure had been placed in position, and added a cuirass, probably of bronze, the holes for the fastening of which are visible on his body. Perhaps this change was felt to be necessary in order to balance the somewhat heavier form of Oinomaos, who wears a cloak over his shoulders. The alertness shown in the attitude of Pelops

literature will be found in Frazer's *Pausanias*, iii. 511, 522. Later references are collected by F. Studniczka, *Olympische Forschungen*, iii, Leipzig, 1923. Treu's arrangement of the west pediment is almost universally accepted. Other arrangements are those of Curtius mentioned above, and of the painter Skovgaard. The latter is criticized by Treu, *Olympische Forschungen*, i, Leipzig, 1907. The reconstruction of the east pediment is far more doubtful. Wernicke, in *Jahrb.* xii. 169, gives illustrations of ten different reconstructions. The last and most valuable discussion of the pediments is that of Studniczka, *op. cit.* He transposes the groups of two figures on either side of Zeus, placing Oinomaos on the right hand of Zeus. The two crouching figures are placed next to the gable figures, and the kneeling boy and maiden take their places in front of the horses.

contrasts strongly with the haughty indifference of Oinomaos, who stands with his right hand placed carelessly on his hip, and his lips half opened almost in a sneer. In contrast to the more youthful Pelops he is bearded. The beard is not rendered plastically, but the surface is left bare for painting. Colour must also have been employed to bring out the double fold of his cloak, and to mark the line of his teeth between the half-open lips.

Next to Pelops and Oinomaos respectively stand Hippo-dameia and Sterope (Figs. 87, 90). The two are clearly distin-guished by their dress and pose. Hippodameia wears a Doric chiton open at the side, and stands with her head slightly inclined towards Pelops and her arms on her breast. Sterope is more richly robed in a closed chiton elaborately draped. She stands erect and proud, her head turned away from her lord. In her left hand, which is raised to the shoulder, she holds a corner of her dress; her right hand, which was also raised, seems to have held some object, possibly, as Treu suggests, a sacrificial bowl or basket. If this suggestion is correct, this is the only hint of the sacrifice which according to tradition Oinomaos offered while Pelops was starting. Both these figures are cut off flat behind without any attempt at modelling; that of Hippodameia is slightly hollowed out, probably in order to reduce its weight.

These five figures form the central group. On either side of them are the chariots, but the space between the horses and the central group is in both cases filled by a connecting figure. That in front of the horses of Oinomaos is, as Pausanias tells us, Myrtilos. He sits with his right leg drawn up, his left leg under him. Head and body are turned towards his horses on his left. His right hand possibly held a halter, his left arm rested on a staff, some such support being necessary to maintain the balance of the figure. He wears a cloak that falls over his left shoulder. The careless finish of his left side, particularly of the left ear, shows that the figure must have been turned towards the left, and this conclusion is confirmed by the shape of the triangular basis. The head is that of an old man, bearded, with crow's feet about his eyes and wrinkled brow. The hair is only roughly outlined in broad masses, all details being left to the painter.

On the opposite side, in front of the horses of Pelops, crouches a boy in a similar attitude but reversed. In this case it is the right side, the side nearest the horses, that

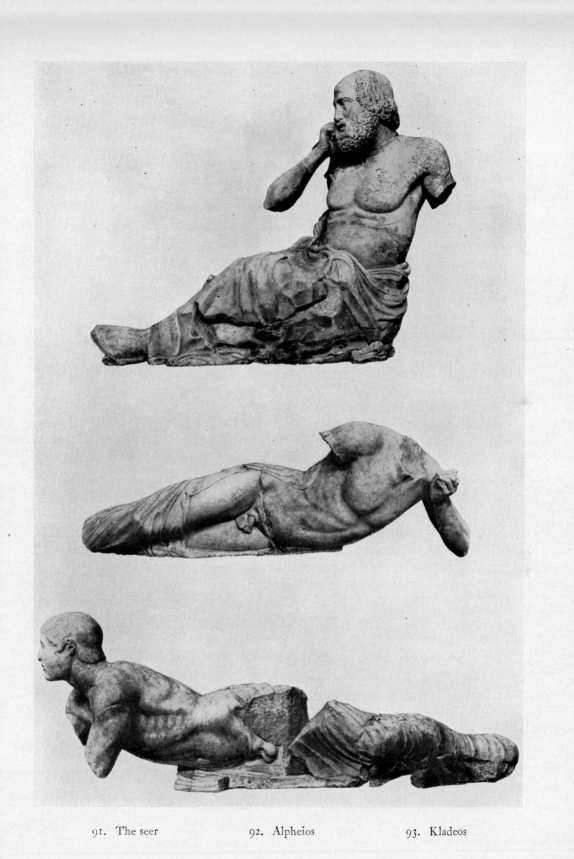

91. The seer   92. Alpheios   93. Kladeos

EAST PEDIMENT OF TEMPLE OF ZEUS

is carelessly worked. He too wears a cloak over his left shoulder and rests his right hand on the ground. His right leg, which is drawn under him, is the worst piece of modelling in the pediments. Not only is the thigh shorter than that of the left leg, but it is absolutely shapeless. We must remember, however, that the sculptor never intended it to be seen from the same level, much less to be seen from above as in the museum. Seen from below and at a distance only the point of the knee can have been visible, and the carelessness may therefore in part be due to the economy of labour that characterizes the work of the pediments.

According to Pausanias this boy is the charioteer of Pelops, Killas or Sphairos. But in this he seems to have been misled by the analogy of Myrtilos. The real charioteer can only be the elder of the two kneeling figures behind the chariot (Fig. 89). His bent back and outstretched arms leave no doubt of his identity. He is grasping the chariot reins and is ready to start immediately. The boy behind him, whose head is reproduced in Fig. 96, is probably a groom. Both these figures are less carefully finished on the left side than on the right, and it is certain therefore that they were turned towards the left.

Of the horses of both chariots considerable remains were found. The outer trace horse was modelled in the round, the other three in high relief. Colour must have been largely used: there are traces of rich brown colour on the horses' tails, and most of the harness was represented by paint. Of the chariots nothing is left, but that they existed is clear from the holes left for the chariot poles. Whether they were of marble or bronze we cannot say.

In comparing the two groups we notice that while the chariot of Pelops is ready to start, the preparations are less advanced on the part of Oinomaos, whose charioteer is still seated at his horses' heads. Thus the sculptor subtly suggests the feature in the legend that the suitor was always allowed a start, while Oinomaos waited till he had completed his sacrifice.

Behind the chariot of Oinomaos are an old man (Fig. 91) and a kneeling maiden (Fig. 88). Pausanias wrongly describes them as grooms. The position of the old man is certain, for his right foot is cut away to make room for the basis of the chariot. He is the most realistic and lifelike figure in the pediment. His head (Fig. 104) is heavy and much wrinkled, somewhat bold in front with wavy locks hanging down behind ending in a row of close curls, his beard being represented by similar curls. Details were brought out by colour, traces of which were visible on the beard. The body is heavy with deep rolls of flesh, and his legs are covered with a thick mantle. He sits with his left hand on the ground and his chin resting on his right hand, gazing on the preparations with a far-off, melancholy look as if foreboding some evil. Expression and attitude suggest that he is a seer,[1] perhaps one of the Iamidai. The introduction of the seer would be very appropriate, but some authorities regard him as a mere retainer of the house of Oinomaos. The girl behind him (Fig. 88) must be some handmaiden of Sterope. She crouches with bowed head and hands clasped over her feet in the typical attitude of a slave girl. The angles were filled by two youthful figures stretched at full length watching the scene (Figs. 92 and 93). Pausanias tells us that they are river-gods, on the spectator's left Alpheios, on the right Kladeos. Treu is inclined to regard them as mere attendants. But such local personifications are common in Greek art, and there seems no reason to doubt the traditional interpretation that Pausanias gives us. The noble dignity of the two figures and the flowing lines of the drapery and muscles are quite in accord with this interpretation. The head of the figure to the right (Fig. 95), in its calm, majestic strength, is far more worthy of a river-god than of an attendant.

THE WESTERN PEDIMENT

The story of the Centaurs and the Lapiths came originally from Thessaly, whence with many another legend it was brought to the western Peloponnese, where it found a new home in the mountains of Pholoe. Peirithoos, king of the Lapiths, had invited the Centaurs to attend his marriage with Deidameia. At the marriage feast Eurytion, king of the Centaurs, heated with wine, endeavoured to carry off the bride. A fight ensued in which the Lapiths with the help of Theseus were victorious. The subject was a very favourite one with artists of the fifth century, and was represented not only at Olympia but on the metopes of the Parthenon and on the frieze of the Temple of Apollo at Bassai.

Very different is the turmoil of this scene from the calm dignity of the eastern pediment. Yet the same strict symmetry

[1] Mr. Baker-Penoyre calls my attention to the close resemblance of this figure to the attitude of the Seer on the Amphiaraos vase (*Mon. In.* x, Pl. IX, iv. v). Here his name is given as Palamedes, and over his head is a serpent.

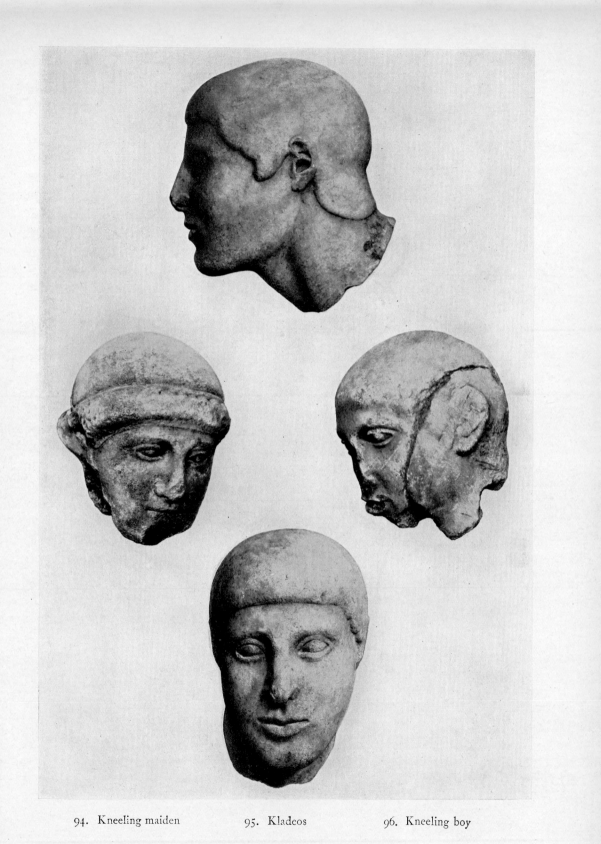

94. Kneeling maiden   95. Kladeos   96. Kneeling boy

HEADS FROM EAST PEDIMENT

governs the composition. In the centre stands a powerful athletic figure of more than mortal stature; in the angles are two pairs of women reclining. Between the angle figures and the central figure are two evenly balanced scenes of conflict, each consisting of eight figures, divided into three groups. Nearest to the angles a kneeling Lapith is struggling to overcome a Centaur who tries to carry off a Lapith woman. Next comes a group of two figures, a Centaur and a Lapith, represented almost upright and full face. Finally another group of three, a standing hero striking with a weapon at a Centaur who has seized a struggling Lapith woman.

It is obvious from this description that the position of most of the figures is determined beyond any doubt by the height and shape of the groups. The only possible variation is in the case of the groups nearest the centre. In the museum at Olympia the Lapith woman is next to the central figure. But Treu has brought forward convincing arguments to prove that these groups should be reversed, so that the place next to the centre is occupied by the hero. Thus arranged, the slope of the heads corresponds to the slope of the gable, a principle that seems to be consistently observed on both pediments. If, on the other hand, the hero were placed farther back, his weapon would appear to be striking at the geison above him, a most unpleasing effect. Moreover, the movement of the group in this case would be towards the central figure, not away from him, and the god's outstretched right hand would appear to be grasping the Centaur's hair, a motive quite inconsistent with the dignity of his attitude. Lastly, Treu's arrangement is certainly implied by Pausanias. ' Peirithoos ', he says, ' is in the centre, and on one side of him Eurytion trying to carry off Deidameia and Kaineus coming to his assistance, on the other side Theseus with his battle-axe laying about among the Centaurs.'

In his identification of the central figure (Fig. 97) it is generally agreed that Pausanias is mistaken. His stature, his commanding gesture, his calmness, the analogy of the eastern pediment, prove that he is no mortal, much less the injured husband thus coolly looking on while his bride is being carried off. He is a god, and we cannot mistake the type. He is no other than Apollo, the fabled ancestor of the Lapiths. He stands erect, naked save for a cloak that falls over his right shoulder, and is draped round his arm. This arm is fully extended to the right, and the head is

turned in the same direction. In his left hand he seems to have
held some object, probably a bow. His figure is tall, well proportioned, and muscular, yet free from all hardness or exaggeration. The draping of his cloak is simple and dignified. There
were traces of dark-red paint on it when first found. The head
(Figs. 102, 103) is treated with the same severe simplicity and
freedom from all affectation. As in the other heads of the
pediments, there are traces of archaism in the modelling of the
eyes and mouth. The chin is somewhat heavy ; the hair falls
very low on his forehead, and is worked in wavy locks bound by
a diadem, possibly of gold, and ending in a row of close curls.

If the central figure is Apollo, the heroes on either side of
him must be Peirithoos and Theseus, and as the god is turned
towards his right, Peirithoos, as the most important figure in
the legend, will be naturally on this side. Of Peirithoos only the
head and a few fragments have been found. He is striding to
the right with right leg advanced, and his mantle that has fallen
from his shoulders twisted round his legs. His right arm was
raised, and probably held a sword with which he was striking at
Eurytion. The Centaur has already a deep gash in his head, but
in spite of his wound he still clasps Deidameia with a look of
maudlin drunkenness and lustfully clutches at her breast (Fig. 98).
Throwing her weight backwards she tries to loosen his grip, and
with her left elbow forces back his head. Eurytion is distinguished from the other Centaurs by a crown of vine or ivy leaves,
the marks of which are visible on his head. Colour must have
been freely used for his hair and the gaping wound in his head,
and also for his huge beard, only the edge of which is carved.
Deidameia wears a long closed chiton that has been torn off
her left shoulder. Her hair is bound with a μίτρα fastened on
the forehead, and is arranged in heavy masses the surface of
which has been roughened as a preparation for paint. The
head is excellently preserved. The features are clear cut and
firm, the expression calm, almost cold. There is no sign of
emotion, but in the bend of the neck and the slight contraction
of the eyes and mouth the sculptor has finely suggested her
obstinate resistance to her hateful ravisher.

To the right of this group—the spectator's left—is a group
of two figures mentioned by Pausanias, a Centaur carrying off
a beautiful Lapith boy, possibly a cup-bearer. Only the central
portion of the figures is preserved, enough to show us that they

97. APOLLO

West pediment

are represented full face, that the horse-body of the Centaur is thrown into the background, and that the boy is making a vigorous resistance.

The next group is far better preserved, and in design and execution is one of the most successful in the pediment (Fig. 101). A Lapith has brought a Centaur on to his knees and tries to force him to the ground. The Centaur tries to support himself with his right arm, while with his left he still grasps the hair of a Lapith maiden. The tense effort of the Lapith is admirably conceived and rendered as he throws himself forward on one knee with all the muscles of the trunk strained to the uttermost and his head slightly bent down, and with both hands clasping the Centaur's head brings his whole weight to bear upon him. In strong contrast is the cowering attitude and piteous expression of the maiden as she tries to free herself from the grip of the bestial monster.

We return now to the central figure. To the left of Apollo is the hero identified by Pausanias with Theseus (Fig. 105). He is the exact counterpart of Peirithoos, striding forward with his left foot, and his legs entwined in his cloak. The head is well preserved, and from the position of the muscles on either side of the neck we can see that he is raising both arms ; as Pausanias tells us, he is wielding an axe. The Centaur whom he is attacking has his fore-leg clasped round a richly robed Lapith woman who is thrusting him away, with one hand clutching his beard, with the other his hair. The success of her efforts is shown in the expression of pain on the Centaur's face. From her elaborate dress Treu supposes her to be the Nympheutria.

The group of two figures consists of a youthful Lapith struggling with a Centaur, whose body, as in the corresponding group on the other side, is in the background. The young Lapith is an athlete, a pankratiast, as shown by his swollen ear (Fig. 106). He has his right arm round the Centaur's neck, and has already forced him on to his knees. The Centaur vainly tries to break his hold, and in despair viciously bites the encircling arm. The contrast of the two faces is instructive. The Centaur's face is violently distorted with pain and passion : in the Lapith's the strain is indicated with more restraint in the contracted brow and slightly open lips. While the athletic motive is well conceived, the effect of the drapery swathed round the Lapith's legs is particularly unfortunate.

The last group on this side is inferior to its counterpart. In this case the kneeling Lapith is plunging a knife, probably a sacrificial knife, into the Centaur's heart, and the Centaur tries to lift a Lapith woman on to his back. The fanlike drapery of the woman, with its hopeless attempt at realism, and the grotesque position of the Centaur's body, the back curved like that of a sea monster, and the hind legs standing up behind the woman, are most unpleasant in effect. The redeeming feature in the group is the splendid figure of the kneeling Lapith, which, like all the nude figures, is full of life and vigour.

Lastly, we come to the angle figures—in each angle a young woman stretched at full length and slightly in front of her an older woman with her body resting on a cushion (Fig. 99). The cushions belong perhaps to the couches of the feast. Who the women are we cannot say. It has been suggested that the younger women are local nymphs, and the analogy of the eastern pediment favours this view. But, as Treu points out, they are dressed precisely like the Lapith women, and like them their dresses are torn off one shoulder, leaving one-half of the body bare. It seems probable, then, that they are merely Lapith women who have escaped from the fray and anxiously await the issue. In this case the two elder women were probably the aged attendants of the family such as we might expect to see at a marriage feast. Their heads (Fig. 107) are modelled with the same lifelike realism as the head of the old attendant on the eastern pediment.

A peculiarity of these figures is that while all the rest of the sculptures are of Parian marble, three of these and an arm of the fourth are of Pentelican marble. The explanation seems to be that these figures were like the rest originally of Parian marble, but at some later period were damaged and replaced by copies in Pentelican marble. This is confirmed by the differences in style that they exhibit, notably in the overlapping of the upper eyelid, the flat and feeble modelling of the hair, the fullness of the flesh with its realistic folds. All these are marks of a later period. At the same time a comparison of the young woman at the south end of Parian marble with the other of Pentelican shows that the copier, though working in the style of his own age, faithfully copied the original types. We have seen that these repairs to the pediments were probably executed about 40 B.C., when the roof of the temple was damaged by earthquake.

98. Eurytion and Deidameia

99. Lapith woman (Pentelican marble)

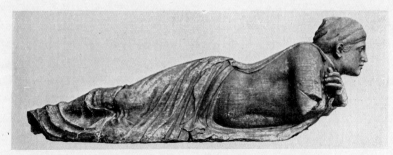

100. Lapith woman (Pentelican marble)

WEST PEDIMENT OF TEMPLE OF ZEUS

THE GREATNESS OF THE SCULPTURES OF THE PEDIMENTS

The real greatness of these magnificent sculptures has not been as much appreciated as it deserves. We are apt to compare them with the matchless marbles of the Parthenon and feel disappointed, forgetting that they were produced some twenty years earlier, and in the artistic history of the fifth century twenty years is a long period. The inequality of execution and the defects are obvious to the most casual observer and are increased by the actual condition of the statues. Some of the defects, for example in the treatment of drapery and of the horses, may be due to the inability of the sculptors. More are due to the economy of labour which led the artists to neglect those parts which owing to their position would be invisible to the spectator. Other parts were left unfinished because the artist relied on the use of colour, to bring out, for example, details of the hair or to mark the difference between the flesh and the clothing. This brings us to the real cause of our want of appreciation. None of us, none even of those who have seen the sculptures themselves at Olympia, has ever seen them as they should be seen. It is not only that all trace of colour, all the accessories, have been lost, but that we only see them in a museum on a level with our eyes, not as they were intended to be seen, raised aloft over the mighty pillars of the colonnade in the clear light of a Greek sky.[1] Could we see them thus we should realize not only the greatness of the conception that inspired them but the grandeur of the composition and the skill of the craftsmen. These sculptures have not of course the wonderful finish of the Parthenon statues. But, as Vasari says, speaking of Della Robbia and Donatello, ' Experience shows that things that are to be seen at a distance, whether pictures or sculptures, have more effect in a bold sketch (*una bella bozza*) than when finished.' Moreover, the artists of Olympia never forgot how their sculptures were to be seen. The recumbent figures in the angles, the kneeling Lapiths in the west pediment, are so arranged that they can only be fully appreciated when seen from below. How much of the beauties of the Theseus or the three Fates were visible to the Athenian spectator ?

[1] Some idea of what the sculptures looked like seen from below can be obtained from the beautiful photographs published recently by Richard Hamann in his *Olympische Kunst*.

In these pediments we see embodied the very spirit of Olympic religion and of the Olympic games. Take first the eastern pediment. In the centre the majestic figure of Zeus, lord of Olympia and of Hellas, the giver of victory and arbiter of strife. By his side Pelops, who had his shrine within the Altis itself, chief of the heroes of Olympia as Zeus was chief of the gods. On the other side of Zeus Oinomaos, representing perhaps a yet older régime before Zeus or Pelops came to Olympia. Then in the angles the river-gods Alpheios and Kladeos, older than all, but ever young in their graceful strength, emblems of the richness and beauty of the land. Between them and the centre the chariots ready for the contest, with their crouching grooms and charioteers. There is no allusion to the discordant elements in the story, to the treachery of Myrtilus, or his love for Hippodameia. Only in the wistful face of the old seer do we see any hint of the tragedy. Rather the chariots suggest those races that drew kings and nobles from all parts of Hellas to compete for the olive crown. Above all we recall the solemn scene in the council-house before the games, when competitors and trainers took an oath before the awful image of Zeus Hokios to observe all the rules of the games and abstain from anything dishonourable. In the dignity and restraint of the whole composition is expressed the very spirit of Olympic religion. No less does the western pediment express the spirit of the games, of the contest. For to the Greeks the struggle of Lapiths and Centaurs typified the superiority of Greek over barbarian, of the trained athlete over brute force. For the Lapiths, as we have pointed out, are athletes, pankratiasts, and in their struggle against their monstrous foes they employ the arts of the wrestling school. To their aid comes Theseus, the hero of athletics, who was said himself to have invented the art of wrestling; and over all stands the calm figure of Apollo, the ideal of physical beauty and athletic manhood.

The composition of both pediments is, as we have seen, governed by the same strict principle of symmetry. In both we have twenty-one figures, in both the central figure is a god invisible to the actors, in both the god is placed between two groups that balance each other figure for figure. Each group is self-centred. In the chariot groups all the figures turn towards the chariots in the centre ; on the western pediment two groups of three figures move towards the central group of two. In both, too, the god forms with the standing figures on either

side of him a cross-group that unites with the main groups, a group almost architectural in its symmetry and severity, the lines of which seem to continue the lines of the fluted columns and triglyphs. The angles of both pediments are filled by reclining figures. Thus there is a regular gradation in the height of the figures corresponding to the slope of the geison, and a similar gradation is noticeable on the ground plan, the central figure being set close to the back wall, the angle figures brought out to the very edge of the geison. Yet in this close symmetry there is no slavish monotony. Each of the figures has its own individuality, distinguishing it from its counterpart, and the variety of pose and expression shows a remarkable originality and power of observation.

It is in the treatment of the nude that the sculptors of the pediments show their supreme skill. The modelling is strong and severe, free from all artificiality or exaggeration. The figures are finely proportioned, tall and strong, but there is no heaviness about them. The muscles, whether in rest or in action, are clearly and truthfully rendered, but without any of the harshness of archaic art. This is the more remarkable when we consider the extraordinary variety in pose and action, so different from the limited range of the Aeginetan pediments. No two figures are alike, and yet every figure is natural. The finest figure of all perhaps is the Apollo of the western pediment; but the artists knew the difference between the torso of a young man and of an old man, and almost equally fine is the treatment of the torso of Zeus and of the aged seer. Yet more remarkable is the knowledge shown of the difference between the appearance of the muscles at rest and in action. Compare, for example, the torso of the Apollo with that of the kneeling Lapith (Fig. 101), or take the recumbent figure of Kladeos in the western pediment and mark how the forward position of the arms stretches the skin over the muscles covering the ribs, while the muscles of the abdomen are soft and relaxed. And compare this figure with the much softer and more rounded lines of the young Lapith woman in the western pediment (Fig. 100). There can be no doubt that the sculptors who made these statues must have been trained in an athletic school that taught them to observe and to represent truthfully and naturally all the positions and movements of the human body as seen in the wrestling school and on the racecourse.

There is the same wonderful variety in the treatment of

the heads, which exhibit a combination of archaic severity with an extraordinary realism. The archaism is apparent in the treatment of the eyelids, which form a uniform ridge round the eyes, or in the slight droop of the mouth. The hair is sometimes rendered in wavy locks ending in spiral curls finished in the centre with a drill : sometimes the whole head is covered by these curls : sometimes the hair is merely outlined in broad masses, all details being shown by colour. Probably colour was used more or less in all cases, for we can hardly suppose that some heads were painted, some not. The realism is evident in the extraordinary variety of feature : every face is different and every face is lifelike. Most realistic of all are the heads of old people. Compare for example the head of Oinomaos (Fig. 86) and the head of the seer (Fig. 104). The heads of the aged Lapith women on the western pediment are equally lifelike, but possibly they may be the work of a later period. One of them (Fig. 107) bears no little resemblance in type to the portrait of an Elean lady (Fig. 35). The barbarous centaurs, too, have each their own individuality. The maudlin sensuality of the centaur trying to carry off Deidameia (Fig. 98) is totally different from the cruel bestiality of the centaur struggling against a young Lapith in the left corner of the pediment. There is the same individuality in the heads of women. What can be more unlike than the head of the kneeling handmaid of the eastern pediment (Fig. 94) and the kneeling Lapith girl (Fig. 108). In the heads of the young we should expect to find more uniformity. But the differences here are perhaps still more remarkable, even in the heads of gods and heroes. Apollo, Theseus (Fig. 105), Kladeos (Fig. 95), are perfectly distinct in type from one another. Still more so are the young Lapith (Fig. 106) and the kneeling groom (Fig. 96). Only in their self-restraint and dignity and in the absence of emotion do these heads resemble one another. Pain and fear are expressed by a slight contraction of the eyes and mouth. It was not that the artists could not represent violent emotion, but they regarded its expression as undignified, and only in the case of the barbarous centaurs did they permit themselves to represent faces distorted by passion or by pain.

The modelling of drapery is far less effective. Indeed, the sculptors are rarely successful except when treating it conventionally in straight folds in figures at rest, as for example in the figures of Hippodameia and Sterope. Generally the drapery

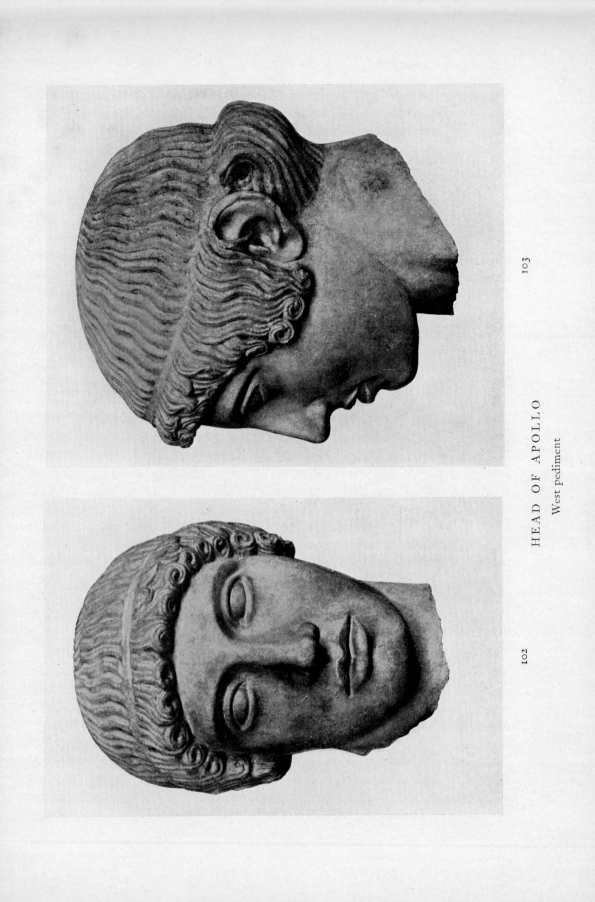

103

102

HEAD OF APOLLO
West pediment

is heavy, and all feeling of the human form is lost beneath it. Sometimes it is treated as mere decorative ornament. Sometimes it is swathed round the lower limbs so as to form a sort of pedestal, a particularly unpleasing effect. Some of the young Lapiths appear to be hopelessly entangled in their robes. It is in the treatment of drapery that the inferiority of the Olympic sculptures to those of the Parthenon is most apparent. Yet even this is not wholly the fault of the sculptors, for the heavy drapery that they reproduce was the ordinary dress of the Peloponnese, where the softer Ionian dress was unknown.

The sculptors are hardly more successful in their representation of horses and of the centaurs. The bodies of the horses, as far as we can judge from their broken remains, were heavy and clumsy, though there is some careful rendering of the muscles. The problem of combining the horse body and the human body has completely baffled the sculptors. The centaurs of Olympia are impossible monsters, while the artists of the Parthenon, by decreasing the size of the horse and enlarging the human torso and representing it full face, have with an incredible skill almost succeeded in making us believe in their reality.

Who were the Artists of the Pediments?

We are now in a position to discuss the question of the authorship of the pediments. Were they, as Pausanias tells us, the work of Paionios and Alkamenes? If not, to whom should we assign them or to what school? There are serious difficulties in accepting the statement of Pausanias. With regard to Paionios we know that he executed the figure of Nike set up by the Messenians not earlier than 424 B.C. This statue we possess, and so different is it in style from the sculptures of the eastern pediment that many critics refuse to believe that they can have been produced by the same artist. Still, the possibility must be admitted that the pediments were the work of his youth, the Nike of his mature art. A more serious difficulty is that Paionios, in his own inscription on the basis of the Nike, claims to have been victorious in a competition for the erection of the akroteria of the temple. That he should make no reference to the far more important sculptures of the pediment if he were really the artist seems incredible. Much less can we suppose that by akroteria he meant pediments, or even that Pausanias so understood it.

At the same time the existence of this inscription may well have given rise to a popular tradition that the unknown artist of the pediment was the famous Paionios.

The difficulty with regard to Alkamenes is different. He was a pupil of Pheidias, and considered by some second only to his master. Many of his works are mentioned by ancient authors, but no extant statue can with certainty be assigned to him. The latest of his works were two statues of Herakles and Athene set up by Thrasybulos at Thebes after the fall of the thirty tyrants in 403 B.C. Now the temple of Olympia was probably finished about 457 B.C. If Alkamenes therefore was the artist of the western pediment he must have had an artistic career of over fifty years. Though not impossible, it is hardly probable that an artist so young and at the time unknown would have been entrusted with so important a work. It is possible that he might have been employed as an assistant to Paionios, but an artist responsible for a whole pediment is somewhat more than an assistant. Possibly we may find the clue to the tradition in the vanity of the official guides who, when asked who was the artist of the pediment, might well be tempted to assign it to an artist so closely connected with Pheidias and so highly esteemed by antiquity.

What light do the actual remains of the pediments throw upon the problem? In the first place the two pediments are so similar in composition and execution, in their excellences and their defects, that we cannot avoid the conclusion that they were the work of the same sculptor or at least of the same school of sculptors. And this conclusion is confirmed by the fact that the metopes also exhibit the same characteristics. If the similarity were confined to peculiarities of execution, it might be explained by the supposition of a school of local sculptors working under the two masters. But the similarity here extends to the whole composition. One-half of Pausanias's statement must be wrong, and in view of the difficulties stated above with regard to both Paionios and Alkamenes we are justified in rejecting the whole statement.

If we refuse to ascribe the sculptures either to Alkamenes or Paionios, to what sculptor or school of sculptors can we assign them? Certainty is impossible, nor does space allow me to discuss the various solutions that have been conjectured. But if I may venture to express my own opinion, the evidence seems

104. Head of seer (E. pediment)

105. Head of Theseus (W. pediment)

106. Head of Lapith boy (W. pediment)

107. Head of aged Lapith woman
(W. pediment)

108. Head of Lapith maiden
(W. pediment)

109. Head of Athene, from Metope of
Nemean Lion

in favour of the view, which is gradually gaining ground, that the sculptures of the pediments and of the metopes are the work of a native Elean school. The temple was in part a monument of the newly established power of Elis. Libon, the architect, was himself an Elean, and we should naturally expect that he would associate with himself Elean sculptors. We have seen that there must have existed for centuries a school of local craftsmen who produced the bronzes and terra-cottas which were used as votive offerings. The art of sculpture was practised in all parts of Greece in the fifth century. The only Elean sculptor of the period known to us is Kallon, two of whose works were set up in the Altis. We may be sure, however, that the demand for athletic statues must have produced a local school of sculptors, even if none of them attained especial eminence. Now the characteristics of the pediments are precisely those that we should expect to find in an Elean school, originality and realism combined with a certain archaic severity, excellence in the modelling of the nude, weakness in the rendering of drapery. We have seen that from the first the votive offerings of Olympia were to a marked degree distinguished by originality and realism, and we should expect to find the same qualities in the local sculpture. Again, no place in Greece can have been more open to the influence of the great athletic school of sculpture that had its centre in Argos and Sikyon. This school almost owed its existence to the demand for statues of victorious athletes. The works of its greatest masters were to be seen in the Altis, the sculptors themselves must have been attracted to the games in the hopes of securing patrons, and many of them may, like Pheidias, have preferred to execute on the spot the works that were to be set up there. The characteristics of this school were severity and simplicity. From such examples the local artists could hardly fail to acquire that mastery in the modelling of the nude which we find in the sculptures of the pediment. But while no place was so rich as Olympia in athletic art, it was conspicuously poor in examples of female statues. There was little demand there for the masterpieces of Ionian art which had so strong an influence on the sculptors of Athens, and in the treatment of drapery the sculptors of Olympia, having no models to hand, were thrown back on their own resources. Thus, if the pediments were the work of local artists, their merits and defects alike admit of a simple explanation.

THE SCULPTURES OF THE METOPES

The metopes, representing the labours of Herakles, were placed over the entrance to the pronaos and opisthodome. Fragments of all have been recovered, though much mutilated. Some of the most important were found by the French expedition and are now in the Louvre. Pausanias gives a list of the subjects. At the west end were (1) the Amazon's girdle, (2) the Kerynean stag, (3) the Cretan bull, (4) the Stymphalian birds, (5) the Lernaean hydra, (6) the Nemean lion. Pausanias enumerates them from south to north : in reality the series begins at the north with the Nemean lion. Beginning again at the south end of the east end he mentions (1) the Erymanthian boar, (2) the horses of Diomede, (3) Geryon, (4) Atlas, (5) the Augean stables. One metope has fallen out of the list ; the excavations have shown that it represented Cerberus. This metope was placed between those of Atlas and the Augean stables. The place of honour was assigned to the latter because it was the only labour connected with Elis. It was after his victory over Augeias, according to Pindar, that Herakles founded the Olympic Games.

The metopes are 1·60 metres high and 1·508 broad. Like the pediments they are made of Parian marble, and colour was freely used. The colour of the background was determined by that of the principal figures. Thus the blue coils of the hydra stood out against a red background, the red bull against a blue. In the upper surface of the figures are numerous holes which held iron spikes in forks intended to prevent the birds from building their nests in the metopes.

The figure of the *Nemean Lion* is in the Louvre : the heads of Herakles and of a goddess are at Olympia. The lion lies dead with its head on its fore-paws and tongue lolling out, while Herakles stands with his right foot on its body and his head resting on his arm in an attitude of utter weariness. In this metope alone his face is beardless, and he has the pankratiast's swollen ear. Opposite stands a goddess. It can be none other than Athene, who looks down on him with a look of troubled sympathy finely indicated by a furrow on her brow. In its delicacy, in its combination of dignity and kindliness, it is the most beautiful of all the heads in the metopes (Fig. 109). Behind Herakles stood a third figure, possibly Hermes.

The contrast between this and the metope of the Augean

stables is striking. Here the youthful Herakles stands weary after his first labour, while Athene encourages her protégé with kindly sympathy. There full of vigour he is completing his last task, and Athene, majestic in full panoply, directs his work. The relief is exceptionally high, almost in the round. The lion is carved from a separate block of marble, inserted after the metope was placed in position. Possibly the original metope was injured during its erection. The lion was painted yellow. The hair of Herakles and Athene was merely blocked out, the surface left rough. The hair of Herakles was painted with reddish brown, details being picked out in black : the eyes and eyebrows were similarly treated.

The very scanty remains of the *Lernaean Hydra* show that Herakles was represented lopping off the heads of the monster, which, supporting itself by a tree-trunk, fills the whole field with its coils. Seven heads have been put out of action and hang limply down. The other two were poised for the attack. This must have been one of the least successful of the metopes ; the field is overcrowded, while the lifeless attitude of Herakles suggests, as has been truly said, that of a hedger lopping off branches with his sickle.

Very different is the metope of the *Stymphalian Birds* (Fig. 110), most of which is in the Louvre. On the left is Athene wearing her aigis, seated on a rock and looking towards Herakles, who is holding out to her a bird. Her attitude is singularly graceful, though perhaps somewhat wanting in dignity for a goddess, and there is a peculiar charm about the beautifully modelled face and neck (Frontispiece). The head of Herakles is strong and dignified, and one of the finest in the series. Here, too, red was used for the hair.

The metope of the *Cretan Bull* (Fig. 111) is one of the best preserved, and in its composition and execution perhaps the best of all the metopes. The sculptor has here an athletic motive thoroughly suited to his abilities, and he has made the most of it. Herakles has captured the bull and fastened to it a rope, the hole for which is visible in its nostrils. The animal is trying to break away to the right, and Herakles holding the rope in his left hand throws all his weight and strength in the opposite direction. His right hand is raised and probably held a club, to be used in case of necessity. The contrast between the action of the bull and Herakles is finely rendered, and must have been greatly enhanced by the use of colour. The naked body of the hero stood out against the red of the bull, which in its turn was thrown up against a bright blue background. The attitude of Herakles is excellent, much superior to that of the bull; the strained muscles of the trunk are admirably rendered, but the lower part of the abdomen is less successful, the roll of flesh on the right flank being too heavy and the inguinal line unduly prominent for such a strained position.

Of the metopes of the *Kerynean Stag* and the *Amazon's Girdle* very little is left. In the former Herakles was represented kneeling on the stag and pulling back its horns. Of the latter all that we know is that the Amazon was lying on the ground.

Passing on to the metopes of the east end, and beginning at the south side, we have first the slaying of the *Erymanthian Boar*. The head of Herakles and the body of the boar are in the Louvre. A jar from which emerge the head and shoulders of Eurystheus is at Olympia. The sculptor has adopted the scheme so frequently represented on vases. Eurystheus has taken refuge in a jar which occupies the right-hand corner of the field, and Herakles advances towards him bearing on his shoulders the boar, which he threatens to hurl upon him.

The fragmentary remains of the metope of the *Horses of Diomede* show that the treatment of this scene was similar to that in the corresponding metope of the Theseion and also in the metope of the Cretan bull. One of the horses is prancing to the right, and Herakles, holding it by the bridle, strains to the left.

The *Geryon* metope is better preserved. The most important part of it is in the Louvre. The scheme is somewhat similar to that of the hydra metope. Herakles advances from the left. Two of Geryon's bodies have been slain and their heads hang down lifeless, their shields lying on the ground. The third, beaten to his knees, holds up his right hand like a pankratiast acknowledging defeat, while Herakles strides forward and, planting his left foot on his thigh, prepares to give him the finishing blow with his club. The composition is ineffective and the execution seems careless.

The best-known and perhaps the finest of all the metopes is that of *Herakles receiving from Atlas the apples of the Hesperides* (Fig. 112). Pausanias describes the subject as Herakles about to receive what Atlas carries (τὸ φόρημα) by which he seems to mean

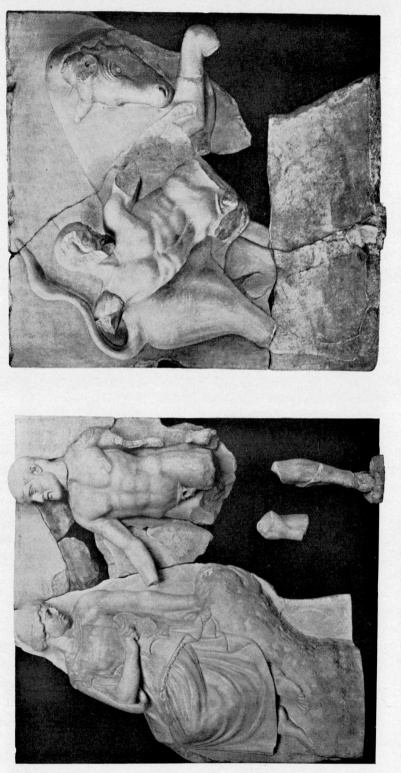

111. HERAKLES AND THE CRETAN BULL

110. HERAKLES AND STYMPHALIAN BIRDS

METOPES OF TEMPLE OF ZEUS

merely the apples and not, as is sometimes stated, 'the burden of the heavens'. In the centre stand Herakles. He is naked, and with bowed head and raised arms supports a cushion on which rest the heavens. These were probably represented by an irregular block of marble suggesting by its wavy outline a mass of cloud. Possibly stars were painted on it. In front of him stands Atlas holding in each hand three golden apples. He is bearded and an older man of heavier build than Herakles. His hair is confined by a diadem and falls in waving locks over his temples and neck. Both figures are finely modelled and quite free from exaggeration. There is a touch of irony in the way in which he offers the apples which the hero is quite unable to take. Behind Herakles stands a draped woman who raises her left hand to ease the hero of his burden. Her right hand held some staff-like object that Treu supposes to have been a spear. Who is she? She is generally regarded as one of the Hesperides offering her friendly but feeble help. But though this interpretation seems quite in keeping with the naïve humour of the scene, there is no suggestion of weakness in her stately form or of uselessness in her action, and I am inclined therefore with Treu to identify her with Athene coming as a very present aid to the hero in his difficulty. If we compare her with the Athene in the Augeias metope, the resemblance is obvious. It is true she has no helmet, but neither has she on the metope of the Stymphalian birds. There she is sufficiently distinguished by her agis : here, if Treu is right, by her spear.

In the *Kerberos* metope we can reconstruct the figure of Herakles. Kerberos occupies one right-hand corner. Herakles moving to the left is trying to drag him away by means of a chain which he has fastened to him. Another figure of which only the foot is left occupied the centre of the field. Treu conjectures that it is Hermes, who would naturally find a place in this scene.

The last metope represents the cleansing of the *Augean stables* (Fig. 113). To the left is Herakles with both arms extended backwards and holding a pole, probably the handle of a broom. With this he pushes with all his might at the pile of dung before him. To the right stands Athene fully armed and pointing downwards with her spear as if directing his work. The vigour and determination of the hero, the stately dignity of the goddess, are admirably rendered. Modern sensitiveness is apt to be shocked at the sight of a hero engaged in such a task, but this false refinement was unknown to the Greek artist, whose treatment of the subject is simple and dignified.

If we compare the metopes with the pediments we notice that in spite of a greater softness and delicacy of finish there is a close resemblance in style. The absence of the grosser faults that disfigure the pediments is due to the fact that the sculptors were engaged in a far easier task. Sculpture in relief does not present the same difficulties as sculpture in the round, and the problem of the metope is far simpler than that of the pediment. It was indeed the same problem that had presented itself to the painters of the panels on black-figured vases, and the labours of Herakles were a favourite subject of those painters. Moreover, the superior finish of the metopes was probably due to the fact that they were intended to be seen closer and at a less height. Yet, in spite of these differences, the essential characteristics of the work are the same. There is the same combination of archaism and realism, of convention and originality ; there is the same treatment of hair, eyes, and mouth, the same skill in rendering the nude, the same use of colour to supply details. The metopes were, as we have seen, contemporary with the building of the temple, and we may therefore assign them to the same group of local artists who produced the pediments.

NOTE

Hans Schrader's *Pheidias* came into my hands too late for me to make use of it, nor can I discuss in a note his revolutionary theories. According to him Pheidias executed his Zeus 460–450 B.C. Paionios had made the model for the sculptures of the temple *c.* 475 : he executed the Nike 450–440 B.C., and also designed and executed the west pediment of the Parthenon ; Alkamenes was responsible for the three figures in Pentelican marble of the west pediment at Olympia, and designed and executed the east pediment of the Parthenon.

112. HERAKLES AND ATLAS   113. HERAKLES CLEANSING THE AUGEAN STABLES

METOPES OF TEMPLE OF ZEUS

XV

The Official Buildings of Olympia

THERE was no town at Olympia. Consequently it was necessary to establish some form of administration on the spot and to provide accommodation for the officials. This consisted at first of business quarters such as were found in most Greek towns. Residences for officials were not provided till the fifth century or later. The two essential buildings were a Prytaneion and a Bouleuterion.

THE PRYTANEION

The Prytaneion [1] in a Greek state was the successor of the king's palace, the religious and political centre of the city. It was the seat of the chief magistrates and contained the hearth of Hestia on which burnt the sacred fire which might alone be used for sacrifices. Thus it was no less essential to a sanctuary than to a city. Pausanias [2] tells us of the hearth of Hestia in the Prytaneion at Olympia, where libations were offered and hymns sung before the processions started to sacrifice on the altars. Once a year at the spring equinox the hearth was cleansed ; the ashes were removed to the Altar of Zeus, and the new fire was kindled in the ancestral manner, possibly by means of a fire-drill. The Prytaneis of Olympia were the priestly officials, especially the Priest of Zeus and the Seers, the Theokoloi, and the Libation pourers. Like the magistrates of a city they probably had the right of dining in the Prytaneion, where a share of the sacrifices was allotted to them. We may surmise that during the festival the Hellanodikai enjoyed the same privileges, just as the Athlothetai did at Athens during the Panathenaic festival. [3] As, elsewhere, distinguished visitors and citizens were feasted in the Prytaneion, so at Olympia the victors in the games were feasted in a banqueting hall that formed part of the building.

[1] Dar. Sag. s.v. ; Frazer, *Pausanias*, ii, p. 170.   [2] v. 15. 8.
[3] Aristotle, *Pol. Ath.*, 63.

The Prytaneion [1] formed a square of 32·80 metres, or exactly 100 Pheidonian feet. Its entrance was in the centre of the south side, probably through a pillared doorway. This gave access to a long narrow vestibule, to the right of which was an altar of Pan. This vestibule opened to right and left into two long halls or colonnades, and in the centre into a chamber 6·80 metres square, in which we may undoubtedly recognize the shrine of Hestia. During all the alterations made in the building this chamber remained unchanged. Of the hearth itself not a vestige remains.

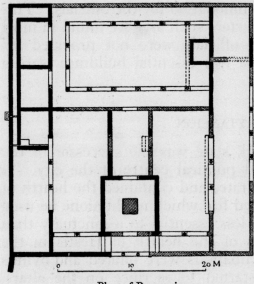

114. Plan of Prytaneion

It was probably like that of Neandria, a square walled enclosure which could contain the accumulated ashes, provided on one side with steps for the use of those who tended the fire. We do not know if it was roofed : if it was, there must have been an aperture to allow the smoke to escape.

North of this chamber was a narrower one which perhaps served as vestibule to the great court beyond. On either side were open courts facing two long colonnades. The wall of the western colonnade and the foundations of some of the pillars still exist. Its northern half was divided into several small rooms. The presence of water-channels and traces of a hearth suggest that here was the kitchen, which was an essential part of a Prytaneion. Quantities of culinary utensils, kettles, cauldrons, pans, and wire ladles were found in this part of the ruins. The kitchen was conveniently situated, for the southern part of the same colonnade probably served as the dining hall of the officials. In Roman times it was paved with mosaics, and remains of two of the couches of the Triclinium were found there.

The eastern colonnade was on a higher level and differed from the western in that instead of an outer wall it had a row of columns opening on the Hill of Kronos. Possibly it was through this

[1] *Olympia*, ii, p. 58 ; Weniger, *Klio*, vi. 1 ff.

colonnade that the processions passed out to sacrifice in the Altis.

The large court to the north seems to have been completely surrounded by colonnades, the pillars of which are of very curious construction. They are built of thick semicircular bricks, two of which together form a drum. The date of these pillars is quite unknown, nor do we know whether the court was covered or open. It is probable that this was the banqueting hall mentioned by Pausanias, where the victors were feasted : here, too, we may suppose, the hymns and dances took place, and here the processions mustered before passing through the eastern colonnade into the Altis.

In Roman times considerable alterations and extensions were made along the west and south sides. A colonnade was built along the whole length of the latter. But through all its history the central hearth of Hestia remained unchanged. It is a curious illustration of religious conservatism and a proof of the antiquity and importance of the building that no clamps of metal were used in either the Greek or Roman walls.

It is impossible to determine the date of the building. The one certain fact is that the Greek building and the Roman extension must have been in existence respectively at the time when the Greek and Roman walls of the Altis were built. For the course of the western walls was determined by the western wall of the Prytaneion. Some fifth-century Doric capitals may possibly belong to the Greek building. But there is evidence that the Prytaneion was far older than the fifth century. In the western colonnade there are walls and foundations belonging to an earlier building, and at a considerably greater depth were found wide foundations of pebble similar to those under the Heraion. The numerous objects of all periods found within the Prytaneion include archaic bronzes, primitive figurines of animals, and early Corinthian pottery. Such evidence suggests that the Prytaneion was one of the oldest buildings of the site.

THE BOULEUTERION

Before we consider the Bouleuterion it will be well to sum up what we know of the Olympic Boule, its constitution and functions.[1]

---

[1] Wernicke, *Jahrb.* ix, pp. 127–35 ; Dyer, *Harvard Studies*, xix, pp. 32 ff.

We hear of it first in two fragmentary inscriptions of the sixth century which appear to deal with regulations for the sanctuary and penalties for their breach. One of them ends with the words ἄνευς βωλὰν καὶ ζᾶμον πλαθύοντα, the other contains the converse formula σὺν βωλᾶι πεντακατίων καὶ δάμοι πλαθύοντι.[1] If these inscriptions refer to the Olympic council, they imply that regulations or alterations in the regulations required the consent of the Boule and of a mass meeting of the people assembled at the festival. But the inference is highly problematical. A more convincing proof of the importance of the Boule is the fact that a special council-house was built for them as early as the sixth century or earlier.

In the first place, as we have seen, the council exercised control over the Altis and its buildings. In the later inscriptions[2] the council appears regularly as the authority that decrees or authorizes the erection of honorary statues. Sometimes it is named alone, sometimes it is coupled with the city of Elis, the Demos of Elis, the Synedroi or senate of Elis, sometimes with the Hellanodikai. It is described generally as ' the Olympic Council ', sometimes with the additional epithet ' most sacred ' (ἱερωτάτη) or ' most illustrious ' (λαμπροτάτη).

Secondly, the council must have exercised some sort of control over the Olympic festival and its programme. It was in the council house that a sort of dokimasia took place on the first day of the games for competitors and officials.[3] Here they took a solemn oath before the awe-inspiring statue of Zeus Horkios. The Hellanodikai swore to give judgement impartially and not to reveal the reasons for their decisions, a most wise provision. As a consequence we find the Boule acting as a court of appeal in disputes. An example of this has been already mentioned, when in 396 B.C. Leon of Ambrakia appealed to the council against the Hellanodikai.[4] The evidence as to the functions of the council is scanty, but clear enough as far as it goes. A fuller idea of its activities may be gained from comparison with the council of the Hieromnamones at Delphi. The latter, however, seems to have been a much smaller body, and its members exercised many functions which at Olympia devolved on the Hellanodikai and other executive officers.

The duties of the Hieromnamones are known to us from a very

[1] *Olympia*, v, nos. 3, 7. [2] *Ib*., pp. 406 ff., *passim*.
[3] P. v. 24. 9. [4] P. vi. 3. 7.

interesting Amphictyonic law of the year 380 B.C.[1] Each of the
Hieromnamones seems to have exercised a more or less independent authority, perhaps in matters which concerned his own state.
Similarly, it is probable that each Hellanodikas could in certain
cases act independently. The inscription begins with the oath
of the Hieromnamon. He swears to give his decisions in accordance with the written law, or, where there is no written law, to
the best of his judgement, not to receive bribes, nor to embezzle
the property of the league. The scribe, who swears to obey the
Hieromnamones, administers the oath to them and to the
Kerukes. The latter seem to be responsible for collecting the
tribute and the sacrifices. The Hieromnamones are every Pythiad
to go the round of the sacred territory and punish all whom they
find unlawfully cultivating it. Then follow regulations as to the
housing of visitors. The colonnades (τὰς παστάδας) are to be
open to all free of charge, but no one may stay in them more
than thirty days, nor may any woman reside there. The Hieromnamones are responsible for the observance of these regulations.
Further, they are every Pythiad to inspect the statues, temples,
the racecourse, and the fountain, and to carry out any repairs
necessary. They are to see to the upkeep of bridges and roads
leading to Delphi, each in his own district. Finally, they are
to hold the Pythian festival in the month of Boukatios, and send
out men to announce the festival in the month of Bysias, i.e.
six months in advance. If they omit to do so they are to be
fined. Any city that does not accept the Sacred Truce is to be
excommunicated.

Of the constitution of the council we know nothing. The
early inscription already quoted suggests that it consisted of
500 members. From the analogy of the Hellanodikai and Delphi
we should conjecture that it was more or less representative,
originally of the Pisatan Amphictyony, later of the tribes of Elis.

The Bouleuterion consists of two long wings, each terminating
at the west end in an apse, parallel to one another and united by
a square central chamber. The two wings are similar in dimensions and arrangement. They are 30·65 metres long and 13·78
metres wide. In each the apse is separated from the main hall
by a cross-wall, and is itself divided by another wall into two
rooms opening into the main hall. Each building was divided
by a central row of seven slender pillars, unfluted and probably

[1] C.I.G., 1688 ; Ditt., Syll.[3] i. 145.

of the Doric order. At the east end were three Doric pillars set between antae. Each hall was raised on a basement of two

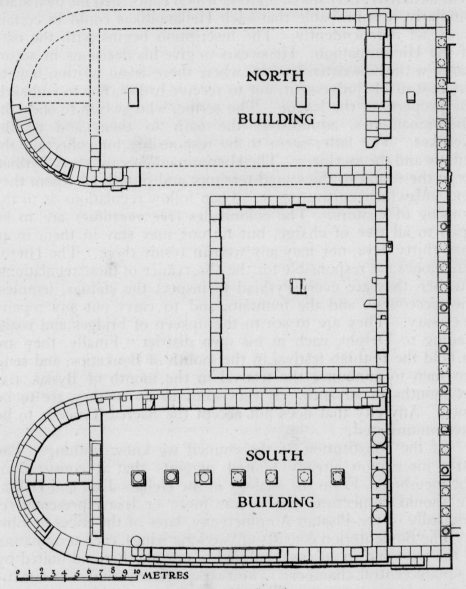

115. Plan of Bouleuterion

steps and was surrounded by a Doric entablature, parts of which still exist. The central building is 14 metres square and seems, like the wings, to have opened eastwards. In the centre is a square foundation, probably for a statue. An Ionic colonnade of twenty-seven columns extended along the front, connecting the three buildings. In Roman times a large open court surrounded by colonnades was built to the east. Underneath it the remains of a circular Greek altar were found.

These three buildings are constructed of different varieties of poros stone and are certainly of different dates. The central building is undoubtedly later than the wings, and is perhaps contemporary with the Ionic colonnade, which probably belongs to the third century B.C. The southern wing is the best preserved. From the remains of its pillars and entablature it appears to be contemporary with, or perhaps a little earlier than, the Temple of Zeus. The scanty remains of the northern wing seem to indicate a considerably earlier date, probably the middle of the sixth century.

The plan of the Bouleuterion presents certain features of exceptional interest. Besides the apse and the central row of pillars, the south wing has the further peculiarity that its walls are slightly curved, especially towards the apse, so that it presents the appearance of a long ellipse with one end cut off. Moreover, the apse itself is slightly pointed.

The central row of columns, which is an arrangement remarkably inconvenient for a council hall, is characteristic of several early temples. We find it in the earliest temple of Artemis at Sparta and in the early temple at Thermon. Similarly the apse, in the light of recent discoveries, is an archaic feature. Elliptical buildings exist both at Thermon and Olympia. It seems, then, that the plan of the Bouleuterion preserves a very ancient architectural tradition in western Greece, and this suggests a possible explanation of the elliptical form of the southern wing. Is it not possible that it stood on the site of a much earlier building, elliptical or semi-elliptical, that in the sixth century this building had fallen into decay and was replaced by a building farther north, similar but with straight walls, that, when in the fifth century further accommodation was required, this old building was rebuilt, the line of the earlier foundations being preserved? This is merely a conjecture. The antiquity of the site is proved by the quantity of archaic bronzes found there, similar to those found in the Prytaneion and south-east building.

What was the purpose of these three buildings?[1] We know little more than that the whole block was called the Bouleu-

[1] v. Wernicke, *l. c.*

terion, that it contained the statue of Zeus Horkios, and that it served as head-quarters to the officials who administered the games.

The only possible explanation of the central building is that of Flasch, that it contained the statue of Zeus Horkios. Oaths were generally taken in the open air, and it is probable that the building was not roofed. If this is so we can understand why no enclosure was erected till a late period, when unity was given to the whole group by the building of the Ionic colonnade. The northern wing must have been the council chamber proper, and the southern wing was probably added in the fifth century to provide increased accommodation for the executive officials, the new board of nine or ten Hellanodikai. The rooms in the apses undoubtedly served for the storage of the archives and the funds, and possibly for the use of the Grammateus.

THE PROEDRIA

Immediately to the south of the Bouleuterion lies the southern colonnade,[1] which I have identified with the Proedria. It is parallel to the south wing and separated from it only by a street. It is built on the extreme edge of the ridge that runs southward from the Heraion. To south and east there is a sudden drop in the level of the ground. A few yards from the east end is the ancient waterway that marks the line of the road that led from the Alpheios to the Altis. The waterway is at this point 6 feet below the level of the Stoa. Similarly, while the foundations of the north wall are only three courses deep, those of the front wall consist of seven courses of stone beside the steps. Thus the hall formed a raised terrace overlooking the Alpheios valley, and as such was naturally utilized by the builders of the Byzantine fortress as the southern wall of that building.

The Stoa was 78.15 metres long and 11.56 broad, with thirty-four columns along the south side and five at either end. The back was closed by a wall except at the ends, where a pillared opening gave access to the road. At the east end this road seems to have been bridged by an archway connecting the Stoa with the Bouleuterion. The pillars and entablature are of a typically late Doric type, and the terra-cotta sima is an obvious imitation of that of the Leonidaion. Down the centre was a row of Corinthian

---

[1] *Olympia*, ii, pp. 79 ff.

columns : from their inartistic and careless workmanship it is probable that they were added in Roman times.

From the above details the close connexion of the Stoa with the Bouleuterion is obvious, and it is quite possible that it was built at the same time as the Ionic colonnade in front of that building. The provision of a Stoa for the use of the Hellanodikai close to their official quarters in the south wing of the Bouleuterion finds its analogy in the city of Elis ; close to the Hellanodikeon, where the Hellanodikai lived and were trained, was a Stoa where, says Pausanias, they pass most of their days.

These Stoai were a distinctive feature of Greek life. We find them in all places of public resort, in or around the Agorai, or the Gymnasia, in sanctuaries like Olympia and Delphi. They served many purposes. They were lounges or promenades where people could walk sheltered from the heat or the rain and watch the busy scenes outside. The Echo Colonnade at Olympia commanded, as we have seen, a unique view of all the ceremonies in the Altis; the Stoa of the Athenians at Delphi stood by the side of the Sacred Way by which the processions passed. From a Delphic inscription already quoted we learn that visitors were even allowed to sleep in the colonnades (παστάδες). Sometimes the Stoai served as meeting-places for discussion or for business. The Stoic school took its name from the Stoa Poikile where Zeno taught at Athens, the Stoa Basilike served as the court of the king Archon, and the Stoai of the Peiraeus as exchanges or marts.

We can readily understand the advantages of such a Stoa reserved for the use of the council and officials. Much of their business could be transacted there far better than in the council house. Among their duties, for example, was the scrutiny of competitors, the classification of athletes and horses. We can picture the Hellanodikai standing on its steps and watching the parade of horses and chariots below, or drawing lots for the heats in the sight of competitors and their friends assembled in the plain. The scene from the Stoa was full of animation and interest. It commanded the Agora, crowded with booths and tents. East and west and south it commanded important roads. In front of it was the main approach to the Hippodrome, part perhaps of a sort of outer circle of the Altis. While the Great Procession doubtless followed the ancient processional road farther north, there may have been many another procession that, starting from the Gymnasion or Palaistra, followed the longer route, passing before the Stoa on its way to the Altis or the Hippodrome. Thus the Stoa well deserved its name Proedria, whether that word signifies merely the place of the Proedroi, or also implies a seat of honour at the festival.

THE HELLANODIKEON

Arguing from the analogy of Elis city Wernicke [1] conjectures that the Hellanodikai had an official residence, and that this was the so-called south-east building. There is no proof of either conjecture. All that we can say is that the purpose of this building is otherwise unknown, that there is some evidence that it was a dwelling-house and that it was an official residence, and that no more appropriate site could have been selected for the residence of the Hellanodikai, seeing that its colonnade faced the Altis and it was close to the start of the Stadion and the Hippodrome.

The building was completely destroyed in Roman times and converted into a Roman villa, probably for the use of Nero. Only the stylobate of the front is left. It consists of four square rooms arranged in a line, surrounded on three sides by a Doric colonnade. We do not know how the rooms opened on to the colonnade, or if there were other rooms at the back. Probably there were, and in that case the plan of the building may have been similar to that of the Theokoleon, which was certainly a dwelling-house, and was also converted into a Roman villa. Like the Theokoleon it contained a well. That the site was occupied at an early date, and that the building had an official character, is proved by the numerous fragments of bronze and pottery found there. These finds are similar to those found under the Prytaneion and Bouleuterion, and include numbers of tripods, kettles, basins, weights, and lamps. Finally, if it was the official residence of the Hellanodikai, we can understand its conversion into a villa for Nero when he usurped the presidency of the Olympic Games.

The date of the building must be placed between that of the Stoa Poikile in the fifth century and the rebuilding of the Stoa in the time of Alexander. Its front wall was aligned to the original Stoa ; its northern colonnade was completely blocked by the building of the Macedonian Stoa. If it was really the Hellano-

[1] *l. c.* ; *Olympia*, ii, p. 73.

dikeon, it probably formed part of the reconstruction of the Altis in the fifth century.

The building is of great importance for the history of Doric architecture. Its stones and terra-cottas were built into the walls of the Roman villa, and their colours are preserved with extraordinary freshness.[1] From them we learn that the shafts of the columns, the echinus, and abacus of the capitals, were not decorated with painted patterns, though possibly tinted with yellow or some light colour. The cornice of the gable was painted with a band of bright blue leaves and red spines on a yellow

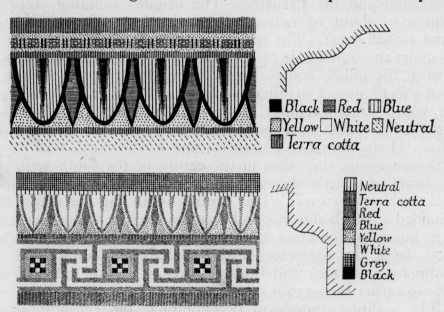

116. Painted cornices from Hellanodikeon

ground. The mutules were very dark blue, the spaces between them red. The triglyphs were also dark blue, the metopes being merely coated with white stucco. The terra-cotta sima was decorated with maeander, palmette, and leaf patterns brightly painted on a black background. Comparing these with the early terra-cottas of the Treasuries, we notice a change similar to that from the black-figure to the red-figure vases.

The conversion of the building into a Roman villa can be dated with certainty owing to the discovery of a leaden water-pipe stamped with the words NERONIS AUG. The arrangement of the building confirms the conjecture that it was intended for

[1] *Olympia*, ii, pp. 185, 197, Figs. 15, 16, 17, 18, Pl. CXXI.

the emperor's use. From the long portico which was actually within the Altis a broad door led directly into the Atrium, while another colonnade connected it with the Triumphal Arch erected as an entrance into the Altis. A fine mosaic pavement was found in one of the rooms.

THE THEOKOLEON

The only official residence mentioned by Pausanias is the Theokoleon,[1] or house of the Theokoloi. It lay between the Leonidaion and the Palaistra. The original building occupied a square of about 19 metres. It consisted of eight rooms built round a small court. The central rooms on each side opened into this court through a pair of pillars flanked by antae. The spaces between the pillars and the antae were closed by stone screens about 3 feet high. The pillars were Doric, fluted only in the upper half, with a straight echinus, but the epistyle was Ionic. The four corner rooms must have been lighted by windows in the outer walls. There were two entrances, one in the north wall of the north-east room, the other in the centre of the south wall. In the corner of the paved court is a cylindrical draw-well carefully lined with stone-work. The central room on the south side contained a hearth and was probably the kitchen. The excellence of the building shows that it belonged to a good period of architecture: from the character of the capitals and antae, and the combination of Doric and Ionic features, it may be inferred that it is not earlier than 350 B.C.

The building underwent two complete reconstructions, one in Greek, the other in Roman times, the date of which cannot however be fixed more definitely. In the first case the accommodation was increased by the addition of three rooms on the east side. The new rooms naturally opened eastwards, and accordingly the open space in front was laid out as a garden-court surrounded on the other three sides by cloisters and rooms. This new court measured 40·36 metres from north to south, 26·65 metres from east to west.

In Roman times this garden-court was extended and converted into a fine quadrangle almost square. In the centre was a paved court surrounded by a colonnade of eight pillars on each side. In the south of this court was a raised platform bearing a large

[1] *Olympia*, ii, p. 107.

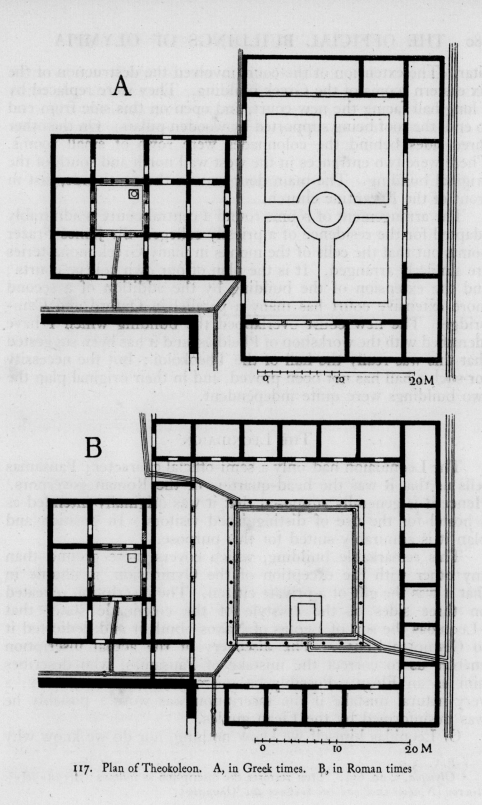

117. Plan of Theokoleon. A, in Greek times. B, in Roman times

altar. The extension of the court involved the destruction of the six eastern rooms of the Greek building. They were replaced by a long hall facing the new court, and open on this side from end to end, the roof being supported by wooden pillars. On the other three sides behind the colonnades were rows of small rooms. There were two entrances in the west wall north and south of the original building. The main door was on the south side, just in front of the Byzantine church.

The arrangement of rooms round a central court is admirably adapted for the residence of a priestly college. Sir James Frazer points out that the cells of the monks in many Greek monasteries are similarly arranged. It is the plan of our own college courts ; and the extension of the building by the addition of a second more extensive court has many a parallel in Oxford and Cambridge. The new court overlapped the building which I have identified with the workshop of Pheidias, and it has been suggested that this was really the hall of the Theokoloi ; but the necessity for such a hall has not been proved, and in their original plan the two buildings were quite independent.

THE LEONIDAION

The Leonidaion had only a semi-official character ; Pausanias tells us that it was the head-quarters of the Roman governors.[1] Hence it is generally supposed that it was originally intended as a hostel for the use of distinguished visitors. In position and plan it is admirably suited for this purpose.

This remarkable building, which covers more ground than any other with the exception of the Gymnasion, is unique in that it was the gift of a private citizen. The inscription repeated on three sides of the epistyle of the colonnade states that ' Leonidas the son of Leotas of Naxos [2] built it and dedicated it to Olympian Zeus '. The discovery of the actual inscription enables us to correct the mistake of Pausanias, who describes him as an Elean. Possibly he misread ΝΑΞΙΟΣ as ΗΛΕΙΟΣ, a very natural mistake if the inscription was worn ; possibly he was misinformed by the Elean guides.

Of Leonidas himself we know nothing, nor do we know why

---

[1] P. v. 15. 2.

[2] *Olympia*, v, no. 651. Treu restores the inscription as follows : $Λ[ε]ω[ν]ΐδ[η]ς$ $Λεώτου\ [Ν]άξιος\ ἐποί[ησε\ καὶ\ ἀνέθηκε\ Διὶ\ Ὀλυμπίῳ].$

he bestowed this princely gift upon Olympia, or why the Arkadians of Psophis honoured him with a statue. From the inscriptions it is inferred that he lived in the second half of the fourth century, and this date is in accord with the architectural evidence of the Leonidaion. There is no known connexion between Olympia and Naxos unless it be through the marble trade. Marble was sparingly used in the earlier buildings of Olympia, but tiles of island marble, either Parian or Naxian, were used for the roof of the Temple of Zeus, and Pausanias ascribes the invention of these tiles to Byzes of Naxos. In Macedonian times, however, marble

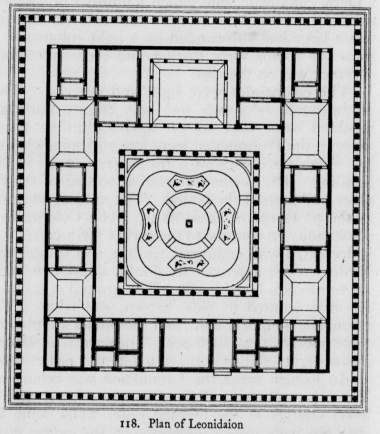

118. Plan of Leonidaion

begins to be freely used for buildings. Is it possible that Leonidas had enriched himself in this trade, and that the Leonidaion was a token of his gratitude?

A spacious building,[1] measuring 74 by 80 metres and surrounded by an Ionic colonnade of 138 columns, it stood at the junction of the main roads to Olympia. Opposite to its northeast corner was the processional entrance to the Altis. The road along its eastern front was a continuation of the processional road, and was lined with statues, probably of Roman officials: the marks of chariot wheels are still visible on its surface. Along its

[1] *Olympia*, ii, p. 83.

south side ran the great road from Arkadia, and the road to the north leading directly to the processional entrance was possibly the sacred road from Elis.

The arrangement of the interior was similar to that of the Theokoleon. In the centre was an open court surrounded by a Doric colonnade, into which a number of rooms opened. The principal rooms were on the west side, in the centre of which was a large hall surrounded by a light colonnade. On the other sides the rooms were smaller and more numerous. The main entrance was on the east.

The colonnades were light and graceful. The Ionic pillars of the outer colonnade had only twenty flutings ; their richly moulded bases were set on square plinths ; their capitals, like those of the Philippeion, were low and somewhat cramped. The low entablature without a frieze gave an air of lightness to the building. The geison was similar to that of the Philippeion and other buildings of the period. The terra-cotta sima [1] is noticeable as the prototype of those of the Echo Colonnade and the south colonnade. In contrast to the earlier terra-cottas it is straight, and is decorated with embossed tendrils and volutes with a maeander border. The antefixes are double palmettes, and between them are terra-cotta lions' heads. The ground is yellow, and the decoration is painted in reds, brown, and white. The inner Doric colonnade is equally light, and the pillars are placed at intervals of three instead of two metopes. The narrow architrave, low capitals, and straight echinus point to a date not earlier than 350 B.C.

In Roman times the Leonidaion was rebuilt and rearranged. The new walls were built of concrete faced with brick, only the lower courses of the original outer walls being kept. Spacious entrance halls were constructed in the centre of the north, east, and probably also the south walls. On the north side the rooms on either side of the entrance hall were rearranged so as to form a group of six centred round an open court or atrium with an impluvium in the centre. The south side has not been completely excavated, but it is probable that it was similarly arranged. The open hall on the west side was preserved with certain alterations, and likewise the rooms on either side of it. Thus the building contained within itself four suites of rooms forming typical Roman residences.

The central court was at the same time converted into an

---

[1] *Olympia*, ii, pp. 87, 198, Pl. CXXIII.

elaborate water-garden. In the centre was a circular island surrounded by a ring-shaped pond, while another pond of more irregular shape encircled the whole court. The ponds were spanned by wooden bridges, and the terrace and islands were laid out with shrubs and flowers and statues. The water for the ponds was supplied by the reservoir close to the Altis door. As this reservoir

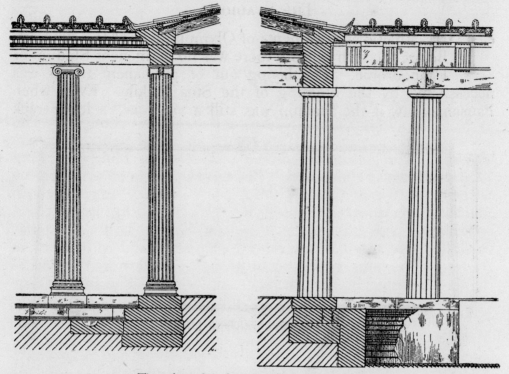

119. The colonnades of the Leonidaion reconstructed

appears to depend on the water system provided by Herodes Atticus we seem justified in assigning the rebuilding of the Leonidaion to this same period. If, as Borrman believes, the Leonidaion had already been rebuilt when Pausanias visited Olympia, the rebuilding must have taken place between A.D. 160 and 174.

At a considerably later period, probably in the third century A.D., a second rebuilding took place, which can be distinguished from the first by its poorly built walls of *opus incertum*. The object appears to have been to provide more accommodation on a smaller scale. The spacious rooms of the earlier building were subdivided, and even the great central hall on the west side was converted into a residence with atrium and impluvium.

XVI

The Athletic Buildings

THE STADION

THE athletic arrangements of Olympia were of the simplest. Before the fifth century there was no permanent Stadion or Hippodrome. The laying out of permanent tracks was necessitated by the building of the Stoa Poikile. Even when Pausanias saw it the Stadion was still a γῆς χῶμα,[1] a level track

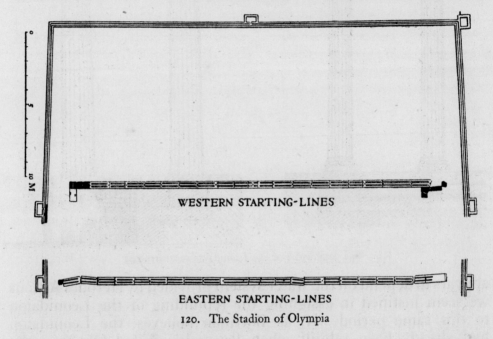

WESTERN STARTING-LINES

EASTERN STARTING-LINES

120. The Stadion of Olympia

surrounded by embankments, partly natural, partly artificial, on which the spectators stood or sat. Only the Hellanodikai were provided with seats, placed apparently in the middle or at the east end of the south side, opposite to an altar of white stone from which the priestess of Demeter Chamyne was privileged to watch the games.

[1] P. vi. 20. 8. For a fuller discussion of the Olympia and other Stadia v. *Gk. Athletics*, pp. 252 ff. ; *Olympia*, ii, p. 63 ; *J. H. S.* xxiii, p. 261, xxviii, p. 253.

The running-track was a parallelogram some 212 metres long and 32 metres broad, formed by levelling the ground at the foot of the Hill of Kronos. It was 10 feet below the level of the Altis. A low stone barrier surrounding it prevented the soil from being washed on to the course. Inside this barrier, at a distance of about a metre, was an open stone gutter opening at intervals into stone basins. This gutter, fed by the conduit which ran along the foot of the Treasury terrace, provided competitors and spectators with a supply of water that they sorely needed, and also carried away the rain-water. The two sides were slightly curved, so as to prevent spectators in the centre from obscuring the view of those at the ends.

The finish and start of the course were marked by stone sills 192·27 metres or 200 Olympic feet apart. These sills are 18 inches

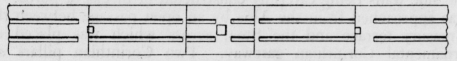

121. Centre of western Aphesis

wide and are divided at intervals of 4 feet by square sockets in which posts were set. Between each pair of sockets were two parallel grooves cut in the stone about 7 inches apart. They marked the place for the runners' feet.[1] There are twenty such sections in the western sill, twenty-one in the eastern. Thus there was room for twenty runners in the stade race. The posts undoubtedly served to keep the runners straight, but there is no evidence that the course was roped. It is uncertain how they were used in the diaulos or two-stade race. In the long race the runners raced round the central posts at either end. In the western sill this central post has a larger socket.

Pausanias speaks of the starting-place of the Stadiodromoi as at the far end of the course, i. e. the eastern end. If he is using the word in its technical sense—runners of the stade race—the finish must have been at the west end. It is more probable that he is speaking of the runners generally, in which case, as the majority of races started and finished at the same end, the east end would be both start and finish. This is the more probable, because the seats of the Hellanodikai cannot possibly have been at the west end.

[1] Gk. Athletics, p. 272.

On the north the slopes of the Hill of Kronos formed a natural stand for spectators. The artificial embankments on the other sides were originally quite low ; that on the south extended some 30 yards with a gradient of 1 in 13. Borrman calculates that there was room for 20,000 spectators. At a later period the embankment was raised to a height of 6½ metres and extended to a distance of 40 metres, providing accommodation for at least 40,000 spectators.

From the above description it is clear that the Stadion was accessible on all sides. A special entrance was provided for the Hellanodikai and competitors in the north-east corner of the Altis. Pausanias calls it the κρυπτὴ εἴσοδος, which is somewhat unfortunately translated ' the secret entrance '. It is in reality a vaulted tunnel 32·10 metres long, 3·70 wide, and 4·45 high, the side walls being carefully constructed of blocks of poros. It was approached from the Altis by an open passage between the Treasury terrace and the Stoa, across which was placed an ornamental Corinthian gateway. Two Corinthian pillars set between two half-pillars supported a low entablature. Their capitals were richly painted in yellow, green, and red, and resemble those of the Temple of Vesta at Tivoli. At the east end of the tunnel was another open passage, communicating with the Stadion and lined with walls of rubble (Fig. 122).

These rubble walls were probably the original walls of the passage and extended along its whole length. They were sufficient to support the first low embankment. This original passage was at a lower level, for a stone bench belonging to it was found under the floor of the later tunnel. The raising of the embankment in Macedonian times [1] necessitated the building of the existing stone walls. The vault and the Corinthian archway were added in the first century B.C., probably in the second half, when under the patronage of Augustus Olympia was beginning to recover something of her popularity.

Immediately outside of the entrance is a row of twelve bases which supported the Zanes [2] erected in Ol. 98 and 112. Two more bases were found inside the passage, and another pair stood on either side of the gateway.

[1] For the chronology v. *J. H. S.* xxviii, p. 255.
[2] P. v. 21 ; *Olympia*, ii, p. 151.

122. ENTRANCE TO STADION

123. PORTICO OF GYMNASION

THE HIPPODROME

Not a trace of the Hippodrome [1] survives. It must have been laid out about the same time as the Stadion. The southern embankment of the Stadion formed part of its northern boundary, and it stretched eastwards as far as a low spur of the hills on which stood the Temple of Demeter Chamyne. Elsewhere it was surrounded by an artificial embankment which afforded the only accommodation for spectators and protected the course from the floods of the Alpheios. The main entrance was at the west end, along which ran a colonnade called the Stoa of Agnaptos. In front of this colonnade was an elaborate *aphesis* devised by one Kleoitas the son of Aristokles [2] and improved by one Aristeides. Towards the east end a cutting in the embankment provided a convenient exit for horses and chariots, especially for such as came to grief at the turn.

The dimensions of the Hippodrome are preserved in a manuscript found at Constantinople.[3] Its length was 3 stades 1 plethron (609 metres), its width 1 stade 4 plethra (320 metres). These appear to be outside measurements, the actual course being probably only half the width. Horses

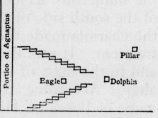

124. Aphesis of the Hippodrome

and chariots raced up and down the course turning sharply round a pillar at either end. The distance from pillar to pillar was 3 stades. Whether the pillars were connected by ropes or any temporary barrier we cannot say. Certainly there was no permanent spina as in the Roman circus.

The aphesis is described by Pausanias [4] as a structure in the shape of a prow with its beak pointing down the course. Each side was 400 feet long. Its base, parallel to the Stoa of Agnaptos, extended over the southern half of the course. Along the sides were constructed pairs of stalls, one on each side. Here the competing chariots or horses were placed with a rope stretched in front of each, their positions being determined by lot. In the centre of the triangle an altar of unbaked brick, whitewashed, was set up every Olympiad, and on the altar was placed a bronze

---

[1] P. vi. 20.
[2] Kleoitas is assigned by Overbeck to the fifth century, but his date is uncertain.
[3] v. *Gk. Athletics*, pp. 452 ff.   [4] vi. 20.

eagle with outstretched wings. At the apex of the aphesis a bronze dolphin was set up. When the official touched a piece of mechanism the eagle rose in the air, and the dolphin dropped to the ground. This was the signal for the start, but I conjecture that it was not given till all the chariots were in line. The manner of starting was as follows. First the ropes in front of the pair of chariots nearest to the base were withdrawn, and they started. As they drew level with the next pair, the ropes in front of these were withdrawn, and so on till the whole field was started. The object of this very complicated starting arrangement was chiefly spectacular, and the race did not actually begin till the chariots were in a line level with the beak.

Pausanias mentions numerous altars in the Hippodrome. The most interesting of these is that of Taraxippos, which was supposed to inspire the horses with terror and was the cause of the numerous accidents in the race. It stood near the east end of the south side of the course, close therefore to the point where the chariots made their first turn and where accidents were most frequent. It was this circumstance which gave rise to the name and to the mass of superstitious legends that gathered round this altar. According to Pausanias Taraxippos is merely another name of Poseidon Hippios.

THE PALAISTRA

There was no resident population at Olympia, and it was only during the festival or perhaps for a month before it that competitors resided there. Hence there was no real need for a gymnasion or palaistra. Neither was built before the third century B.C., and even then they were characterized by the same practical simplicity as the Stadion. They were not, like similar buildings in cities, the daily resort of the inhabitants, nor could they ever become educational establishments for the training of epheboi, where philosophy or rhetoric rivalled or even eclipsed athletics.[1]

All athletic buildings require water, and the site chosen at Olympia was in the north-west between the Altis and the Kladeos, the upper springs of which were till the time of Herodes Atticus the only reliable source of water supply. The floods of this river, while sweeping away the western side of the Gymnasion,

---

[1] v. *Gk. Athletics*, ch. xxii.

covered the Palaistra with a thick layer of sand, and thus helped to preserve its remains.

The Palaistra [1] consists of a court 41 metres square surrounded by a colonnade of Doric pillars on to which numerous rooms open. The colonnade, which was 4·70 metres deep, probably served as a sheltered running-track. The two principal entrances are at either end of the south wall; a third door in the north com-municated with the Gymnasion. The southern en-trances, which were in the form of pillared vestibules, led into small ante-rooms, between which was a long shallow hall faced by a row of fifteen Ionic pillars. It was probably the Apoduterion, or undressing room, which was usually close to the en-trance and served as a sort of meet-ing-place for ath-letes and their friends.

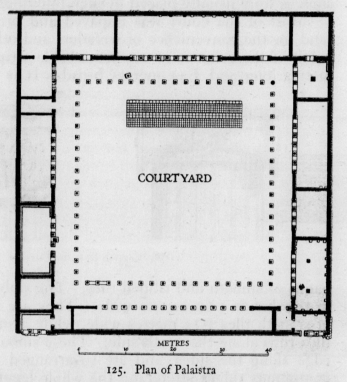

COURTYARD

METRES

125. Plan of Palaistra

Opposite in the centre of the north wall was another large hall, in which we may perhaps recognize the Ephebeum of Vitruvius, a sort of club-room for the use of Epheboi; at Olympia it must have been for the use of the competitors. In the north-east corner was a bathroom: it contained the remains of a brick-lined bath of Roman date, 4 metres square and 1·38 metres deep. It is impossible to determine the uses of most of the rooms. Some of them opened into the court by doorways, but only one of these, that in the south-west corner, had a door. Possibly it was the porter's lodge. The other rooms probably served for the storage of oil, sand, and athletic apparatus. Most

[1] Olympia, ii, p. 113.

P p

of the rooms were open in front with two or more Ionic pillars between antae. These pillars are not of uniform pattern, and are mostly fluted only on the side facing the court. Six of the rooms have stone benches, and one at least a concrete floor. They probably served as lounges where visitors could sit and gossip and watch the competitors practising. In several rooms there were bases which supported statues of gods, heroes, or athletes, such as were usually placed in such buildings.

Most of the court was unpaved and probably covered with sand for the convenience of wrestlers and other athletes. In the north of the court is a very remarkable strip of pavement 24·20 metres long and 5·44 metres broad. It is formed of alternate

126. Capitals from the Palaistra

bands of smooth and ribbed tiles. The ribbed tiles are arranged in two bands 1·60 metres wide. They are separated by a band of smooth tiles 1·12 metres wide, while a single band of smooth tiles runs along the north side. These smooth tiles have a raised edge along the sides, and are so arranged that the edges form continuous ridges stretching the whole length of the platform.

The object of this curious pavement is uncertain. We may reject the delightfully humorous suggestion that the ribbed tiles were covered with sand and used as a wrestling ring, or the equally humorous conjecture that they were a jumping track. A more reasonable conjecture is that it was a platform for the use of officials or trainers, but why they should need such a platform is not apparent. The most likely explanation is that it was a sort of bowling alley. A somewhat similar pavement was found in the larger Thermae at Pompeii, and on it some heavy stone balls.

The architecture is thoroughly eclectic. Doric, Ionic, and Corinthian pillars are used, and some of them are of very curious types (Fig. 126). Thus the so-called Corinthian pillars of the southern porches are fluted, and stand directly on the thresholds without any bases.[1] Further, the capitals at each corner have a heavy volute, and between each pair of volutes is a single stiff leaf resembling a palmette. It is a type that belongs rather to Asia Minor, and lends support to the suggestion that the Palaistra was built by one of the Diadochoi. Again, the Ionic pillars in front of one of the rooms are very unusual.[2] The flutings are replaced by raised ridges, and the ends of the capitals resemble bell-shaped flowers with their stalks intertwined in the centre. Similar capitals are found in the house of the Faun at Pompeii. This eclectic style of architecture points to a date not earlier than the third century B.C.; at the same time the careful workmanship makes a date later than the close of this century improbable. There is no evidence for connecting it with Philadelphos or any other of the Diadochoi.

THE GYMNASION

The Gymnasion[3] formed originally a large quadrangle extending as far as the Kladeos, and was surrounded on three sides at least by colonnades. Only the southern and eastern of these can be traced. The southern colonnade consisted of a single row of Doric columns parallel to the north wall of the Palaistra. It was 5·23 metres broad and was closed at the east end by a wall. From the manner in which this wall abuts on that of the Palaistra, it is clear that the Gymnasion was built later than the Palaistra.

The eastern colonnade was not in line with the east wall of the Palaistra, but deflected slightly to the west so as to avoid the slope of the hill. It was 210 metres long and nearly 12 metres broad. On the east it was enclosed by a massive wall. It was divided down the centre by a row of sixty-six slender Doric pillars, and opened to the west through a similar row. This colonnade was the Xystos or covered running-track, which was an essential part of all Hellenistic gymnasia. Near the third column from the south there was a stone sill similar to those found in the Stadion, and we may conjecture that there was another sill at the third pillar from the north end, the distance

---

[1] Marquand, *Gk. Architecture*, p. 196, Fig. 228.
[2] *Ib.*, p 95, Fig. 100.   [3] *Olympia*, ii, p. 127 ; P. vi. 21. 2.

between these points being exactly an Olympic stade. The floor of the colonnade was of loose earth. Thus runners could practise in excessive heat or in bad weather under precisely the same conditions as on the actual race-course. From the fact that the Xystos was provided with stone sills we may infer that the

127. Entrance of Gymnasion reconstructed

Greek sprinter paid as much attention to practising starts as does the modern runner.

On the western side of the Gymnasion were rooms for the accommodation of competitors during the games and perhaps another Xystos. There were doubtless one or more uncovered tracks or paradromides, and ranges for throwing the diskos or the spear. In the centre was a stone platform or κρηπίς, probably a stand for the convenience of spectators.

From the architecture it appears that the date of the Gymnasion was slightly later than that of the Palaistra. The great entrance [1] which we see to-day on the way to the Altis was a later addition (Fig. 123). It consisted of a Corinthian porch raised on three tiers of stone steps. At either end was a façade of four Corinthian columns supporting a gable roof. The architrave and frieze were decorated with alternate rosettes and bulls' heads linked together by festoons. The sides were enclosed by walls, and the passage was divided by two rows of four Corinthian columns aligned to those of the façades. The shafts were fluted and rested on low bases. The capitals were of moderate height, somewhat heavy in outline, and coarsely moulded. They resemble those of the Stadion entrance. Borrman assigns the gateway to the close of the second century. But the architectural evidence is quite in keeping with a later date, and it seems to me more probable that it was built in the latter part of the first century.

[1] *Olympia*, ii, p. 121.

XVII

The Exedra and the Water Supply

ἄριστον μὲν ὕδωρ.

THE Exedra[1] is the only building of imperial times that can be dated with certainty, and it is the only one that calls for special description. As already stated, it was not really an Exedra at all, but a covered water-tank forming the termination of the aqueduct by which Herodes carried the waters of the Alpheios to the Altis.

The problem of supplying water to the vast crowds assembled for the festival must always have been a difficult one. The heat and drought of Olympia in summer were proverbial: the spectators suffered severely and sometimes even died from thirst. The efforts made by the authorities to deal with the problem are shown by the fact that no fewer than a hundred and twenty water-channels and pipes of various types and dates were discovered during the excavations, while outside the Altis were ten wells.[2]

These wells, which depended for their supply on the level of the Alpheios water, were constructed of semicircular brick tiles or of poros and covered with stone slabs. They were placed for the most part near the line of ancient roads. One of the oldest is north-west of the Prytaneion near the road that led along the valley of the Kladeos. Another was just to the north of the Heroon, where perhaps passed the sacred road from Elis. Two more are east of the Bouleuterion on the line of the great southern road.

Except for these wells the water supply until the time of Herodes was derived entirely from the valley of the Kladeos. As the level of the Altis was considerably above the level of the surrounding plain the water was collected in a reservoir a little above the north-west corner of the Heraion. From this reservoir it was distributed partly by means of the three open water-

---

[1] *Olympia*, ii, p. 134. [2] *Ib.* ii, pp. 170 ff.

channels already noticed, which served to drain the Altis. One of these ran eastwards along the foot of the terrace wall to the Stadion, another diagonally across the Altis to the Bouleuterion, the third due south to the Sacred Olive-tree to the east of the Temple of Zeus. For the purpose of storing the water stone basins were provided at intervals along these channels. Other conduits led from the same reservoir westwards. Here the ground sloped away, and it was possible to supplement the supplies from

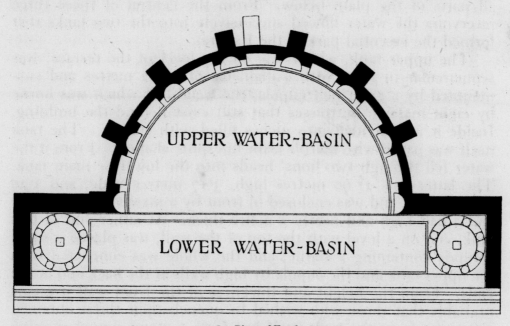

128. Plan of Exedra

the Heraion reservoir by water brought direct from the springs in the upper part of the Kladeos valley.

But the supply of water from the Kladeos must have been always limited and unreliable in summer, and quite inadequate for the needs of the festival. Finally the system seems to have broken down completely. A new reservoir was built, slightly higher up, to which water was brought by a tunnel cut along the western side of the Hill of Kronos. But this does not seem to have been really successful. Consequently when Herodes set himself to provide a really efficient water system, he abandoned the Kladeos and utilized the more distant but more copious springs in the side valleys of the Alpheios. Not far from the village of Miraka, about a mile and a half from Olympia, one of the pillars

of his aqueduct is still standing. Thence it followed the lower
slopes of the hills till it reached the Hill of Kronos immediately
above the Treasury of the Geloans. Here it entered a tunnel
placed above and slightly in front of the retaining wall at the
back of the Treasuries. This tunnel is 0·40 metres wide and
0·83 metres high, lined with tiles and with a semicircular roof.
It runs along the whole length of the Treasuries and ends in
three open reservoirs from which the water was distributed to
all parts of the plain below. From the central of these three
reservoirs the water flowed successively into the two tanks that
formed the essential part of the Exedra.

The upper tank, which was on the level of the terrace, was
semicircular in form with a diameter of 16·62 metres and surmounted by a great half cupola, the weight of which was borne
by eight massive buttresses that still exist behind the building.
Inside it was divided into niches filled with statues. The tank
itself was paved with marble slabs but quite shallow. From it the
water fell through two lions' heads into the lower or main tank.
The latter was 21·90 metres high, 3·17 metres wide, and 1·20
metres deep, and was enclosed in front by a massive wall a metre
and a half high and nearly a metre thick. At either end of this
tank, and on a level with the top of the wall, was placed a small
rotunda containing a statue, and the whole was connected with
the upper tank and the cupola by high walls at the back and at the
ends. From the height and thickness of the front wall it seems
probable that those who wished to quench their thirst obtained
water not from the tank itself but from a stone runnel running
outside along the foot of the tank, into which the water flowed.

The walls and the cupola were built of brickwork and stone
with a core of rubble and mortar. Stone and brick appear to
have been used without any definite principle. The blocks of
stone were roughly and carelessly cut, with the exception of some
that were taken from earlier buildings. The bricks are of
different sizes, and some of them are stamped with the name of
Herodes. All parts of the building that were visible from the
front were covered with a thick layer of stucco or with marble
slabs. The interior of the cupola was decorated with marble
encrustation of different colours, white, grey, red, and green,
and also with architectural details, bases and capitals of pillars,
and architraves carved on thin slabs of marble. At some height
from the floor it was divided into a series of niches. There were

eight semicircular niches corresponding to the eight buttresses on the outside, and between them seven oblong niches of about twice the size. The former contained statues of the members of the imperial family, the latter those of the family of Herodes.

The two tiny rotundas at either end of the tank were only 3·80 metres in diameter. Each of them consisted of eight small Corinthian pillars standing on three steps and supporting a conical roof. They were built entirely of Pentelic marble except the pillars, which were of Carystian marble. The workmanship of the capitals is unusually careful and good for the period. The marble tiles of the roof were carved to represent olive leaves which overlapped each other like scales. Each rotunda contained the basis for a statue.

In the centre of the front wall of the tank stood a marble bull, which was found lying in the tank. It bears the following inscription on its flank :

Ῥήγιλλα ἱέρεια
Δήμητρος τὸ ὕδωρ
καὶ τὰ περὶ τὸ ὕδωρ τῷ Διί.

'Regilla, priestess of Demeter, dedicated the water and all connected with it to Zeus.' From this we learn that the Exedra was dedicated by Herodes in the name of his wife, and that she held at Olympia the honoured office of priestess of Demeter Chamyne.[1]

We have seen that the apse of the Exedra contained eight semicircular and seven oblong niches. Each of the latter contained two bases. There were therefore twenty-two bases for statues, or if we include the bases in the two rotundas twenty-four. Corresponding to these the remains of fourteen statues were found in the Exedra, and also the remains of fourteen inscribed bases of Pentelic marble. Most of the latter had been cut into slabs and used for the pavement of the Byzantine church. Of these bases five are inscribed with the names of members of the imperial family, the remaining nine with those of members of Herodes' family. The two sets of bases differ slightly in form. Moreover, the imperial statues were dedicated by Herodes himself, those of Herodes and his family by the city of Elis. Hence it may be regarded as certain that one set occupied the semicircular, the other the oblong niches, and as there are nine bases

---

[1] *Olympia*, v, no. 610 ; cp. nos. 456, 485.

Q q

of the second set it follows that they must belong to the oblong niches, and that the imperial statues filled the semicircular niches.

The members of the imperial family named in the inscriptions are the following :

1. Antoninus Pius (Ins. 617).
2. Faustina the elder, wife of Antoninus (Ins. 613). The upper part of her statue was also found.
3. Faustina the younger, wife of Marcus Aurelius (Ins. 614).
4. Titus Aelius Antoninus and Annia Galeria Aurelia Faustina, children of Marcus Aurelius (Ins. 615, 616). The statues of these two children stood on one basis.
5. Lucius Aelius Aurelius Commodus, afterwards the Emperor Verus (Ins. 618).

To these we may add the Emperor Hadrian, whose statue was found complete, and undoubtedly also Marcus Aurelius, to whom Treu assigns the torso of a mailed man. If we could be sure that these occupied seven of the eight niches we should have little hesitation in assigning the eighth place to Sabina, the wife of Hadrian. There is, however, a difficulty. The name of Antoninus is inscribed on a thin slab of marble that cannot possibly have formed part of a solid marble basis, but must have served as a veneer for a brick or rubble basis of the usual Roman type. Probably, then, it stood in one of the rotundas, and in that case we may conjecture that the other rotunda was occupied by the statue of Marcus Aurelius. In these circumstances it is obviously impossible to determine the order in which the statues were placed.

Passing on to the family of Herodes we have inscriptions referring to the following :

1. Herodes Atticus (Ins. 622).
2. Vibullia Alcia Agrippina, mother of Herodes (Ins. 621).
3. Marcus Atilius Atticus, eldest son of Herodes (Ins. 623).
4. Elpinice, eldest daughter of Herodes (Ins. 624).
5. Regillus and Athenais, the two youngest children of Herodes (Ins. 625, 626). They occupied the same basis.
6. Appius Annius Gallus, father of Regilla (Ins. 619).
7. M. Appius Bradua, grandfather of Regilla (Ins. 620).

8. L. Vibullius Hipparchus, son-in-law of Herodes and husband of Athenais (Ins. 627).
9. Athenais, daughter of Hipparchus (Ins. 628).

To these must of course be added Regilla herself, the remaining four bases belonging probably to the father and grandfather of Herodes, the mother of Regilla, and her grandfather on the father's side. The statues of Hipparchus and Athenais were undoubtedly added some years after the completion of the Exedra. The other statues of the family of Herodes were dedicated by the city of Elis, but in these two inscriptions the name of the dedicator is omitted. Hence we may infer that they were set up by Hipparchus himself.

The latest possible date for the building of the Exedra is determined by the death of Regilla in A.D. 161, the earliest date by the fact that statues were erected in it to two children of Faustina and Marcus Aurelius. As the latter were married in A.D. 145 the earliest date for the Exedra is two years later, A.D. 147. The arguments for fixing the date more precisely are not conclusive. It is urged that at the time of its building Marcus and Faustina can have had only these two children living, and therefore that it was built before A.D. 150 or 151, when Anna Lucilia was born to them. But for all we know there may have been statues of Anna or other children on one of the lost bases. Again, Adler conjectured that Herodes built the aqueduct and Exedra in gratitude for the honour shown to Regilla by the Eleans when they appointed her priestess of Demeter. But it is not by any means certain that Regilla held this office in A.D. 153 as Adler states, and it is just as probable that the Eleans conferred this honour upon Regilla in gratitude for the Exedra as vice versa.

XVIII
The Olympic Festival

Ἤδη γὰρ αὐτῷ πατρὶ μὲν βωμῶν ἁγισθέντων διχόμηνις ὅλον χρυσάρματος
ἑσπέρας ὀφθαλμὸν ἀντέφλεξε Μήνα
καὶ μεγάλων ἀέθλων ἁγνὰν κρίσιν καὶ πενταετηρίδ᾿ ἁμᾷ
θῆκε ζαθέοις ἐπὶ κρημνοῖς Ἀλφεοῦ.

Pindar, Ol. iii. 19.

NO work on Olympia would be complete without some account of the festival itself. Yet to describe it is no easy task. Our information is fragmentary, derived from various periods, many of them late, and the details are often obscure and disputed.[1] Here I can only attempt to describe it such as it appears to me to have been in the middle of the fifth century, the most glorious period in the history of Olympia.

Some months before the date of the festival the ' heralds of the seasons, the truce-bearers of Zeus ', left Elis. East and west they travelled, and in every state they were welcomed. The magistrates received them in the Prytaneion, and there on the Hearth of the city they poured libation, proclaimed the Sacred Truce, and invited the citizens to join in the festival. From that time the territory of Elis was sacrosanct, none might bear arms within it, and whatever wars were going on there was safe-conduct for all who travelled to Olympia whether as private citizens or as representatives of the states.

A month or more before the festival athletes and trainers, chariots and horses, owners and jockeys, began to gather at Elis. Competitors, it seems, had to give in their names a month before-hand, and there, under the eyes of the Hellanodikai, they under-went their last month's training. The training was especially severe, and the Hellanodikai enforced their orders by means of the rod. This month was a very valuable time for these officials. In it they had the opportunity of testing the competitors, rejecting the unfit, satisfying themselves of their parentage and right to compete, above all of judging the claims of boys and colts to

---

[1] For discussion of the date, duration, and arrangements of the games v. *Gk. Athletics*, ch. ix. 194 ff., and Weniger, in *Klio*, 1904, pp. 126.

compete in these classes. A few days before the festival the whole company of officials and competitors left Elis for Olympia. The procession followed the sacred road along the coast to the fountain of Piera, the boundary of Elis and Pisatis. There they halted and performed certain rites of lustration. They passed the night at Letrinoi and the next day made their entrance to Olympia.

Meanwhile crowds were gathering at Olympia. Along the coastal road from the gulf of Corinth poured a constant stream of visitors of every class, driving, riding, or on foot. Conspicuous among them were the state embassies, each striving to outdo the others. Up the Alpheios rowed barges bringing splendid equipages from the princes of Italy and Sicily. Along every valley and over every pass came the hardy peasants from the Peloponnese. Some came from love of sport or to see their friends compete, others for profit or advertisement. There were princes and politicians, philosophers and rhetoricians, poets and sculptors, merchants and horse-breeders from Elis, and with them all the crowd of those who catered for the needs of the assembly, peasants loaded with wine-skins and baskets of fruit or fish, shepherds driving in victims for the sacrifices, vendors of wreaths and fillets, of amulets and votive offerings, tumblers, acrobats, mountebanks. Outside the Altis the plain was full of tents and hastily constructed booths, but for most of the crowd there was no shelter and they had to sleep under the open sky or in the corridors.

The festival lasted five days, from the 12th to the 16th of the month. The first day was given up to preliminary business. The chief event was the final scrutiny of competitors in the Bouleu-terion. Between the two wings of this building stood the Altar of Zeus Horkios. In either hand he held a thunderbolt as a warning to evil doers. Before this awe-inspiring statue competitors, their fathers, brothers, and trainers took their stand. A pig was sacrificed, and with uplifted hand they swore that they would use no unfair means in the coming games. The competitors themselves further swore that for ten months they had strictly observed the rules of training. Next the judges, whose duty it was to decide on the claims of boys to compete as such, swore to give their decision justly and without bribes, and not to reveal the reasons of their judgement. Not till then could the final list of entries be made out. The heats and ties were drawn, the order of the runners was settled, and the names perhaps were pasted on a white board.

On this as on the other days there were various sacrifices both public and private, but of these little is known. The daily sacrifice to Zeus of course was duly offered, and we can hardly doubt that on this opening day special sacrifices were offered at the six double altars. In the evening of this day, or possibly of the day before, an offering of blood was poured on the mound of Pelops. The competitors, too, and their friends, would offer their vows and sacrifices to gods and heroes whose favour they hoped to win, and would try to obtain from the seers and sooth-sayers some omen of success. Some perhaps would go off to the Stadion for a last practice. Everywhere crowds followed them. But there were other attractions than the athletes. There were the temples and treasuries to be seen, the monuments and statues. In the opisthodome of the temple were orators, philo-sophers, poets to be heard. Elsewhere there were sculptors and painters exhibiting their works, and for the common folk the booths around the Agora provided all the attractions of a fair.

On the second day the games began. First came the chariot-race. Early in the morning the low embankments of the Hippo-drome[1] were filled with an eager crowd who occupied every point of vantage, especially at the ends facing the pillars round which the chariots turned. Meanwhile the procession had been marshalled, probably at the Prytaneion. First came the Hellanodikai robed in purple with garlands on their heads, the herald, trumpeter, and other officials, then the competitors, the chariots, and the horses. Skirting the Altis they entered the Hippodrome at the west end by the Porch of Agnaptos. As the competitors passed before the spectators the herald proclaimed each man's name, the name of his father and of his city, and asked if any man had any charge to bring against them. Then in solemn terms he proclaimed the opening of the games, and the chief Hellanodikas or some other distinguished person addressed the competitors.

Now all was ready and the chariots took their places in the stalls along either side of the aphesis, their places being assigned by lot. Then the trumpet sounded, the ropes in front of each pair of chariots were withdrawn, and they moved forward slowly till they were level with the beak of the aphesis. Then from the altar in the centre a golden eagle rose, and the dolphin at the

---

[1] *Gk. Athletics*, pp. 451 ff.

beak dropped and the race began. The fields were large, sometimes as many as forty, but the race was long, twelve times the
length of the double course, 72 stades or nearly 9 miles, and the
pace must have been slow at first. Yet even so the excitement
must have been intense from start to finish. For the chariots
had to negotiate twenty-three turns round the pillars, and
skilful driving was sorely needed to avoid losing ground at the
turn and to avoid collisions. Accidents were frequent, as we
know from the *Elektra* of Sophokles. There in a field of ten
only one reached the goal in safety, and Pindar tells us that
Arkesilas of Kyrene was the sole survivor out of a field of forty.
During the last lap the excitement of the spectators knew no
bounds, they shouted, leapt from their seats, waving their arms
or their clothes and embracing their neighbours in their joy.

When the race was over the owner of the victorious chariot
came forward and bound a fillet round the head of his charioteer.
Then, leading perhaps his chariot, he advanced to the place where
the Hellanodikai sat. Beside them was set the gold and ivory
table wrought by Kolotes, and on it were the olive crowns cut
from the sacred olive-tree. Then the herald proclaimed the
name of the victor, his father, and his city, and the chief Hellanodikas placed upon his brow the crown, while the people pelted
him with flowers and branches. If the race was a dead heat, the
crown was not awarded but was dedicated to the god.

After the chariot-race came the horse-race. It was started in the
same manner, but the distance was only a single lap or 6 stades.
The jockeys rode without saddle or stirrups. In the first half
of the fifth century there was also a riding race for mares and
a mule chariot-race, but both these events were discontinued in
444 B.C. The two-horse chariot-race was not introduced till
the close of the century, and the various competitions for colts
at a still later date.

No sooner was the last race over than the spectators hurried
over the embankment to secure places to witness the pentathlon.[1]
This was the most characteristic of all Greek athletic competitions. Its object was to test the all-round athlete. The five
events of which it was composed, running, jumping, throwing the
diskos and the javelin, and wrestling, were the basis of all physical
education among the Greeks. The three events which were
peculiar to the pentathlon, the jump, the diskos, and the

[1] *Gk. Athletics*, p. 358 ; *J. H. S.* xxiii. 54.

javelin required that rhythmical, harmonious movement which appealed especially to the Greek, and perhaps for this reason these exercises were performed both in practice and in competition to the accompaniment of the flute.

The competition must have taken considerable time, especially if the field was large, and three Hellanodikai were especially appointed to judge it. It is difficult to say how it was decided. It is certain that a competitor who was first in three events won outright, and it seems also that a victor in the pentathlon was commonly described as a triple victor ($\tau\rho\iota\acute{\alpha}\kappa\tau\eta\rho$). But it must often have been the case that no one won more than two events or perhaps one. Thus Philostratos, describing the mythical origin of the pentathlon, narrates how five heroes each won one event, and the prize was awarded to Peleus because, having won the wrestling, he was second in the other four events.[1] Further, it seems certain from a passage in Xenophon[2] that wrestling was the last event and that some sort of elimination took place before the wrestling and only those who had qualified in the first four events were entitled to wrestle. What was the method of elimination and what the system of marking formerly seemed insoluble mysteries. A solution, however, has been recently put forward by a Finnish athlete, Captain Lauri Pihkala[3] which seems to me to satisfy all the conditions. He suggests that in the first four events the performance of each competitor was compared with those of each of his fellow competitors individually, and that any competitor who had been defeated by any single other in three events was cut out of the contest. If any one was absolutely first in three of the four events, or if he had defeated every one else in three, not necessarily the same three events, he would be the sole survivor and therefore the winner of the pentathlon. More often it would happen that from two to four were left in who had tied by defeating all their rivals in two events. These alone were permitted to wrestle and the winner of the wrestling was therefore the winner of the whole pentathlon, ' the triple victor ' who had defeated every rival in three events.

The pentathlon began with a foot-race, the length of which was a single stade. Then came the jump[4]. It was a long jump

[1] Philostratos, *Gym.* 3.   [2] Xen. *Hell.* vii. 4. 29 ; *Gk. Athletics*, p. 368.
[3] A full statement of this theory is to appear in the next volume of the *J. H. S.* I am indebted to Captain Pihkala for leave to publish it.
[4] *Gk. Athletics*, p. 295 ; *J. H. S.* xxiv. 70, 179.

and the jumpers used jumping weights, *halteres*, of stone or metal.
Some of these may be seen in our museums. They vary in shape,
and in weight from $2\frac{1}{2}$ lb. to 10 lb. A stone *halter* was found at
Olympia $11\frac{1}{2}$ inches long and slightly over 10 lb. in weight (Fig.
129). The jumper seems to have taken a short, springy run,
swinging the weights backwards and forwards once or twice
as he ran. At the moment of taking off he swung them vigorously
forward, so that in mid-air arms and legs were almost parallel.
Just before landing he swung them sharply backwards, a movement which helped to lengthen the jump and also to secure a firm,
even landing, a point of style to
which the Greek attached great
importance. The jump possibly
took place at the end of the racecourse, in which case the stone
sills may have served as the take
off ($\beta\alpha\tau\acute{\eta}\rho$). In front of this a
pit ($\sigma\kappa\acute{\alpha}\mu\mu\alpha$) was dug, the ground
being carefully loosened and
levelled. Each jump was marked
by a peg, and when all had
jumped the jumps were measured
with a rod ($\kappa\alpha\nu\acute{\omega}\nu$). On a vase
in the British Museum we see

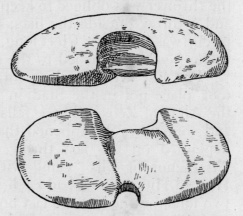

129. Jumping weight found at Olympia

a jumper in mid-air, and underneath him are three pegs representing the jumps of previous performers.

Throwing the diskos was the next event.[1] The diskos was
a circular plate of metal or stone. Existing specimens vary from
$6\frac{1}{2}$ to 9 inches in diameter, and from 3 to 9 lb. in weight. The
$\beta\alpha\lambda\beta\acute{\iota}s$, from which it was thrown, was marked out by lines in
front and on the sides, which the thrower might not overstep.
The object was to throw the diskos as far as possible. The
drawings of the diskos thrower on vases show a considerable
variety of style, but the principle of the throw is always the
same ; it is that represented in Myron's Diskobolos. The thrower,
after rubbing the diskos with sand, took his stand a short distance
behind the front line holding the diskos in his left hand with his
right foot advanced. He then swung it forward and upward in
both hands till it was on a level with or higher than his head, at
the same time moving the left foot to the front. Next he swung

---

[1] *Gk. Athletics*, p. 313 ; *J. H. S.* xxvii. 1.

it vigorously downward and backward, drawing the left foot back again till at the end of the swing he reached the position represented by Myron. Then with a vigorous lift the whole body was straightened, and as the diskos swung forward the left leg was once more advanced. The whole movement was backward and forward like that of a pendulum, and thereby differed from the circular swing of the modern diskos thrower.

The stone sills of the Stadion probably served as the βαλβίς for both the diskos and the javelin. In the pentathlon the javelin [1] was not thrown at a target but for distance only. At the same time the thrower was obliged to keep within certain limits on either side, and a throw outside the lists, ἔξω ἀγῶνος, was disqualified. The javelin was about 5 or 6 feet long, and was thrown by means of a short thong (ἀγκύλη) attached to the shaft near the centre of gravity.

The last event in the pentathlon, the wrestling competition, took place not in the Stadion but in the open space in front of the Altar of Zeus. Three falls were necessary to secure victory, and sometimes it happened that victory in the whole pentathlon depended on the last throw. Thus Herodotos [2] tells us that Tisamenos of Elis ' came within a single throw of winning '. He and Hieronymos had each won two events, each had secured two falls, but he lost the last bout.

' Then in the evening, the lovely shining of the fair-faced moon beamed forth, and all the precinct sounded with songs and festal glee.' Victors and their friends wreathed with fillets and garlands held revelry. To the sound of flute and lyre they went in glad procession round the Altis, singing as they went the old triumphal hymn of Herakles written by Archilochos, or some new song written for them by Pindar or Bacchylides. Banquets followed given by the victors to their friends. Sometimes the victor would feast the whole assembly and the revels would last the whole night.

The third day, the day of the full moon, was the great day when the official sacrifice was offered to Zeus. Of the procession we can form some idea from the frieze of the Parthenon. First came the officials, the Hellanodikai in their purple robes, the seers and priests, the attendants leading the victims for the sacrifice : then came the Theoriai, the official deputations from the states of Hellas, bearing in their hands rich vessels of silver and gold : after them the competitors, chariots, horsemen,

---

[1] Gk. Athletics, p. 338 ; J. H. S. xxvii, pp. 249–73.　　　　[2] Hdt. ix. 33.

athletes, trainers, friends. The procession started from the Prytaneion. Following the processional road it moved southwards past the Temple of Zeus, then turning east passed between the temple and the council house, whence it made its way through an avenue of statues past the east end of the temple to the Great Altar. The priest of Zeus, the seers and their ministers, mounted the ramp that led up to the platform or prothysis, and there in the sight of all the people the victims were slain. The thighs were taken up to the top of the altar and there burnt; the rest of the flesh was removed to the Prytaneion.

The sacrifice took place in the morning. In the afternoon the competitions for boys were held, a foot-race, wrestling, and boxing. We do not know for certain what was the age limit for boys. At the Augustalia at Neapolis,[1] which were modelled on the Olympic Games, boys had to be over seventeen and under twenty. But the Greeks had no registers of births, and the Hellanodikai doubtless exercised considerable discretion, taking account not merely of a boy's declared age but of his physical development. Thus we hear of a boy of eighteen who was disqualified from competing among boys, and who thereupon entered for the men's competition and won it.

Most of the athletic events were reserved for the fourth day. The programme began in the morning with the foot-races.[2] They were three in number, the stade race of 200 yards, the double stade race or diaulos, and the long race of twelve laps or approximately three miles. Each event was proclaimed by the herald. The finish was probably at the east end, near which were the seats of the Hellanodikai. The stone starting-lines have been already described. Each runner occupied one of the divisions. He took his stand with his feet close together, the position of the feet being determined by the two grooves cut in the stone sills, with his body bent slightly forward, but not, like the modern runner, starting off his hands. The start was given by the herald with the word 'go' (ἄπιτε). Just as to-day, runners tried to poach at the start, but Greek discipline was drastic. 'Runners who start too soon', says Adeimantos to Themistokles, 'are beaten with rods.'

The starting-lines at Olympia provided room for twenty runners. If there was a larger number of competitors, preliminary

[1] *Olympia*, v, no. 56 ; *Gk. Athletics*, p. 271.
[2] *Gk. Athletics*, p. 270 ; *J. H. S.* xxiii, p. 261.

heats were held, the winner of each heat running in the final. The stade race was a single length of the course. The diaulos or double race was so called because the course resembled a double flute. Hence each runner probably ran straight to the post opposite his starting-place, turned round it to the left, and returned on the parallel track. In the long race it seems probable that all the posts were removed except the centre one at each end, and that the runners raced up and down round these posts just as did the chariots in the Hippodrome. It is reasonable to conjecture that the posts were connected by ropes, but there is no evidence for this. The style of the Greek runners, if we may judge from the drawings on Panathenaic vases, did not differ much from that of the modern runner. The conventional drawing of the sprinters with the right arm and right leg working together has led writers who are not conversant with the conventions of Greek vases to infer that the Greek sprinter advanced by a series of awkward leaps, in fact that he did not know how to run. But as the same conventionality occurs in the drawing of horses, it would be equally reasonable to infer that the Greek horse did not know how to trot.

The foot-races were over before midday, and now there was a rush back to the Altis to witness the most exciting of all events, the competitions in wrestling, boxing, and the pankration. These events took place in the open space in front of the Altar of Zeus. Here the ties [1] were drawn in the presence of the spectators and the Hellanodikai. Lots marked with letters of the alphabet were put into a silver urn : there were two marked A, two B, two Γ, and so on according to the number of entries. If there was an odd number of competitors a single lot was put in for the bye. Each competitor, after uttering a prayer to Zeus, drew a lot, holding it in his hand but not looking at it until all were drawn. Then the Hellanodikas went round and examined the lots, pairing off the competitors accordingly. To draw a bye in such a contest was naturally a great advantage, and it was regarded as an additional honour to win one of these events without ever drawing a bye. The number of entries probably rarely exceeded sixteen, requiring four rounds. Occasionally a famous athlete was allowed a walk over.

Wrestling was perhaps the most popular of all Greek sports, and was an essential part of physical education. The very name

---

[1] Lucian, *Hermotim*, 39.

Palaistra signifies the wrestling school. The style of wrestling employed was described by the Greeks as ὀρθὴ πάλη or upright wrestling, as opposed to ground wrestling, which was only allowed in the pankration. The object was to throw an opponent, and a wrestler was considered thrown if he touched the ground with any part of his body above the knees. Whether a wrestler who fell on his knee was thrown is a point hard to determine. As a wrestler in throwing another over his head is sometimes depicted as sinking on one knee, it seems to me probable that this did not count as a fall. Three throws were necessary to secure victory, and if both wrestlers fell together it appears that nothing was scored. A wonderful variety of grips and throws are represented on the vases. All holds seem to have been allowed, but from the nature of the competition there was little opportunity for leg holds. Tripping was freely used. Among the throws represented are the heave, the flying mare, and the cross buttock.[1]

Boxing [2] came next. Neither in boxing nor in wrestling was there any classification according to weight. This was one of the causes that led to the deterioration of these sports, and especially of boxing. But we must not be misled by the descriptions of boxing in Virgil and other Roman writers who knew nothing of athletics. The deadly cestus of the Romans, heavy with lead and iron, had no place in Greek sport, though the Greek gloves of the fourth century with their ring of hard leather round the knuckles were sufficiently formidable weapons. But the boxing thongs (ἱμάντες) represented on vases of the fifth century are merely strips of soft leather some 10 feet or more long, wound round the fingers and across the back of the hand and fastened round the wrists. They served rather to protect the knuckles than to decrease the force of the blow. Boxing scenes on these vases suggest that the young Greek boxer had considerable knowledge of foot-work, and used both hands with effect. But the absence of classification according to weight quickly led to deterioration, and this was hastened by two other causes. The Greek ring was large, and there were no rounds. The fight went on till one or other boxer acknowledged defeat by holding up his hand. Hence cautious tactics prevailed, the boxer adopted a stiff guard with the left hand and boxing became

[1] *Gk. Athletics*, p. 375 ; *J. H. S.* xxv. 14, 263.
[2] *Gk. Athletics*, p. 402 ; *J. H. S.* xxvi. 213.

a matter of endurance. Perhaps with the idea of making it more lively, more formidable gloves were introduced. If so, the remedy was worse than the disease.

The most exciting of all the contests was the pankration,[1] in which, as the name denotes, each competitor tried to force his opponent to acknowledge defeat by any means in his power. These means included boxing with bare hands, wrestling upright or on the ground, kicking. Twisting the arm, throttling, kicking in the stomach were some of the methods employed, and we should naturally regard it as mere brutality did we not know that the Greeks considered it to be a contest of pure skill and ascribed its invention to Herakles. Perhaps if we knew the laws that governed it we should find that it was no more brutal than the prize fight, or than jiu-jitsu. As it is, the only regulation that we know is one forbidding biting and gouging (ὀρύττειν). The latter expression seems to denote digging the fingers into the eye or other tender parts of the body.

The fight usually began with sparring and attempts to secure a wrestling grip, especially a leg hold. But soon both competitors were on the ground and the contest consisted mostly in ground wrestling, though hitting was still allowed. Sometimes a wrestler would intentionally take to the ground with the intention of throwing his opponent heavily by a stomach throw, or of seizing his ankle and twisting it. The struggle went on as in boxing till one of the two acknowledged defeat. Occasionally it happened that a pankratiast died before he would give in. Thus it is related that one Arrhichion died at the moment when his opponent gave in, and thus though dead was awarded the Olympic crown.

The programme closed with the race in armour, a popular and picturesque event which afforded a welcome relief after the excitement of the fighting events. Like the modern obstacle race, it was a practical military exercise, and appealed to the citizen soldier rather than to the specialized athlete. The race was a two-stade race, and the runners wore helmets and greaves and carried round shields.[2] The fields were large; twenty-five shields were kept at Olympia for use in this race. If, as seems probable, the whole field raced together up the track and turned round a single post, it must have been an amusing race to watch, and

---

[1] *Gk. Athletics*, p. 435 ; *J. H. S.* xxvi. 4.
[2] Greaves were not worn after 450 B. C.

marking as it did the connexion between athletic training and real life, it formed an appropriate finish to the games.

The last day of the festival was spent in feasting and rejoicing. The victors paid their vows at the altars of the gods, and in the evening were entertained at a banquet in the Prytaneion. Already the crowd was beginning to disperse. All was hurry and confusion. The booths and tents were taken down. There were provisions to be bought for the journey, horses, mules, and vehicles to be hired, and the country folk did a roaring trade. Many who had no mule or vehicle of their own or could not hire them had to start off on foot or stay behind. But all were happy as a Derby crowd—all save the defeated. Greeks, we fear, had little sympathy with defeat. ' By back ways ', says Pindar,[1] ' they slink away sore smitten by misfortune.' ' No sweet smile graces their return.' As for the victors, rejoicing friends brought them to their homes, there to be received in triumph by their fellow citizens, and with dance and song to be escorted to the temple of their city to dedicate to god or hero their crown of victory. And so ended the Olympiad.

[1] Pindar, *P.*, viii. 86.

INDEX

A

Achaian League, 142 ff.
Achaians in NW. Peloponnese, 51, 77.
Africanus, 86, 167.
Agora, position of, 189.
Aitolian League, 142 ff.
Aitolian migrations into Elis, 42.
Aleision, 23.
Alexander of Macedon, 130.
Alkamenes and sculptures of Olympia, 245, 260.
Alkibiades at Olympia, 113, 118.
Alpheios and its tributaries, 19 ; altar of, 198 ; represented in pediments, 250.
Altars, 193 ; ash, 195 ; double, 198 ; Zeus, 193 ; Hera, 196 ; Herakles, 220 ; Gaia, 49, 196, 221.
Altis, topography of, 7, 175 ; boundaries of, 176 ; walls and entrances of, 135, 179, 185.
Amber at Kakóvatos, 38.
Anolympiads, 85, 122.
Antiquarianism in legends, 59, 170.
Antiquaries of Elis, 61.
Apollonios of Tyana, 168.
Archelaos of Cappadocia, 156.
Archilochos of Paros, 91.
Architecture :
  ground-plans, rectangular : Heraion, 208 ; Zeus Temple, 234 ; Metroon, 123 ; Treasuries, 219 ; Prytaneion, 268 ; Hellanodikeon, 276 ; Theokoleon, 278 ; Leonidaion, 281 ; Palaistra, 289 ; Stoai, 108, 136, 274.
  —, semi-elliptical : prehistoric houses, 27 ; Bouleuterion, 273.
  —, circular : Philippeion, 131 ; Heroon, 204 ; Exedra, 295.
  columns and entablature : Corinthian, 132, 286, 291, 292 ; Doric, 123, 209, 225, 232, 236, 278, 282 ; Ionic, 132, 282, 291.
  roof : Philippeion, 132 ; Heraion, 208 ; Zeus Temple, 237 ; Geloan Treasury, 224 ; Megarian Treasury, 228 ; Sikyonian Treasury, 232. (v. Terracottas.)
  steps, undercutting of, 132, 137.
  asymmetry : Heraion, 209 ; Zeus Temple, 236.
  use of colour, 132, 224, 228, 232, 236, 277, 286.
  use of marble, 128, 281.
  use of wood in Heraion, 209.
Arene, 24.
Arethousa, 17, 41.
Argos and Olympia, 51, 88, 116, 124, 208.
Arkadia and Olympia, 115, 120, 138.
Arkadians, ethnology of, 18, 43.
Asklepiades, diskos of, 59.
Athens and Olympia, 91, 97, 109, 111, 115, 124.
Athletics, Greek : secular and military, 67 ; why connected with religion, *ib.* ; national character of, 96 ; history of, 96, 106, 119, 139, 149, 153, 165, 170 ; corruption and professionalism in, 119, 150, 154, 165 ; the Olympic ideal, 166, 170 ; the pentathlon, 303 ; foot-races, 307 ; boxing and wrestling, 308.
Augustus, 159.

B

Balkans, migrations from, 33.
Basilai, 42, 54.
Bosanquet, Prof. R. C., 38.
Boule of Olympia, 102, 164, 270.
Bouleuterion, 271.
Bronzes : pre-geometric, 78 ; geometric, 92 ; orientalizing, 93.
  statuettes : Aphrodite, 95 ; Artemis, 95 ; Zeus, 100, 207.
  head of Zeus, 100 ; of athlete, 99.
Bybon, weight thrown by, 97.
Byzantine church, 3 ; fortress, 3.

C

Calendar, 68 ff. ; solar and lunar years, 70 ; octennial cycle and penteteris, 71 ; names of Elean months, 68, 200.
Chariot-race, 66, 82, 160, 302.
Claudius Rufus, inscription of, 152, 166.
Coins of Elis, 102, 104, 116, 120, 241.
— of Pisa, 122.
Colonies and Olympia, 90.

Cook, A. B., 64, 69.
Cornford, F. M., 54, 64.
Cretan religion, 41, 48.
Cretan Zeus, legend of, 42, 48, 61.
Crete and the NW. Peloponnese, 17, 36, 39, 61, 124.
Curtius, Ernst, 7, 214.

D

Decoration, systems of : prehistoric pottery, 32 ; pre-geometric bronzes, 80 ; orientalizing bronzes, 93 ; Tremolierstich, 80 ; imitation brickwork, 132. (*v. also* Architecture, Terra-cottas.)
Delphi and Olympia, 49, 57, 62, 129.
Dion Chrysostom, 109, 166.
Dionysios of Syracuse at Olympia, 113.
Diskos, 304.
Dodona and Olympia, 47 ff.
Dörpfeld, Dr. W., 11, 27, 85, 183, 216.
Dropion, inscription of, 142.
Dyer, Louis, 189, 217.
Dyspontion, 22.

E

Elean art, continuity of, 80 ; coins, 102 ; sculpture, 260.
Elean kings, genealogy of, 46 ; end of monarchy, 101.
Elean nobility, inscriptions of, 154 ; offices held by, 201.
Eleans, character of, 16 ; immigrants from Aitolia, 45, 76.
Elis, fertility of, 16 ; sanctity of, 17, 74 ; violated, 116, 121, 137.
Elis and Pisa, 76, 83, 85, 101.
Elis city, 23, 105.
Epeians in Homer, 45.
Ephyra, 23.
Epidamnian Treasury, 231.
Epinikia, 66, 98, 106, 168.
Evelyn-White, H. G., 242.
Exainetos, 66.
Exedra, 173, 295.

F

Farnell, Dr. L. R., 42, 72.
Fluteplayers, inscriptions in honour of, 174.
Förster, Hugo, 87.
Frazer, Sir James, 64, 69, 190.
Funeral games, 63.
Furtwängler, A., 78.

G

Gardner, Prof. E. A., 242.
Gardner, Prof. Percy, 102, 116.
Geloan Treasury, 222.
Gorgias, 113, 127, 183.
Gymnasion, 144, 291.

H

Hadrian, 166, 172.
Hallstatt, 31, 83.
Halteres, 305.
Hellanodikai, 84, 90, 101, 103, 105, 122, 170, 189, 270.
Hellanodikeon, 108, 276.
Heraia, 21 ; treaty with Elis, 85.
Heraion, date of, 11 ; description of, 207 ff. (*v.* Religion.)
Herakleia, 23.
Herakles, legends of, 39, 42, 43, 50 ; the Idaean, 48, 61 ; founder of Olympic games, 60 ; in art, 94 ; statues of, 111 ; 'Successors of', 149, 154, 166.
Heralds, competitions for, 119 ; inscriptions of, 174.
Heroa, 133, 203.
Heroon, 204.
Hero-worship, 57, 65, 67, 133.
Herodes Atticus, 172, 274 ff.
Herodotos, 37, 85, 96, 103, 306 ; at Olympia, 126, 238.
Herod the Great, 156.
Hieratic cults, 198.
Hieromnamones of Delphi, 270.
Hippias of Elis, 86, 126.
Hippodameia, 55.
Hippodameion, 191.
Hippodrome, 287.
Homer, 16, 27, 44, 48, 51, 53
Hyde, Walter, 98, 177.

I

Iamidai and Klytiadai, 58, 201.
Iamos, 49.
Idaean Cave, 48, 220.
Inscriptions : Ϝράτραι, 21, 101 ; regulations for sanctuary, 68, 102, 194, 270 ; Proxenia, 120, 122, 140 ; lists of officials, 157, 200 ; Exedra, 297 ; Heroon, 205 ; Leonidaion, 280 ; Metroon, 161 ; Nike, 117 ; Asinius Quadratus, 170 ;

Asklepiades, 59 ; Bybon, 97 ; Demokrates, 139 ; Gorgias, 127 ; Kallikrates, 147 ; Lakon, 162 ; Philonides,
131. (*v. also* Victor Statues, Honorary
Statues.)
Iphitos, 60 ; diskos of, 62, 74 ; truce of,
83.
Iron at Kakóvatos, 38.
Isokrates, 112, 114.

K

Kakóvatos, excavations at, 27, 35.
Kallikrates, 146.
Kaukones, 42.
Kleidhi, 35.
Kolotes, prize table of, 110.
Korakou, 28, 31.
Koukoura, 22, 26.
Kouretes, 50, 61, 65.
Kypselos, chest of, 53, 213 ; statue of
Zeus, 91.
Kyrene, Treasury of, 229.

L

Leaf, Dr. W., 38, 57.
Leleges, 40.
Leocharis, basis of statues, 131.
Leonidaion, 137, 281.
Leonidas of Naxos, 181, 280.
Lepreon, 24, 74, 115.
Leukas, pottery of, 12, 27, 28, 30.
Lucian, 167, 169, 173.
Lykaion, Zeus worship at, 48, 49.
Lysias at Olympia, 112.

M

Macedonia, incised pottery of, 33.
Macedonian kings and Olympia : Arche-
laos, 129 ; Alexander, 130 ; Philip,
129 ; Demetrios Poliorketes, 141 ;
Antigonos Gonatas, 141 ; Antigonos
Doson, 144.
Megarian Treasury, 225.
Melankomas, 166.
Messenia and Olympia, 88, 117, 120.
Metapontine Treasury, 225.
Metroon, 123, 160.
Minyai, 43, 45.
Minyan cities, 37, 43.
Minyan pottery, 34.
Miraka, 21, 27.

Mosaics in Zeus Temple, 238 ; in Ther-
mai, 172.
Mummius, 147, 185.
Myron of Sikyon, 91, 232.

N

Nero, 67, 163 ff. ; Triumphal Gate of,
186 ; villa of, 276.

O

Octennial Cycle, 70.
Officials, Lists of, 157, 200 ; alytarches,
170 ; epimeletes, 201 ; epispondorchestai, 201 ; exegetes, 169, 201 ;
hiaromaoi, 103 ; kathemerothytes,
201 ; manteis, 169, 194 ; proxenoi,
194 ; spondophoroi, 201 ; theokoloi,
103, 200.
Oinomaos, 53, 64.
Olenian rocks, 23.
Olive crown, 60, 63.
Olive tree, the sacred, 188.
Olympia and its communications, 19 ;
accessibility of, 25.
—, art and literature at, 126, 168 ; commerce at, 126, 168 ; a Roman tourist
resort, 169.
—, Panhellenic character of, 90, 112 ;
political importance of, recognized by
tyrants, 91, by Macedon, 129, by Rome,
158 ; exclusiveness of, 129 ; athletic
ideal of, 96. (*v.* Religion.)
—, battle of, 121, 175.
Olympia, the Nymph, 122.
Olympic Festival, origin of, 58 ; ancient
legends, 59 ; funeral games theory, 64 ;
kingship theory, 64 ; the penteteris,
68 ; octennial cycle, 71 ; lustration
rites, 72 ; military character of games,
73 ; the Sacred Truce, 73 ; exclusion
of women, 75 ; national exclusiveness,
76 ; end of, 3, 174.
—, Presidency of : Pisatan, 59 ; dual
control, 84 ; usurped by Pheidon, 88 ;
Elean control, 103, 104 ; Pisatan usurpation in *Ol.* 104, 121.
—, Programme of games, 87, 91, 98.
—, Competition at games, 88, 97, 106,
119, 138, 153, 165.
Oracle of Earth, 48, 49 ; of Zeus, 49, 58,
115, 169.
Oxylos, 46.

P

Paionios, Nike of, 115, 117, 179 ; akroterion of Zeus Temple, 238 ; pediment, 259.
Palaistra, 144, 288.
Panainos, 110, 242.
Paroreatai, 43.
Pausanias : description of Olympia, 5, 167 *passim* ; accuracy of, 7, 181, 245, 280.
Peet, Prof. T. E., 31.
Peisistratos, 98.
Peloponnese, NW., geography of, 13 ; connexion with North and West, 17 ; with Italy, 32, 38 ; with Aitolia and Thessaly, 45 ; aloofness from Aegean and Crete, 17, 39 ; history of, 18 ; ethnology of, 40.
Pelops, legends of, 53 ; cult and shrine of, 203.
Penteteris, 68, 86.
Peregrinus at Olympia, 168, 173.
Pheidias, 109, 240 ; workshop of, 243.
Pheidon of Argos, 84, 88, 207.
Philip of Macedon, 129.
Philippeion, 131.
Philonides, inscription of, 131, 181.
Philostratos, 168.
Phlegon, 63, 86, 167.
Phrixa, 21.
Piera, fountain of, 23.
Pindar, 19, 42, 49, 51, 59, 106, 234.
Pisa, 21, 26, 53 ; destruction of, 85.
Pisatis, 15, 53.
Pithoi burials, 28.
Polybios, 146, 148, 149.
Pottery of Olympia : prehistoric, 28 ; affinities of, with Italian, 31 ; Balkan, 32 ; Minyan, 34 ; Macedonian, 33.
— of Pylos (Kakóvatos), L. M. II, 36.
Poulsen, F., 93.
Praxiteles, Hermes of, 213.
Prehistoric village at Olympia, 11, 26.
Processional Entrance, 188.
— Road, 178, 180, 187.
Proedria, 182, 189, 274.
Prytaneion, 267.
Ptolemies and Olympia, 140, 143, 150.
Pylians a Minyan race, 43.
Pylos : Elean, 23 ; Triphylian, 24. (*v.* Kakóvatos.)

R

Register, the Olympic, 85, 138 ; used for chronology, 86.
Religion of Olympia : national character of Zeus worship, 58, 90, 109 ; supremacy of Zeus, 124 ; tendency to monotheism, 91, 172 ; intrusion of eastern cults, 124 ; conservatism, 150 ; the Philippeion and apotheosis, 133, 135 ; worship of Rome and Emperors, 160, 162 ; Pantheon of Twelve Gods, 198 ; hero-worship, 203.
Cults :
  Aphrodite, 8, 188.
  Apollo, 47.
  Artemis, 41, 198 ; ἀγοραία, 188.
  Athene, 111, 198.
  Charites, 45.
  Demeter Chamyne, 8, 75 ; priestess of, 172, 173, 297.
  Dionysos, 45, 214.
  Eileithyia, 8, 220.
  Gaia, 48, 54 ; the Gaion, 196, 220.
  Hades, 45.
  Hera, introduced from Argos, 51, 116, 124, 208 ; altar of, 196 ; festival of, 214 ; the Sixteen Women, 214 ; Colossal Head of, 212.
  Hermes, 40, 110.
  Hestia, 178.
  Kybele and Rhea, 123 ; mother and child, 221.
  Kronos, 42.
  Pan, 40, 41.
  Poseidon, 44.
  Sosipolis, 125, 220.
  Zeus, northern origin of, 47 ; at Olympia and Dodona, 48 ; as sky god, 48 ; as god of oracles, 49 ; as god of trees, 49 ; as war god, ἄρειος, 50, 73 ; ἀγοραῖος, 124, 188 ; ὅρκιος, 190, 271.
Lustration rites, 42, 70, 121, 195.
Sacrifices, to Pelops, 203 ; to Zeus, 195 ; monthly offerings, 197.
Ridgeway, Sir William, 64.
Robert, C., 220.
Rome and Olympia, 145, 152 ff.
Roman officials, statues of, 153, 184.
Rose, Prof. H. J., 63.

S

Salmone, 23.
Salmoneus, 54.
Samikon, 24, 26.
Sculpture at Olympia, 9, 110.
  Honorary statues, 126, 131, 140, 143, 181 ; of Roman officials, 153, 184 ; Elean nobles, 154, 164 ; and ladies, 165, 214 ; Roman Emperors, 162, 172, 297.
  Remains of statues found at Olympia : Nike of Paionios, 115 ; Hermes of Praxiteles, 213 ; head of Hera, 212 ; of Zeus, 100 ; of Aphrodite, heads of athletes, 99 ; portrait head of athlete, 99 ; of Elean lady, 165.
  Victor statues, 66, 98, 110, 126, 154, 160 ; portraits, 99 ; position of, 177, 181, 184.
  Votive offerings : statues of Zeus, 91, 99, 110, 114, 177 ; of other gods, 110, 177 ; sculptured groups, 100, 111, 177.
Sculpture, Architectural : Megarian Treasury, 228 ; Kyrenean Treasury, 229 ; Zeus Temple, 245.
Selinuntine Treasury, 230.
Seltman, C. T., 102.
Sikyonian Treasury, 231.
Sparta and Olympia, 89, 115, 162.
Stade race, 86.
Stadion, 108, 285.
Stepped wall of Treasury Terrace, 107.
Stoa : Poikile, 108, 136 ; Southern, v. Proedria ; use of Stoai, 275.
Stratification, 10.
Sulla, 152.
Sybaris, Treasury of, 230.

T

Taraxippos, altar of, 288.
Temenos, boundary of, 175.
Terra-cotta figurines, 78.
Terra-cottas, architectural : different styles of, 7 ; Heraion, 211 ; Geloan Treasury, 223 ; veneering, 224 ; Megarian Treasury, 226 ; Proedria, 274 ;

Hellanodikeon, 277 ; Leonidaion, 282 ; method of manufacture, 224.
Terramare, pottery of, 31.
Theatron at Olympia, 107, 178.
Theokoleon, 137, 278.
Thermai, 172.
Thermon and Olympia, 27, 30, 38, 46.
Thessaly : prehistoric houses, 27 ; pottery, 34 ; legends, 45, 54.
Thompson and Wace, 27 ff.
Trade routes, 17, 38, 81.
Treasuries, 91, 100, 107, 134, 217 ff.
Treaties and settlements recorded at Olympia, 100, 112, 142, 146, 156.
Triphylia, 15, 24.
Troy, pottery of, 33.
Truce, the Sacred, 73, 83, 112, 116.
Typaian Rock, 24, 75.

V

Victors, honours paid to, 65, 98 ; hero-worship of, 67. (v. also Epinikia, Victor Statues.)
Votive offerings, 10, 115, 123 ; before 700 B.C., 78 ; after 700 B.C., 92. (v. Sculpture.)

W

Wace, A. J. B., 31.
Water-channels, 176.
Water supply, 294.
Weege, 27, 34.
Weniger, L., 68, 123, 192, 216, 220.
Wernicke, K., 189, 276.
Women, taboo on, 75, 194 ; statues of, 165 ; sports for, 214.

X

Xenombrotos, inscription of, 181.
Xenophon, 121, 175, 178.
Xystoi, 165, 291.

Z

Zanes, 120, 123, 150, 154, 166, 170, 286.
Zeus, altar of, 27, 193 ; temple of, 107, 157, 234 ff. ; throne of, 242 ; statue of, 108, 147, 171, 241. (v. Religion.)

Printed in England at the Oxford University Press